Honolulu, Waikiki & O'ahu

North Shore & Central O'ahu
p246

Windward Coast
p214

Pearl Harbor & Leeward O'ahu
p174

Honolulu
p82

Waikiki
p136

Southeast O'ahu
p196

Craig McLachlan, Ryan Ver Berkmoes

PLAN YOUR TRIP

ON THE ROAD

LAURA SAN FILLIPO / GETTY IMAGES ©

HANAUMA BAY P207

Contents

BREACHING HUMPBACK
WHALE P300

COVID-19

We have re-checked every business in this book
before publication to ensure that it is still open after
2020's COVID-19 outbreak. However, the economic
and social impacts of COVID-19 will continue to be
felt long after the outbreak has been contained, and
many businesses, services and events referenced
in this guide may experience ongoing restrictions.
Some businesses may be temporarily closed, have
changed their opening hours and services, or require
bookings; some unfortunately could have closed per-
manently. We suggest you check with venues before
visiting for the latest information.

Right:
Waimanalo
Beach (p217)

WELCOME TO

Honolulu, Waikiki & O'ahu

I have a much-treasured love for O'ahu. Besides being an island paradise, this is the most multicultural, happy, family-friendly place I've encountered; I knew I was somewhere exceptional when we enrolled our hapa (mixed heritage) kids at Waikiki School, where every child feels the aloha. I love bodyboarding or lolling in the waves at Waimanalo Beach, watching beaming couples and their entourages arrive for 'beach weddings.' O'ahu has a wonderful experience waiting for everyone who shows up to make the most of it.

by Craig McLachlan, Writer

📷 yuricraig

For more about our writers, see p320

PPICTURES / SHUTTERSTOCK ©

O'ahu

Surfing the North Shore
World-renowned surfing
mecca (p246)

Waimea Bay
Gorgeous arc of sand
and surf (p253)

Hiking to Ka'ena Point
Easy ocean-side trail
with wildlife (p268)

USS Arizona Memorial
Monument commemorating
the Pearl Harbor attack (p177)

Bishop Museum
Rich cultural and natural-
history storehouse (p100)

Honolulu's Chinatown
Vibrant history, restaurants
and nightspots (p94)

Sunset at Waikiki Beach
Traditional Hawaiian
song and dance (p139)

Kahuku
Point
Kaihalulu
Beach

Kamehameha Hwy

Sunset Beach Park
Sunset
Beach
'Ehukai Beach Park
Kulalua Point
Pupukea Beach Park
Pupukea
Kahuku
Forest
Reserve
Waimea Bay Beach Park
Waimea
Pu'u Ka'inapua'a ▲
(2361ft)
Laniakea Beach
Waimea Valley
Hale'iwa Ali'i   Pua'ena
Beach Park   Point
83
Kawailoa
Forest
Reserve
Mokule'ia
Army Beach
Mokule'ia
Beach
Park
Waialua
Bay
Hale'iwa
Mokule'ia
Ka'ena
Point
Kuaokala Game
Management
Area
930
Waialua
Ka'ena Point
State Park
Dillingham
Airfield
Farrington Hwy
Kamehameha Hwy
Yokohama
Bay
Makua
Military
Reservation
Mokule'ia
Forest
Reserve
Kaukonahua Rd
803
Makua
Beach Park
Wai'anae Range
Mt Ka'ala
(4025ft) ▲
99
Makua Valley
Makua
Kea'au
Forest
Reserve
Schofield Barracks
Military Reservation
Wahiawa
Kea'au
Beach Park
Makaha Valley
Wai'anae Kai
Forest Reserve
Kolekole Pass
(1724ft)
Wheeler
Army
Airfield
Kepuhi Point
Makaha Beach Park
Honouliuli
Forest
Reserve
Kunia
Lahilahi Point
Poka'i Beach Park
Makaha
Wai'anae
750
Mililani
H2
Kane'ilio Point
93
Lualualei
Naval
Reservation
Kunia Rd
Pea
Cit
Ma'ili Beach Park
Ma'ili
99
Waipahu
Wai'anae Coast
Ma'ili Point
Nanakuli
Forest
Reserve
Nanakuli
Farrington Hwy
Kahe Point & Hawaiian
Electric Beach Park
Makakilo
'Ewa
H1
Ko Olina
93
76
Kapolei
Barbers Point
Naval Air Station
'Ewa
Beach
Pu'uloa
Beach
Park
Barbers
Point
Barbers Point
Beach Park
South Shore

North Shore

Kaua'i Channel

KO'OLAU

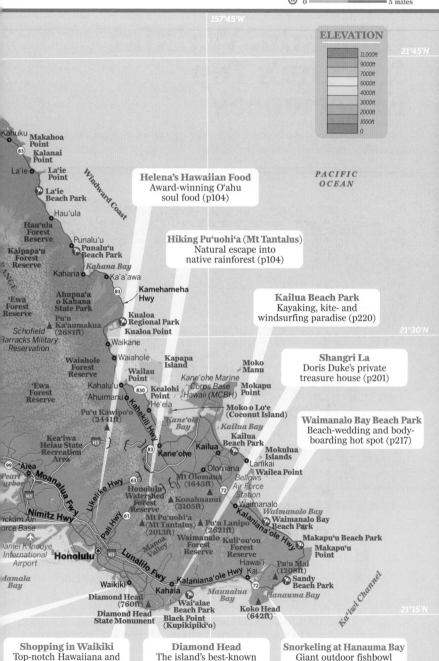

ELEVATION

11,000ft
9000ft
7000ft
5000ft
4000ft
3000ft
2000ft
1000ft
0

Helena's Hawaiian Food
Award-winning Oʻahu
soul food (p104)

Hiking Puʻuohiʻa (Mt Tantalus)
Natural escape into
native rainforest (p104)

Kailua Beach Park
Kayaking, kite- and
windsurfing paradise (p220)

Shangri La
Doris Duke's private
treasure house (p201)

Waimanalo Bay Beach Park
Beach-wedding and body-
boarding hot spot (p217)

Shopping in Waikiki
Top-notch Hawaiiana and
souvenirs (p168)

Diamond Head
The island's best-known
landmark (p199)

Snorkeling at Hanauma Bay
Giant outdoor fishbowl
and playground (p207)

PACIFIC
OCEAN

Kahuku
Makahoa
Point
Kalanai
Point
Laʻie
Laʻie
Point
Laʻie
Beach Park
Hauʻula
Hauʻula
Forest
Reserve
Kaipapaʻu
Forest
Reserve
Punaluʻu
Punaluʻu
Beach Park
Kahana
Kahana Bay
Kaʻaʻawa
Ahupuaʻa
o Kahana
State Park
Puʻu
Kaʻaumakua
(2681ft)
Kamehameha
Hwy
Kualoa
Regional Park
Kualoa Point
Waikane
Waiahole
Forest
Reserve
Waiahole
Kapapa
Island
Wailau
Point
Moko
Manu
ʻEwa
Forest
Reserve
Kahaluʻu
Kealohi
Point
Kaneʻohe Marine
Corps Base
Hawaii (MCBH)
Mokapu
Point
Ahuimanu
Heʻeia
Puʻu Kawipoʻo
(2441ft)
Kaneʻohe
Bay
Moko o Loʻe
(Coconut Island)
Keaʻiwa
Heiau State
Recreation
Area
Kailua Bay
Kailua
Beach Park
Mokulua
Islands
Kane'ohe
Kailua
Olomana
Lanikai
Wailea Point
Mt Olomana
(1643ft)
Bellows
Air Force
Station
Honolulu
Watershed
Forest
Reserve
Konahuanui
(3105ft)
Waimanalo
Waimanalo Bay
Mt Puʻuohiʻa
(Mt Tantalus)
(2013ft)
Puʻu Lanipo
(2621ft)
Waimanalo Bay
Beach Park
Waimanalo
Forest
Reserve
Kuliʻouʻou
Forest
Reserve
Makapuʻu Beach Park
Makapuʻu
Point
Honolulu
Hawaiʻi
Kai
Puʻu Mai
(1208ft)
Waikiki
Kahala
Sandy
Beach Park
Diamond Head
(760ft)
Waiʻalae
Beach Park
Koko Head
(642ft)
Hanauma Bay
Diamond Head
State Monument
Black Point
(Kupikipikiʻo)
Maunalua
Bay
Kaʻiwi Channel

Schofield
Barracks Military
Reservation
ʻEwa
Forest
Reserve
Moanalua Fwy
Pearl
Harbor
Nimitz Hwy
ʻAiea
Hickam Air
Force Base
Daniel K Inouye
International
Airport
Mamala
Bay
Likelike Hwy
Pali Hwy
Lunalilo Fwy
Manoa
Valley
Kalanianaʻole Hwy
Kalanianaʻole Hwy
Kalanianaʻole Hwy
Windward Coast
Kahekili Hwy

157°45'W
21°45'N
21°30'N
21°15'N

0   10 km
0   5 miles

Honolulu, Waikiki & O'ahu's Top Experiences

JOHN SEATON CALLAHAN / GETTY IMAGES ©

1 SUN & SAND

Let's face it, most visitors to O'ahu come to hit the beach and there are some doozies right around this Pacific island paradise. If you're staying in Waikiki, they're virtually right outside your hotel door, while if you're willing to get adventurous and head further afield, it's not hard to find that perfect stretch of sand with decidedly fewer sun-worshippers. You may well discover that beach of your dreams. Above: Hanauma Bay (p207)

Waikiki

The 2-mile stretch of white sand that everyone calls Waikiki Beach runs from Hilton Hawaiian Village all the way down to Kapi'olani Park, towards Diamond Head. It keeps changing names, personalities and degrees of beachgoer density along the way. Claim your spot! p139

Waimanalo Beach

This beauty at the southeastern end of the Windward Coast will take your breath away. A few miles southeast of Kailua Beach, Waimanalo is a lengthy stretch of real Hawaiian fantasy. p217

North Shore

Everyone has heard of the North Shore's winter waves and surfing wonders, but in quieter times, beaches along the 'Seven-Mile Miracle' such as Waimea Bay (pictured) and Sunset Beach exhibit a spectacular split personality and are top spots to hit the sand. p247

2 ON THE WATER

O'ahu is the stuff of dreams for those into activities involving water, wind and waves. The waves are legendary, especially those of winter on the North Shore, one of the world's surfing meccas. Reliable trade winds make the Kailua Bay area on the Windward Coast similarly popular among windsurfers and kitesurfers. Bodyboarders, paddleboarders and kayakers have top spots all over from which to pick. Or go sailing, wakeboarding or parasailing.

Surfing

Modern-day surfing began on O'ahu and surfers worldwide dream of hitting the waves on the North Shore's 'Seven-Mile miracle'. There are plenty of surf spots all over though and no shortage of rental boards and surf schools.

➡ **Banzai Pipeline** p255

Above left: Bodyboarding in Queen's Surf Beach (p144)

Above right: Kayaks on Kailua Beach (p222)

Left: Banzai Pipeline (p255)

Bodyboarding

Also known as boogie-boarding, beginners can pick it up in no time. Try in Waikiki before heading to Waimanalo Beach;once your confidence is up, Makapu'u Beach is the top spot. Sandy Beach, with its pounding waves, is for experts only.

➡ **Makapu'u Beach Park** p211

Kayaking

Tour operators and rental companies abound, with top spots in Waikiki, Kailua, Hale'iwa and Hawai'i Kai. Consider paddling out to lovely offshore islands from Kailua with Kailua Beach Adventures, which also offers paddleboarding and kitesurfing options.

➡ **Kailua Beach Adventures** p222

3 HISTORY & CULTURE

O'ahu has a fascinating history, from the arrival of the Polynesians through to European 'discovery' by Captain Cook, the fall of the monarchy, immigrant laborers, Pearl Harbor, statehood, and right through to today. Engross yourself in WWII history, the finest Polynesian anthropological museum in the world, the USA's only royal palace and surprisingly top-class art museums.

Far left: Bishop Museum (p100)

Left: Honolulu Museum of Art (p96)

Below: USS Arizona Memorial (p177)

Hawaiian History

Exhibits on Polynesian history at Bishop Museum are extraordinary. The museum is a rich cultural and natural-history storehouse for Hawaii and wider Polynesia. Inspect rare artifacts such as the feathered cloak worn by Kamehameha the Great.

➡ **Bishop Museum** p100

Remembering WWII

Around 1.6 million tourists visit Pearl Harbor National Memorial annually, taking in an evocative series of memorials and museums such as the USS Arizona Memorial. Also worth a visit is Punchbowl (National Memorial Cemetery of the Pacific).

➡ **USS Arizona Memorial** p177

Art in Abundance

The spectacular Honolulu Museum of Art could be the biggest surprise of your visit; it also runs trips to Shangri La, Doris Duke's spectacular sanctuary and Islamic art collection out past Diamond Head.

➡ **Honolulu Museum of Art** p96

PLAN YOUR TRIP TOP EXPERIENCES

4 HIT THE TRAILS

JAMISON LOGAN / SHUTTERSTOCK ©

First-timers are often surprised at the mountainous nature of Oʻahu, offering a plethora of hiking opportunities. Surprisingly close to sandy beaches are verdant valleys, towering cliffs and forested mountains. Climb up high, whether that be up volcanic cones or the central peaks, and you'll be rewarded with spectacular views. Alternatively, stick to the valleys and enjoy the lush vegetation, or scramble around bits of rugged coastline.

Diamond Head

Just a short walk from Waikiki you'll find the trail up the island's most recognizable landmark, Diamond Head, offering a short, sharp climb and incomparable views out over Waikiki and southeast Oʻahu. p199

Coastal Wanders

Besides just wandering along the beach in bare feet, consider the challenging hike out to Oʻahu's westernmost tip on the Kaʻena Point Trail.

➡ **Kaʻena Point State Park** p193

Into the Forest

While there are forest walks on all sides of the island, close to Honolulu and Waikiki are the Puʻuohiʻa (Mt Tantalus) hiking trail network and the ever-popular Manoa Falls Trail, a rewarding 1.6-mile round-trip walk through lush rainforest.

➡ **Manoa Falls Trail** p102

Above: Kaʻena Point State Park (p193)

Left: Manoa Falls Trail (p102)

Below: Kalawahine Trail (p104)

Below right: Diving off
Hawai'i Kai (p206)
Top left: Kuhio Beach
Park (p144)
Bottom left: Snorkeling in
Hanauma Bay (p208)

5 IN THE WATER

The water is warm. Expect Waikiki sea temperatures of around 27°C (80°F) in the peak month of September and 24°C (75°F) in the coldest month of February. There's lots to look at in the water, whether you're near the surface or below it.

Swimming

You can swim all around O'ahu, though you'll want to observe all lifeguard warnings; there are 41 staffed lifeguard towers around the island. If you're staying in Waikiki, you're not far from the beach.

➡ **Kuhio Beach Park** p144

Snorkeling

The water is warm, shallow reefs and nearshore waters are awash with colorful fish and corals, and underwater visibility is generally exceptional. Hanauma Bay is a beginners' snorkeling paradise.

➡ **Hanauma Bay** p207

Diving

O'ahu has plenty on offer, from lessons to boat, night, reef, cave and wreck dives. You'll find popular dive shops in Hawai'i Kai. Some offer beginner trips with no certification required.

➡ **Hawai'i Kai** p202

6 EAT LOCAL

EQROY / SHUTTERSTOCK ©

RINGOSOUNDS / SHUTTERSTOCK ©

Poke (poh-keh)

Bite-sized seasoned raw fish (pictured left), an art form in itself, with *poke* chefs taking pride in developing their own flavors. It's available everywhere, but the take-out options at Tamura's are sensational.

➡ **Tamura's Fine Wine & Liquors** p119

Farmers Markets

All over the island, farmers bring their produce to town, offering the freshest of fruit and veg. KCC Farmers Market is an extravaganza.

➡ **KCC Farmers Market** p202

Classic Tiki Bars

For tiki-head swizzle sticks and tiny umbrellas in your cocktails, try the 1950s time-warp classic La Mariana Sailing Club, out on Sand Island.

➡ **La Mariana Sailing Club** p124

'Ono grinds (god eats) can be found all over O'ahu. Think tropical fruit such as mango and papaya, tasty seafood and multiethnic offerings introduced by waves of immigrant laborers from a swath of countries. A 'plate lunch' typically features a scoop or two of sticky rice with fried mahimahi, Korean-style *kalbi* short ribs, Filipino pork adobo or Japanese-style chicken *katsu* (deep-friend fillets). O'ahu has an 'eat homegrown' movement and top-quality local produce.

Top right: Windward
Coast (p214)
Bottom right: Honolulu
from Pu'uohi'a (Mt
Tantalus)
Left: Pali Hwy on the
Southeast O'ahu Loop
(p35)

7 ON THE ROAD

The best way to really explore and enjoy the whole island is to rent a car and drive. Rental outlets are plentiful, both at the airport and in Waikiki, so hitting the road is fairly simple, allowing you to explore beautiful O'ahu at your own pace. O'ahu isn't huge, so you won't be racking up the miles and there are so many interesting things to see and do along the way.

Circle the Island

It's less than 100 miles of driving to take on this day trip around the island. Highlights are Hale'iwa, the North Shore's 'Seven-Mile Miracle' and the Windward Coast. Travel in either direction. p32

Southeast O'ahu

Allow at least half a day to drive the spectacular loop from Honolulu east to Hawai'i Kai, around the volcanic lookouts, past Makapu'u Point, Waimanalo Beach, Kailua and back over the Pali Hwy. p35

Head Up for Views

From downtown Honolulu, this one-hour drive up to Punchbowl, Pu'uohi'a (Mt Tantalus) and Round Top Drive offers an exciting climb and descent plus stupendous views. p134

KARA KNIGHT / SHUTTERSTOCK ©

MELISSA TSE / GETTY IMAGES ©

Below: Ala Moana Center
(p127)

8 HAWAIIANA SHOPPING

THEODORE TRIMMER / SHUTTERSTOCK ©

While you can shop till you drop in Waikiki and at the Ala Moana Center, claimant to the title of world's largest open-air shopping center, there are also opportunities to pick up unique Hawaiiana and souvenirs at one-off stores and galleries all over O'ahu – everything from handcrafted ukuleles to koa wood carvings, tropical fashion items and flip-flops.

Aloha Wear

Bailey's Antiques & Aloha Shirts boasts the finest collection in the islands. Peruse over 15,000 shirts split among new, used and vintage, going right back to the 1930s!

➡ **Bailey's Antiques & Aloha Shirts** p170

Vintage Treasures

Search out tiny stores and galleries in Chinatown such as Tin Can Mailman, known for its Hawaiian treasures, antiques and history. Old postcards, framed photos and out-of-print books enthrall.

➡ **Tin Can Mailman** p128

Unique Local Art

See fresh fish being printed on paper in Kane'ohe at Gyotaku by Naoki, a hard-to-find workshop and gallery. You'll spot the fabulous art prints island-wide in restaurants and bars

➡ **Gyotaku by Naoki** p229

Need to Know

For more information, see Survival Guide (p303)

Currency
US dollar ($)

Language
English, Hawaiian

Visas
For Visa Waiver Program (VWP) countries, visas are not required for stays of less than 90 days.

Money
ATMs are all over the place and credit cards are accepted just about everywhere.

Cell Phones
Among US providers, AT&T, Verizon, T-Mobile and Sprint are good; international travelers need multiband phones.

Time
Hawaii-Aleutian Standard Time (GMT/UTC minus 10 hours)

When to Go

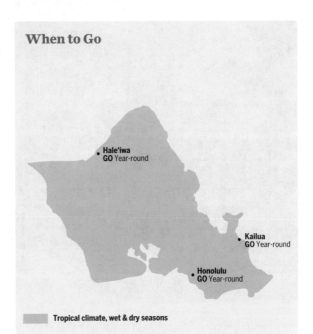

Hale'iwa
GO Year-round

Kailua
GO Year-round

Honolulu
GO Year-round

Tropical climate, wet & dry seasons

Winter High Season
(Jan–Apr)

➡ Snowbirds arrive en masse, escaping high-latitude winters.

➡ January and February are the rainiest months of the year.

➡ Spring break makes things even busier.

Summer High Season
(Jul & Aug)

➡ Family summer-vacation travel is at a peak.

➡ Expect accommodation prices to be at a premium.

➡ Sunny, hot weather continues.

Low Season
(Sep–Dec)

➡ The weather is ideal and families aren't traveling.

➡ Trade winds and travel bargains abound.

➡ Waves build on the North Shore, leading to the Triple Crown of Surfing in November and December.

Useful Websites

Lonely Planet (www.lonely planet.com/usa/honolulu-and-waikiki) Destination information, hotel bookings, traveler forum and more.

Hawaii Tourism Authority (www.gohawaii.com/islands/oahu) O'ahu's official site.

Honolulu Magazine (www.honolulumagazine.com) For everything Honolulu.

Honolulu Star-Advertiser (www.staradvertiser.com) Daily newspaper.

This Week Hawaii (www.this weekhawaii.com/oahu) What's going on this week.

Alternative Hawaii (www.alternative-hawaii.com) Indie travel website.

Important Numbers

Emergency (police, fire, ambulance)	✔911
Local directory assistance	✔411
Long-distance directory assistance	✔1-(area code)-555-1212
Toll-free directory assistance	✔1-800-555-1212
Operator	✔0

Exchange Rates

Australia	A$1	$0.69
Canada	C$1	$0.76
Europe	€1	$1.12
Japan	¥100	$0.92
New Zealand	NZ$1	$0.64
UK	£1	$1.29

For current exchange rates, see www.xe.com.

Daily Costs

Budget: Less than $100

➡ Waikiki hostel: $25–35

➡ Bus fare: $2.75

➡ Local-style plate lunch: $8–10

➡ Tap beer: $3.50–6

Midrange: $100–250

➡ Waikiki budget hotel: $100–160

➡ Car rental for a couple of days: $80–100

➡ Activities such as surfing or stand-up paddling: $80–120

➡ Restaurant meals: $15–30

Top end: More than $250

➡ Full-service resort room: from $250

➡ Top-chef-made meals: from $25

➡ O'ahu helicopter tour: $240

➡ Evening cocktails and entertainment: from $30

Opening Hours

The following standard hours apply; variances are noted in listings.

Banks 8:30am to 4pm Monday to Friday; some to 6pm Friday and 9am to noon or 1pm Saturday.

Bars and clubs Noon to midnight; some to 2am Thursday to Saturday.

Businesses and government offices 8:30am to 4:30pm Monday to Friday; some post offices open 9am to noon Saturday.

Restaurants Breakfast 6am to 10am, lunch 11:30am to 2pm, dinner 5pm to 9:30pm.

Shops 9am to 5pm Monday to Saturday, some also noon to 5pm Sunday; malls keep extended hours.

Arriving in Honolulu, Waikiki & O'ahu

Daniel K Inouye International Airport (p309) You can reach Honolulu or Waikiki by airport shuttle, public bus or taxi/Uber/Lyft (fares $35 to $45). For other points around O'ahu, it's more convenient to rent a car.

Roberts Hawaii Airport Shuttle (p309) Operates 24-hour shuttles to Waikiki hotels departing every 20 to 60 minutes.

TheBus You can reach downtown Honolulu, the Ala Moana Center and Waikiki via TheBus routes 19 or 20. Buses run every 20 minutes from 6am to 11pm; the regular fare is $2.75. Luggage is restricted to what you can hold on your lap or stow under the seat (maximum size 22in by 14in by 9in).

Language

Hawaii has two official languages: English and Hawaiian.

There's also an unofficial vernacular called pidgin, whose colorful vocabulary permeates everyday local speech.

While Hawaiian's multisyllabic, vowel-heavy words may look daunting, the pronunciation is actually quite straightforward.

The *okina* punctuation mark (') is the Hawaiian language's glottal stop; it signifies a short break in the middle of a word.

For much more on **getting around**, see p309

What's New

O'ahu is a mosaic of cultures with a Hawaiian heart. It's one of the most multiethnic places on the planet and it's always changing. There are forward-looking attitudes to sustainability and an understanding that the island needs more than just its number-one earner of tourism to thrive.

Made in Hawaii

Over the last few years there's been a massive increase in the number and quality of Hawaii-made products and souvenirs. While bobble-head dashboard hula dolls are still out there in every ABC Store, consider purchasing Hawaii-made soaps, ocean-safe sunscreens, cosmetics, coffee, chocolate, and locally designed and made clothing. There's a big push toward a sustainable tourism industry, and the locals are buying into it more and more – so buy local!

Farm-to-Table Movement

The growing 'farm to fork' movement is really taking off on O'ahu, with many restaurants committing to use locally farmed products as much as possible, rather than just produce flown in from the mainland.

It's part of the Hawaiian concept of *malama 'aina*: caring for the land so that it can give back all that is needed to sustain life for present and future generations. Part of the movement is rediscovering farming practices from before the mass conversion of the land to sugar and pineapple plantations.

Biki Bikeshare

O'ahu is now in on the worldwide phenomenon of bike sharing, with 130 Biki (https://gobiki.org) stations around Honolulu. Unlock a bike using your credit card, the Biki app or a Biki Pass, cycle to any other Biki stop and leave the bike there. Biki is run by the nonprofit Bikeshare Hawaii, funded by Honolulu County, the state of Hawaii and various partners.

LOCAL KNOWLEDGE

WHAT'S HAPPENING IN O'AHU

Craig McLachlan, Lonely Planet writer

It's hard not to be upbeat when you live in a Pacific paradise, but the aloha of native Hawaiians on O'ahu is being put to the test as the number of homeless increases and protests over issues that Native Hawaiians hold close to their hearts intensify. Activism against the Thirty Meter Telescope planned for Mauna Kea on the Big Island is strong, as is opposition to the development of Waimanalo's Sherwood Forest and an increase in the number of wind turbines at Kahuku. While you'll see plenty of Hawaiian state flags flying upside down as a signal of distress, you'll see more and more Kanaka Maoli, the yellow, red and green flag seen by many Hawaiians as establishing a separate identity. It's hard not to feel empathy for these proud Polynesian people, but if visitors don't venture out of Waikiki, they may never know that there's a different side of O'ahu out there.

Ala Moana Center Expansion

The Ala Moana Center (p127) has sprouted a new Ewa Wing, with 30 shops, Bloomingdale's and Nordstrom department stores, the Shirokiya Japan Village Walk and a Foodland Farms supermarket. Along the front of the center, the 215-unit Park Lane Ala Moana condominium complex consists of seven eight-story buildings. You may keel over when you see the prices, though.

Kaka'ako Development

Planned redevelopment of the Kaka'ako district west of the Ala Moana Center is rocketing along, with new residential buildings (some that could reach 700ft high!) going up and out-of-date buildings such as Ward Warehouse coming down to make way for more development. Locally owned shops such as Hungry Ear Records (p128) and T&L Muumuu Factory (p132) are moving into the neighborhood; other O'ahu businesses such as Lonohana Estate Chocolate (p130) are moving to the trendy Salt at Our Kaka'ako (p127) shopping center; and more and more breweries and restaurants with creative and locally sourced food are turning up, too.

Honolulu Rapid Transit Project (HART)

When it was agreed on in 2008, Honolulu's elevated, 20-mile rapid transit line, with 21 stations to link East Kapolei with the Ala Moana Center, was a $4-billion project to be partly usable by 2018 and completed by 2020. However, it has more than doubled in cost and won't be completed until 2025 at the earliest. Traffic congestion on the H-1 will be around for a while yet.

Southwest Airlines Hawaii

There's a lot more competition in the interisland flying market now that Southwest Airlines has jumped in with cheap flights between O'ahu and the other major Hawaiian islands.

Vacation Rentals Law

In 2019 the Honolulu government enacted a new law severely restricting the number of holiday rentals and B&B-style establishments across O'ahu. The law, particularly aimed at Airbnb and the like, is the result of lobbying by local hotels and resorts as well as the hospitality workers union. Many neighborhood groups also oppose short-term rentals aimed at tourists, as they make it more difficult for locals to find rentals. How strictly the law will be enforced is anyone's guess.

Pearl Harbor National Memorial

The World War II Valor in the Pacific National Monument underwent a name change in 2019 to become the Pearl Harbor National Memorial (p177). The move was via a bipartisan act of Congress to focus the park on what it is most known for. Likewise, the Pacific Aviation Museum is now the Pearl Harbor Aviation Museum (p179).

LISTEN, WATCH & FOLLOW

For inspiration, visit https://www.lonely planet.com/usa/hawaii/oahu.

@gohawaii Instagram account with inspirational images.

Hawaii Publi Radio (www.hawaiipublic radio.org) News and information.

Honolulu Civic Beat (www.civilbeat.org) Online O'ahu news.

Honolulu Magazine (www.honolulu magazine.com) The scoop on Honolulu.

Have Aloho Will Travel (https://sound cloud.com/havealohawill travel) Local O'ahu podcast.

FAST FACTS

Food trend '*ulu* (breadfruit)

Number of beaches 125

Number of snakes There are no snakes!

Pop 980,000

Accommodations

Find more accommodations reviews throughout the On the Road chapters (from p81)

PRICE RANGES

Unless otherwise stated, prices indicate high-season rates for a double-occupancy room. These days there seems to be no standard rate at many places – look for discounted rates early and online. Quoted rates generally don't include taxes of 14%. Unless noted, breakfast is not included and bathrooms are private.

$	under $100
$$	$100–$250
$$$	over $250

Most of O'ahu's traditional accommodation options such as hotels and resorts are packed into Waikiki and this is where most visitors stay. O'ahu is a small island; it's easy to see the whole of it while staying in one spot. Of late, less traditional places such as rooms, condos and entire houses all over O'ahu are available online.

Accommodation Types

Hotels and resorts There are plenty of top-class hotels and resorts run by the likes of Hilton, Starwood and Marriott in Waikiki, plus a Four Seasons and Disney's Aulani hotel-resort out west in Ko Olina, and Turtle Bay Resort on the North Shore. Most cheaper hotels are in Waikiki.

Vacation rentals and condominiums This section of the industry has been growing exponentially. Online offerings include rooms, condos and entire houses all over the island. A 2019 vacation-rental law (p111) could severely restrict offerings in the future, though.

Hostels O'ahu has only two hostels associated with Hostelling International, but a number of privately run hostels, most of them in Waikiki, cater to backpackers and provide decent-quality low-cost accommodations.

B&Bs and inns There are still a few traditional B&Bs, but the success of online companies such as Airbnb means that it's very competitive out there.

Camping You can pitch a tent at many county and some state parks around the island, many of which are at gorgeous beaches. Expect basic facilities: restrooms, open-air showers and some picnic tables or grills.

Best Places to Stay

Best on a Budget

If your wallet ain't fat, head for the backstreets of Waikiki, still only a short walk from the beach. There are some good options back here near the Ala Wai Canal and also at the Diamond Head end of Waikiki. Consider camping, though that will be further afield, and also rooms on sites such as Airbnb.

➡ Beach Waikiki Boutique Hostel (p154), Waikiki

➡ Polynesian Hostel (p155), Waikiki

➡ Waikiki Central Hotel (p157), Waikiki

➡ 'Ilima Hotel (p157), Waikiki

Best for Families

O'ahu, with oh so much to do, is great for families. It's hard for kids to get bored in

Waikiki, where there are lots of good accommodations near the beach and a plethora of activities. The Ko Olina resorts offer a slightly more controlled environment where you could stay in the one resort for a week if your heart (and family) so desired.

➡ Hilton Hawaiian Village (p155), Waikiki

➡ Aulani, A Disney Resort (p186), Ko Olina

➡ Coconut Waikiki Hotel (p158), Waikiki

➡ Ilikai Hotel (p155), Waikiki

Best for Solo Travelers

If you're craving a bit of everything bar solitude, Waikiki is the place to be. Lots of eating, drinking and shopping options, with the beach and associated activities at your fingertips. Waterfront hotels offer grace and sophistication, while those a tad further back aren't bad either. For solitude, investigate options in other parts of O'ahu.

➡ Surfjack Hotel & Swim Club (p158), Waikiki

➡ Halekulani (p156), Waikiki

➡ Moana Surfrider (p156), Waikiki

➡ 'Alohilani Resort Waikiki Beach (p157), Waikiki

Best Outside of Waikiki

There are surprisingly few traditional accommodations such as hotels and resorts outside of Waikiki. Ko Olina offers three popular resorts in Leeward O'ahu, while Turtle Bay is it for the North Shore. There are a few business-type hotels in Ala Moana and Honolulu and a nice, secluded resort in Kahala. Without doubt, the heart of the action is in Waikiki.

➡ Turtle Bay Resort (p251), North Shore

➡ Kahala Hotel & Resort (p201), Kahala

➡ Four Seasons Resort Oahu at Ko Olina (p186), Ko Olina

➡ Manoa Valley Inn (p110), Honolulu

Booking

Book accommodations early for busy seasons January to April plus July and August. National holidays also get busy. Deals can be had in the slower times of May and June and September through December.

JOSHUA RAINEY PHOTOGRAPHY / SHUTTERSTOCK ©

Aulani, A Disney Resort (p186)

Lonely Planet (lonelyplanet.com/hotels) Find independent reviews, as well as recommendations on the best places to stay – and then book them online.

Airbnb (www.airbnb.com) O'ahu residents have embraced Airbnb; offerings include rooms, condos and entire houses all over the island.

Flipkey (www.flipkey.com) Has a mix of condominiums and houses all over O'ahu.

Captain Cook Resorts (www.captaincookresorts. com) Condos are usually much larger than hotel rooms and are well equipped, so that owners can live in them but rent them out when they're not there.

VRBO (www.vrbo.com) Vacation Rentals by Owner. Lots and lots of options in Waikiki and around O'ahu.

Honolulu Department of Parks & Recreation (www.honolulu.gov/parks/beach-parks/camping. html) Administers beach parks and their campgrounds across O'ahu. Apply for camping permits online.

Hawaii Division of State Parks (https://dlnr. hawaii.gov/dsp/camping-lodging/oahu) Administers state parks and recreation areas. Apply for camping permits online.

Getting Around

For more information, see Transportation (p309)

If you want to get out and explore this exciting island during your visit to O'ahu – and it would be a waste not to – the best way to do it is to rent some wheels, hit the road and stop when you feel like it.

Traveling by Car

Getting around O'ahu is relatively easy, especially if you've come from mainland USA or another right-hand-side-of-the-road driving country.

Car Hire

All the big car-hire companies are here. The easiest way to get from the airport to your hotel, then around O'ahu during your stay, is to rent a car at the airport when you arrive. For this to work efficiently, you'll want to prebook.

If you only want a rental car for a few days and want to avoid prohibitive parking charges at your hotel, take a taxi/Uber/Lyft or shuttle to your hotel and get a rental car by the day once you're there. This is easy enough

to do, but day rates tend to be higher than longer-term rentals.

Driving Conditions

Slow, courteous driving is the rule on O'ahu. Locals usually don't honk, don't follow close and let other drivers pass and merge. Do the same, and you may get an appreciative *shaka* (Hawaiian hand greeting sign) from other drivers.

There's heavy traffic heading into Honolulu in the morning and away from

RESOURCES

Hawaii News Now (www.hawaiinews now.com/traffic) Up-to-date traffic and driving conditions on O'ahu's roads.

Go Akamai (http://goakamai.org/) Hawaii's interactive traffic-map app.

Federal Highway Administration Hawaii (www.fhwa.dot.gov/trafficinfo/hi.htm) Roadwork information and traffic cameras.

Honolulu Parking (https://parking.com/honolulu) Figure out your parking before you go.

TheBus (www.thebus.org) O'ahu's bus system is extensive and easy to use.

American Automobile Association (AAA; www.hawaii.aaa.com) Membership benefits include 24-hour roadside assistance.

Department of Transportation Bike Maps (http://hidot.hawaii.gov/high ways/bike-map-oahu) Bike maps and tips for the whole of O'ahu.

Franko's Maps (http://frankosmaps.com) Legendary physical guide, recreation, surfing and diving maps for O'ahu.

Honolulu in the afternoon. In particular, the H-1 freeway, which runs along the urbanized south coast from near the Ko Olina resorts in the west to Kahala in the east, gets clogged.

Two Wheels

If two wheels are more your thing, check out these guys:

Hawaii Harley Rental.Com (www.hawaiiharleyrental.com) Rent a Harley!

Hawaiian Style Rentals (www.hawaiianstylerentals.com) For mopeds and scooters.

Asking for Directions

You're in Hawaii! Here are some handy tips for interpreting replies from locals when you've asked for directions on O'ahu:

➡ *Mauka* (mao-kah) means 'toward the mountains.'

➡ *Makai* (mah-kigh) means 'toward the sea.'

So, 'go *mauka*' means that you should head inland.

Compass directions often get dropped in favor of place names. If you are in downtown, you might be told to:

➡ 'Go 'Ewa' – this means 'go west', as 'Ewa is west of downtown.

➡ 'Go Diamond Head' – this means 'go east', as Diamond Head is east of downtown.

It can be a tad confusing at first, especially if you mix up your *mauka* and your *makai*, but it doesn't take long to catch on and it's part of the charm of O'ahu.

No Car?

Bus

O'ahu's public bus system, TheBus (p311) is extensive and easy to use. The Ala Moana Center is Honolulu's central bus transfer point.

The system covers most places on the island along the main roads, and it's a great way to experience the island's best trips, such as the classic North Shore and Windward Coast loop. However, many trailheads, wilderness areas and viewpoints are not served.

Buses run regularly on major routes, seven days a week and from early morning into the evening. The website has full schedule and route info. All buses are wheelchair accessible.

Bicycle

It's possible to cycle around O'ahu, but consider taking TheBus to get beyond Honolulu metro-area traffic. All buses have front-loading racks that accommodate two bicycles at no extra charge – just let the driver know first. Cyclists will find O'ahu to be a fairly rider-friendly place. There are many local cyclists on the roads and drivers are

---

DRIVING FAST FACTS

➡ Drive on the right.

➡ Seatbelt and child-restraint use required by law.

➡ No texting while driving.

➡ Minimum age for full license: 18 years.

➡ Carry your license at all times.

➡ Blood-alcohol limit is 0.08%.

ROAD DISTANCES (MILES)

	Honolulu	Waikiki	Hale'iwa	Kailua
Waikiki	3			
Hale'iwa	31	34		
Kailua	13	15	39	
Wai'anae	31	33	33	40

Halona Cove (p210), on the Southeast O'ahu Loop

used to seeing people riding along the shoulder.

Biki (p133; https://gobiki.org/) is a new bike-share system, with pickup and drop-off points all over Honolulu and Waikiki.

Driving Tours

Circle Island Tour Drive around O'ahu. It's less than 100 miles and there's plenty to see and do.

Southeast O'ahu Loop Take a day to explore the best of Southeast O'ahu and the southern Windward Coast.

Leeward Coast Head to the least visited side of the island, away from the crowds.

Punchbowl, Pu'uohi'a & Round Top Drive This loop heads high above Honolulu, taking in magnificent tropical vegetation and views.

Off the Beaten Path Check out Central O'ahu, then head to the northwestern tip of the island on the North Shore.

Diamond Head to Makapu'u Beach From one of O'ahu's most iconic lookouts, head east along the dramatic coastline.

Driving up the Windward Coast Beaches, stunning mountains, more beaches and great food are the highlights of this tropical drive.

Month by Month

January

The busy season kicks in as mainlanders arrive en masse. The Martin Luther King Jr holiday on the third Monday is particularly busy. Typically the rainiest month of the year.

☆ Chinese New Year

Around the time of the second new moon after the winter solstice, usually between late January and mid-February, Chinatown in Honolulu celebrates the lunar New Year with more than a week's worth of lion dances, firecrackers, street fairs and parades.

☆ O'ahu Fringe Festival

Held in January on alternate years, O'ahu's Fringe Festival presents uncensored performing arts, often off the cuff. Expect the unexpected.

February

One of the best months to spot humpback whales migrating past the island. Valentine's Day (February 14) and Presidents' Day (third Monday) are booked solid at resorts. Winter storms bring rain and cooler temperatures.

🏃 Great Aloha Fun Run

This popular 8.15-mile race from the harbor-front Aloha Tower to Aloha Stadium takes place on the third Monday in February. There's a free nine-week training program leading up to the event.

March

It's still winter elsewhere, so it's still peak season on O'ahu. Note that college students take spring break in March or April, making things even busier – and families turn up for Easter.

☆ Honolulu Festival

Music, dance and drama performances at various venues in Honolulu and Waikiki take place for three days in early March. The Asia Pacific cultural festival also features an arts-and-crafts fair and a grand parade followed by a fireworks show.

April

Winter rains abate about the same time as the tourist crush does. Any time after Easter is a low-key, and possibly lower-priced, time to visit. And there's plenty going on.

☆ Waikiki Spam Jam

One of Waikiki's wackiest street festivals is held in late April or early May. The Spam Jam celebrates the state's favorite meat product. Try Spam served as sushi, in spring rolls, atop nachos, in tacos, mixed with pasta – even as a popsicle flavoring.

☆ 'I Love Kailua' Town Party

A giant block party takes over Kailua town's main street one Sunday in late April. Local bands and hula schools turn out to perform, while the community's artists vend their wares and area restaurants cook up a storm.

May

May Day, the first, is Lei Day in Hawaii, when the tradition of stringing together and wearing tropical flowers, leaves and seeds is celebrated. Crowds thin, though Memorial Day weekend is busy.

🎏 Wahiawa Pineapple Festival

On a Saturday in early May everything pineapple is celebrated at this small-town community fair at Wahiawa District Park on California Ave. A parade, music, food sales, games and demonstrations are all included.

🎏 Shinnyo Lantern Floating Hawaii

On the last Monday in May, the souls of the dead are honored with a Japanese floating-lantern ceremony after sunset at Magic Island in Ala Moana Beach Park.

June

Calmer currents prevail; it's relatively safe to assume that you can swim instead of surf on the North Shore. It's before summer-vacation time, so take advantage of the weather and discounts on hotels and flights.

☆ Pan-Pacific Festival

Expect outdoor hula shows and *taiko* drumming as part of the mid-June Asian and Polynesian performing-arts showcase in Honolulu and Waikiki. Don't miss the huge *ho'olaule'a* (celebration) block party and parade that takes place along Kalakaua Ave.

🎏 King Kamehameha Day Celebrations

The state holiday is June 11. A ceremony at the king's statue in Honolulu is followed by a parade and a street party. Later in the month, a hula festival is held in his majesty's honor.

☆ Sailor Jerry Festival

Held in Chinatown, this festival features music, stand-up comedy, movies and tattooing. Sailor Jerry (aka Norman Collins) was a legendary tattoo artist who inked Honolulu-stationed WWII sailors and soldiers.

July

Towns around the island welcome Independence Day, July 4, with fireworks and festivities. Family summer-vacation travel is at a peak around the holiday, as are lodging prices. Temperatures rise and rain is scarce.

🎏 Duke Kahanamoku Challenge

Outrigger-canoe and stand-up paddle-surfing (SUP) races, island-style food, and traditional Hawaiian games, art and crafts, and entertainment on a Sunday in early March at Duke Kahanamoku Lagoon & Beach, Waikiki.

☆ Prince Lot Hula Festival

On the third Saturday in July, one of O'ahu's premier Hawaiian cultural festivals features noncompetitive hula performances at Moanalua Gardens in Honolulu. The former royal-retreat setting provides an even more graceful, traditional atmosphere.

🎏 Hale'iwa Arts Festival

Artists gather at Hale'iwa one weekend in July to show and sell wares. There's painting, photography, printmaking, ceramics, woodwork, jewelry, leatherwork, sculpture, glass and more. Music, food, cultural tours and hands-on demonstrations are also scheduled.

☆ Ukulele Festival

Since 1971 this has been one of the world's premier festivals celebrating the ukulele. This is a don't-miss celebration in mid-July.

🏃 Hawaii Dragon Boat Festival

Colorful and fierce Chinese dragon boats race to the beat of island drummers at Ala Moana Beach Park in late July.

August

Sunny weather continues nearly everywhere. On Statehood Day, the third Friday of the month, some celebrate, some protest – but everyone takes the day off work. Families taking summer vacations keep things busy.

☆ Hawaiian Slack Key Guitar Festival 'Waikiki Style'

Lay out a picnic blanket at Waikiki Aquarium and enjoy free Hawaiian guitar and ukulele shows. Top performers take the stage, plus there are food vendors and an arts-and-crafts fair.

☆ Na Hula Festival

Well into its eighth decade, this festival features local hula *halau* (schools), which gather for music and dance celebrations at Kapi'olani Park in early August.

September

Trade winds blow in, but the temperature is still ideal, making this an excellent time to explore the island without the crowds.

🎊 Aloha Festivals

Begun in 1946, the Aloha Festival is the state's premier cultural festival. The signature events are Waikiki's royal court procession, block party and floral parade. Activities take place throughout the month.

🏃 Na Wahine O Ke Kai

Hawaii's major women's outrigger-canoe race is held near the end of September. It starts at sunrise on Moloka'i and ends 41 miles later at Waikiki's Kahanamoku Beach.

October

Travel bargains abound during one of the year's slowest times for visiting O'ahu. The weather is reliably sunny, but it's very humid when the trade winds don't blow. Plenty of events aimed at the locals.

🍴 Hawaii Food & Wine Festival

Star chefs, sustainable farms and food-lovers come together for food and wine. Events in Honolulu and beyond highlight local bounty and may include gala dinners, farm-to-table tastings, traditional Hawaiian feasts, luncheon discussions, and wine-, chocolate- and coffee-pairing sessions.

🎊 Honolulu Pride

Hawaii's largest LGBTIQ event features a huge pride parade that begins on Magic Island in Ala Moana Regional Park and follows Kalakaua Ave to Kapi'olani Regional Park, where there's music and a festival. Dozens of additional events in the days before and after.

🏃 Moloka'i Hoe

The men's outrigger-canoe world championship is held in mid-October. The fastest teams take less than five hours to race the 41 miles from Moloka'i to Waikiki.

🎊 Halloween

In the weeks leading up to and including Halloween (October 31), look for themed performances, haunted houses, costume contests and local festivals.

November

Surfers descend on the North Shore for the epic winter wave season. It can get cool at night. Thanksgiving can be a pricey time to visit.

☆ Hawaii International Film Festival

Screenings of imported Pacific Rim, Asian, mainland American, European and even a few Hawaii-related films roll at venues in Honolulu and Waikiki. This highly regarded event is popular, so book tickets ahead. For full schedules, see www.hiff.org.

🏃 Triple Crown of Surfing

This world-class surfing competition takes place from mid-November to mid-December at the North Shore's Hale'iwa surf break, Sunset Beach and Banzai Pipeline. The start date depends on the surf. Be ready, and bring your binoculars!

🎊 King Kalakaua's Birthday

Victorian-era decorations and a concert of monarchy-era music by the Royal Hawaiian Band at 'Iolani Palace on November 16.

December

Despite the occasional chill, Santas all over the island are putting on their best aloha shirts. Early on, locals have the place to themselves; Christmas and New Year bring crazy-high prices and crowds.

🏃 Honolulu Marathon

On the second Sunday in December the Honolulu Marathon attracts more than 30,000 runners (more than half hailing from Japan), making it one of the world's top marathons. Runners trace a route from downtown Honolulu to Diamond Head.

🎊 Christmas

The island celebrates Christmas all month. Many communities host parades, including a floating regatta originating at Hawai'i Kai Marina. Honolulu City Lights starts in early December with a parade and concert and finishes with fireworks for the New Year.

Itineraries

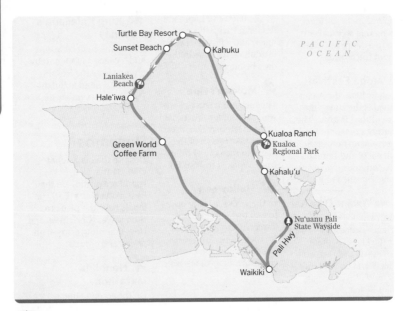

Turtle Bay Resort
Sunset Beach
Kahuku
PACIFIC OCEAN
Laniakea Beach
Hale'iwa
Kualoa Ranch
Green World Coffee Farm
Kualoa Regional Park
Kahalu'u
Nu'uanu Pali State Wayside
Pali Hwy
Waikiki

1 DAY Circle Island Tour

Either rent a car or join a tour for this one-day adventure circling O'ahu. All up, you're in for less than 100 miles of driving. Don't forget towels, sunscreen and bathing suits. Traveling in either direction is fine.

From **Waikiki**, cross to the Windward Coast on the Pali Hwy, making sure to stop at the **Nu'uanu Pali State Wayside** at the pass. Halfway down, turn left onto Rte 83, and from **Kahalu'u** you'll be heading up the coast. Take a break at **Kualoa Regional Park** to check out Mokoli'i Island (Chinaman's Hat) and the magnificent Kualoa mountains. **Kualoa Ranch** beckons with all sorts of activities.

The drive and scenery are mesmerizing. Break for lunch at the shrimp trucks at **Kahuku**, a classy restaurant at **Turtle Bay Resort** or at Ted's Bakery at **Sunset Beach**. You're hitting the 'Seven-Mile Miracle' that surfers dream of: the North Shore stretch of waves and sand from Sunset Beach to Hale'iwa township. See if the turtles are visiting at **Laniakea Beach**.

After checking out **Hale'iwa**, down a pick-me-up at **Green World Coffee Farm** in Central O'ahu before taking the H-2 and H-1 freeways back to **Waikiki**.

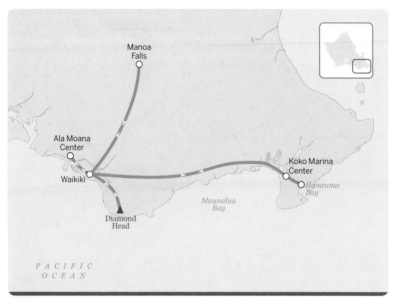

Waikiki, Hanauma Bay & Diamond Head

Into the outdoors? Make sure to hit these spots if you've got limited time on O'ahu. There's plenty to see and do within a few miles of **Waikiki**, including swimming, snorkeling, sailing and hiking. Get out there and do it! And a bit of retail therapy won't hurt either.

On day one, shake out the cobwebs with an early-morning swim at Kuhio Beach Park, followed by a stroll down to Kaimana Beach and around gorgeous Kapi'olani Regional Park. This will set you up for a good look around Waikiki. Head into the legendary diner Eggs 'n' Things for brunch, then when you're ready, head up inland past the University of Hawai'i and into the Manoa Valley for a fun short hike up to **Manoa Falls**. Remember, it could be raining up here, even if the sun's shining in Waikiki. Back in Waikiki late afternoon, enjoy a refreshing swim, then cocktails, followed by the Kuhio Beach Torchlighting & Hula Show or slack-key guitars in the evening.

Day two has an early start as you'll want to get to spectacular **Hanauma Bay** for snorkeling before the crowds arrive – as a bonus, entry is free before 7am! Get there at 9am and the car park is likely to be full. Don't leave without spotting Hawaii's state fish, the *humuhumunukunukuapua'a*. Stop off at Kokonuts at the **Koko Marina Center** for refreshments after. Back in Waikiki, enjoy some solid beach time and an afternoon catamaran cruise from right on the beach before heading out to House Without a Key at Halekulani.

Get an early start on day three to climb **Diamond Head**, as it gets hot in the middle of the day. Spectacular views from the top make the climb worthwhile. Stop off at Bogart's or Da Cove Health Bar & Cafe on Monsarrat Ave for an acai bowl on your way back to Waikiki. Take a dip at the beach, freshen up, then head to the **Ala Moana Center**, the world's largest open-air shopping center, with more than 340 stores and restaurants. Eat at Ala Moana tonight or head a bit inland to one of Honolulu's hidden gems, Sweet Home Café, on King St just northeast of the Ala Moana Center.

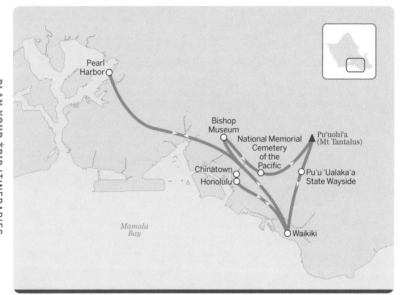

Honolulu & Pearl Harbor

4 DAYS

For those into history, art and culture, Oʻahu is a treasure trove. While millions of visitors turn up to see Pearl Harbor, others will be captivated by the quality of the city's museums, the intrigue of its historical district and Chinatown, and the proximity of verdant mountain scenery.

From your base in **Waikiki**, spend at least a day at **Pearl Harbor**. The Pearl Harbor National Memorial is one of the USA's most significant WWII sites. It narrates the history of the Pearl Harbor attack and commemorates fallen service personnel. Visit the USS Arizona Memorial, the Battleship Missouri Memorial, the USS Bowfin Submarine Museum & Park and the Pearl Harbor Aviation Museum.

For another day, visit the **Bishop Museum**, undoubtedly the world's top Polynesian anthropological museum and Hawaii's version of the Smithsonian Institute. There's lots going on here, but on your way back, make time to drive into the **National Memorial Cemetery of the Pacific**, better known as Punchbowl. Some 50,000 people are buried in this volcanic crater. Views of Honolulu from the rim are superb. Going back to Waikiki, drive the Punchbowl, Puʻu ʻOhiʻa & Round Top Drive scenic route and take a stop at **Puʻu ʻUalakaʻa State Wayside** to view the city and Waikiki.

For a third day, head into **Honolulu**. The Honolulu Museum of Art is exceptional and may be the biggest surprise of your trip to Oʻahu. Book ahead and join a tour out to Shangri La, Doris Duke's hideaway at Black Point. The only way to see Shangri La is on a tour from here. Next, **Chinatown** beckons! Wander the streets and markets, check out the galleries, then stick around for dinner at a local hot spot such as Lucky Belly or Pig & the Lady. Later on, Dragon Upstairs may be calling.

Downtown and Honolulu's Historical District are worth a day, too. Check out the only royal palace in the USA, ʻIolani Palace, then the State Capitol with its unusual design. There's thought-provoking art from Hawaii's multiethnic communities at the Hawaiʻi State Art Museum and more history at the Hawaiian Mission Houses Historic Site. Atmospheric Cafe Julia or Artizen by MW at the State Art Museum are great spots for lunch. Don't forget to go up Aloha Tower.

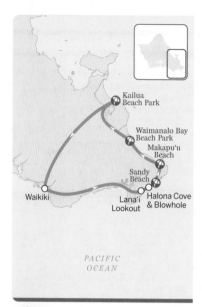

🏅 1 DAY Southeast O'ahu Loop

Spectacular scenery awaits on this trip, for which you'll want your own wheels. In store are great beaches, views, strolling and killer bodyboarding. Take your time and it'll take all day, or buzz around in half that.

From **Waikiki**, head east on Rte 72, the Kalaniana'ole Hwy, from the eastern end of the H-1 at Kahala. If you want refreshments, drop into the Koko Marina Center at Hawai'i Kai. You'll hit Hanauma Bay for snorkeling on a different day (it's a must!), so for now carry on with stops at the **Lana'i Lookout**, **Halona Cove and Blowhole** and **Sandy Beach**. You'll need confidence to bodyboard here, as the waves crash right onto the beach!

Makapu'u Lookout reveals unreal views of **Makapu'u Beach**, Waimanalo Bay and magnificent *pali* (cliffs). **Waimanalo Bay Beach Park** is *the* place to pull out that boogie board. Otherwise, carry on to Kailua township or its amazing golden-sand **beach park**. Strolling, swimming, kayaking, windsurfing and kitesurfing are all here. Get a shave ice at Island Snow Hawaii.

Getting late in the day? Head back over to Waikiki on the Pali Hwy (Rte 61) to complete the loop.

🏅 1 DAY Leeward Coast

You'll want your own wheels for this road less traveled. Past the Ko Olina resorts, the Leeward Coast feels like forgotten O'ahu. That said, there are magnificent white-sand beaches, Native Hawaiian pride is alive and well, and there are good spots to hike.

Take the H-1 west from **Honolulu**, and for a look at what **Waipahu** used to be like, make a stop at the Plantation Village. This outdoor museum tells the story of life on the sugar plantations and of Waipahu, one of O'ahu's last plantation towns.

From the freeway, spot the construction of HART, the mostly elevated Honolulu rapid-transit project that will eventually link East Kapolei with the Ala Moana Center. At the end of the H-1, visit the upscale **Ko Olina** resorts and golf course, which feel a bit out of place here in western O'ahu.

Heading up the coast now, if you're ready to eat, stop in at Coquitos Latin Cuisine, roadside in **Wai'anae**. Further up, take a dip at magnificent **Makaha Beach**, or at **Keawa'ula Beach**, renowned for its sunsets. From the end of the road, hike out to **Ka'ena Point** and back. The return journey to Honolulu will take a tad over an hour.

Off the Beaten Track

KUNIA ROAD

If you're not in a hurry on your way to Wahiawa in Central O'ahu (and why would you be?), consider taking scenic Kunia Rd through rural plantations at the foot of the mountains. (p269)

MAKAHA BEACH

Surprisingly free of tourists, away from most visitor action on the leeward coast, spectacular Makaha Beach is where big-wave surfing got its start in the 1950s. (p191)

HELENA'S HAWAIIAN FOOD

A few blocks southeast of the Bishop Museum, Helena's is a top spot to come if you want to eat 'local'. (p104)

LA MARIANA SAILING CLUB

Time warp! Who says all the great tiki bars have gone to the dogs? Irreverent and kitschy, this 1950s joint by the lagoon is filled with yachties and long-suffering locals. (p124)

ETHEL'S GRILL

One of the greatest hole-in-the-wall restaurants in Honolulu, Ethel's has the tastiest food and a homely atmosphere. (p114)

Kahuku Point
Kuilima Point
Sunset Beach
North Shore
Kulalua Point
Pupukea
Kahuku Forest Reserve
Pu'u Ka'inapua'a (2361ft)
Waimea
Kaua'i Channel
Waimea Valley
Pua'ena Point
Waialua Bay
Hale'iwa
Mokule'ia
Kawailoa Forest Reserve
Ka'ena Point
Kuaokala Game Management Area
Waialua
Yokohama Bay
Makua Military Reservation
Mokule'ia Forest Reserve
Mt Ka'ala (4025ft)
Schofield Barracks Military Reservation
Wahiawa
Makua Kea'au Forest Reserve
Wai'anae Kai Forest Reserve
Kolekole Pass (1724ft)
Wheeler Army Airfield
MAKAHA BEACH
Makaha
Honouliuli Forest Reserve
Kunia
Mililani
Wai'anae
Lualualei Naval Reservation
Kane'ilio Point
Ma'ili
Ma'ili Point
Nanakuli Forest Reserve
KUNIA RD
Pearl City
Nanakuli
Wai'anae Coast
Waipahu
Kahe Point
Makakilo
'Ewa
Ko Olina
Kapolei
Barbers Point Naval Air Station
'Ewa Beach
Barbers Point
South Shore

N
0 ———————— 10 km
0 ———————— 5 miles

PACIFIC OCEAN

GYOTAKU BY NAOKI

You'll probably spot Naoki's magnificent *gyotaku* (Japanese-style fish prints) all over O'ahu, but there's nothing like watching him print up a freshly caught fish in his own studio in Kane'ohe. (p229)

LIKEKE FALLS

Ready for a hidden waterfall, and maybe even being lucky enough to have it to yourself? The family-friendly Likeke Falls Trail winds through a forest of native and exotic trees into the lush Ko'olau Range. (p223)

BAILEY'S ANTIQUES & ALOHA SHIRTS

Bailey's has the finest aloha-shirt collection on O'ahu, possibly the world! Racks are crammed with thousands of collector-worthy vintage shirts in every conceivable color and style. (p170)

Kahuku
Makahoa Point
La'ie Point
La'ie
Hau'ula
Kaipapa'u Forest Reserve
Punalu'u
Kahana Bay
Kahana
Ka'a'awa
'Ewa Forest Reserve
Ahupua'a o Kahana State Park
Kualoa Point
Pu'u Ka'aumakua (2681ft)
Waikane
Waiahole Forest Reserve
Waiahole
Wailau Point
Kahalu'u
'Ahuimanu
He'eia
Kane'ohe Bay
Kane'ohe Marine Corps Base Hawaii (MCBH)
Windward Coast
KO'OLAU RANGE
GYOTAKU BY NAOKI
Kane'ohe
LIKEKE FALLS
Kailua Bay
Kailua
Lānikai
Olomana
Mt Olomana (1643ft) ▲
Waimanalo Bay
'Aiea
Honolulu Watershed Forest Reserve
Konahuanui (3105ft) ▲
HELENA'S HAWAIIAN FOOD
Mānoa Falls
Waimanalo
Pearl Harbor
Honolulu International Airport
ETHEL'S GRILL
Pu'u Lanipo (2621ft) ▲
Honolulu
LA MARIANA SAILING CLUB
BAILEY'S ANTIQUES & ALOHA SHIRTS
Hawai'i Kai
Makapu'u Point
Mamala Bay
Waikiki
PIONEER SALOON
Diamond Head (760ft) ▲
KONA BREWING COMPANY
Koko Head (642ft)
Ka'iwi Channel

PIONEER SALOON

It's simple stuff, but the locals can't get enough of Pioneer Saloon's Japanese fusion plate lunches, with everything from grilled ahi (yellowfin tuna) to fried baby octopus to *yakisoba* (fried noodles). (p163)

KONA BREWING COMPANY

This Big Island import, on the water in Hawai'i Kai, is known for its microbrewed beers, especially the Longboard Lager, the Pipeline Porter and the Big Wave Golden Ale. (p207)

Spam *musubi* (p4◆

Eat & Drink Like a Local

'Dis is seriously broke da mout!' That's the ultimate local compliment: the food's so delicious that it breaks the mouth. Honolulu, Waikiki, Waimanalo, Kahuku and the North Shore are just some of the places you'll find exceptional – often creative – fare. So eat everything in sight. It's all *'ono grinds* (good eats).

The Year in Food

Mild, tropical weather year-round ensures that it's always a good time to eat on O'ahu.

Winter (December–February)
Peak tourist season means that you will want to book ahead for top restaurants in Honolulu and Waikiki. Crowd-pleasing avocados, tangerines and strawberries are ripe.

Spring (March–May)
Tropical fruits such as mango, papaya and pineapple hit their prime. Look for festivals celebrating food all over the island.

Summer (June–August)
What *isn't* in season during the dry, warm days of O'ahu's summer? With little notice you should be able to book a top table anywhere.

Autumn (September–November)
The Hawai'i Food & Wine Festival (p109) is a lovefest for great food held in Honolulu in October.

Local Specialties

Cheap, tasty and filling, local *grinds* (food) is the stuff of cravings and comfort. There's no better example than the classic plate lunch, a fixed-plate meal of 'two scoop' rice, macaroni or potato salad and a hot protein dish reflecting Hawaii's polyglot food heritage, such as fried mahi-mahi, teriyaki chicken, Korean-style *kalbi* short ribs, Filipino pork *adobo* or Japanese-style *katsu* pork or chicken.

Often eaten with disposable chopsticks on disposable plates, these meals pack a flavor (and caloric) punch: fried, salty and meaty. Nowadays healthier plates come with options for brown rice and salad greens, but in general the backbone of the plate lunch is those two scoops of rice and potato/macaroni salad.

Sticky white rice is more than a side dish in Hawaii. It's a culinary building block, an integral partner in everyday meals. Without rice, Spam *musubi* (rice balls) would just be a slice of canned meat. The *loco moco* would be nothing more than an egg-and-gravy-covered hamburger patty. Just so you know, sticky white rice means exactly that. Not fluffy rice. Not wild rice. And definitely not instant rice.

One must-try local *pupu* (snack or appetizer) is *poke* (poh-keh), a savory dish of bite-size raw fish (typically ahi – yellowfin tuna), seasoned with *shōyu* (soy sauce), sesame oil, green onion, chili-pepper flakes, sea salt, *ogo* (crunchy seaweed) and *'inamona* (a condiment made of roasted, ground *kukui* – candlenut tree – nuts). Few foodstuffs short of a raw oyster can match *poke* when it comes to evoking the flavors of the ocean. *Poke* chefs take pride in developing their own signature flavors, such as tongue-twisting garlic.

Another favorite local food is *saimin*, a soup of chewy Chinese egg noodles swimming in Japanese broth, garnished with green onion, dried *nori* (Japanese dried seaweed), *kamaboko* (steamed fish cake) and *char siu* (Chinese barbecued pork).

On a hot day, nothing beats a mound of snowy shave ice packed into a cup and drenched with sweet syrups in an eye-popping rainbow of hues. Purists stick with just ice, but for added decadence ask for sweet azuki beans, *mochi* (sticky, sweet Japanese pounded-rice cakes) or ice cream underneath, or maybe *haupia* (coconut pudding) or a dusting of powdered *li hing mui* (dried salted plums) on top.

Spam

Hawaii may be the only US state where you can eat Hormel's iconic canned meat with pride. Here in the nation's Spam capital, locals consume around seven million cans per year.

During the plantation era canned meat was cheap and easy to prepare for *bento* (Japanese-style boxed lunches) taken to the fields. But Spam itself wasn't introduced to the islands until WWII, when fresh meat was replaced by standard US military rations. By the time the war ended, residents had developed an affinity for the fatty pork-based meat product.

How you feel about Spam is, of course, an entirely different affair – many visitors to O'ahu have a hard time getting the quivering processed meat past their lips, or they simply associate the stuff with the worst memories of school lunches. But in many ways, eating Spam is as true to experiencing Hawaii on a culinary level as devouring a plate of poi (steamed and mashed taro).

And Spam looks and tastes different in Hawaii. It's always eaten cooked (typically fried to a light crispiness in sugar-sweetened *shōyu*), not straight from the can. It's commonly served for breakfast with eggs and rice. One very popular preparation is Spam *musubi*: a block of rice with a slice of cooked Spam on top (or in the middle) and wrapped with *nori*. Created in the 1960s, it has become a classic, and thousands of *musubi* are sold daily at O'ahu grocers, lunch counters and convenience stores.

Don't miss the Waikiki Spam Jam festival (p153) in late April or early May.

Shave ice (p39)

CRACK SEED

Forget candy bars. Hawaii's most popular snack is crack seed, sold prepackaged in O'hu's supermarkets and convenience stores or by the pound at specialty shops. It's an addictive, mouthwatering Chinese invention that can be sweet, sour, salty, spicy or some combination of all four. Like Coca-Cola or curry, the various flavors of crack seed are impossible to describe. Just one taste and you'll be hooked.

Crack seed is usually made from dried fruit such as plums, cherries, mangoes or lemons. The most popular flavor – which is also the most overwhelming to the uninitiated – is *li hing mui*. These days powdered *li hing mui* – sour enough to pucker the most stoic of faces – is used to spice up just about everything, from shave ice to fresh-fruit margaritas.

Kaimukī Crack Seed Store (p131) could keep you going every day for a month with something new to try.

Native Hawaiian Food

With its earthy flavors and Polynesian ingredients, Native Hawaiian cooking is a distinct culinary genre. But it's not necessarily easy for visitors to find – look for it at roadside markets, plate-lunch vendors and island diners.

Kalua pig is traditionally roasted whole underground in an *imu*, a pit of red-hot stones layered with *ti* and banana leaves. Cooked this way, the pork is smoky, salty and succulent. Nowadays *kalua* pork is hugely popular; it's typically oven roasted, and seasoned with salt and liquid smoke. At a commercial luau, a pig placed in an *imu* is usually only for show (it couldn't feed 300-plus guests anyway).

Poi – a purplish paste made of pounded taro root, often steamed and fermented – was sacred to ancient Hawaiians. Taro is highly nutritious, low in calories, easily digestible and versatile to prepare. Tasting bland to mildly tart or even sour, poi is usually not eaten by itself but as a starchy counterpoint to strongly flavored dishes such as *lomilomi* salmon (minced, salted salmon with diced tomato and green on-

Laulau

ion). Fried or baked taro chips are widely sold at supermarkets and convenience stores. They make a tasty contrast to potato chips.

A popular main dish is *laulau*, a bundle of pork or chicken and salted butterfish wrapped in taro or *ti* leaves and steamed until it has a soft, spinach-like texture. Other traditional Hawaiian fare includes baked *'ulu* (breadfruit), with a mouthfeel similar to potato; *'opihi* (limpet), tiny mollusks picked off reefs at low tide; and *haupia*, a yummy coconut-cream custard thickened with arrowroot or cornstarch.

In general, Native Hawaiian cuisine is very filling, if not the most flavorful – there's a lot of emphasis on starch and meat. If you've dined elsewhere in Polynesia, it has a very similar ingredient and flavor profile to sister Polynesian cuisines across the ocean.

Luau

In ancient Hawaii, a luau commemorated auspicious occasions such as births, war victories or successful harvests. Modern luau that celebrate weddings or a baby's first birthday are often large banquet-hall or outdoor gatherings with the *'ohana* (extended family and friends). Although the menu might be daring – including Hawaiian delicacies such as raw *'a'ama* (black crab) and *'opihi* – the entertainment is low-key.

Hawaii's commercial luau started in Waikiki in the 1970s. Today these shows offer the elaborate pseudo-Hawaiian feast and Polynesian dancing and fire-eaters that many visitors expect. But the all-you-can-eat buffet of luau standards is usually toned down for the mainland palate, with steamed mahi-mahi, teriyaki chicken, and paste-like poi that gives the authentic stuff a bad name. Most commercial luau are pricey and touristy, but they're fun for all that – it's one of those experiences you check off the list and probably don't need to repeat.

You'll find luau many nights of the week at the resort centers of Waikiki and Ko Olina.

Hawaii Regional Cuisine

In the early 1990s a pioneering movement dubbed Hawaii Regional Cuisine took off. This type of cooking incorporates fresh island ingredients from local farmers, ranchers and fishers; borrows liberally from Hawaii's ethnic groups; and is marked by creative fusion combinations such as Peking duck in ginger-*liliko'i* (passion fruit) sauce.

Once Hawaii Regional Cuisine hit the foodie radar, some of its founding chefs, including Alan Wong, Roy Yamaguchi and Sam Choy, became celebrities (and all three still have O'ahu restaurants). Many more O'ahu chefs have found inspiration and gone in their own direction. One delicious example: George Mavrothalassitis has paired modern Hawaiian with classic French at his Chef Mavro (p117).

The best Hawaii Regional Cuisine still focuses on seasonally fresh, locally grown and often organic ingredients. Upscale restaurants are still the mainstay for Hawaii's star chefs, but now you'll find neighborhood bistros and even plate-lunch food trucks serving dishes inspired by this inventive fare, with O'ahu farms lauded like designer brands on menus.

How to Eat & Drink

Informal dining is O'ahu's forte. For local food such as the ubiquitous plate lunches, swing by retro drive-ins and diners with Formica tables, open from morning till night. Across the island you'll find food trucks (sometimes called *kaukau* wagons or lunch wagons). These range from the famous shrimp vendors of Kahuku to idiosyncratic trucks run by visionary chefs. Also look for great little cafes with healthy and interesting menus that are run with passion.

For inventive cuisine by Hawaii's star chefs, explore Honolulu – Hawaii's cutting-edge foodie trends all start in the capital city, and you'll find excellent options at any price point. Waikiki also has good top-end options, but it's besieged by expensive resort restaurants and chains as well.

Outside Honolulu and Waikiki, restaurants close earlier in the evening (often by 9pm). Open from *pau hana* (happy hour) until late, bars usually serve tasty *pupu* such as *poke*, shrimp tempura or *edamame* (fresh soybeans in the pod). The casual Hawaii dress code means that T-shirts and flip-flops are commonly worn, except at Honolulu's most upscale restaurants and at Waikiki's luxury resorts. The older generation of locals tends toward neat, modest attire, which for men generally just means an aloha shirt and slacks.

For groceries, head first to the many farmers markets with their huge variety of locally produced fare. However, most groceries are still imported from the mainland and beyond (including foods that can be grown on O'ahu, such as bananas and even some pineapples!). You can get virtually anything you want, but the prices average 30% more than on the US mainland, so prepare for some sticker shock.

Drinks
Coffee, Tea & Juice

Hawaii was the first US state to grow coffee. The finest coffee beans come from the Big Island, where 100% Kona coffee has worldwide cachet. But O'ahu is also in on

---

O'AHU'S HOMEGROWN BOUNTY

In recent years every island in Hawaii has become known for various locally produced foods renowned for their quality. O'ahu is no exception. Among the island's great bounty, look for salad greens from Nalo Farms in Waimanalo and Ili'ili Farms; organic mushrooms from Small Kine Farm; tomatoes from North Shore Farms; Wailalua Estate coffee, vanilla and chocolate; Manoa Honey; sweet corn and farm-raised shrimp from Kahuku; 'Ewa-grown melons; and orange-flesh Kamiya papayas, especially those from Kahuku Farms (p240).

You can find these items and more at O'ahu's many farmers markets, including these good ones: KCC Farmers Market (p202) in Diamond Head and Kailua Farmers Market (p226). For a guide to O'ahu farmers markets, see www.hawaiiliving.com/blog/farmers-market-guide.

Top: Traditional Hawaiian food

Bottom: Beers from Honolulu Beerworks (p123)

YI-CHEN CHIANG / SHUTTERSTOCK ©

THE BASICS

An entire island whose culture is the perfect fit for a relaxed vacation – what could be better? Rarely will you dine at an establishment where shorts or a skirt and an aloha shirt won't fit right in. O'ahu places to eat take three main forms.

Restaurants Can be excellent, usually with outdoor seating, sometimes with ocean views.

Cafes From humble to offbeat, these are where you can find island staples such as the plate lunch, or more esoteric, creative fare.

Food trucks All the rage; many offer short and superb menus. Find them at beaches, by the roadside and in tiny villages.

the action. Waialua Estate (www.waialua estate.com) coffee is grown on O'ahu's North Shore. It can be found in island restaurants and at supermarkets such as Whole Foods Markets.

Ancient Hawaiians never got buzzed on coffee beans, which were first imported in the early 19th century. Hawaii's original intoxicants were plant-based Polynesian elixirs: 'awa (kava), a mild sedative and intoxicant, and noni (Indian mulberry), which some consider a cure-all. Both are pungent in smell and taste. Look for them in the crunchier natural-foods stores and juice joints.

Tea growing was introduced to Hawaii in the late 19th century, but it never took hold as a commercial crop due to high labor and production costs.

Not surprisingly, fruit trees thrive on O'ahu. Alas, most supermarket cartons contain imported purees or sugary 'juice drinks' such as POG (passion fruit, orange and guava, which are more flavorings than actual juice). It's tasty, but it's also just fruity enough to fool you into thinking you're drinking something healthy – you're not (although in a pinch, mix it with rum, add ice and you'll be smiling).

Look for real, freshly squeezed and blended juices at island cafes, health-food stores, farmers markets and roadside fruit stands. The best will proudly note which fruits are island sourced. In stores big and small you'll find tasty, refreshing drinks from Waialua Soda Works (www.waialua sodaworks.com), which bottles old-fashioned soda pop that's naturally flavored by tropical fruit such as liliko'i.

Beer, Wine & Cocktails

Several microbreweries are now firmly established on O'ahu. Brewmasters claim that the mineral content and purity of Hawaii's water makes for excellent beer. Another hallmark of local craft beers is the addition of a hint of tropical flavors, such as Kona coffee, coconut or liliko'i.

Among the local brewers, two stand out. At Beer Lab (p124), superbly talented hobbyists have become professional brewers. Over at Honolulu Beerworks (p123), you can try 10 or more of its great beers in a warehouse setting. Some of the best breweries on neighbor islands have also set up shop on O'ahu. The excellent Kona Brewing Company (p207), from the Big Island, has a very inviting restaurant at Hawai'i Kai that's good at sunset. The equally top-notch Maui Brewing Co (p165) has recently opened huge bars in Waikiki and Kailua.

It seems as though every beachfront and hotel bar mixes tropical cocktails topped with fruit garnish and a toothpick umbrella. But there's more here than just a cliché. There's a trend among better bars island wide to put some creativity into their cocktails. Look for menus that list interesting and creative takes on standards such as the ever-popular mai tai.

Most bars have pau hana before 5pm and many complement these with another after 8pm. In Waikiki, these later happy hours often come with live Hawaiian music. Top-end restaurants usually have extensive and pricey wine lists of bottles imported from the mainland and worldwide.

Bodyboarding in Waikiki (p150)

Plan Your Trip

On the Water

If you want to get wet, O'ahu is the place for you. Surfing is the obvious option, but there's also all the other ways you can ride the waves as well as go exploring above and below the surface.

Best on the Water

Waimanalo Bay Beach Park
Bodyboarding is the best at this Windward Coast beauty (p217).

Hale'iwa Beach Park
Keep an eye out for turtles while stand-up paddling on the Anahulu River (p260).

Kailua Beach Park
Paddle out to uninhabited islands in kayaks from gorgeous Kailua Beach (p221), or make the most of steady winds to learn kite- or windsurfing.

Waikiki
Enjoy the sights of Waikiki (p139) and Diamond Head from the sea while catamaran sailing.

Hawai'i Kai
Enjoy wakeboarding, banana boats, parasailing and jet packs at this water-sports bonanza (p202).

Swimming

O'ahu has distinct coastal areas, each with its own peculiar seasonal water conditions. As a general rule, the best places to swim in winter are in the south, and in summer, to the north.

A word of warning: approximately 10 days after a full moon, box jellyfish swim into the shallow waters, especially around Waikiki, and stay for a day or two. The Waikiki Aquarium has an online calendar (www.waikikiaquarium.org/interact/box-jellyfish-calendar) of times when the jellyfish peak.

ALTERNATIVE ADVENTURES

Beyond swimming and surfing, O'ahu offers other adrenaline-fueled aquatic options. Hawai'i Kai (p202) in Southeast O'ahu offers parasailing, waterskiing, banana-boat rides and more.

Bodysurfing & Bodyboarding

Bodysurfing is a great way to catch some waves, sans equipment. There's a bit of a knack to it, but once you've found the groove, it's good times ahead. The ideal locations are sandy shore breaks where the inevitable wipeouts aren't that painful.

If you're just getting started, Waimanalo Bay Beach Park (p217) and Bellows Field Beach Park (p217) in windward O'ahu have gentle shore breaks. If you know your way around the surf, head to Sandy Beach Park (p209) in Southeast O'ahu, where contests are regularly held and where the shore is often lined with spectators.

Bodyboarding has myriad choices. If you want to see and be seen, the island's most popular bodyboarding site is Kapahulu Groin in Waikiki's Kuhio Beach Park (p144). Otherwise, if you're keen for shore breaks, try the aforementioned bodysurfing waves. If you want something a bit bigger, have a look at the surfing spots.

Stand-up Paddleboarding (SUP)

Where there's surfing, there's usually stand-up paddle-boarding (SUP). Waikiki (p150) in particular is an SUP haven, and it's easy to rent gear and get lessons. Kailua Beach Park (p221) actually gets many more people on SUPs than on surfboards, while all across the North Shore you'll find SUPs at every surf beach.

Kayaking

The top kayaking destination is undoubtedly Kailua Beach Park (p221) on the Windward Coast, which has three uninhabited islands within the reef that are made for exploring via kayak and paddle. Landings are allowed on two of the islands: Moku Nui, which has a beautiful beach good for sunbathing and snorkeling; and Popoi'a Island (Flat Island), where there are some inviting walking trails.

Twogood Kayaks Hawaii (p223) offers tours, lessons and rentals.

Other good places where you can rent a kayak and go for a paddle include the Kane'ohe Bay Area (p229), the North Shore's Hale'iwa (p260), and Fort DeRussy Beach (p142) in Waikiki.

Kitesurfing & Windsurfing

Kite- and windsurfing action on O'ahu centers on Kailua on the Windward Coast, where you'll find the vast majority of rentals and lessons. Kailua Beach Park (p221) has persistent year-round trade winds and superb conditions for all levels in different sections of the bay. The speed and jumps at Kuilei Cliffs Beach Park (p199) below Diamond Head in Southeast O'ahu are also popular with local kite- and windsurfers. Mokule'ia Beach Park (p267) is known for its consistent North Shore winds.

It's all innovation out on the water these days, with kite foiling and windsurf foiling all the rage, especially in places such as Kailua. You'll need some skills to get up on the foils, though.

Outrigger Canoeing

There's not much in Hawaii that's more traditional then outrigger canoeing. First used by the Polynesian settlers who came to inhabit Hawaii, it has since become a popular activity for people who want a thrill ride on the ocean.

You can book a trip from vendors at Kuhio Beach Park (p144) in Waikiki, where you can ride right from the sand and surf the waves back in. The round trip will cost around $110 for four people and is very popular with kids. You can also enjoy a ride in Kailua (p222).

CHARLOTTERABOFF / SHUTTERSTOCK ©

Stand-up paddleboarder, Waikiki

PLAN YOUR TRIP ON THE WATER

Whale-Watching

Catching a view of a whale on O'ahu isn't a fluke. Between December and May humpback whales and their newly birthed offspring visit the harbors of northern and western O'ahu. Hawaiian spinner dolphins are year-round residents of the Wai'anae Coast in Leeward O'ahu. Whale- and dolphin-watching boat trips depart from Honolulu (p102), Hale'iwa (p260) on the North Shore, and from Ko Olina (p186) and Wai'anae (p191) on the Leeward Coast.

Learn more about Hawaii's humpback whales and find out how to volunteer to participate in one of three annual whale counts at the Hawaiian Islands Humpback Whale National Marine Sanctuary (www.hawaiihumpbackwhale.noaa.gov). Note that you don't always need a boat; look for whales from land along the North Shore at Turtle Bay (p249) or from Ka'ena Point (p193), and from Makapu'u Point Lighthouse (p211) and above the Spitting Cave (p202) in Southeast O'ahu.

Honu (green sea turtles)

Diving & Snorkeling

Of the 700 fish species that live in Hawaii's waters, nearly a third are found nowhere else. Divers and snorkelers can also often see spinner dolphins, green sea turtles and manta rays. The waters hold hard and soft corals, anemones, unusual sponges and a variety of shellfish. Then there's the plethora of beautiful tropical fish. You may not want to come up for air.

Best Diving & Snorkeling

Hanauma Bay

The bay (p207) is one of the top spots to snorkel and dive on the planet.

Sharks Cove

Great snorkeling here and in the tide pools at Pupukea Beach Park (p256).

Waikiki

Don your mask and snorkel and head out in front of the Sheraton Waikiki (p151).

Queen's Surf Beach

Decent snorkeling in Waikiki (p144) at Queen's and at Kaimana Beach, both opposite Kapi'olani Park.

Three Tables

Good snorkeling and diving off Pupukea Beach Park (p256) on the North Shore.

Makaha Caverns

Popular dive spot off Makaha Beach (p192) on the Leeward Coast.

Diving

Whether you're an old pro or a beginner, O'ahu has plenty to offer under the sea: lessons, boat dives, shore dives, night dives, reef dives, cave dives and wreck dives. The water temperatures are perfect for diving, with yearly averages ranging between 72°F (22°C) and 80°F (27°C). Even better than the bathwater temperatures is the visibility, which is usually perfect for seeing the abundance of fish, coral and other sea creatures. Because of its volcanic origins, the island also has some cool underwater caves and caverns.

Two-tank boat dives average $130 to $150 and include all gear (subtract about $20 if you have your own gear). Many operators offer a beginners' 'discover scuba' option, an introductory course that includes brief instruction, and possibly swimming-pool practice, followed by a shallow beach or boat dive. The cost is generally $130 to $180, depending on the operation and whether a boat is used. Full, Open Water Professional Association of Diving Instructors (PADI) certification courses can be completed in as little as three days and cost around $500.

You'll find many dive shops in Waikiki (p151). You can arrange trips here that cover all the dive spots around the island as well as rent anything you might need. Shops can also be found on the north coast at Hale'iwa (p260), and southeast at Hawai'i Kai (p202).

O'ahu's top summer dive spots include the caves and ledges at Three Tables and Sharks Cove (p256) on the North Shore, and the Makaha Caverns (p192) off Makaha Beach in Leeward O'ahu. For wreck diving, the sunken 165ft ship *Mahi* (p190), also off Makaha Beach, is a prize.

Numerous spots on the south coast going east from Honolulu provide winter diving. The best is Hanauma Bay (p207), which, while known for snorkeling, is also a fine site for diving. In fact, you'll have the whole bay to play in, with crystal-clear water, coral gardens and sea turtles.

Good sources of info include the following:

Franko's Maps (www.frankosmaps.com) Produces a color illustrated O'ahu dive map that's widely sold around the island and lists dive sites and descriptions. It also offers a handy laminated fish card that you can take with you underwater so you can identify just what you're seeing.

Divers Alert Network (www.diversalertnetwork. org) Provides advice on diving insurance, emergencies, decompression services, illness and injury.

To-Hawaii (www.to-hawaii.com/underwater-world.php) Has a detailed and illustrated online guide to local fish.

Hanauma Bay Fish Identification Card Produced by the University of Hawai'i, this is a free download and provides pictures and descriptions of the fish you'll likely see in the bay and elsewhere around O'ahu. Just do an online search for 'Hanauma Bay Fish Identification Card pdf'.

Snorkeling

There's no excuse not to go snorkeling on O'ahu. The water is warm, the currents are generally gentle and the underwater visibility is awesome. Shallow reefs and nearshore waters are awash with fish and colorful corals. You can expect to spy large rainbow-colored parrotfish munching coral on the sea floor; schools of silver needlefish glimmering near the surface; brilliant yellow tangs; odd-shaped filefish and ballooning puffer fish. In addition, look for striped butterfly fish, Moorish idols and gape-mouthed moray eels. Neon-colored wrasse have more species (43) than any other Hawaiian reef fish. The saucy wrasse mate daily and change sex (and color) as they mature; most start female and become male.

As activities go, this is about as cheap as it gets, with mask and snorkel rentals available nearly everywhere for around $15 a day. If you're staying at a vacation rental or condo, one or two sets are usually free for guest use. Some resorts even offer gear for free as well.

The year-round snorkeling mecca is Hanauma Bay Nature Preserve (p207) in Southeast O'ahu, a mere 30-minute (or less) drive east of Waikiki. With turquoise waters ringed by the remnants of an ancient volcano, this is O'ahu's most-loved snorkeling spot. The legally protected bay offers a giant outdoor fishbowl to splash around in, plus a coral reef that's thousands of years old. Pull a snorkel mask over your eyes – you'll be amazed by the diversity of sea life visible just below the surface of the nature preserve's glimmering waters. If you're lucky, a green sea turtle will paddle by.

When summer waters are calm on the North Shore, Waimea Bay (p253) and Sharks Cove (p256) in Pupukea provide top-notch snorkeling in pristine conditions, and far less human activity than at Hanauma.

But if you're staying in Waikiki you needn't go far to explore O'ahu underwater. Kaimana Beach (p144) and Queen's Surf Beach (p144) are smaller snorkel sites at the eastern end of Waikiki, while you may be surprised to find that the snorkeling right out in front of the Sheraton Waikiki is superb.

Spinner dolphins

Responsible Diving & Snorkeling

The popularity of underwater exploration is placing immense pressure on many dive sites. Please consider the following tips when diving and snorkeling to help preserve the ecology and beauty of reefs.

Don't touch the turtles Minimize your disturbance of marine animals. It is illegal to approach endangered marine species too closely; these include whales, dolphins, sea turtles and the Hawaiian monk seal.

Don't feed the fish Doing so disturbs their normal eating habits and can encourage aggressive behavior; besides, you might feed them food that is detrimental to their health.

Be conscious of the coral Take care not to touch coral with your body (never stand on it) or drag equipment across the reef. Polyps can be damaged by even the gentlest contact. If you must hold on, only touch exposed rock. Be conscious of your fins; even without contact, the surge from heavy strokes near the reef can damage delicate organisms. When treading water in shallow reef

Snorkelers at Hanauma Bay (p207)

areas, take care not to kick up clouds of sand. Settling sand can easily smother reef organisms.

Take only pictures Resist the temptation to collect coral or shells from the seabed. Buy an underwater camera and take pictures instead.

Pack it out Ensure that you remove all your trash and any other litter you may find. Plastics in particular are a serious threat to marine life. Turtles can mistake plastic for jellyfish and eat it.

Practice proper buoyancy Major damage can be done by divers descending too fast and colliding with the reef. Make sure you are correctly weighted and that your weight belt is positioned so you stay horizontal. Be aware that buoyancy can change over an extended trip.

Care for caves Spend as little time in underwater caves as possible; your air bubbles may be caught under the roof and thereby leave previously submerged organisms high and dry.

Safe Space for Dolphins

In the wild, acrobatic spinner dolphins are nocturnal feeders that come into sheltered bays during the day to rest. Although it may look tempting to swim out and join them, these intelligent animals are very sensitive to human disturbance, so it's illegal to approach them.

Some tour boats on O'ahu allow snorkelers and swimmers to approach closer than the recommended guideline of 50yd. Even if wild dolphins appear 'happy' to see you and frolicsome, encountering humans tires them out, according to many marine biologists, so the dolphins may not have enough energy later to feed or defend themselves.

Repeated encounters with humans have driven some dolphins out of their natural habitats into less safe resting places.

If you're booking a boat trip that promises a dolphin encounter, ask this simple question: 'Are people in the water kept further than 50yd from the dolphins?'

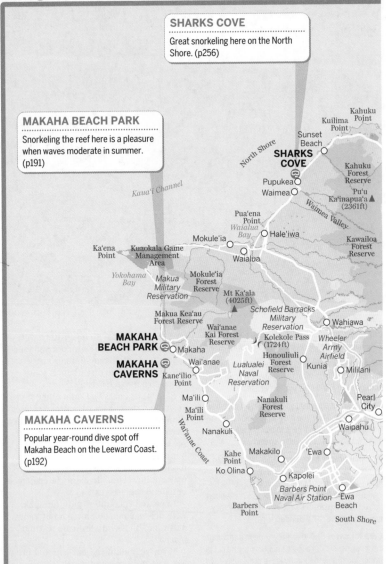

SHARKS COVE

Great snorkeling here on the North Shore. (p256)

MAKAHA BEACH PARK

Snorkeling the reef here is a pleasure when waves moderate in summer. (p191)

MAKAHA CAVERNS

Popular year-round dive spot off Makaha Beach on the Leeward Coast. (p192)

Kahuku Point

Kuilima Point

Sunset Beach

SHARKS COVE

Kahuku Forest Reserve

North Shore

Pupukea

Waimea

Pu'u Ka'inapua'a ▲ (2361ft)

Waimea Valley

Pua'ena Point

Waialua Bay

Hale'iwa

Kawailoa Forest Reserve

Kaua'i Channel

Mokule'ia

Waialua

Ka'ena Point

Kuaokala Game Management Area

Yokohama Bay

Makua Military Reservation

Mokule'ia Forest Reserve

Mt Ka'ala (4025ft) ▲

Schofield Barracks Military Reservation

Wahiawa

Makua Kea'au Forest Reserve

Wai'anae Kai Forest Reserve

Kolekole Pass (1724ft)

Wheeler Army Airfield

MAKAHA BEACH PARK

Makaha

MAKAHA CAVERNS

Kane'ilio Point

Wai'anae

Lualualei Naval Reservation

Honouliuli Forest Reserve

Kunia

Mililani

Ma'ili

Ma'ili Point

Nanakuli Forest Reserve

Pearl City

Wai'anae Coast

Nanakuli

Waipahu

Kahe Point

Makakilo

'Ewa

Ko Olina

Kapolei

Barbers Point Naval Air Station

'Ewa Beach

Barbers Point

South Shore

0 · · · · · · · · · 10 km
0 · · · · · · · · · 5 miles

PACIFIC OCEAN

Kahuku
Makahoa Point
La'ie Point
La'ie
Hau'ula
Windward Coast
Kaipapa'u Forest Reserve
Punalu'u
Kahana Bay
Kahana
Ka'a'awa
'Ewa Forest Reserve
Ahupua'a o Kahana State Park
Kualoa Point
Pu'u Ka'aumakua (2681ft)
Waikane
Waiahole Forest Reserve
Waiahole
Wailau Point
KO'OLAU RANGE
Kahalu'u
Ahuimanu
Kane'ohe Marine Corps Base Hawaii (MCBH)
Pu'u Kawipo'o (2441ft)
He'eia

KANE'OHE BAY

Head out for aquatic fun and snorkeling tours. (p229)

KANE'OHE BAY
Kane'ohe
Kailua Bay
Kailua
Likeke Falls
'Aiea
Honolulu Watershed Forest Reserve
Olomana
Lānikai
Pearl Harbor
Konahuanui (3105ft)
Mt Olomana (1643ft)
Waimanalo Bay
Hickam Air Force Base
Manoa Falls
Waimanalo
Daniel K Inouye International Airport
Pu'uohi'a (Mt Tantalus) (2013ft)
Pu'u Lanipo (2621ft)
Makapu'u Point
Mamala Bay
Honolulu
Hawai'i Kai
Pu'u Mai (1208ft)
Waikiki
Kahala
Maunalua Bay
HANAUMA BAY
Ka'iwi Channel

QUEEN'S SURF BEACH
Diamond Head (760ft)
Black Point (Kupikipiki'o)
Koko Head (642ft)

HANAUMA BAY

Some of Hawaii's best snorkeling and diving. (p207)

QUEEN'S SURF BEACH

Waikiki's best snorkeling, here and at Kaimana, both opposite Kapi'olani Park. (p144)

Makaha Beach (p19)

Plan Your Trip

Surfing

Modern surfing began on O'ahu and continues to thrive to this day.
Go to Waikiki to rent a board and learn to ride a wave; go to the
North Shore to become a star. It's why so many vacations here
have turned permanent.

Best Surfing

Hale'iwa

There's a good reason Hale'iwa (p260) hosts the first round of the Triple Crown of Surfing.

Sunset Beach

Legendary surf beach (p253) that's home to the Van's World Cup of Surfing.

Banzai Pipeline

In the surfing world, this is the holy grail (p255); monster waves in winter.

Makaha Beach

Big-wave surfing got its start here (p191) on the Leeward Coast in the 1950s.

Ala Moana Beach

Good surfing at this beach (p85), right out front of the Ala Moana Center.

Waikiki

Learn to surf where the sport was born (p150) and good waves can break anytime (especially summer).

Where to Surf

Wonderful Waikiki

Duke Kahanamoku grew up on the sands of Waikiki where, along with a handful of others, he swam, fished, dove and rode the reefs on traditional boards (which were all that remained of a traditional Hawaiian sport that had largely died out). Their derring-do caught the attention of outsiders near the beginning of the 20th century. In succeeding years Kahanamoku spread the gospel of surfing, traveling the world demonstrating the Hawaiian 'Sport of Kings.'

Over 100 years later, surfing is alive and well where Duke saved it from extinction – it's the very heart of tourism on O'ahu and the entire state. Scores of surf schools and board-rental places line the streets. Many of Waikiki's residents live here simply because they can surf every day. After thrilled beginners ride a wave for the first time, they buy a lei and toss it over the outstretched arm of the iconic Duke Kahanamoku statue.

The surf breaks (p150) are packed tightly together, but like the fruit at the buffet of one of the resorts overlooking the waves, their flavors can be very different. The best-known breaks include the following:

Ala Moana Bowls Where the locals surf; has a great tube section and can get heavy.

Canoes Right off the beach; untold scores of people have learned to surf here.

Populars A top spot for long-boarders.

Publics Slightly out of the crowded breaks; very reliable.

Queens The first break everyone masters after Canoes.

Techniques A tight break that inspired the development of hollow, maneuverable boards in the 1930s.

Threes A solid break that's a long paddle from shore; locals don't seem to mind.

The Southeast

Go east of Diamond Head and the wealth of surf breaks at Waikiki thin out. Diamond Head Cliffs (p199) is reliable because the surf can come from multiple directions. It lacks the amateur-hour shenanigans you find just west.

The other place popular with surfers is Sandy Beach Park (p209), although the waves can be savage and break close to shore, so it's mostly the domain of bodysurfers and bodyboarders.

Honolulu

With so many harbors and the like, it's easy to get lost offshore of the capital (p106).

Kewalos Gets crowded with intermediates in summer. The westernmost of the breaks is out front of Ala Moana Beach Park.

Point Panic & Flies Less experienced surfers favor these neighboring breaks.

Tennis Courts Good 3ft to 5ft waves all summer long, out from Ala Moana Beach Park.

Legendary North Shore

When it comes to surf, nowhere on the planet gets as much attention as O'ahu's North Shore. Starting at the small town of Hale'iwa and running approximately 7 miles east on the Kamehameha Hwy to Sunset Beach (p253), this stretch of coastline has been dubbed surfing's mecca.

While the South Shore of O'ahu gets quiet in winter, the North Shore roars to life. During this time, powerful storms in the Gulf of Alaska send intense northwest swells in the general direction of the 'Seven-Mile Miracle,' where occasionally the surf can top 30ft on the outer reefs. For three months pro surfers from all over the world arrive, hoping to catch a piece of the action. If you're just starting off, this isn't the time or the place to learn.

On November 7, 1957, after years and years of spectating, a group of California surfers paddled out at Waimea Bay and ushered in the era of big-wave riding. Large waves had been surfed for a few years by this time, most visibly on the west side of O'ahu at Makaha, but Waimea was in a different league. The bravado and ability of Greg Noll, Pat Curren, James Jones, Eddie and Clyde Aikau, and a host of others would become the stuff of legend.

Several miles up the road and fewer than 10 years later, San Diego–born Butch Van Arsdalen rode the Banzai Pipeline (p255) for the first time. By the late 1960s and early '70s Gerry Lopez and Rory Russell had emerged as the ultimate Pipeline stylists, defining the term 'getting tubed.'

Today there's no better place to watch all the action than at the Pipeline. Breaking less than 100yd from shore, the cavernous tubes that detonate over a coral shelf in less than 3ft of water tempt surfers every year, sometimes with lethal consequences.

Other North Shore breaks:

Backyards (p255) If you're OK with wind, you'll love this break as much as the windsurfers do.

Chun's Reef (p255) Great all-around break; can get crowded with surfers from beginner to expert.

Hale'iwa (p262) Part of the Triple Crown of Surfing contest. Conditions here vary: at times beginners love it, at other times it's experts only.

Laniakea (p255) One of the North Shore's only true point breaks, it's even popular with sea turtles.

Leftovers, Rightovers & Alligator Rock (p255) A troika of uncrowded breaks good for advanced surfers.

Pua'ena Point (p262) The favored break of many of O'ahu's surf schools.

Pupukea (p255) A high-performance right that's for experts only.

Sunset Point (p254) Intermediate surfers love this very popular break.

Velzyland (p254) Good for diverse groups: some can surf, others can swim here.

Every year surfers amass on the North Shore for a shot at winning the Vans Triple Crown of Surfing (www.vanstriple crownofsurfing.com). The three-contest series, held in November and December, has men's and women's events. It's a huge draw for spectators and anybody who is anybody in the world of surfing. Sunny Garcia won the Triple Crown a record six times from 1992 to 2004. An O'ahu native, he learned to surf in Wai'anae on the Leeward Coast.

Windward Coast

For all its beauty and other attributes, O'ahu's Windward Coast is not prime surfing territory. The 'wind' in the name offers the clue: water sports dependent on wind power are in their prime here, especially on Kailua Bay. But the island shelters the ocean, and breaks are modest at best. Flat Island (p223) is on the bay and next to its

O'AHU SURF ETIQUETTE

When it comes to dealing with the resident surfing populace, remember one simple word: respect. The rules of surfing etiquette are important and not very complicated; the gist is don't be a wave hog, and don't get in the way of other people while they're riding. If you're taking lessons, ask your instructor to explain the etiquette to you. Or if you're fending for yourself, don't be afraid to ask somebody in the water – they'll probably be happy to help and could end up giving you some local insight. Basically, be humble, be kind, share and always surf with a smile (even if you're on the verge of drowning).

Banzai Pipline (p255)

namesake island. It's reliable and good for beginners.

Leeward Coast

Before there was a North Shore (in terms of surfing!) there was O'ahu's Leeward Coast. The northern stretch known as the Wai'anae Coast is where big-wave surfing got its start, specifically at Makaha (p192). Beginning after WWII, locals learned how to deal with the winter waves, which reach 15ft. Today the break still attracts experts, but it's not the same glossy scene you'll find on the North Shore. Innovative changes to surfboards in the 1960s, particularly the move from heavy redwood boards to lighter balsa-wood boards and the addition of a surfboard fin, made tackling the North Shore's giant waves more feasible, so the scene shifted there.

Two other breaks worth noting in west O'ahu are Tracks (p189), which is reliably gentle year-round, and 'Ewa Beach (p186), a hard-core local spot on the scraggly coast west of Pearl Harbor.

Gauging Surf Conditions

Knowing how big the next swell is and when it's coming are essential. This is where streaming webcams, surf reports and forecasts come in. For O'ahu, the following sources are very useful; and don't forget common sense – if conditions look intimidating, stay on shore.

Hawaii News Now Surf Report (www.hawaii newsnow.com/weather/surf-report) A quick and easy graphical summary of conditions.

Live Surf Cam Hawaii (www.livesurfcamhawaii. com) An index to scores of live surf cams on O'ahu and across the state.

National Weather Service (www.weather.gov/ hfo/SRF) The official wave conditions and surf report for O'ahu.

Surfer (http://forecasts.surfer.com) Has surf reports and forecasts.

Surfline (www.surfline.com) Great omnibus site with massive amounts of information.

Surfing

BANZAI PIPELINE

In the surfing world, this is the holy grail; monster waves in winter. (p255)

SUNSET BEACH

Legendary surf beach that hosts the Van's World Cup of Surfing. (p253)

HALE'IWA

Hosts the first round of the Triple Crown of Surfing for good reason. (p260)

MAKAHA BEACH

Big-wave surfing got its start here on the Leeward Coast in the 1950s. (p191)

ALA MOANA

Good surfing right out front of the Ala Moana Center. (p85)

Kahuku Point
Kuilima Point
Kaua'i Channel
North Shore
SUNSET BEACH
Sunset Beach
BANZAI PIPELINE
Kahuku Forest Reserve
Pupukea
Waimea
Pu'u Ka'inapua'a (2361ft)
Waimea Valley
HALE'IWA
Waialua Bay
Hale'iwa
Kawailoa Forest Reserve
Mokule'ia
Ka'ena Point
Kuaokala Game Management Area
Waialua
Yokohama Bay
Makua Military Reservation
Mokule'ia Forest Reserve
Mt Ka'ala (4025ft)
Schofield Barracks Military Reservation
Wahiawa
Makua Kea'au Forest Reserve
Wai'anae Kai Forest Reserve
Kolekole Pass (1724ft)
Wheeler Army Airfield
MAKAHA BEACH
Makaha
Honouliuli Forest Reserve
Kunia
Mililani
Lahilahi Point
Wai'anae
Lualualei Naval Reservation
Kane'ilio Point
Ma'ili
Nanakuli Forest Reserve
Pearl City
Ma'ili Point
Waipahu
Wai'anae Coast
Nanakuli
Kahe Point
Makakilo
'Ewa
Ko Olina
Kapolei
Barbers Point Naval Air Station
'Ewa Beach
Barbers Point
South Shore

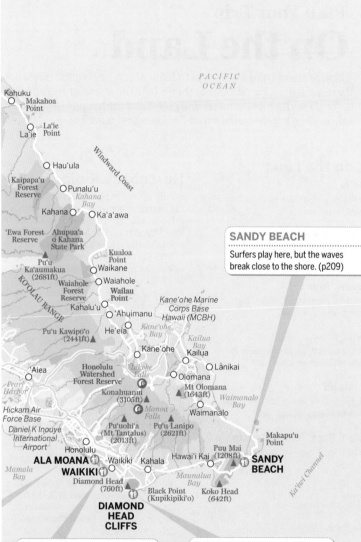

N
0 ——————— 10 km
0 ——————— 5 miles

PACIFIC
OCEAN

Kahuku
Makahoa
Point

La'ie
Point
La'ie

Hau'ula

Windward Coast

Kaipapa'u
Forest
Reserve
Punalu'u

Kahana
Bay
Kahana
Ka'a'awa

'Ewa Forest
Reserve
Ahupua'a
o Kahana
State Park

Pu'u
Ka'aumakua
(2681ft)
Kualoa
Point
Waikane

Waiahole
Forest
Reserve
Waiahole

KOOLAU RANGE
Wailau
Point

Kahalu'u
'Ahuimanu

Kane'ohe Marine
Corps Base
Hawaii (MCBH)

Pu'u Kawipo'o
(2441ft)
He'eia
Kane'ohe
Bay

Kailua
Bay

'Aiea
Honolulu
Watershed
Forest Reserve
Lulkeke
Falls
Kane'ohe
Kailua

Olomana
Lānikai

Pearl
Harbor
Konahuanui
(3105ft)
Mt Olomana
(1643ft)

Manoa
Falls
Waimanalo
Waimanalo
Bay

Hickam Air
Force Base
Pu'uohi'a
(Mt Tantalus)
(2013ft)
Pu'u Lanipo
(2621ft)

Daniel K Inouye
International
Airport
Honolulu

Puu Mai
(1208ft)
Makapu'u
Point

Mamala
Bay
ALA MOANA
WAIKIKI
Waikiki
Kahala
Hawai'i Kai
SANDY
BEACH

Diamond Head
(760ft)
Maunalua
Bay
Ka'iwi Channel

Black Point
(Kupikipiki'o)
Koko Head
(642ft)

DIAMOND
HEAD
CLIFFS

> **SANDY BEACH**
> ....
> Surfers play here, but the waves
> break close to the shore. (p209)

> **WAIKIKI**
> ....
> Learn to surf where surfing was born
> and good waves can break any time
> (especially in summer). (p139)

> **DIAMOND HEAD CLIFFS**
> ....
> Reliable waves off Kuilei Cliffs
> Beach Park. (p199)

On the Land

Think of Hawaii and it's natural to think of sun, sand and waves, but there's a surprising number of things to do on the land and above it, too. O'ahu is mountainous and green and the locals are fit and active, enjoying life on their mid-Pacific island paradise.

Best on the Land

Mokule'ia
Horseback riding on the beach at Hawaii Polo (p268), west of Hale'iwa.

Bellows Field Beach Park
Superb beach camping (p217) among the ironwood trees at Waimanalo.

Helicopter Tour
Buzz around the island on a 45-minute flight (p108) with unbelievable views.

Skydiving
Jump out of a perfectly good plane above the North Shore at Dillingham Airfield (p267).

Magic Island
Join the locals running around this lovely peninsula at Ala Moana Regional Park (p85).

Kapi'olani Park Tennis Courts
Free courts (p146) in excellent condition with lighting at night.

Horseback Riding

Saddle up and explore rural parts of the island on horseback. Ride through a valley as one of the activities at Kualoa Ranch (p233), or, further up the Windward Coast, explore a ranch in La'ie (p238). On the North Shore, trot beachside at the polo club in Mokule'ia (p268) or plod along the mountainside above Pupukea (p257). A 1½-hour trail ride costs between $60 and $100.

Bird-Watching

Most islets off O'ahu's Windward Coast are sanctuaries for seabirds, including terns, noddies, shearwaters, Laysan albatrosses, boobies and 'iwa (great frigate birds). Moku Manu (Bird Island), off the Mokapu Peninsula near Kane'ohe, has the greatest variety of species, including a colony of 'ewa'ewa (sooty terns) that lays its eggs in ground scrapes.

Bird-watchers can visit Moku'auia (Goat Island; p239), offshore from Malaekahana State Recreation Area on the Windward Coast. In Kailua, the Kawai Nui Marsh (p221) is another place to see Hawaiian water birds in their natural habitat. On the edge of the North Shore, James Campbell National Wildlife Refuge (p240) encompasses a native wetland habitat protecting some rare and endangered water-bird species.

Hikers who tackle O'ahu's many forest-reserve trails, especially around Pu'uohi'a

(Mt Tantalus; p104), can hope to see the *'elepaio* (Hawaiian monarch flycatcher), a brownish bird with a white rump, and the *'amakihi,* a yellow-green honeycreeper, the most common endemic forest birds on O'ahu. The *'apapane,* a bright-red honeycreeper, and the *'i'iwi,* a scarlet honeycreeper, are rarer.

For birding checklists and group field trips, contact the Hawaii Audubon Society (www.hawaiiaudubon.org).

Golf

With more than 40 courses to choose from, you're spoiled for golfing choice on O'ahu. You'll find PGA-level courses with the atmosphere of a private club, resort courses, and municipal greens with lower fees, a relaxed atmosphere and similarly spectacular surrounds.

For a full list of O'ahu courses, log on to www.hawaiigolf.com. Green fees run from about $30 to $250 for 18 holes. Discounted rates are often available if you don't mind teeing off in the afternoon or reserve in advance online.

The City and County of Honolulu (www.honolulu.gov/des/golf.html) runs six 18-hole municipal golf courses. Reservations can be made online.

Tennis

O'ahu has 181 public tennis courts throughout the island; for locations, see www.honolulu.gov/rep/site/dpr/dpr_docs/tenniscourts.pdf. If you're staying in Waikiki, the most conveniently located are the courts at the Diamond Head Tennis Center at the eastern end of Kapi'olani Park, and the Kapi'olani Regional Park Tennis Courts (p152), opposite the Waikiki Aquarium. The courts at Ala Moana Regional Park (p108) are also close by. Many courts have free lighting.

Running

In the early hours of the morning you'll see joggers aplenty in parks, on footpaths and

ABOVE THE LAND

Dillingham Airfield (p267) on the North Shore is the base for exciting activities in the air, such as skydiving, gliding and trike flights. Helicopter tours such as those on offer from Blue Hawaiian Helicopters (p108), in Honolulu, and Paradise Helicopters (p251), which operates out of Turtle Bay on the North Shore, are also a highlight.

on beaches all around the island. Running on O'ahu is huge. Kapi'olani Park, the Ala Wai Canal and Magic Island at Ala Moana Regional Park are favorite jogging spots in Waikiki.

O'ahu has about 75 road races each year, from 1-mile fun runs and 5-mile jogs to competitive marathons, biathlons and triathlons. For an annual schedule of running events, check out the Running Room (www.hawaiirunningroom.com) and click on 'Races.'

The island's best-known race is the Honolulu Marathon, which has mushroomed from 167 runners in 1973 to become one of the largest in the US. Held in mid-December, it's an open-entry event, with an estimated half of the roughly 30,000 entrants running their first marathon. For information, contact the Honolulu Marathon Association (www.honolulumarathon.org).

Camping

You can pitch a tent at many county and some state parks around the island, but none are close to Waikiki. Many, however, are at gorgeous beaches.

Walk-in camping permits are not available at state or county campgrounds; you must get permits in advance from one of the following:

Hawaii Division of State Parks (www.dlnr.hawaii.gov/dsp/camping-lodging/oahu) Offers camping at four areas on O'ahu.

Honolulu Department of Parks & Recreation (www.honolulu.gov/parks/beach-parks/camping) Runs campgrounds in 14 City and County of Honolulu parks.

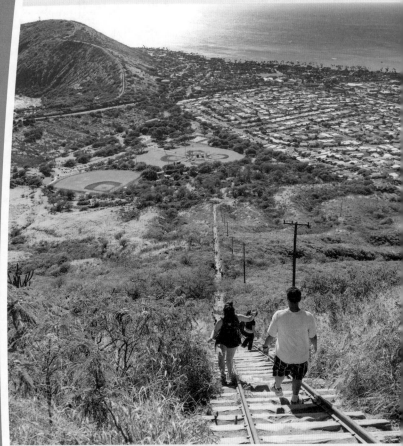

Hikers on the Koko Crater Trail (p206

Plan Your Trip

Hiking & Biking

Even though O'ahu is Hawaii's most populous island, nature sits right outside Waikiki's door. About 25% of the island is protected natural areas. The coastline is dotted with beaches, the mountainous interior is carved by hiking trails, and roads are generally in good shape for cyclists. Mountain biking is growing.

Best Hiking & Biking

Manoa Falls

Lovely short walk through lush vegetation to the head of the Manoa Valley (p102).

Diamond Head

Magnificent views are the reward for perseverance at O'ahu's best-known landmark (p199).

Koko Crater

A good slog up countless stairs at this Southeast O'ahu volcano (p206).

Seven-Mile Miracle Cycle

Get on your bike (p272) and check out the North Shore's incredible beaches.

Ka'ena Point

Walk to the island's western tip (p193) from the North Shore or Leeward Coast.

Punchbowl, Pu'uohi'a & Round Top Drive

Cycle a strenuous route (p134) up, followed by an exhilarating descent above Honolulu.

Hiking

Trails

Even if you don't have a lot of time, plenty of hikes can be accessed near Waikiki. The island's classic hike, and its most popular, is the short but steep trail to the city overlook at the crater's summit in Diamond Head State Monument (p199) in Southeast O'ahu. It's easily reached from Waikiki and ends with a panoramic city view. Also in the island's southeast corner, investigate the Kuli'ou'ou Ridge Trail (p206): the views are worth the sturdy climb.

In Honolulu, the Manoa Falls Trail (p102) is another rewarding excursion. Two miles further is the Nu'uanu Valley Lookout (p104), which has a similar flavor and makes for a good double shot. Also only a few miles from downtown Honolulu, the forested Pu'uohi'a (Mt Tantalus; p104) and Makiki Valley (p104) area has an extensive trail network, with fine overlooks of Honolulu and surrounding valleys. Wa'ahila Ridge Trail (p105) provides a different perspective on the area and good birdwatching possibilities.

Just west of Honolulu in the Pearl Harbor area, the 'Aiea Loop Trail (p194) is popular with hikers and mountain bikers. It's contained within Kea'iwa Heiau State Recreation Area, so there's an opportunity to visit an ancient temple.

Traveling a bit further afield to the Windward Coast, the Maunawili Trail system (p242) near Kailua provides a varied walk that covers a lot of different territory. Outside Kailua, a short, tree-shaded climb will take you to lesser-known Likeke Falls (p223).

For an excellent beach stroll, take to the sands outlining Kailua Bay. North up the coast, there are several quiet upland hikes in Ahupua'a o Kahana State Park (p234) and above Hau'ula (p243); all take you deep into the forest and are worth exploring.

On the North Shore, the mixed sand-and-rock coastline at Turtle Bay makes for a pleasant trek. Further west, above Pupukea, the Kaunala Loop Trail (p256) was considered sacred by Hawaiian royalty – it's no wonder, since the view is awesome.

Far from anywhere else, one of the most stunning of the island's hikes starts in Ka'ena Point State Park (p193) at the northwest edge of Leeward O'ahu. The trail hugs the coastline, as blue ocean crashes against dark volcanic rocks below and craggy cliffs rise above. Expect to see shorebirds, and maybe monk seals, in the windswept natural reserve on the uninhabited tip of the island.

Note that other ridge climbs and more challenging trails exist; this is not meant to be a comprehensive list. Search the excellent website administered by the Nā Ala Hele Trail & Access Program (https://hawaiitrails.hawaii.gov/trails) for trails, printable topo maps and announcements of recently developed or reopened paths.

Maps by the US Geological Survey (www.usgs.gov) are available in some island bookstores and can be ordered, or downloaded free online.

Hiking Preparation & Safety

Overall, O'ahu is a very safe place to hike, but there are a few things to keep in mind:

Hike with at least one other person At the very least, tell a reliable individual where you are going and when you expect to be back.

Take along plenty of liquids Anywhere in Hawaii, hiking can be a sweaty experience, so drink liquids along the trail and, above all, avoid dehydration. Allow 4 pints (2L) of water per person for a full-day hike.

Wear a hat and sunscreen and start out early It can get very hot in the middle of the day.

Wear sturdy footwear Good traction is a must here; it often gets muddy.

The weather is very changeable Even when the sun is shining in Waikiki, it can be pouring with rain only a few miles inland, so be prepared.

Ridges can be exposed to strong winds Take an extra layer of clothing for ridge hikes.

Dangerous flora and fauna You won't find any snakes, poison oak or poison ivy or many wild animals to contend with. There's the slim chance you might encounter a wild boar, but – as exciting and death defying as that sounds – unless they're cornered they're rarely a problem.

Flash floods Streams can rise quickly during thunderstorms, so use common sense in heavy rain.

Landslides Be alert to the possibility of landslides and falling rocks. Swimming under non-maintained waterfalls can be dangerous, as rocks may dislodge from the top. Be careful on cliff edges, as rocks here tend to be crumbly.

Leptospirosis This is a bacterial disease found in freshwater ponds and streams that have been contaminated with mouse, rat or mongoose urine. It's nasty, so never drink stream water; avoid getting cuts by wearing long trousers; and don't go swimming in ponds.

Nightfall Darkness falls fast once the sun sets, and ridgetop trails are no place to be caught unprepared at night. Always carry a flashlight just in case.

Biki bikes (p310)

Hike Like a Local

To find hiking trails island-wide, visit the website of the government-sponsored Nā Ala Hele Trail & Access Program (https://hawaiitrails.hawaii.gov/trails). For group hikes, check the calendar of the following organizations:

Hawaiian Trail & Mountain Club (www.htmc1910.org) Volunteer-run hiking club that arranges intermediate to challenging group hikes on weekends all over the island. Trail descriptions and safety tips available online.

Sierra Club (www.sierracluboahu.org) The Hawaii chapter of this nonprofit national organization leads weekend hikes and other outings around O'ahu, including volunteer opportunities to rebuild trails and combat invasive plants.

Guided Hikes

Local guided hikes provide entry to otherwise inaccessible private land in spots such as the valleys of Kualoa Ranch (p233) on the Windward Coast, and out of Hale'iwa and in the Waimea Valley (p254) on the North Shore. The **Hawai'i Nature Center** (www.hawaiinaturecenter.org) in

Waikiki Beach and Honolulu from Diamond Head (p203)

the Makiki Forest Recreation Area, near Honolulu, leads family-oriented hikes by reservation.

Outfitters offer guided hiking tours whose main advantage is that bus transportation from Waikiki is included. On tours, it's always a good idea to ask what, if any, food or water is provided.

Cycling & Mountain Biking

A lot of people usee pedal power, both for transportation and for fun, on O'ahu. Biki (p310; www.gobiki.org) is Honolulu's new bike-share system, with 130 stations.

The Bike Shop (p106), with locations in Honolulu, 'Aiea and Kailua, is the place to go to get your bike. It rents a variety of high-quality bicycles, including electric-assist, road, racing and mountain bikes,

and can give you advice and maps of cycling routes to match your skill level. It organizes group rides throughout the year – check the website for details.

Mountain biking is still an emerging sport on the island. In Hau'ula, the loop trail is a fun track; the Maunawili Trail system is a scenic 9.5-mile ride that connects the mountain Nu'uanu Valley Lookout with sea level in Waimanalo – both are on the Windward Coast (p242). In Southeast O'ahu, check out the Kuli'ou'ou Ridge Trail (p206) for great views and a challenging climb, and in Pearl Harbor there's the 'Aiea Loop Trail (p194), part of Kea'iwa Heiau State Recreation Area.

The **Hawaii Bicycling League** (www. hbl.org) is a local club that holds group road-cycling rides most weekends, from 10-mile jaunts to 60-mile travails. **Bike Hawaii** (www.bikehawaii.com) offers tours and activities, including downhill and mountain biking.

KA'ENA POINT TRAIL

Most head out to O'ahu's western-most tip from the Leeward Coast. Walk the return trip or carry on around to the North Shore as a railway and road used to. (p195)

SEVEN-MILE MIRACLE CYCLE

Cruise along the North Shore's spectacular stretch of sun, sand and waves from Hale'iwa to Sunset Beach and back. Not only surfers drool over this gorgeous coastline. (p272)

Kahuku Point
Kuilima Point
Sunset Beach
Kahuku Forest Reserve

North Shore

Pupukea
Waimea
Pu'u Ka'inapua'a (2361ft)

Kaua'i Channel

SEVEN-MILE MIRACLE CYCLE

Waialua Bay Hale'iwa

Waimea Valley

Mokule'ia

Kawailoa Forest Reserve

Ka'ena Point
Kuaokala Game Management Area

Waialua

KA'ENA POINT TRAIL

Makua Military Reservation

Mokule'ia Forest Reserve

Mt Ka'ala (4025ft)

Schofield Barracks Military Reservation

Wahiawa

Makua Kea'au Forest Reserve

Wai'anae Kai Forest Reserve

Kolekole Pass (1724ft)

Wheeler Army Airfield

Kepuhi Point

Makaha
Lahilahi Point
Kane'ilio Point

Wai'anae

Honouliuli Forest Reserve

Kunia

Mililani

Lualualei Naval Reservation

Ma'ili
Ma'ili Point

Nanakuli Forest Reserve

Pearl City

Waipahu

Nanakuli

Wai'anae Coast

Kahe Point

Makakilo

Ko Olina

'Ewa

Kapolei

Pearl City

PU'UOHI'A (MT TANTALUS) CYCLE

For a strenuous workout on a road bike, try the Punchbowl, Pu'uohi'a & Round Top driving tour. A steep climb, fantastic views and a quick descent. (p134)

Barbers Point Naval Air Station 'Ewa Beach

Barbers Point

South Shore

DIAMOND HEAD CLIMB

Stunning views await those who make the effort to climb Hawaii's most iconic landmark. Persevere through tunnels and up staircases to the former military observation station at the 760ft summit. (p203)

N 0 — 10 km
0 — 5 miles

HAU'ULA LOOP TRAIL

Good for both novice hikers and mountain bikers, this popular 2.5-mile loop trail winds its way through native vegetation and introduced species. Both shady and scenic. (p243)

'AIEA LOOP TRAIL

Hikers and mountain bikers alike will enjoy the sweeping vistas of Pearl Harbor, Diamond Head and the Ko'olau Range on this 4.8-mile trail. (p194)

MAUNAWILI TRAIL

This scenic 9.5-mile one-way hiking and mountain-biking trail winds along the back side of the Maunawili Valley, following the base of the lofty Ko'olau Range. (p242)

MANOA FALLS TRAIL

Honolulu's most rewarding short hike, this 1.6-mile round-trip trail runs above a rocky streambed before ending at a pretty little cascade. Expect lush vegetation, and possibly a muddy track. (p102)

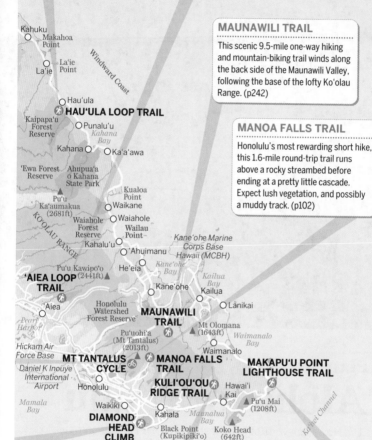

Kahuku
Makahoa Point
La'ie Point
La'ie

Windward Coast

Hau'ula
HAU'ULA LOOP TRAIL

Kaipapa'u Forest Reserve
Punalu'u
Kahana Bay
Kahana
Ka'a'awa

'Ewa Forest Reserve
Ahupua'a o Kahana State Park
Kualoa Point
Pu'u Ka'aumakua (2681ft)
Waikane
Waiahole Forest Reserve
Waiahole
Wailau Point
Kahalu'u
'Ahuimanu

Kane'ohe Marine Corps Base Hawaii (MCBH)

Pu'u Kawipo'o (2441ft)
He'eia
Kane'ohe Bay

'AIEA LOOP TRAIL

'Aiea
Honolulu Watershed Forest Reserve
Kane'ohe
Kailua Bay
Kailua
Lānikai

Pearl Harbor
Pu'uohi'a (Mt Tantalus) (2013ft)
MAUNAWILI TRAIL
Mt Olomana (1643ft)
Waimanalo Bay

Hickam Air Force Base
MT TANTALUS CYCLE
MANOA FALLS TRAIL
Waimanalo

Daniel K Inouye International Airport
Honolulu
KULI'OU'OU RIDGE TRAIL
Hawai'i Kai
MAKAPU'U POINT LIGHTHOUSE TRAIL

Mamala Bay
Waikiki
Kahala
DIAMOND HEAD CLIMB
Maunalua Bay
Pu'u Mai (1208ft)

Black Point (Kupikipiki'o)
Koko Head (642ft)

Kaiwi Channel

KO'OLAU RANGE

KULI'OU'OU RIDGE TRAIL

One for both hikers and mountain bikers, this trail climbs forest switchbacks, then along a ridgeline to a windy summit and magnificent 360-degree views. (p206)

MAKAPU'U POINT LIGHTHOUSE TRAIL

An easy walk on a mile-long paved service road that climbs to the red-roofed Makapu'u Point Lighthouse. Can get hot and windy in summer. Spot whales in winter. (p211)

Wind farm (p2...)

Plan Your Trip
Aloha for Oʻahu

The Hawaiian word 'aloha' means love, respect and compassion. It has deep cultural and spiritual significance to Native Hawaiians, and you'll hear it said everywhere during your time on the islands. It's not just a greeting or a type of brightly colored shirt but an emotion, expressing a love and respect for the land and the sea, the people, the community, Oʻahu and Hawaii. Show some aloha – it's the essence of a visit to this Pacific paradise.

Green Strategies

Recycling & Composting

You'll find recycling bins at beaches, public parks and some museums and tourist attractions. A good number of local restaurants now provide compostable and biodegradable to-go containers.

The Department of Environmental Services operates a three-cart curbside recycling program: **blue** is for mixed recyclables that go to produce new products; **green** is for green waste that goes to make compost; **gray** is for general trash that is incinerated to produce energy.

Turning Waste into Power

Around 10% of O'ahu's electricity is now trash powered. The island's H-POWER waste-to-energy facility incinerates trash to produce electricity, which is then sold to Hawaiian Electric.

Show Aloha for O'ahu

Sustainable Travel

Around nine million visitors land on O'ahu's shores every year – outnumbering residents by nine to one – and tourism, either directly or indirectly, provides one out of every three jobs in Hawaii. Pressures from tourism can be intense, as corporations seek to build more condos and hotels, to irrigate golf courses and to, well, sprawl. Sustainable travel practices can help ensure the island stays a paradise in the years to come.

Tread Lightly

Every step we take has an impact, but we can minimize the effect by being aware of our surroundings. Staying on trails helps preserve the area's plant life. Coral is a living creature: touching it, standing on it and bumping into it can kill the delicate polyps.

Seeds caught in the soles of shoes or bugs hiding in the bottom of backpacks potentially pose a threat. Cleaning thoroughly before you arrive helps to fight the introduction of invasive species.

Tap water on the island is safe and drinkable. Buying a refillable bottle from a local business can help reduce waste (and it's a cool souvenir).

Local reusable grocery bags are also available at every drugstore and supermarket for just a dollar or two. Choose one with a tropical design – or a funny illustrated diagram of a *poke* (cubed raw fish) bowl – and you'll get a mini vacation every time you shop at home.

Support Ecofriendly Businesses

Show some aloha for O'ahu and do some ecofriendly planning before you come. Check out **Sustainable Tourism Hawaii** (www.sustainabletourismhawaii.org). *Pono* means 'to do what is right'. To travel *pono* is to travel consciously and respectfully. These guys encourage visitors to explore Hawaii in a manner that is respectful of Native Hawaiian culture, the wildlife and environment, and local residents.

Check out O'ahu

There's no doubt that you can have a great vacation without leaving Waikiki. There are superb restaurants, cafes, stores and accommodations within a few blocks of the beach – but that would be doing O'ahu an injustice. This mid-Pacific paradise is worth exploring, worth contributing to, worth understanding and well worth the effort.

Show Aloha for the Land & Sea

With nearly one million people living on this small island, there's a lot of pressure on resources, in particular, energy.

Sources of Energy

Due to its isolation and a lack of fossil-fuel resources, Hawaii relies on imports of petroleum and coal for power generation, although renewable energy production is increasing. In 2017, 62% of Hawaii's electricity came from oil, the highest for any US state, while 26% was generated from solar, wind, hydro, geothermal and other renewable sources. The state has the highest electricity prices in the US, with the average cost of electricity 2.5 times that of the US average.

While everyone on O'ahu agrees that the island needs to increase its levels of renewable energy, in late 2019 there were considerable protests in Kahuku against the expansion of a local wind-farm project that would increase the number of turbines in the town from 12 to 20, and bring the total number of turbines on O'ahu to 50. Local arguments against the expansion included that the small town shouldn't have to host 40% of the island's noisy turbines in its backyard. Protesters said that rooftop solar-power generation was a much better way to go, at least until better technology produces a less obtrusive way to generate power from the wind.

Collecting recyclables

Conservation

Hawaii's ecosystem is fragile – so fragile, in fact, that 25% of all the endangered species in the US are endemic to the Hawaiian Islands. Vast tracts of native forest were long ago cleared to make way for the monocrop industries of sugarcane and pineapple. In the 1960s the advent of mass tourism posed new challenges to the environment with the rampant development of land-hungry resorts and water-thirsty golf courses, which now number more than 40. Additionally, the large military presence has come into question for its environmental practices. Just the sheer number of visitors to the island puts immense pressure on the ecosystem.

That said, some notable progress has been made. The waters around the island have been declared part of the Hawaiian Islands Humpback Whale National Marine Sanctuary; approaching within 100yd of a whale is illegal. Overfishing is still a problem, but the killing of sea turtles by the longline industry has been banned and there are efforts afoot to further restrict the laying of gill nets.

Though invasive species still threaten endemic ones, there are strong efforts to identify any brown tree snakes that stow away aboard aircraft. There are no snakes on O'ahu and this species poses a severe threat to the island's bird populations, as experienced on Guam, where the snake, which is native to Australia and Papua New Guinea, was accidentally introduced after WWII.

Some local conservation groups have united to work toward restoring habitats in their neighborhoods. For example, a Maunalua Bay project removed more than 3 million lb of invasive algae by organizing community *huli* (pull) parties.

Keep up with the Issues

Though O'ahu lags a little behind some of her sisters, environmental consciousness has taken root on this, the most densely populated and heavily militarized and touristed of the Hawaiian Islands. A wide coalition of scientists, activists and residents has made conservation efforts a slow but steady success.

For the latest environmental issues facing the island, check out the following:

Native Hawaiian people at Prince Kuhio Day celebrations in Honolulu

Environment Hawaii (www.environment-hawaii.org)

Hawai'i Conservation Alliance (www.hawaiiconservation.org)

Show Aloha for Native Hawaiians

There is no doubt that Native Hawaiians feel that they've had a raw deal since Queen Lili'uokalani was overthrown in 1893.

In the 1970s Hawaiian culture, battered by colonization, commodified and peddled to tourists, was ready for a revival; it just needed the spark. In 1976 a replica of the ancient Polynesian sailing canoe *Hokule'a* successfully sailed to Tahiti using only the sun, stars, wind and waves for a compass, bringing a burst of cultural pride. That same year a group of Hawaiian activists occupied Kaho'olawe, which the US government had used for bombing practice since WWII. A Native Hawaiian rights movement soon emerged.

When the state of Hawaii held its landmark Constitutional Convention in 1978, it passed a number of amendments, such as making Hawaiian an official state language (along with English) and mandating that Hawaiian culture be taught in public schools. In the community, traditional arts such as *lauhala* (traditional Hawaiian leaf weaving), *kapa* (bark cloth) making, wood carving, hula and *la'au lapa'au* (plant medicine) experienced a revival. Heiau (ancient stone temples) and fishponds started to be restored as well.

Traditional Hawaiian culture remains an important part of island life and identity, reflected in ways both large and small: in spontaneous hula dancing on an airplane, an *oli* (chant) sung before political ceremonies in Honolulu or a *lomilomi* (traditional Hawaiian massage; known as 'loving touch') at a healing spa.

Native Hawaiians Today

It hasn't been plain sailing since the Hawaiian renaissance for many Native Hawaiians. Visitors who venture out of Waikiki today will see plenty of upside-down state flags (signaling distress),

Hawaiian royal flags, and Kanaka Maoli flags, the red, green and yellow flag popular among Hawaiian activists.

At the time of research there were three major protests going on, all involving much angst and many arrests:

➡ against the 100ft telescope on Mauna Kea on Hawai'i (the Big Island)

➡ against development of Sherwood Forest at Waimanalo on O'ahu

➡ against another eight wind turbines in Kahuku on O'ahu's upper Windward Coast

The predicament of Native Hawaiians could clearly be seen by the line of tents of homeless people along the highway outside Waimanalo Beach Park.

The depth of pride and emotions of Native Hawaiians can be heard in the music of Hawaiian band Ekolu, who sing about using aloha as a way to fight back.

Show Aloha for the Community

Immigration by people from around the globe over 150 years has produced one of the most multiethnic populations on the planet, and for the most part everyone lives together in great harmony. It's part of the aloha of O'ahu. Help them out.

HAWAI'I 2050 INITIATIVE

Even the government has gotten into the green swing of things, creating the Hawai'i 2050 (www.planning.ha waii.gov/sustainability/hawaii2050) sustainability plan. This evolving statewide program combines community input with a governmental task force to formulate economic, social and environmental policies that focus on renewable energy, living sustainably within the bounds of the islands' natural resources, and striking a balance between profitable tourism and Hawaiian cultural preservation. That's a tall order, but as the plan itself states, this is 'not an academic or political exercise; it is a matter of the survival of Hawai'i as we know it.'

Eat Local

Every food product not made on O'ahu has been imported. The great distances involved and the amount of fuel required make the 'locavore' or 'eat local' movement sound even more appetizing. More and more restaurant menus these days sound like agricultural report cards. Creative island chefs love featuring island-grown produce such as Nalo greens, North Shore grass-fed beef and locally caught seafood – and telling you so. It's part of the Hawaiian concept of *malama 'aina*, meaning to care for and nurture the land so that it can give back all that is needed to sustain life for present and future generations.

Farmers markets, too, are booming on O'ahu. They're all over the island, sell the freshest fruit and vegetables, and, if you've got basic kitchen facilities where you're staying, can save you a bundle. How about pineapple, papaya, mango and apple bananas for breakfast?

Buy Local

Avoid foreign-made trinkets as souvenirs of your visit and purchase locally made products that have been crafted with pride and aloha. There's been a huge increase in the number and quality of Hawaii-made products, such as soaps, ocean-safe sunscreens, cosmetics, coffee, chocolate, and locally designed and made clothing. It's part of the push for a sustainable tourism industry – so buy local!

Keeping the Country Country

Spend some time exploring O'ahu and you'll notice bumper stickers and hand-painted signs with antidevelopment slogans such as 'Keep the Country Country.' The North Shore is almost completely devoid of condos, as locals have opposed each new proposal with solidarity. This is not just a Native Hawaiian attitude. There is a strong belief among those living in more rural parts of O'ahu, on the North Shore and Windward Coast in particular, that they'd like to keep things as they are – as a steadfast part of the countryside, not an extension of Honolulu.

Top: Carambola (star fruit)

Bottom: Avocados at a farmers market

Plan Your Trip
Family Travel

With so much surf and sand, O'ahu's coastline could be likened to a giant, free water park. Traveling families have been coming to the island for decades; local resorts, hotels and restaurants are well prepared. So stop for a shave ice and relax; *keiki* (children) are most welcome here.

Keeping Costs Down

Accommodations

Children under 18 often stay for free when sharing a hotel room with their parents if they use existing bedding. Look to fit the family in one room; roll-away beds are usually available (for a surcharge) at hotels and resorts.

Transportation

Kids ride cheaply on TheBus. Children under five ride for free, while kids aged six to 18 ride for $1.25 (and can get a day pass for $2.50). Walking is the cheapest transportation around – if you're staying in Waikiki you can walk to Diamond Head or Kaimana Beach.

Eating

Many restaurants have children's menus. Food trucks and other outdoor eateries are family faves, as they're super casual and the location may provide space for kids to roam. Many beach parks have picnic tables. Sandwiches and meals to go are readily available at cafes, drive-ins and grocery stores.

Activities

There's lots to do on O'ahu that won't break the bank, starting with the beach. Investing in some snorkeling gear, a bodyboard or a ball that floats will probably keep kids busy for days. Short hikes also make cost-effective activities.

Children Will Love...

Beaches

Hanauma Bay, Southeast O'ahu (p207) Technicolor tropical fish and some of the best snorkeling around.

Pupukea Beach Park tide pools, North Shore (p256) Great for the whole family, with sea creatures in a safe environment.

Waimanalo Bay Beach Park, Windward Coast (p217) A great spot to learn to bodyboard and bodysurf.

Kuhio Beach Park, Waikiki (p144) Plenty of sun, sand and surf in the heart of Waikiki.

Short Walks

Manoa Falls, Honolulu (p102) Try a rewarding hike through lush tropical forest to picturesque falls.

Diamond Head, Southeast O'ahu (p199) Climb to the highest point for unbelievable views of Waikiki and Honolulu.

Makapu'u Point Lighthouse Trail, Southeast O'ahu (p211) An adventure on a sealed road to an isolated lighthouse.

Likeke Falls Trail, Windward Coast (p223) Fun family hike on the windward side of the island.

Attractions

Waikiki Aquarium, Waikiki (p145) Who doesn't love eyeballing spectacularly colorful fish through the glass?

Hawaii Children's Discovery Center, Honolulu (p93) Lots of fun things to do on a rainy day.

Honolulu Zoo, Waikiki (p146) Tropical greenery and a petting zoo for kids.

Bishop Museum, Honolulu (p100) Planetarium shows and exploding faux volcanoes.

Fun Rides

Kualoa Ranch, Windward Coast (p233) Explore movie and TV filming locations or ride a horse.

Atlantis Submarine, Waikiki (p153) How many kids on this earth don't want to ride in a submarine?

Wet 'n' Wild Hawaii, Leeward O'ahu (p184) Waterslides and a wave pool out west.

Dole Plantation, Central O'ahu (p270) Pineapple garden maze, Pineapple Express train ride and pineapples to eat.

Food & Drink

KCC Farmers Market, Southeast O'ahu (p202) Incredible selection of tasty (and healthy) eats!

Matsumoto's Shave Ice, North Shore (p264) Generations have been stopping for shave ice in Hale'iwa on circle-island tours.

Leonard's, Waikiki (p163) The *malasadas* (Portuguese-style fried doughnuts) at Leonard's bakery are the bomb.

Da Cove Health Bar & Cafe, Waikiki (p164) Try an incredibly delicious acai bowl next to Waikiki School.

Region by Region

Honolulu

There are plenty of fun things for kids to do in Honolulu, though not so much that's beach oriented. Head to the Hawaii Children's Discovery Center (p93) for educational and fun activities; the same goes at the Bishop Museum (p100). Ala Moana offers its beach park (p85) and tennis courts, or shopping, eating and exploring at the Ala Moana Center (p127). There's hiking up to Manoa Falls (p102), or to the Nu'uanu Valley Lookout (p104) for a longer trek.

Waikiki

Soooo much to do in Waikiki. For a start, there's the sea and learning to surf, bodyboard or snorkel. Or go under the waves in a submarine! You can also check out tropical fish at the Waikiki Aquarium (p145) and animals at Honolulu Zoo (p146). Hit tennis balls in Kapi'olani park (p146), take a catamaran ride, or watch a free hula show and Hilton Hawaiian Village's Friday-night fireworks (p167). And there's lots of ice cream.

Pearl Harbor & Leeward O'ahu

Ko Olina offers up its Disney Aulani resort (p186), plus good fun and snorkeling at its sandy lagoons. Hit the waterslides at Wet 'n' Wild (p184), ride the historic Hawaiian Railway (p183) or, at the top end of the Leeward Coast, hike out to Ka'ena Point (p268). Older kids may find the history of Pearl Harbor engrossing, and they can clamber around the battleship *Missouri* (p178) or the USS Bowfin Submarine Museum (p179).

Southeast O'ahu

There are some great options for outdoor adventures in the southeast, such as climbing Diamond Head (p199) and snorkeling at Hanauma Bay (p207). KCC Farmers Market (p202) offers up all sorts of fun eats on Saturday morning, while Kahala Mall (p202) has air-conditioned comfort and movie theaters. Water sports abound at Hawai'i Kai (p202), while watching pro bodysurfers at Sandy Beach (p209) and hiking to Makapu'u Point Lighthouse (p211) are fun things to do around the coast.

Windward Coast

Waimanalo Bay Beach Park (p217) is the place to learn to bodyboard, while Kailua Beach Park (p221) offers all sorts of water-sports options, such as kayaking and learning to wind- or kitesurf. Hike into Likeke Falls (p223) or on the Ka'iwa Ridge (Lanikai Pillboxes) Trail (p222). Up the coast, Kualoa Ranch (p233) offers all sorts of outdoor adventures, while the Polynesian Cultural Center (p238) at La'ie is a fun learning experience. Eat shrimp in Kahuku (p240), where older children will love the ziplines at CLIMB Works Keana Farms (p240).

North Shore & Central O'ahu

On offer here are gorgeous beaches and learn-to-surf territory, though not when the big waves are rolling in.

Try kayaking, stand-up paddleboarding or just lolling in the waves in summer. Sharks Cove (p256) and the tide pools offer snorkeling and exploring options, while you can go biking, sailing or fishing out of Hale'iwa (p260).

Dole Plantation (p270), near Wahiawa, has everything pineapple, including a pineapple maze and a Pineapple Express train to ride.

Good to Know

Look out for the 🖪 icon for family-friendly suggestions throughout this guide.

Breastfeeding Mothers in Hawaii have the right to breastfeed in public.

Changing facilities Available in shopping malls, in big hotels and at sights.

Childseats State law requires children under the age of four to ride in a child safety seat and children aged four through seven to ride in a child safety seat or a booster seat when traveling in a motor vehicle.

Cribs (cots) Usually available; check ahead with the hotel.

Diapers (nappies) Sold island-wide at grocery, drug and convenience stores.

High chairs Usually available.

Kids' menus Widely available.

Seat belts Hawaii's universal seat-belt law requires that all front- and back-seat motor-vehicle occupants buckle up.

Kids' Corner

Say What?

Aloha.	Hello.
Mahalo.	Thank you.
lei	a string of flowers
hula	a dance

Did You Know? ℹ

- 79 movies, including *Godzilla* and *Jurassic Park*, have been filmed at Kualoa Ranch.

Have You Tried?

Spam *musubi*
Spam on rice – like sushi!

Waikiki Aquarium (p145)

Strollers Bring your own, or rent online and have it delivered to your hotel.

Transportation Reserve car seats with rental agencies in advance or bring your own. Most car-hire companies rent child safety seats from $10 per day.

Online services Deliver rented car seats, strollers, playpens, cribs and more right to your door. Try:
➡ Paradise Baby (www.paradisebabyco.com)
➡ Baby's Away (www.babysaway.com)
➡ Baby Aboard (www.babyaboardhawaii.com)

Useful Resources

Lonely Planet Kids (www.lonelyplanetkids.com) Loads of activities and great family-travel blog content.

Hawaii Tourism Authority (www.gohawaii.com/experiences/family-fun) Family fun in Hawaii.

Hawaii Travel Activity Book and Journal: For Kids! (www.amazon.com) Information on history, sights and the natural environment in the Hawaiian Islands.

Hawaii: Kids Coloring and Activity Book (www.amazon.com) For kids aged five to seven.

Regions at a Glance

Ready to get out and explore O'ahu? While the beaches, restaurants and shops of Waikiki could keep you happy for days, there's so much to do around the island that it would be a shame not to explore further. Gorgeous beaches dot the coastline, while inland, verdant mountains and *pali* (cliffs) beckon. The Windward Coast faces the trade winds from the east, while the less windy leeward coast is sheltered by the mountains. Honolulu and Waikiki are on the south coast, and the North Shore's monster winter waves are the stuff of legend. It's not all about the magnificent natural environment, though. Bustling state capital Honolulu has museums, multiethnic restaurants, an intriguing history and a captivating Chinatown. Seriously, you could play on O'ahu for weeks.

Honolulu

Culture
History
Food

Multicultural Modernism

Honolulu lets you take the pulse of multiracial O'ahu, which confounds census categories with one of the world's great melting pots. East, West and everywhere else intermingle as ancient Hawaiian traditions greet a mix of immigrant groups from all over the globe.

Historical Hot Spot

Hit Honolulu's historical district, museums and Chinatown for a wonderful look into the fascinating stories that got the 50th state to where it is today. Brawling, womanizing whalers, Protestant missionaries, Hawaiian kings and queens, and the USA's only royal palace are in the mix.

Endless Feast

Honolulu is a multiethnic foodie capital, with everything from food trucks to farmers markets to fusion menus by Hawaii's star chefs. Eating provides endless pleasure to the locals, who chow down on an incredible variety of cuisine, mostly introduced by the various immigrant groups.

p82

Waikiki

Beaches
Entertainment
Shopping

Sand & Surf

Gorgeous sand and warm waters virtually on your hotel doorstep make Waikiki a wondrous destination. Take a surfing lesson, bodyboard on friendly waves, sail on a catamaran, soak in temperate waters, teach the kids to swim or just loll on the beach and enjoy it!

Hula & Ukuleles

There's no lack of things going on. Enjoy swaying hula performances and the strumming of ukuleles and slack-key guitars while sipping cocktails in atmospheric bars under sprawling tree canopies. It isn't all for show: Hawaiians are proud of their aloha culture.

Shop till You Drop

Anything and everything you could possibly want to take home is in Waikiki. Designer boutiques and brand-name stores are everywhere. For those with lighter wallets, the ubiquitous ABC Stores have it all, from snacks and sunblock to souvenir dashboard hula girls.

p136

Pearl Harbor & Leeward O'ahu

History
Country
Resorts

Solemn Tributes

One of the USA's most significant war sites, Pearl Harbor National Memorial has museums narrating the history of the Pearl Harbor attack and commemorates fallen service members. Be sure to visit the USS Arizona Memorial and the Battleship Missouri Memorial.

Off the Beaten Path

Leeward O'ahu sees fewer visitors than the rest of the island, mainly because the Farrington Hwy up the coast culminates in a dead end. There are lovely beaches, and while the townships may feel a tad rough around the edges you'll find plenty of interest.

Ko Olina Resorts

Some come to the southwest tip of O'ahu to bunker down at Ko Olina's resorts. Families thrive at Disney's Aulani; others stay at the impressive Four Seasons; and golfers swear by the Ko Olina Golf Club.

p174

Southeast O'ahu

Activities
Driving
Hiking

Adventure in Paradise

So much to do in the water! While snorkeling or diving at Hanauma Bay is a must, experienced bodyboarders rave about Sandy Beach and Makapu'u Beach Park. Hawai'i Kai operators offer everything from parasailing to banana boats, wakeboarding and jet packs.

Road Trip

Rent a car for a spectacular drive from Diamond Head to Makapu'u Point. The Halona coast is a highlight, featuring the Lana'i Lookout and Fishing Shrine, Halona Cove and Halona Blowhole, and stunning views out to Maui and Moloka'i. Spot migrating whales in winter.

Hit the Track

There's a lovely mix of places to walk here, from climbing the volcanic cones of Diamond Head or Koko Head to tackling the tough Kuli'ou'ou Ridge Trail or wandering out to Makapu'u Point Lighthouse. Savor the geographical masterpiece that is Southeast O'ahu.

p196

Windward Coast

Activities
Countryside
Driving

Play in the Sea

The name Windward Coast implies wind, and that's something that kite- and windsurfers revel in, especially in Kailua Bay. Kayakers and stand-up paddleboarders get out before the wind gets up, while bodyboarders play all day at Waimanalo Bay. Further north, swim at Malaeka-hana Beach.

Ranches & Farms

With plenty of rainfall, this is O'ahu's lushest and most verdant coast. Things grow! Waimanalo farms produce vegetables and leafy greens for the island's top restaurants, while up the coast are rural communities, working cattle ranches, fruit orchards and shrimp ponds.

The Coast Road

Circle O'ahu by car and you'll find the highway up the coast to be a highlight. There's a different view around each corner, from craggy cliffs to massive mountains, beaches that look ready to invade the road, and tiny, isolated offshore islands.

p214

North Shore & Central O'ahu

Beaches
Activities
Country

The Seven-Mile Miracle

The 7-mile stretch of waves and sand from Hale'iwa to Sunset Beach has been dubbed the 'Seven-Mile Miracle' and has surfers drooling with its monster winter waves. This is home to the Triple Crown of Surfing, considered the world's premier surf event.

Land, Sea & Air

You're in fun country here! Surf, kite- or windsurf, bodyboard, SUP, snorkel or dive in the sea, go hiking, check out pineapples and coffee on the land, or try skydiving, gliding or trike flights up top. This is a place to play.

Keeping it Country

Locals love their laid-back and simple life and have steadfastly resisted proposals for resorts and condos that they believe would make the North Shore just an extension of Honolulu. It's this attitude that helps makes the North Shore such a gem to visit.

p246

On the Road

AT A GLANCE

POPULATION
405,000

STATE LEGISLATURE
Hawaii State Capitol Building (p89)

BEST LOCAL LUNCH
Helena's Hawaiian Food (p104)

BEST TIKI BAR
La Mariana Sailing Club (p124)

BEST MICROBREWERY
Beer Lab Hawaii (p124)

WHEN TO GO
Sep Enjoy Aloha Festivals statewide, with celebrations of Hawaiian music, dance and history.

Jan–Feb Chinatown rocks with Chinese New Year parades, lion dances and fireworks.

Oct A foodies dream come true at the Hawai'i Food & Wine Festival.

Downtown Honolulu (p86)
CHRISTIAN MUELLER / SHUTTERSTOCK ©

Honolulu

I n Honolulu, you get to rub elbows with the real Hawaii. A boisterous, vibrant Polynesian capital, Honolulu delivers an island-style mixed plate of experiences.

The city is steeped in history, from the extraordinary Victorian-era royal buildings to tombs that date from before the monarchy was dethroned and a sovereign nation was stolen. Tour these surprising sites and then plunge into the warren that is Chinatown, the city's oldest neighborhood, which brims with surprises where 19th-century whalers once brawled and immigrant traders thrived.

Explore Kakaʻako, the neighborhood near downtown and the waterfront, with hip cafes and breweries. Or wander old Kaimuki, an appealing district of shops, restaurants and pubs.

On the shore, ocean breezes rustle palm trees along beaches, while in the cool, mist-shrouded Koʻolau Range and valleys, tropical forest hiking trails offer postcard city views.

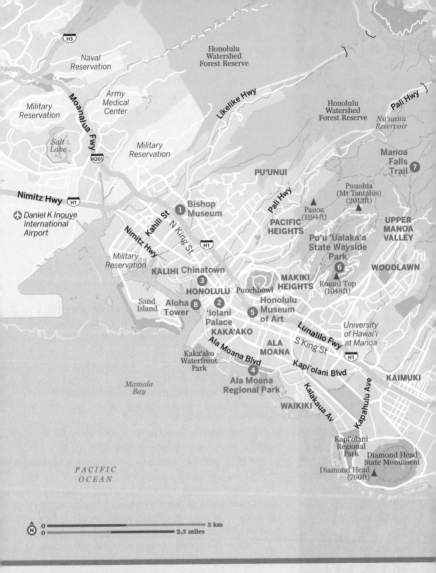

Honolulu Highlights

1 Bishop Museum (p100) Delving into the extraordinary history and cultures of Hawaii.

2 'Iolani Palace (p87) Inspecting the genteel surrounds of the USA's only royal palace.

3 Chinatown (p94) Exploring the narrow alleyways of the city's oldest neighborhood.

4 Ala Moana Regional Park (p85) Frolicking in the sun at the city's largest beach park.

5 Honolulu Museum of Art (p96) Wandering this exceptional fine-arts museum with treasures from around the world.

6 Pu'u 'Ualaka'a State Wayside Park (p101) Taking in all of Honolulu from high above the city.

7 Manoa Falls Trail (p102) Hiking through O'ahu's green heart.

8 Aloha Tower (p89) Taking the lift up for harbor and downtown views.

History

In 1793 the English frigate *Butterworth* became the first foreign ship to sail into what is now Honolulu Harbor. In 1809 Kamehameha the Great moved his royal court from Waikiki to Honolulu (Sheltered Bay) to control the vigorous international trade taking place there, but it didn't replace Lahaina on Maui as the official capital of the Kingdom of Hawai'i until 1845.

In the 1820s Honolulu's first bars and brothels opened to crews of whaling ships. Hotel St, a lineup of bars and brothels a few blocks from the harbor, became the city's red-light district. Christian missionaries began arriving around the same time and were somewhat unimpressed. Today, Hawaii's first missionary church still stands just a stone's throw from the royal palace.

In 1893 a small group of citizens, mostly of American missionary descent, seized control of the kingdom from Queen Lili'uokalani and declared an independent republic, imprisoning the queen in downtown Honolulu's 'Iolani Palace. After political machinations and backroom deals that reached Washington, DC, Hawaii was formally annexed by the USA in 1898.

During the first half of the 20th century, Honolulu was the sleeping center of an island economy built on sugarcane and pineapples. Tourism was limited to the wealthy, who could afford long sea voyages or very expensive air travel, but World War II brought immense change. The population expanded greatly, due to vast numbers of military personnel being stationed on O'ahu, many of whom wished to return to the beautiful island during peacetime. The revolution of jet travel in the 1960s made Hawaii a destination that was both affordable and reachable for Americans with limited vacations. Waikiki rapidly expanded to accommodate the massive influx of visitors and increasingly Honolulu's economy became dependent on tourism.

As plantations closed in the 1980s and 1990s, they were replaced by housing developments for a growing population working in an economy based on tourism, trade and the military.

🏖 Beaches

Ala Moana Regional Park BEACH
(Map p96; ☎808-768-4616; 1201 Ala Moana Blvd; ⓟ🚻) Opposite the Ala Moana Center mall, this city park boasts a broad, golden-sand beach nearly a mile long, buffered from passing traffic by shade trees. Ala Moana is hugely popular, yet big enough that it never feels too crowded. This is where Honolulu residents come to go running after work, play beach volleyball and enjoy weekend picnics. The park has full facilities, including light tennis courts (p108), ball fields, picnic tables, drinking water, restrooms, outdoor showers and lifeguard towers.

The peninsula jutting from the southeast side of the park is **Magic Island**. You can take an idyllic sunset walk around the peninsula's perimeter year-round, within an anchor's toss of sailboats pulling in and out of neighboring Ala Wai Yacht Harbor.

Sand Island State Recreation Area BEACH
(Map p86; http://dlnr.hawaii.gov/dsp/parks/oahu; Sand Island Pkwy; ⏰7am-7:45pm Apr-Aug, to 6:45pm Sep-Mar; ⓟ) A barely visited half-mile ribbon of sand hides in plain sight from much of Honolulu. Industrial Sand Island, sitting between the airport and the port, is home to this large urban park. The beach faces the open Pacific and has fine-grained sand. It's backed by vast lawns dotted with trees and public facilities such as restrooms.

From the sand there are fine views of planes taking off (wave to the morose faces overhead winging their way home) and of the high-rises of downtown and Waikiki. On the downside, the park suffers from shabby maintenance and there's a few people wandering about who clearly have no place else to go. It's also a bit of a trek to reach the beach. From the intersection where the Sand Island Access Rd heads southwest from the Nimitz Hwy (Hwy 92), it's about a 4-mile drive, as you have to drive all the way to the east end of the island before hooking back to the beach.

Kaka'ako Waterfront Park BEACH
(Map p86; end of Ohe or Kolua Sts, off Ala Moana Blvd; ⏰6am-10pm; ⓟ) Near downtown, Kaka'ako Park feels far away from the urban jungle, attracting experienced surfers in the morning and picnickers in the afternoon. In-line skaters roll along the rock-fringed promenade, offering clear views of Diamond Head and Honolulu Harbor. It's not a safe swimming spot and there's no sandy beach, but Point Panic (p106) is a killer bodysurfing break offshore. Limited facilities include restrooms, drinking water and picnic tables.

Greater Honolulu

Sights

Honolulu's compact downtown is just a lei's throw from the harborfront. Nearby, the buzzing streets of Chinatown are packed with food markets, antiques shops, art galleries and hip restaurants. Between downtown and Waikiki, Ala Moana has Hawaii's biggest mall and the city's best beach.

The University of Hawai'i campus is a gateway to the lush and historic Manoa Valley. Various outlying sights, including the fabulous Bishop Museum, are worth putting into your schedule.

Downtown

This area was center stage for the political intrigue and social upheavals that changed the fabric of Hawaii during the 19th century. Major players ruled here, revolted here, worshipped here and still rest, however restlessly, in the graveyards. You can take in a lot of Hawaii history on a short stroll.

Note that the Fort St pedestrian mall suffers from all the social problems that bedevil Honolulu, including many homeless people.

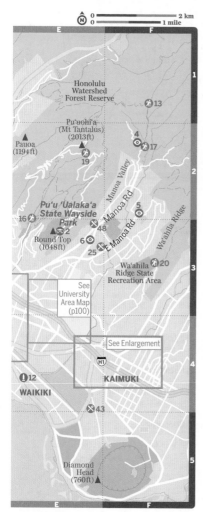

issaries here. Although the palace was modern and opulent for its time, it did little to assert Hawaii's sovereignty over powerful US-influenced business interests, who overthrew the kingdom in 1893.

Two years after the coup, the former queen, Lili'uokalani, who had succeeded her brother David to the throne, was convicted of treason and spent nine months imprisoned in her former home. Later the palace served as the capitol of the republic, then the territory and later the state of Hawaii. In 1969 the government finally moved into the current state capitol, leaving 'Iolani Palace a shambles. After a decade of painstaking renovations, the restored palace reopened as a museum, although many original royal artifacts had been lost or stolen before work even began.

Visitors must take a self-guided or docent-led tour (no children under five) to see the grand interior, including re-creations of the throne room and residential quarters upstairs. The palace was modern by Victorian standards. Every bedroom had its own bathroom with flush toilets and hot running water, and electric lights replaced the gas lamps years before the White House in Washington, DC, installed electricity. If you're short on time, you can independently browse historical exhibits in the basement, including royal regalia, historic photographs and reconstructions of the kitchen and chamberlain's office.

The palace grounds are open during daylight hours and are free of charge. The former **barracks** of the Royal Household Guards, a building that looks oddly like the uppermost layer of a medieval fort, now houses the ticket booth. Nearby, the domed Keliiponi Hale **pavilion**, originally built for the coronation of King Kalakaua in 1883, is still used for state governor inaugurations. Underneath the huge banyan tree, allegedly planted by Queen Kapi'olani, the Royal Hawaiian Band gives free concerts on most Fridays from noon to 1pm, weather permitting.

Reserve tickets in advance online during peak periods.

Keliiponi Hale   HISTORIC BUILDING
(Coronation Pavilion; Map p90) The Keliiponi Hale was erected in front of 'Iolani Palace in 1883 as a pavilion for the coronation of King Kalakaua. As there was no other ranking person to perform the duty, Kalakaua placed the crown on his own head. The pavilion was later moved to its present site and used as a bandstand. These days, the Royal Hawaiian Band (p125) plays free concerts near the pavilion at noon on most Fridays.

★ **'Iolani Palace**   PALACE
(Map p90; ☎ 808-522-0822; www.iolanipalace. org; 364 S King St; grounds free, basement galleries adult/child $5/3, self-guided audio tour $20/6, guided tour $27/6; ☺ palace 9am-4pm Mon, from 10:30am Tue-Thu & Sat, from noon Fri, basement galleries 9:30am-4pm Mon-Sat, tours 9-10am Tue-Thu & Sat, to 11:15am Fri) No other place evokes a more poignant sense of Hawaii's history. The palace was built under King David Kalakaua in 1882. At that time, the Hawaiian monarchy observed many of the diplomatic protocols of the Victorian world. The king traveled abroad, meeting with leaders around the globe, and received foreign em-

Greater Honolulu

★ **Hawai'i State Art Museum**   MUSEUM
(Map p90; ☎808-586-0900; http://hisam.ha
waii.gov; 2nd fl, No 1 Capitol District Bldg, 250 S Hotel St; ⊙10am-4pm Mon-Sat & 6-9pm 1st Fri of month) 🅵 **FREE** With its vibrant, thought-provoking collections, this public art museum brings together traditional and contemporary art from Hawaii's multiethnic communities. The museum inhabits a grand 1928 Spanish Mission Revival–style building, formerly a YMCA and today a nationally registered historic site. The museum is also home to a fine gift shop and an excellent cafe, Artizen by MW (p111).

Upstairs, revolving exhibits of paintings, sculptures, fiber art, photography and mixed media are displayed around themes, such as the island's Polynesian heritage, modern social issues or the natural beauty of land and sea. Hawaii's complex confluence of Asian, Pacific Rim and European cultures is evident throughout, shaping an aesthetic that captures the soul of the islands and the hearts of the people.

Special events are very worthwhile. On the first Friday evening each month, galleries are open with live entertainment and a family-friendly atmosphere. Drop by at noon on the last Tuesday of the month for free 'Art Lunch' lectures or between 11am and 3pm on the second Saturday for hands-on Hawaiian arts and crafts, often designed with kids in mind.

Hawaii State Capitol NOTABLE BUILDING
(Map p90; ☑808-586-0178, tours 808-586-0034; 415 S Beretania St; ⊙7:45am-4:30pm Mon-Fri) FREE Built in the architecturally interesting 1960s, Hawaii's state capitol is a poster child of conceptual postmodernism: two cone-shaped legislative chambers have sloping walls to represent volcanoes; the supporting columns shaped like coconut palms symbolize the archipelago's eight main islands; and a large encircling pool represents the Pacific Ocean surrounding Hawaii. Visitors can walk through the open-air rotunda and peer through viewing windows into the legislative chambers. Pick up a self-guiding tour brochure from the governor's office, Room 415.

Free 75-minute public tours depart most Wednesdays at 1pm from Room 415. Various online touring guides and resources are available at http://governor.hawaii.gov/hawaii-state-capitol-tours.

★**Aloha Tower** LANDMARK
(Map p90; ☑808-544-1453; www.alohatower.com; 1 Aloha Tower Dr; ⊙9am-5pm; ℗) FREE Built in 1926, this 10-story landmark was once the city's tallest building. In the golden days when all tourists to Hawaii arrived by ship, this pre-WWII waterfront icon – with its four-sided clock tower inscribed with 'Aloha' – greeted every visitor. These days, Hawaii Pacific University occupies the mostly defunct Aloha Tower Marketplace, which was meant to ensnare people arriving at the cruise-ship docks. Take the elevator to the top-floor observation deck for fabulous 360-degree views of Honolulu and the waterfront.

Hawaiian Mission Houses Historic Site MUSEUM
(Map p90; ☑808-447-3910; www.missionhouses.org; 553 S King St; 1hr guided tour adult/child $12/6; ⊙10am-4pm Tue-Sat, guided tours 11am, noon, 1pm, 2pm & 3pm) Occupying the original headquarters of the Sandwich Islands mission that forever changed the course of Hawaiian history, this modest museum is authentically furnished with handmade quilts on the beds and iron cooking pots in the stone fireplaces. It's free to explore the grounds, but you'll need to take a guided tour to see inside any of the buildings.

You'll notice that the first missionaries packed more than their bags when they left Boston – they brought a prefabricated wooden house, called the **Frame House**, with them around the Horn. Designed to withstand New England winter winds, the small windows instead blocked out Honolulu's cooling tradewinds, which kept the two-story house hellaciously hot and stuffy. Erected in 1821, it's the oldest wooden structure in Hawaii.

DON'T MISS

DOWNTOWN'S UNMISSABLE STATUES

Kamehameha the Great Statue (Map p90; 447 S King St) Standing before the Ali'iolani Hale, a bronze statue of Kamehameha the Great faces 'Iolani Palace. Often ceremonially draped with layers of flower lei, the statue was cast in 1880 in Florence, Italy, by American sculptor Thomas Gould. The current statue is a recast, as the first statue was lost at sea near the Falkland Islands. It was dedicated here in 1883, just a decade before the Hawaiian monarchy would be overthrown. The original statue, which was later recovered from the ocean floor, now stands in Kohala on Hawai'i, the Big Island, where Kamehameha I was born.

Queen Lili'uokalani Statue (Map p90; State Capitol) Pointedly positioned between the state capitol building and 'Iolani Palace is a life-size bronze statue of Queen Lili'uokalani, Hawaii's last reigning monarch. She holds a copy of the Hawaiian constitution she wrote in 1893 in an attempt to strengthen Hawaiian rule; 'Aloha 'Oe,' a popular song she composed; and *kumulipo,* the traditional Hawaiian chant of creation.

Father Damien Statue (Map p90; State Capitol) In front of the capitol is a highly stylized statue of Father Damien, the Belgian priest who lived and worked with victims of Hansen's disease (leprosy) who were exiled to the island of Moloka'i during the late 19th century. He later died of the disease himself. In 2009 the Catholic Church canonized Father Damien as Hawaii's first saint, after the allegedly miraculous recovery from cancer in 1988 of a Honolulu schoolteacher who had prayed over Damien's original grave site on Moloka'i.

Downtown Honolulu & Chinatown

0 — 200 m
0 — 0.1 miles

Nimitz Hwy

Iwilei Rd

Nimitz Hwy

Beretania Park

'A'ala St

N Beretania St

'A'ala Park

Nu'uanu Stream

Awa St

River St

Kekaulike St

N King St

Foster Botanical Garden

N Vineyard Blvd

College Walk

River St pedestrian Mall

N Kukui St

Maunakea St

Nu'uanu Ave

S Kukui St

S Beretania St

School St

Lunalilo Fwy

Pali Hwy

Nu'uanu Ave

S Vineyard Blvd

Vineyard St

Kamamalu Park

Queen Emma St

CHINATOWN

N Hotel St (buses only)

Kekaulike St Pedestrian Mall

N King St

Smith St

Ala Moana Blvd

Maunakea St

Pau'ahi St

N Hotel St

Bethel St

Chinatown Gateway Plaza

Maunakea St

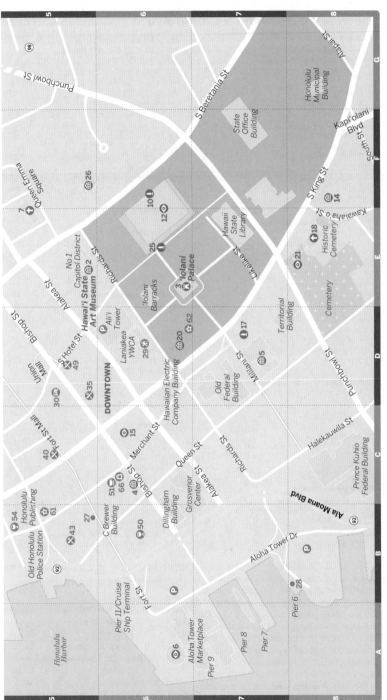

Downtown Honolulu & Chinatown

The 1831 coral-block **Chamberlain House** was the early mission's storeroom, a necessity because Honolulu had few shops in those days. Upstairs are hoop barrels, wooden crates packed with dishes, and the desk and quill pen of Levi Chamberlain. He was appointed by the mission to buy, store and dole out supplies to missionary families, who survived on a meager allowance – as the account books on his desk testify. Nearby, the 1841 **Printing Office** houses a lead-type press used to print the first bible in the Hawaiian language.

Ali'iolani Hale   HISTORIC BUILDING
(Map p90; ☏808-539-4999; www.jhchawaii.net; 417 S King St; ⊙8am-4pm Mon-Fri) **FREE** The first major government building ordered by the Hawaiian monarchy in 1874, the 'House of Heavenly Kings' was designed by Australian architect Thomas Rowe to be a royal palace, although it was never used as such. Today, it houses the Supreme Court of

Hawaii. Don't miss the **King Kamehameha V Judiciary History Center**, where you can browse historical displays about martial law during WWII, the overthrow of the monarchy and the reign of Kamehameha I.

Kawaiaha'o Church CHURCH

(Map p90; ☑ 808-469-3000; www.kawaiahao.org; 957 Punchbowl St; ☺ worship services 9am Sun, 5pm Wed) **FREE** Nicknamed 'Westminster Abbey of Hawaii,' O'ahu's oldest church was built on the site where the first missionaries constructed a grass thatch church shortly after their arrival in 1820. The original structure seated 300 Hawaiians on *lauhala* mats, woven from *hala* (screwpine) leaves. This 1842 New England Gothic–style church is made of 14,000 coral slabs, which divers chiseled out of O'ahu's underwater reefs – a weighty task that took four years. The door is often unlocked during business hours.

The clock tower was donated by Kamehameha III, and the old clock, installed in 1850, still keeps accurate time. The rear seats of the church, marked by *kahili* (feathered staffs) and velvet padding, are reserved for royal descendants today.

The **tomb of King Lunalilo** (Map p90; 🏛), the short-lived successor to Kamehameha V, is found at the main entrance to the Kawaiaha'o Church grounds. Lunalilo died from tuberculosis on February 3, 1874, after a short reign of a year. Due to his popularity and status as Hawaii's first elected monarch, he became known as 'The People's King.' He was an 'elected monarch' as King Kamehameha V, the last of the Kamehameha kings, died in 1872 without naming a successor.

The **cemetery** to the rear of the church offers a who's who of colonial history: early Protestant missionaries are buried alongside other important figures, including the infamous Sanford Dole, who became the first territorial governor of Hawaii after Queen Lili'uokalani was overthrown.

Washington Place HISTORIC BUILDING

(Map p90; ☑ tour reservations 808-586-0248; www.washingtonplacefoundation.org; 320 S Beretania St; ☺ tours by reservation only, usually 10am Thu) **FREE** Formerly the governor's residence, this colonial-style mansion was built in 1846 by US sea captain John Dominis. The captain's son became the governor of O'ahu and married the Hawaiian princess who later became Queen Lili'uokalani. After the queen was released from house arrest inside 'Iolani Palace in 1896, she lived here until her death in 1917. A plaque near the sidewalk is inscribed with the lyrics to 'Aloha 'Oe,' the patriotic anthem she composed. The building is still used for official events. To reserve a tour, phone or visit http://ags.hawaii.gov/washingtonplace/visitor-information.

Cathedral of St Andrew CHURCH

(Map p90; ☑ 808-524-2822; www.thecathedralofstandrew.org; 229 Queen Emma Sq; ☺ usually 9am-5pm Tue-Fri, services 11:30am Wed, 5:30pm Sat, 7am, 8am & 10:30am Sun; P) **FREE** King Kamehameha IV, attracted to the royal Church of England, decided to build his own cathedral and founded the Anglican Church in Hawaii in 1861. The cathedral's cornerstone was laid in 1867, four years after his death on St Andrew's Day – hence the building's name. The architecture is French Gothic, utilizing stone and stained glass shipped from England.

Honolulu Museum of Art at First Hawaiian Center ARTS CENTER

(Map p90; ☑ 808-532-8701; http://honolulumuseum.org; 999 Bishop St; ☺ 8am-4pm Mon-Thu, to 4:30pm Fri) **FREE** First Hawaiian Bank's high-rise headquarters on Bishop St is home to the downtown gallery of the Honolulu Museum of Art (p96), featuring fascinating mixed-media exhibits of modern and contemporary works by Hawaii artists. Exhibits cover several floors and the building itself features a four-story-high art-glass wall incorporating 185 prisms.

Hawaii Children's Discovery Center MUSEUM

(Map p96; ☑ 808-524-5437; www.discoverycenterhawaii.org; 111 'Ohe St; $12; ☺ 9am-1pm Tue-Fri, 10am-3pm Sat & Sun; P ♿) On a rainy day when you can't go to the beach, consider dropping by this hands-on museum for families. Opposite Kaka'ako Waterfront Park, the building was once the city's garbage incinerator, as evidenced by the surviving smokestack. Interactive science and cultural exhibits are geared toward elementary-school-aged children, preschoolers and toddlers. The **Fantastic You!** exhibit explores the human body, allowing kids to walk through a mock human stomach. In the **Your Town** section, kids can drive a play fire engine or conduct a TV interview. **Hawaiian Rainbows** and **Your Rainbow World** introduce Hawaii's multicultural heritage, while **Rainforest Adventures** highlights Hawaii's natural environment and conservation.

Alexander & Baldwin Building HISTORIC BUILDING

(Map p90; 822 Bishop St) The 1929 headquarters of one of Hawaii's most powerful prewar plantation and trading companies, this structure combines powerful authority with tropical flair. Note the height of each floor and the veranda up top that rings the zenith of the palm-fronted and imposing facade.

◉ Chinatown

Chinatown is easily the most pedestrian-friendly Honolulu neighborhood, and you'll make a discovery every few steps. The scent of burning incense still wafts through Chinatown's buzzing markets, fire-breathing dragons spiral up the columns of buildings and steaming dim sum awakens even the sleepiest of appetites.

The location of this mercantile district is no accident. Between Honolulu's busy trading port and what was once the countryside, enterprises selling goods to city folks and visiting ships' crews sprang up in the 19th century. Many of these shops were established by Chinese laborers who had completed their sugarcane-plantation contracts. The most successful entrepreneurial families have long since moved out, making room for newer waves of immigrants, mostly from Southeast Asia.

★ **Foster Botanical Garden**   GARDENS
(Map p90; ☑ 808-522-7135; www.honolulu.gov/parks/hbg; 180 N Vineyard Blvd; adult/child $5/1; ⊙ 9am-4pm, guided tours 10:30am Mon-Sat; ℗)

Tropical plants you've only ever read about can be spotted in all their glory at this spectacular botanic garden, which took root in 1850. Among its rarest specimens are the Hawaiian *loulu* palm and the East African *Gigasiphon macrosiphon,* both thought to be extinct in the wild. Several of the towering trees are the largest of their kind in the USA. The self-guided tour is excellent and gives an introduction to plants and trees found across Hawaii.

Oddities include the cannonball tree, the sausage tree, and the double coconut palm capable of producing a 50lb nut – watch your head! Follow your nose past fragrant vanilla vines and cinnamon trees in the spice and herb gardens, then pick your way among the poisonous and dye plants. Don't miss the blooming orchids or the elegant – and appropriately named – royal palms. The gardens are on the National Register of Historic Places. The free guided tours are expertly led and engaging. Call to reserve a spot.

Hawaii Theatre   HISTORIC BUILDING
(Map p90; ☑ box office 808-528-0506; www.hawaii theatre.com; 1130 Bethel St) This neoclassical landmark first opened in 1922, when silent films were played to the tunes of a pipe organ. Dubbed the 'Pride of the Pacific,' the theater ran continuous shows during WWII, but the development of Waikiki cinemas in the 1960s finally brought down the curtain.

DON'T MISS

HONORING HEROES: PUNCHBOWL

Northeast of downtown Honolulu is a bowl-shaped crater, nicknamed the Punchbowl, formed by a long-extinct volcano. Hawaiians called the crater Puowaina (Hill of Human Sacrifices). It's believed that at an ancient heiau (temple) here, the slain bodies of *kapu* (taboo) breakers were ceremonially cremated upon an altar. Today, the remains of ancient Hawaiians sacrificed to appease the gods share the crater floor with the bodies of well over 50,000 soldiers at the **National Memorial Cemetery of the Pacific** (Punchbowl; Map p86; ☑ 808-532-3720; www.cem.va.gov/cems/nchp/nmcp.asp; 2177 Puowaina Dr; ⊙ 8am-5:30pm Oct-Feb, to 6:30pm Mar-Sep; ℗).

The remains of Ernie Pyle, the distinguished war correspondent who was killed in Okinawa during the final days of WWII, lie in section D, grave 109. Five stones to the left, at grave D-1, is the marker for Ellison Onizuka, the Hawai'i (Big Island) astronaut who perished in the 1986 Challenger space shuttle disaster. Other notables buried here include longtime US senator and WWII vet Daniel K Inouye. Screens at the visitors center at the cemetery entrance let you look up the location of any gravesite.

Even without the war sights, Punchbowl would be worth the drive up for the plum views of the city and Diamond Head. After entering the cemetery, bear left and go to the top of the hill, where there's a sweeping ocean-view lookout. Special events held at the cemetery include Memorial Day ceremonies to honor veterans and a traditional Easter sunrise Christian service. Note the iconic 30ft-tall statue *Columbia* on the central tower, which features in the opening credits of both the old and new *Hawaii Five-0*.

After multi-million-dollar restorations, this nationally registered historic site reopened in 1996 and is now a major venue for live performances (p126). By night, the elaborate neon signage has a seductive glow.

Izumo Taishakyo Mission TEMPLE

(Map p90; ☑ 808-538-7778; www.izumotaisha hawaii.com; 215 N Kukui St; ⊙8:30am-4:45pm) **FREE** This Shintō shrine was built by Japanese immigrants in 1906. It was confiscated during WWII by the city and wasn't returned to the community until the early 1960s. Ringing the bell at the shrine entrance is considered an act of purification for those who come to pray. Thousands of good-luck amulets are sold here, especially on January 1, when the temple heaves with people who come seeking New Year's blessings. The original Izumo Taisha is in Shimane Prefecture, Japan.

Lum Sai Ho Tong TEMPLE

(Map p90; ☑ 808-536-6590; 1315 River St; ⊙temple 8:30am & 2pm) Founded in 1899, the Lum Sai Ho Tong Society was one of more than 100 societies started by Chinese immigrants in Hawaii to help preserve their cultural identity. This one was for the Lum clan hailing from west of the Yellow River. The tiny Tin Hau temple on the 2nd floor opens twice daily for respectful worship and visits. It's thick with incense and smoke.

Chinatown Cultural Plaza PLAZA

(Map p90; cnr Maunakea & N Beretania Sts) Inside this utilitarian mall, covering almost an entire city block, traditional acupuncturists, tailors and calligraphers work alongside travel agencies and dim-sum halls. In the small open-air central courtyard, elderly Chinese people light incense before a **statue of Kuan Yin**. The bland 1970s complex replaced a notorious warren of tiny alleys and back street shops of dubious repute. Outside on the riverside River St Pedestrian Mall, senior citizens practice tai chi after dawn and play checkers, cards and mah-jongg all day.

Hawai'i Heritage Center MUSEUM

(Map p90; ☑ 808-521-2749; www.hawaiiheritage center.org; 1040 Smith St; $1; ⊙9am-1:30pm Mon-Sat, tours 9:30am & 11:30am Wed & Fri) Local

---

DON'T MISS

CHINATOWN MARKETS

The commercial heart of Chinatown revolves around its markets and food shops. Noodle factories, pastry shops and produce stalls line the narrow sidewalks, always crowded with cart-pulling grandmothers and errand-running families. In these busy warrens you'll see the whole range of O'ahu's bounty from both the sea and the land. In addition to the two markets below, don't miss the Maunakea Marketplace (p112), with its popular food stalls.

Kekaulike Market (Map p90; 1039 Kekaulike St; ⊙7am-5pm) Like a daily farmers market, the vendors inside have the full range of whole fish, dry goods, prepared foods and Hawaii's plethora of produce. Out front, vendors hawk fruit and vegetables from a row of displays on the pedestrianized street.

O'ahu Market (Map p90; ☑808-538-6179; 145 N King St; ⊙6am-5pm) An institution since 1904, with everything an Asian-food cook needs: ginger root, quail eggs, jasmine rice, luscious slabs of tuna, long beans and salted jellyfish. It's always crowded with shoppers, from homemakers to office workers. Amid the medley of spice smells, you'll catch a whiff of the harbor just steps away.

---

volunteers with family ties to the community run this crowded gallery that displays changing historical and cultural exhibitions about O'ahu's Chinese, Japanese and other ethnic communities. Ask about the excellent tours of Chinatown.

Kuan Yin Temple TEMPLE

(Map p90; ☑ 808-533-6361; 170 N Vineyard Blvd; ⊙8:30am-2pm) **FREE** With its ceramic-tile roof and bright red columns, this ornate Chinese Buddhist temple is Honolulu's oldest. The richly carved interior is filled with the sweet, pervasive smell of burning incense. The temple is dedicated to Kuan Yin, bodhisattva of mercy, whose statue is the

Ala Moana & Around

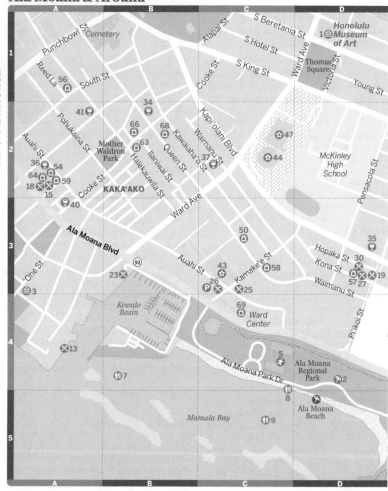

largest in the interior prayer hall. Devotees burn paper 'money' for prosperity and good luck, while offerings of fresh flowers and fruit are placed at the altar.

◉ Ala Moana & Around

Ala Moana means 'Path to the Sea' and its namesake road, Ala Moana Blvd (Hwy 92), connects the coast between Waikiki and Honolulu. Although many people think of Ala Moana only for its shopping mall, Ala Moana Regional Park (p85), which is O'ahu's biggest beach park, makes a relaxing alternative to crowded Waikiki.

A wave of development continues to transform the area with hip loft-style condos and faux-industrial commercial developments.

★ **Honolulu Museum of Art**　MUSEUM
(Map p96; ☑ 808-532-8700; www.honolulumuseum.org; 900 S Beretania St; adult/child $20/free, 1st Wed & 3rd Sun each month free; ⊙ 10am-4:30pm Tue-Sun, tours 10am-noon Tue-Sat, 1-2:30pm Wed & Fri-Sun; P ♿) This exceptional fine-arts museum is among the best of its kind anywhere. The collection is effectively a 'best of' summary of major art movements globally over the last several centuries (eg the Impressionist room includes a Van

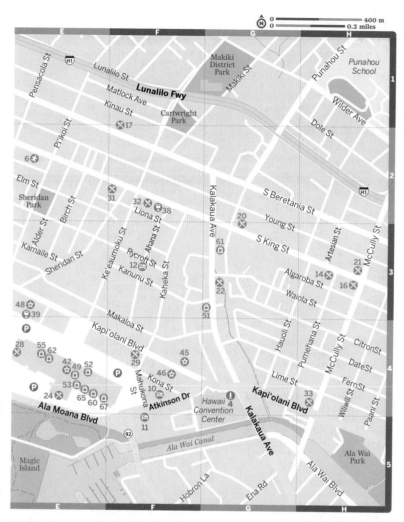

Gogh, a Monet, two Gauguins etc). Plan on spending a couple of hours at the museum, possibly combining a visit with lunch at the Honolulu Museum of Art Café (p116).

The museum, dating to 1927, has a classical facade, with galleries branching off a series of garden and water-fountain courtyards. Beautiful exhibits include one of the country's finest Asian art collections, featuring everything from Japanese woodblock prints by Hiroshige and Ming dynasty–era Chinese calligraphy and painted scrolls to temple carvings and statues from Cambodia and India. Another highlight is the striking contemporary wing with Hawaiian works on its upper level (don't

miss the surfboard crafted by the legendary CJ Kanuha), while the modern art includes Georgia O'Keeffe's Hawaii work. You'll be bewitched by the Pacific and Polynesian artifacts, such as ceremonial masks, war clubs and body adornments.

Admission includes excellent free tours. The morning tours are individual and can be customized for any theme or gallery at the request of the visitor.

Check the museum website for upcoming special events, art lectures, film screenings and music concerts at the Doris Duke Theatre (p127), and evening parties with food, drinks and live entertainment.

Ala Moana & Around

Entry to the lovely shop (p130), the excellent cafe (p116) and the library is free. Parking is diagonally opposite the museum at 1111 Victoria St (enter off Beretania or Young St), and costs $5. From Waikiki, take bus 2 or 13.

Water Giver Statue　　　STATUE
(Map p96; 1801 Kalakaua Ave, Hawaii Convention Center) Fronting the convention center, this magnificent statue was created by local artist Shige Yamada. It symbolically acknowledges the Hawaiian people for their generosity and expressions of goodwill to newcomers. Its sister statue is the Storyteller (p147) in Waikiki.

◉ University Area

At the entrance to the lovely Manoa Valley, the neighborhood surrounding the University of Hawai'i (UH) Manoa campus (also known as Moiliili), has a vibrant feel, with a collection of cafes, eclectic restaurants and one-of-a-kind shops. There's plenty of action around the University Ave and S King St intersection.

University of Hawai'i at Manoa   UNIVERSITY

(UH Manoa; Map p100; ☎808-956-8111; http://manoa.hawaii.edu; 2500 Campus Rd; P) About 2 miles northeast of Waikiki, the main campus of the statewide university system has a contemporary feel offset by towering, ancient trees. Today, its breezy, tree-shaded campus is crowded with students from islands throughout Polynesia and Micronesia. The university has strong programs in astronomy, oceanography and marine biology, as well as Hawaiian, Pacific and Asian studies.

From Waikiki or downtown Honolulu, take bus 4 or 13; from Ala Moana, catch bus 6 or 18. The campus self-guided walking tour (p108) is an excellent way to explore the campus.

East-West Center   CULTURAL CENTER

(Map p100; ☎808-944-7111; www.eastwestcenter.org; 1601 East-West Rd, University of Hawai'i at Manoa) On the eastern side of the UH campus, the East-West Center aims to promote mutual understanding among the peoples of Asia, the Pacific and the US. Changing exhibitions of art and culture are displayed in the EWC Gallery. Savor the Japanese teahouse garden and royal Thai pavilion outside. The center regularly hosts multicultural programs, including lectures, films, concerts and dance performances.

John Young Museum of Art   MUSEUM

(Map p100; ☎808-956-7198; www.hawaii.edu/johnyoung-museum; 2500 Dole St, University of Hawai'i at Manoa; ☉noon-4pm Sun-Fri) FREE A short walk downhill from the UH Campus Center, the John Young Museum of Art features 20th-century Hawaii painter John Young's collection of artifacts from the Pacific islands, Africa, Asia and Mesoamerica, mostly ceramics, pottery and sculpture. The museum has a lovely outdoor courtyard and hosts excellent special exhibitions – often with Hawaii themes.

Hiroshima to Honolulu
Friendship Torii   MONUMENT

(Map p100; cnr S King St & S Beretania St, University area) In a grassy median called the Mō'ili'ili Triangle Park sits a symbol of Honolulu's close ties to Japan. This bright red Shintō gate is a half-size replica of a famous *torii* (traditional gate) at the water's edge of Miyajima island, just south of Hiroshima. Few know that Honolulu and Hiroshima are sister cities, even fewer know that the two cit-

ies' ties go back to the 19th century – when the first wave of Japanese immigrants were drawn from the Hiroshima region.

◉ Upper Manoa Valley & Makiki

Welcome to Honolulu's gardens. Roads into the upper Manoa Valley wind north of the University of Hawaii Manoa campus, passing historic homes and entering forest reserve land in the hills above downtown's highrises. It can be pouring with rain here while beachgoers are basking in the sunshine at Waikiki. Rainbows are frequent and provide the inspiration for names of the UH sports teams. Further west lies Makiki Heights, the neighborhood where former US president Barack Obama spent much of his boyhood.

Lyon Arboretum   GARDENS

(Map p86; ☎808-988-0456; http://manoa.hawaii.edu/lyonarboretum; 3860 Manoa Rd; donation $5, guided tour $10; ☉8am-4pm Mon-Fri, 9am-3pm Sat, tours 10am Mon-Sat; P♿) ✍ Beautiful walking trails wind through this highly regarded 200-acre arboretum managed by the University of Hawai'i. It was originally founded in 1918 by a group of sugar planters growing native and exotic flora species to restore Honolulu's watershed and test their economic benefit. This is not your typical overly manicured tropical flower garden, but a mature and largely wooded arboretum, where related species cluster in a semi-natural state. For a guided tour, call at least 24 hours in advance.

Key plants in the Hawaiian ethnobotanical garden are *'ulu* (breadfruit), *kalo* (taro) and *ko* (sugarcane) brought by early Polynesian settlers; *kukui* (candlenut trees), once harvested to produce lantern oil; and *ti*, which was used for medicinal purposes during ancient times and for making moonshine after Westerners arrived. It's a short walk to Inspiration Point, or keep walking uphill for about 1 mile along a jeep road, then a narrow, tree-root–ridden path to visit seasonal 'Aihualama Falls, a lacy cliffside cascade.

The office has a good selection of books for sale, as well as insect repellent. Parking is a major hassle; get there early to snare one of the scarce spaces. Otherwise, ride bus 5 to the end of the line and then make the 0.6-mile walk up to the arboretum.

Manoa Chinese Cemetery   CEMETERY

(Map p86; 3430 E Manoa Rd) FREE The Lin Yee Chung Manoa Chinese Cemetery is on a knoll nestled on the eastern slopes of the

University Area

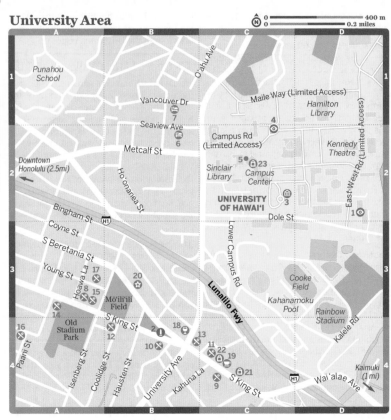

Manoa Valley. Founded in 1852, with all the design elements of a classic Chinese cemetery, it is the oldest and largest Chinese cemetery on the Hawaiian Islands. Stroll among the gates and gravesites for a look into local history and enjoy the views out of the valley mouth to the tall buildings of Waikiki.

Mānoa Heritage Center   GARDEN, TEMPLE
(Map p86; ☑808-988-1287; www.manoaheritage center.org; 2856 O'ahu Ave; adult/child $20/free; ☺tours by reservation only Mon-Fri; 👶) Hidden on a private estate, the centerpiece of this unique site is the ancient, stone-walled Kūka'ō'ō heiau (temple). It's surrounded by beautiful Hawaiian gardens, which include rare native and Polynesian-introduced plants. Walking tours are led by volunteers and staff eager to share island lore and Hawaiian traditions. Book tour reservations online or by phone in advance. No walk-ins are allowed.

◉ Greater Honolulu

★**Bishop Museum**   MUSEUM
(Map p86; ☑808-847-3511; www.bishopmus eum.org; 1525 Bernice St; adult/child $25/17; ☺9am-5pm; 🅿👶) Hawaii's version of the Smithsonian Institute in Washington, DC, the Bishop Museum showcases a remarkable array of cultural and natural history exhibits. It is often ranked as the finest Polynesian anthropological museum in the world. Founded in 1889 in honor of Princess Bernice Pauahi Bishop, a descendant of the Kamehameha dynasty, it originally housed only Hawaiian and royal artifacts. These days it honors all of Polynesia and is an unmissable part of Honolulu's cultural fabric.

The main gallery, the **Hawaiian Hall**, resides inside a dignified three-story Victorian building. The three floors are designed to take visitors on a journey through the different realms of Hawai'i. On the 1st floor is *Kai Akea,* which represents the Hawaiian gods,

University Area

HONOLULU SIGHTS

legends, beliefs, and the world of precontact Hawai'i. One floor up, *Wao Kanaka* focuses on the importance of the land and nature in daily life. The top floor, *Wao Lani,* is inhabited by the gods.

The fascinating two-story exhibits inside the adjacent **Pacific Hall** cover the myriad cultures of Polynesia, Micronesia and Melanesia. It shows how the peoples of Oceania are diverse, yet deeply connected, and is filled with cultural treasures such as canoes, woven mats and contemporary artwork. The **Picture Gallery** features evocative 19th-century paintings depicting Hawaii.

The state-of-the-art, multisensory **Richard T Mamiya Science Adventure Center** is based on better understanding Hawaii's environment. The **Hawai'i Sports Hall of Fame** has photos and memorabilia from outstanding accomplishments by Hawaiian sports legends.

The well-marked **Na Ulu Kaiwi'ula Native Hawaiian Garden** features species important to Hawaiian culture, ranging from endemic plants to those such as breadfruit that were brought to Hawaii by Polynesians centuries ago.

The Bishop Museum is also home to O'ahu's only **planetarium**, which has an ever-changing range of shows, including traditional Polynesian methods of wayfaring (navigation). Check the museum website for upcoming shows.

The **gift shop** sells books on the Pacific not easily found elsewhere, as well as some high-quality Hawaiian art, crafts and souvenirs. There is also a quality **cafe**, open

10:30am to 3:30pm daily. Check the museum website for special events.

From Waikiki or downtown Honolulu, take bus 2 (the 'School St/Middle St' bus) and get off at the intersection of School and Kapālama Sts. Parking is free.

★ **Pu'u 'Ualaka'a State Wayside Park**   VIEWPOINT
(Map p86; www.hawaiistateparks.org; 2760 Round Top Dr; ⊙7am-7:45pm Apr-Aug, to 6:45pm Sep-Mar; P) FREE The best free view in Honolulu! At this hillside park, sweeping views extend from Diamond Head on the left, across Waikiki and downtown Honolulu, to the Wai'anae Range on the right. The airport is visible on the coast and Pearl Harbor beyond that. The blue Pacific is a backdrop to everything. It's less than 2.5 miles up Round Top Dr from Makiki St to the park entrance. Signs detail the area's history as a macadamia nut farm.

Queen Emma Summer Palace   HISTORIC BUILDING
(Hanaiakamalama; Map p86; ☏808-595-3167; www.daughtersofhawaii.org; 2913 Pali Hwy; adult/child $10/1; ⊙9am-4pm Mon-Sat, to 3pm Sun; P) In the heat and humidity of summer, Queen Emma (1836–85), the wife and royal consort of Kamehameha IV, used to slip away from her formal downtown Honolulu home to this cooler hillside retreat in Nu'uanu Valley. Gracious docents from the Daughters of Hawai'i society show off the cathedral-shaped koa cabinet that displays a set of china given by England's Queen Victoria, brightly colored feather cloaks and capes once worn by Hawaiian royalty, and more priceless antiques.

OBAMA'S HAWAII ROOTS

Former US president Barack Obama's wife Michelle once said: 'You can't really understand Barack until you understand Hawaii.'

Obama, who spent his formative years from age 10 to 18 in Honolulu's Makiki Heights neighborhood, has written that 'Hawaii's spirit of tolerance...became an integral part of my world view, and a basis for the values I hold most dear.' The local media and many *kama'aina* (those who were born and grew up in Hawaii) agree that Hawaii's multiethnic social fabric helped shape the leader who created a rainbow coalition during the 2008 and 2012 elections.

Obama has also said Hawaii is a place for him to rest and recharge. 'When I'm heading out to a hard day of meetings and negotiations, I let my mind wander back to Sandy Beach, or Manoa Falls... It helps me, somehow, knowing that such wonderful places exist and I'll always be able to return to them.'

On a more mundane note, he has often spoken fondly of hanging out at the iconic Rainbow Drive-In (p162) near Waikiki as a teenager.

Built in Greek Revival style, the exterior recalls an old Southern plantation home, with its columned porch and high ceilings. Good free tours are offered at various times daily.

Moanalua Gardens GARDENS
(Map p86; ☑ 808-834-8612; www.moanalua gardens.com; 2850a Moanalua Rd; adult/child $5/3; ☉8am-5pm) This 24-acre public park is home to some exceptional trees, including the Hitachi Tree, a massive monkeypod used by Japanese company Hitachi as its corporate symbol. In return, Hitachi makes annual payments that make the park viable. Also here is the Kamehameha V Cottage, originally built in the 1850s by Prince Lot Kapuāiwa, who would later become King Kamehameha V. The gardens host the annual Prince Lot Hula Festival (p109) in July.

Royal Mausoleum
State Monument MAUSOLEUM
(Mauna 'Ala; Map p86; http://dlnr.hawaii.gov/dsp/ parks/oahu/royal-mausoleum-state-monument; 2261 Nuuanu Ave; ☉8am-4pm Mon-Fri) **FREE** Known as Mauna 'Ala (or Fragrant Hills) in Hawaiian, this is the final resting place of Hawaii's two prominent royal families, the Kamehamehas and the Kalakauas. Completed in 1865 for Prince Albert, it's adjacent to the public O'ahu Cemetery. The mausoleum is home to the remains of almost all of Hawaii's monarchs, their consorts, and various princes and princesses. A sacred place to all Hawaiians, the manicured grounds are peaceful and the Gothic Revival chapel is on the National Register of Historic Places.

🏃 Activities

The beaches and the mountains help define Honolulu, meaning that outdoor activities are available for all. Think surfing, bodyboarding, stand up paddling (SUP), swimming in the sea and hiking the inland mountains. Free lit tennis courts dot the city and an abundance of golf courses are close at hand. It's an outdoor activities paradise.

Hiking & Walking

You could spend days enjoying the solitude of the forests and peaks around the city. Some of O'ahu's most popular hiking trails lead into the lush, windy Ko'olau Range just above downtown. Keep in mind that it can be raining in the inland mountains while it's sunny on the beaches – tracks can get both muddy and slippery. For more info on O'ahu's trail system, see http://hawaiitrails. ehawaii.gov.

⭐**Manoa Falls Trail** HIKING
(Map p86; http://hawaiitrails.ehawaii.gov; off Manoa Rd; 🚶) Honolulu's most rewarding short hike, this 1.6-mile, two-hour round-trip trail runs above a rocky streambed before ending at a pretty little cascade. Tall tree trunks line the often muddy and slippery path. Wild orchids and red ginger grow near the falls, which drop about 100ft into a small, shallow pool. It's illegal to venture beyond the established viewing area.

The trail has an 800ft elevation and features myriad plants, including four kinds of tree ferns. Falling rocks and the risk of leptospirosis (a waterborne bacterial infection) make entering the water dangerous.

On public transport, take bus 5 Manoa Valley to the end of the line; from there, it's a half-mile walk uphill to the trailhead. By car, drive almost to the end of Manoa Rd, where a privately operated parking lot charges $5 per vehicle. The cacophony of 'no parking'

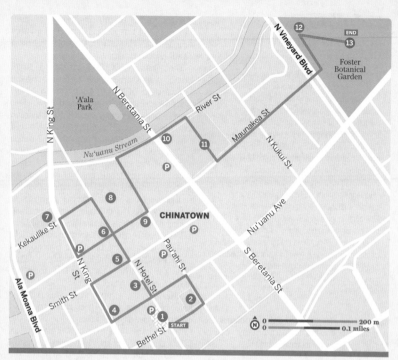

City Walk
Chinatown

START DR SUN YAT-SEN MEMORIAL PARK
END FOSTER BOTANICAL GARDEN
LENGTH 1 MILE; TWO HOURS

Honolulu's most foot-trafficked neighborhood, Chinatown is also steeped in history. Start at **1 Dr Sun Yat-sen Memorial Park** at the stone lions that flank the road. Walk northeast to the restored neoclassical **2 Hawaii Theatre** (p94), then continue around the corner.

Go southwest on Nu'uanu Ave and take a short right onto N Hotel St to find the city's oldest bar, **3 Smith's Union Bar** (p122), where sailors from USS *Arizona* drank before WWII. Back on Nu'uanu Ave, note the avenue's granite-block sidewalks, built with the discarded ballasts of 19th-century trading ships. At the corner of King St, peek into the **4 First Hawaiian Bank**, with its antique teller cages.

Poke your head into the tiny **5 Hawai'i Heritage Center** (p95) before turning left into historic Hotel St, once Honolulu's red-light district and now boasting hip cafes and bars. At the corner of Maunakea St, the ornate facade of the **6 Wo Fat Building** resembles a Chi-

nese temple. The building – and, incidentally, also the villain of the *Hawaii Five-0* TV series – is named after Honolulu's first restaurant, which opened here in 1882.

On King St, continue past the red pillars coiled with dragons outside the Bank of Hawaii to the corner of Kekaulike St and venture inside the buzzing 1904 **7 O'ahu Market** (p95). Cross the road and wander up the pedestrian mall of intriguing markets, then head into the **8 Maunakea Marketplace** (p112) and pick a food stall for a break.

Heading *mauka* (toward the mountains) on Maunakea St, you'll pass fragrant **9 lei shops** where skilled artisans string blossoms. Take Pau'ahi St to River St, passing old shopfronts in various stages of renovation.

By the river, the statue of **10 Dr Sun Yat-sen** (p95) stands over the senior citizens playing checkers outdoors. Cut through the courtyard of the **11 Chinatown Cultural Plaza** (p95). Back on Maunakea St, cross over Vineyard Blvd to the venerable **12 Kuan Yin Temple** (p95), originally built in 1880. Finish with a stroll around the mid-19th-century **13 Foster Botanical Garden** (p94).

HONOLULU ACTIVITIES

DOUBLE-UP ON HAWAIIAN CLASSICS

If you're visiting the Bishop Museum (p100) – and it's well worth the effort – double-up by visiting one of Honolulu's classic Hawaiian eateries, only a few minutes' drive away, for lunch. Walking through the door of Helena's Hawaiian Food (Map p86; ☑808-845-8044; http://helenashawaiianfood.com; 1240 N School St, Greater Honolulu; mains $6-18; ⊘10am-7:30pm Tue-Fri) is like stepping into another era at this legendary institution. Although longtime owner Helena Chock has passed away, her relatives still command the family kitchen, which opened in 1946. Most people order à la carte; cash only. A few blocks southeast of the Bishop Museum, Helena's received a James Beard Award for 'America's Classics.'

signs in the area indicates the problems the neighborhood faces from the many visitors to this at-times-overcrowded trail.

'Aihualama Trail   HIKING
(Map p86; http://hawaiitrails.ehawaii.gov) Just before Manoa Falls, the marked 'Aihualama Trail branches off the falls trail (p102) to the left and scrambles over boulders. The trail quickly enters a bamboo forest with some massive old banyan trees, then contours around the ridge, offering broad and beautiful views of Manoa Valley. After 1.3 miles of gradual switchbacks and a climb of 1200ft, hikers reach an intersection with the Pauoa Flats Trail, which ascends to the right for more than half a mile over muddy tree roots to the spectacular Nu'uanu Valley Lookout. High atop the Ko'olau Range, with O'ahu's steep *pali* (cliffs) visible all around, it's possible to peer through a gap over to the Windward Coast. The total round-trip distance to the lookout from the Manoa Falls trailhead is approximately 5.5 miles. You can also get to the lookout on tracks from the Makiki Valley and Tantalus Dr.

Makiki Valley & Manoa Cliff Trails   HIKING
(Map p86; http://hawaiitrails.ehawaii.gov) A favorite workout for city dwellers, the 2.5-mile Makiki Valley Loop links three Pu'uohi'a-area trails. These trails are usually muddy, so wear shoes with traction and pick up a walking stick. The loop cuts through a lush

tropical forest, mainly composed of non-native species introduced to reforest an area denuded by Hawaii's 19th-century *'iliahi* (sandalwood) trade.

The Maunalaha Trail crosses a small stream, passes taro patches and climbs up the eastern ridge of Makiki Valley, passing Norfolk pine, banyans, bamboo and some clear views. Look out below for the tumbledown remains of ancient Hawaiian stone walls and a historic coffee plantation. After 0.7 miles, you'll reach a four-way junction. Continue uphill on the 1.1-mile Makiki Valley Trail, which traverses small gulches and crosses gentle streams bordered by patches of ginger and guava trees while offering glimpses of the city below. The 0.7-mile Kanealole Trail begins as you cross Kanealole Stream, then follows the stream back down through a field of Job's tears – the bead-like psuedocarps ('false fruit') of the female flowers of this tall grass are sometimes used for lei – to return to the forest baseyard.

Alternatively, a more strenuous 6.2-mile hike beginning from the same trailhead eventually leads to sweeping views of the valley and the ocean beyond. This Manoa Cliffs Circuit, aka the 'Big Loop,' starts on the same Maunalaha Trail, then takes the Moleka Trail to the Manoa Cliff, Kalawahine and Nahuina Trails. At the Kalawahine Trail intersection, you can detour right onto the Pauoa Flats Trail to reach the Nu'uanu Valley Lookout and eventually link up with the 'Aihualama Trail, which will take you down to the Manoa Falls area. From the lookout, backtrack to the Kalawahine Trail, then connect via the Nahuina Trail with the Kanealole Trail, which rolls downhill back to the forest baseyard.

The starting point for both hiking loops is Makiki Valley State Recreation Area, less than 0.5 miles up Makiki Heights Dr from Makiki St. Park in the car park, then follow the signs and walk along the hillside Makiki Arboretum Trail toward the main trailheads near the Hawai'i Nature Center, which organizes family-friendly hikes and outdoor education programs.

Pu'uohi'a (Mt Tantalus) Trail   HIKING
(Map p86; http://hawaiitrails.ehawaii.gov; off Tantalus Dr) Along the Tantalus–Round Top scenic drive, a network of hiking trails littered with fragrant *liliko'i* (passion fruit) offers contemplative forest hikes combined with city views. The hardy Pu'uohi'a Trail, in conjunction with the Pauoa Flats Trail,

leads up to **Nu'uanu Valley Lookout**, traveling almost 2 miles each way. The trailhead hides at the very top of Tantalus Dr, about 3.6 miles up from Makiki Heights Dr. There's a parking turnoff opposite the trailhead, on the *makai* (seaward) side of the road.

The trail begins with reinforced log steps, leading past fragrant ginger, musical bamboo groves and lots of eucalyptus, a fast-growing tree planted to protect the watershed. After 0.5 miles, the trail summits **Pu'uohi'a** (Mt Tantalus, 2014ft), then leads back onto a service road ending at a telephone relay station. Behind that building, the trail continues until it reaches the **Manoa Cliff Trail**, where you'll turn left. At the next intersection, turn right onto the muddy **Pauoa Flats Trail**, which leads up to the Nu'uanu Valley Lookout, high in the Ko'olau Range.

You'll pass two trailheads before reaching the lookout. The first is the **Nu'uanu Trail**, on the left, which runs 0.75 miles along the western side of the upper Pauoa Valley, offering broad views of Honolulu and the Wai'anae Range. The second is the 'Aihualama Trail (p104), a bit further along on the right, which heads 1.3 miles through tranquil bamboo groves and past huge old banyan trees to Manoa Falls.

Wa'ahila Ridge Trail | HIKING

(Map p86; http://hawaiitrails.ehawaii.gov) Popular even with novice hikers, this boulder-strewn trail offers a cool retreat amid the Norfolk pines and endemic plants, with ridgetop views of Honolulu and Waikiki. Rolling up and down a series of small saddles and knobs before reaching a grassy clearing, the 4.8-mile round-trip trail covers a variety of terrain in a short time, making an enjoyable afternoon's walk.

Look for the Na Ala Hele trailhead sign beyond the picnic tables inside Wa'ahila Ridge State Recreation Area, at the back of the St Louis Heights subdivision, east of Manoa Valley.

If you are traveling by car, head to Ruth Pl, which runs west into the park. From Waikiki, bus 14 St Louis Heights stops at the intersection of Peter and Ruth Sts, which is about a half-mile walk from the trailhead.

Hawai'i Nature Center | OUTDOORS

(Map p86; 808-955-0100; http://hawaiinaturecenter.org; 2131 Makiki Heights Dr; fees from $10; ⊙schedule varies; ⊛) Inside the woodsy Makiki Valley State Recreation Area, this small non-profit community center conducts family-oriented environmental education programs,

day camps and guided weekend hikes for ages six and up. Reservations are usually required; check the online calendar for details.

Hawaiian Trail & Mountain Corp | HIKING

(http://htmclub.org; donation per hike $5) ⦿ This volunteer-run hiking club arranges group hikes on weekends all over O'ahu, ranging from novice to intermediate to challenging. A calendar of upcoming hikes, trail descriptions and safety tips are available online.

Sierra Club | HIKING

(Map p90; 808-537-9019; http://sierraclubo ahu.org; 1040 Richards St; donation per hike adult/child $5/1; ⊛) The Hawaii chapter of this nonprofit national organization leads weekend hikes and other outings around O'ahu, including volunteer opportunities to rebuild trails and combat invasive plants.

Surfing

Honolulu and Waikiki have plenty of places to rent surfboards. One shop known for high-quality boards and good advice is Aloha Board Shop (p128).

Surf HNL | SURFING

(Map p96; 808-371-8917; http://surfhnl.com; 1hr lesson from $100, SUP sets rental per hr/day $30/60; ⊙8am-6pm) Surf and stand-up

---

RAINY DAY HONOLULU

Rain showers can happen daily on O'ahu, especially as you move up the green mountainsides and lush valleys. Rainbow imagery didn't become ubiquitous here for no reason!

However, sometimes the rain is part of much larger weather patterns sweeping across the Pacific Ocean and the rain can last for days. Consider the following for their highly recommended and immersive (no pun intended) experiences where the hours will fly by.

Bishop Museum (p100) All of Hawaii's culture, history and nature displayed in deeply engaging exhibits.

Honolulu Museum of Art (p96) Literally an in-your-face Great Art 101 course covering Hawaii and the world.

Pearl Harbor National Memorial (p177) The free museum at the visitors center about the December 7, 1941 attack emphasizes the human side of the story and is up to the highest standards of the National Park Service.

paddling (SUP) lessons are on offer in Ala Moana Regional Park and Poka'i Bay on Leeward O'ahu. Transportation between Waikiki hotels and Ala Moana is included. For surfboard, bodyboard and SUP rentals, delivery to Ala Moana Beach costs $15, Ko Olina is $20. Reserve by phone or online.

Point Panic & Flies
SURFING

(Map p86) These surf breaks are just off Kaka'ako Waterfront Park (p85) at the end of Cooke St and are a good spot for beginner to intermediate surfers in summer. Point Panic is a nice left and right break just west of the Kewalo Basin boat channel, while Flies is a bit further west. Point Panic can be busy with bodyboarders.

Kewalos
SURFING

(Map p96) This surf break off Kewalo Basin Park is good for intermediate surfers in summer, but can get crowded. Kewalos is at the mouth of Kewalo Basin boat harbor, and the westernmost of many breaks out in front of Ala Moana Regional Park (p85). Kewalo means 'Shark's Hole,' so keep an eye out.

Tennis Courts
SURFING

(Map p96) Straight out from, you guessed it, the tennis courts at Ala Moana Regional Park, this surf break is popular when a swell hits between June and September. Good in 3ft to 5ft waves; beginners will want to head to Baby Courts, a bit further inshore, when things get bigger. Both can get crowded.

Cycling

Bike Shop
CYCLING

(Map p96; ☎808-596-0588; www.bikeshophawaii. com; 1149 S King St; bicycle rental per day from $20, car rack $5, delivery from $35; ⊙9am-8pm Mon-Fri, 9am-5pm Sat, 10am-5pm Sun) Rents a variety of high-quality bicycles, including electric-assist, road, racing and mountain bikes, and can give you advice and maps of cycling routes to match your skill level. Road cyclists looking for an athletic workout should pedal the Tantalus–Round Top scenic loop. The Bike Shop also has clothing and accessories, and does maintenance.

Golf

Moanalua Golf Club
GOLF

(☎808-839-2311; www.hawaiigolf.com; 1250 Ala Aolani St; green fees from $41; ⊙8:30am-7:30pm Mon-Fri, from 5:30am Sat & Sun) The oldest golf course in Hawaii was built in 1898 by a Protestant missionary family and has the distinction of once having Amelia Earhart land her aircraft on it! It's a fairly quick

🏃 City Walk
Historic Honolulu

START 'IOLANI PALACE
END REAL GASTROPUB
LENGTH 1.7 MILES; THREE HOURS

Honolulu's historical district is so compact that it's easy to take your time and still inspect all the major sights in a day. There's a lot of intriguing history and art packed into a small area, which is right next to Downtown's tall buildings and only a 10-minute walk from Chinatown. Enjoy this walk at your leisure – it could take anything from one hour to an entire day.

An appropriate place to start is at ❶ **'I-olani Palace** (p87), the only royal palace in the USA. Built under King David Kalakaua in 1882, the grounds are open during daylight hours and are free of charge; you'll have to pay to take a tour of the palace itself though. The former barracks of the Royal Household Guards, a building that looks oddly like the uppermost layer of a medieval fort, now houses the ticket booth. The palace served as the State Capitol after statehood until the present building was completed next door.

At the back of the palace, check out the massive banyan trees, then head *mauka* (toward the mountains) to find the ❷ **Queen Lili'uokalani Statue** (p89) standing between the palace and Hawaii's present State Capitol building. Lili'uokalani was queen at the time of the overthrow of the Kingdom of Hawaii on January 17, 1893. The life-size bronze statue has her holding a copy of the Hawaiian constitution she wrote in 1893 in an attempt to strengthen Hawaiian rule.

Built in the '60s, after Hawaii became the 50th state in 1959, the ❸ **State Capitol** (p89) building is unlike any other state capitol and takes conceptual postmodernism to a new level. Among other features, two cone-shaped legislative chambers have sloping walls to represent volcanoes.

Out front on Beretania St, make sure to check out the impressive stylized statue of ❹ **Father Damien** (p89), the priest who died with his flock of Hansen's disease (leprosy) on Moloka'i in 1889. On the far side of Beretania St street is ❺ **Washington Place** (p93), formerly the governor's official residence. This

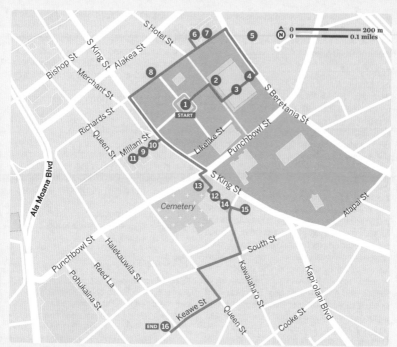

colonial-style mansion was built in 1846. Admire it before carrying on down Beretania St and crossing Richards St. If you think Beretania sounds like an unusual name for a Hawaiian St, you're right. It came from the Hawaiian transliteration of the word Britannia, referring to Great Britain.

Dead ahead, the grand 1928 Spanish Mission Revival–style building is the **6 Hawai'i State Art Museum** (p88). Its vibrant thought-provoking collections bring together traditional and contemporary art from Hawaii's multiethnic communities. Downstairs, **7 Artizen by MW** (p111) is a delicious cafe for a break or a meal.

Carrying on down Richards St, you could also stop for lunch at **8 Cafe Julia** (p112) on the far side of the courtyard in the charming old YWCA building. The outdoor tables are lovely and the food has great island flavors.

Turn left on King St and you'll know you are at **9 Ali'iolani Hale** (p92), now the Supreme Court of Hawaii, when you spot the magnificent gold-helmeted **10 Kamehameha the Great Statue** (p89). Cast in bronze in 1880 in Florence, Italy, by American sculptor Thomas Gould, this is the second such statue. The first was lost at sea near the Falkland Islands (though later recovered!).

Head inside Ali'iolani Hale, through security, to check out the free **11 King Kamehameha V Judiciary History Center** and learn about the course of legal changes in Hawaii's history. There's even a real courtroom, where student groups come to fight mock legal battles.

Next, down S King St is **12 Kawaiaha'o Church** (p93), built in 1842 in New England Gothic style of 14,000 coral slabs and nicknamed the 'Westminster Abbey of the Pacific.' Inspect those walls. They really are made of coral. Don't miss the **13 Tomb of King Lunalilo** (p93) out front, or the **14 small cemetery** to the rear of the church, which is almost like a who's who of local colonial history. The church's side door is usually open.

Just over Kawaiaha'o St is the **15 Hawaiian Mission Houses Historic Site** (p89). The museum is in the original headquarters of the Sandwich Islands Mission, which forever changed the course of Hawaiian history. Admission to the grounds is free, but you'll need to take a tour to look inside any of the buildings. Finish off your tour by walking four blocks southwest to **16 Real Gastropub** (p124), a hip place known for its beer and casual snacks and food.

par-72 course with elevated greens, straight fairways and nine holes that are played twice around from different tees. Reserve a tee time in advance.

Tennis

Ala Moana Regional Park TENNIS
(Map p96; 1201 Ala Moana Blvd) FREE The municipal park has 10 free first-come, first-served public tennis courts. If you hit balls during the day, you can cool off with a dip in the ocean afterwards; if you come at night, the courts are lit.

Tours

Just west of Ala Moana Regional Park, fishing boats, sunset sails, dinner cruises and party boats leave daily from Kewalo Basin. More expensive guided tours may include transportation to/from Waikiki and they advertise various specials in the free tourist magazines available at the airport and around town. Many, such as helicopter flights and food tours, may be cheaper if booked directly online, instead of through a third party such as a hotel concierge. For a deep dive into Chinatown, check with the Hawai'i Heritage Center (p95) for details of their neighborhood walking tours.

Blue Hawaiian Helicopters SCENIC FLIGHTS
(Map p86; ☑808-871-8844; www.bluehawaiian. com; 99 Kaulele Pl; tours from $230) Soar over O'ahu. The 45-minute Blue Skies of O'ahu flight takes in Honolulu, Waikiki, Diamond Head, Hanauma Bay and the whole of the Windward Coast, then the North Shore, central O'ahu and Pearl Harbor. Everything you need to know, including video clips, is on the website. Book well ahead.

Atlantis Cruises WILDLIFE
(Map p90; ☑800-381-0237; http://atlantis adventures.com; Pier 6, Aloha Tower Dr; 2½hr whale-watching tour adult/child from $48/24; ☺whale-watching cruise 11:30am Jan-Mar) Atlantis runs whale-watching cruises with an onboard naturalist on a high-tech boat designed to minimize rolling. Reservations are essential; book online for discounts. There is a 'whale watch guarantee' and transportation is available from select Waikiki hotels ($12). Atlantis also runs a submarine tour (p153) from Waikiki.

Architectural Walking Tour WALKING
(Map p90; ☑808-628-7243; www.aiahonolulu .org; 828 Fort Street Mall; tours $15; ☺usually 9-11:30am Sat) Led by professional architects, these historical-minded walking tours will literally change your perspective on downtown Honolulu's capitol district. The state's business center and financial district also harbors some of Hawaii's most significant and cherished architectural treasures. Reservations required – check the calendar and register online. The printed walking guides ($5) are excellent.

UH Campus Self-Guided Walking Tour WALKING
(Map p100; http://universityofhawaii.myuvn.com/ self-guided-tour; 2465 Campus Rd) Download the map online for a self-guided walking tour of the University of Hawai'i at Manoa's leafy campus. At the Campus Center, ask for a free Campus Art brochure, which outlines outdoor sculptures and other works by notable Hawaii artists.

Courses

⭐**Nā Mea Hawaii** ARTS & CRAFTS
(Map p96; ☑808-596-8885; www.nameahawaii. com; Ward Centre, 1200 Ala Moana Blvd; ☺class times vary) Highly recommended community-oriented bookstore (p129), art gallery and gift shop hosts free classes, workshops and demonstrations in hula dancing, Hawaiian language, traditional feather lei making and *lauhala* weaving, ukulele playing and more. Check the website for schedules and if pre-registration is required. There's at least one cultural class each day.

'Ōlelo Hawai'i Classes LANGUAGE
(Map p100; ☑808-956-4822; http://asuhmanoa. wixsite.com/asuh/lelo-hawai-i-initiative; 2500 Campus Rd) 'Ōlelo Hawai'i means 'Hawaiian language' and you can join these free classes offered at various times of the year by students at the University of Hawai'i at Manoa. Most classes are held at various locations on the university's main campus and beginners are welcomed. You can attend one or more classes and no registration is required. See the website for schedules.

Festivals & Events

Some of Honolulu's biggest festivals spill over into Waikiki, most notably the annual Honolulu Pride parade (p154). A good source of events info is www.hawaii.com/ oahu/events.

O'ahu Fringe Festival PERFORMING ARTS
(www.oahufringe.com; ☺Jan) Part of a Hawaii-wide circuit, O'ahu Fringe Festival presents

uncensored performing arts, often off the cuff. Most venues are downtown.

Chinese New Year CULTURAL
(☺late Jan–mid-Feb) Chinatown's annual swirling new year festivities include a parade with lion dances and crackling firecrackers. Red-colored decorations are everywhere.

Honolulu Festival CULTURAL
(www.honolulufestival.com; ☺early Mar) Three days of Hawaiian and Asian-Pacific cultural exchange with music, dance and drama performances, an arts-and-crafts fair, a parade and fireworks.

Shinnyo Lantern Floating Hawaii CULTURAL
(www.lanternfloatinghawaii.com; ☺May) Held on Memorial Day in May, the souls of the dead are honored with a Japanese floating-lantern ceremony after sunset at Magic Island in Ala Moana Regional Park. More than 5000 lanterns are floated and over 50,000 people turn up to watch.

Pan-Pacific Festival CULTURAL
(www.pan-pacific-festival.com; ☺mid-Jun) Three days of Japanese, Hawaiian and South Pacific entertainment, with music, dancing and *taiko* (traditional Japanese drumming) at the Ala Moana Center and Waikiki.

King Kamehameha Celebration CULTURAL
(☑808-586-0333; http://ags.hawaii.gov/kamehameha; ☺Jun 11) The statewide King Kamehameha Celebration (a holiday for many) includes festivities at 'Iolani Palace, a big downtown parade and a lei-draping ceremony at his statue (p89).

Sailor Jerry Festival CULTURAL
(http://808web.wixsite.com/sailorjerryfestival; ☺Jun) Held in Chinatown, this festival features music, stand-up comedy, movies and tattooing. Sailor Jerry (aka Norman Collins) was the legendary tattoo artist who fulfilled the third part of Honolulu-stationed WWII sailors' and soldiers' proud motto – 'stewed, screwed and tattooed.'

Queen Lili'uokalani Keiki Hula Competition DANCE
(http://keikihula.org; Neal S Blaisdell Center, 777 Ward Ave; ☺Jul) Children's hula troupes from throughout Hawaii compete in a festival to honor Hawaii's last reigning monarch.

Prince Lot Hula Festival DANCE
(http://moanaluagardensfoundation.org; 'Iolani Palace, 364 S King St; ☺Jul) The state's oldest and largest noncompetitive hula event sees Hawaii's leading hula *halau* (schools) perform over a summer weekend.

Hawaii Dragon Boat Festival SPORTS
(www.dragonboathawaii.com; Ala Moana Regional Park, 1201 Ala Moana Blvd; ☺late Jul) Colorful Chinese dragon boats race to the beat of island drummers on one long summer Saturday.

Made in Hawaii Festival FAIR
(www.madeinhawaiifestival.com; Neal S Blaisdell Center, 777 Ward Ave; ☺Aug) A huge annual marketplace for Hawaii-made products, including everything from art to food to furniture to crafts to tacky souvenirs.

Aloha Festivals CULTURAL
(www.alohafestivals.com; ☺Sep) September's statewide cultural festival, a month-long block party, is a celebration of Hawaiian music, dance and history. There are events across Honolulu.

Hawai'i Food & Wine Festival FOOD & DRINK
(www.hawaiifoodandwinefestival.com; ☺Oct) Star chefs, sustainable farmers and food lovers come together for over three weeks of wine tastings, cooking demonstrations, excursions, and dining events highlighting the state's top farmers, fishers, ranchers, bakers, food producers and chefs.

Talk Story Festival LITERATURE
(☺mid-Oct; ♿) Storytellers gather to honor traditional and contemporary storytelling and oral history with Hawaii's best tellers. The venues and website change each year.

Hawai'i International Film Festival FILM
(www.hiff.org; ☺Nov) This celebration of film packs several movie theaters with homegrown and international films. The culmination is a gala awards ceremony.

Honolulu Fashion Week ART
(http://honolulufashionweek.com; Hawaii Convention Center, 1801 Kalakaua Ave; ☺Nov) An opportunity for local designers to parade their creations on the catwalk.

King Kalakaua's Birthday CULTURAL
(www.iolanipalace.org; 364 South King St, 'Iolani Palace; ☺Nov 16) Features a concert of traditional monarchy-era music by the Royal Hawaiian Band (p125) at 'Iolani Palace every November 16, a parade down Waikiki's Kalakaua Ave, and a lei-draping ceremony at the King

Kalakaua statue located at the intersection of Kalakaua Ave and Kuhio Ave in Waikiki.

🛏 Sleeping

Honolulu doesn't have much in the way of accommodations. The vast majority of rooms are in Waikiki (p154), which is really just a Honolulu neighborhood, so staying there means you're still close to much of what the city offers.

There are a few places to stay out near the airport, plus a couple of upscale hotels around Ala Moana Shopping Center that might as well be in Waikiki. You will find vacation rentals and bed and breakfasts in various neighborhoods across the city. Those on the hillsides can have sweeping views, but the vacation rental law means that this type of accommodation is in flux.

🛏 Downtown

Aston at the Executive Centre Hotel   HOTEL **$$**
(Map p90; ☑855-945-4090; www.astonexecutivecentre.com; 1088 Bishop St; r from $190; P🛱♨) Honolulu's only downtown hotel is geared for business travelers and extended stays. The large, modern suites with floor-to-ceiling windows are in a 41-story tower. Studios have kitchenettes, while one-bedroom units have a full kitchen and washer/dryer. A fitness center, heated lap pool and continental breakfast round out the amenities.

🛏 Ala Moana & Around

Central Branch YMCA   HOSTEL **$**
(Map p96; ☑808-941-3344; www.ymcahonolulu.org; 401 Atkinson Dr, Ala Moana; s/d from $65/85, without bath $52/75; 🛱♨) Opposite the Ala Moana Center, the ol' Y lets unfussy budget travelers book basic, well-worn rooms with shared bathrooms or slightly larger ensuite rooms on single-sex or co-ed floors. Perks include an Olympic-sized swimming pool and a gym. The traffic noise, shabbiness and institutional atmosphere are downers, but the location is excellent.

Ala Moana Hotel   HOTEL **$$**
(Map p96; ☑866-956-4262; www.alamoanahotelhonolulu.com; 410 Atkinson Dr, Ala Moana; r from $170; P🌸🛱♨) Looming over the Ala Moana Center mall and convenient to the convention center, this high-rise offers corporate-style hotel rooms without much island flavor. Upper floors may have

straight-on views of the beach – request the Waikiki Tower for a lanai (balcony). It's only a short walk to Ala Moana Regional Park.

Pagoda Hotel   HOTEL **$$**
(Map p96; ☑808-941-6611; www.pagodahotel.com; 1525 Rycroft St, Ala Moana; r from $95; P🌸🛱♨) A few blocks north of the Ala Moana Center, the Pagoda Hotel has a beautiful Japanese garden and a popular restaurant on site. Rooms are clean and offer fridges and microwaves. The pool is like an oasis and there are daily koi (carp) feedings to enjoy. There's a shuttle bus to Waikiki and Ala Moana Center.

🛏 University Area

Hostelling International (HI) Honolulu   HOSTEL **$**
(Map p100; ☑808-946-0591; www.hostelsaloha.com; 2323a Seaview Ave,; dm/r from $30/70; ☺reception 8am-noon & 4pm-midnight; P🔌🛱) Along a quiet residential side street near the UH Manoa campus, this tidy, low-slung house just a short bus ride from Waikiki has same-sex dorms and basic private rooms kept cool by the tradewinds. Some students crash here while looking for apartments, so it's often full. It has a kitchen, a laundry room, lockers and limited free parking.

⭐ **Manoa Valley Inn**   B&B **$$**
(Map p100; ☑808-947-6019; www.manoavalleyinn.com; 2001 Vancouver Dr; rooms from $190; P🌸🛱♨) Listed on the National Register of Historic Places, the Manoa Valley was built in 1912 and is one block west of the University of Hawai'i campus. A Honolulu landmark, it features seven gorgeous rooms filled with antiques, as well as lovely gardens, a heated pool and a sumptuous breakfast.

🛏 Greater Honolulu

The best thing to be said about the airport hotels is that they are convenient for those with very late or very early flights and the rates are fairly low. But most other places to stay in Honolulu are better options – and Waikiki is only a 20-minute cab ride from the airport at night.

Best Western The Plaza Hotel   HOTEL **$$**
(Map p86; ☑808-836-3636; http://book.bestwestern.com; 3253 N Nimitz Hwy, Airport; r from $165; P🌸🔌🛱♨) Nothing special here near the airport terminals: the 274 rooms are basic, view-free and have microwaves and fridges. There's also a cafe.

In 2019, the Honolulu government enacted a new law severely restricting the number of holiday rentals and bed-and-breakfast-style establishments across O'ahu. The law is the result of lobbying by local hotels and resorts as well as the hospitality workers union. In addition, many neighborhood groups oppose short-term rentals aimed at tourists, as they make it more difficult for locals to find rentals.

Of the thousands of short-term rentals listed on sites such as Airbnb and Booking.com, less than 1000 have proper permits allowing this use. Under the law enacted in 2019, renting units without a permit can result in large fines to the unit's owner. However, how this actually plays out remains in flux. In the meantime, visitors should consider the following:

➡ Licensed bed-and-breakfast-style accommodation is limited to rooms in owner-occupied homes.

➡ Short-term rentals of apartments and condos are generally allowed in Waikiki.

➡ Renters should confirm that any potential rental – especially in areas outside Waikiki – has the proper license to help ensure the unit won't suddenly be withdrawn from the market, even if the renter has a confirmed reservation. However, the law imposes no penalties on visitors renting unlicensed units. The legal burden falls on the unit's owner.

Airport Honolulu Hotel HOTEL $$
(Map p86; ☑ 808-836-0661; www.theairporthonoluluhotel.com; 3401 N Nimitz Hwy, Airport; r from $145; 🅿 ✳ 🛜 🌊) If you need to be next to the airport, this nondescript hotel near the noisy freeway has large but bland rooms. Rates include fridge, microwave, infrequent airport-shuttle service and a small fitness center. There is a restaurant on site.

Eating

Honolulu has some of the best places to eat in the US, and its multicutural vibe extends to the restaurants. You'll find superb restaurants with influences from across Asia, the Pacific, the Americas and even Europe. Best of all, the city is the heart of Hawaii Regional Cuisine, with scores of talented chefs interpreting local flavors and produce.

Restaurants range from simple takeout joints to small storefronts to complex, designer destinations. Generally you'll find prices lower and quality much better than in Waikiki. Really, Honolulu's food scene is reason enough to visit the city.

✖ Downtown

Weekday cafes for office workers and students abound Downtown. You'll find choices more limited at night and on weekends, but the many great options in Chinatown are close by.

⭐**Artizen by MW** HAWAIIAN $
(Map p90; ☑ 808-524-0499; www.artizenbymw.com; 250 S Hotel St, Hawai'i State Art Museum; mains $8-16; ⊙ 7:30am-2:30pm Mon-Fri) This impressive cafe at the Hawai'i State Art Museum is the perfect spot for breakfast or lunch, or just for a coffee break while perusing the museum's stunning collections. There are ready-made grab-and-go *bentō* (Japanese-style boxed lunches), or sit and try the avocado toast, Artizen burger or seared ahi salad. After a walking tour, the mango-peach iced tea is a joy.

Gochi Grill HAWAIIAN $
(Map p90; ☑ 808-585-8558; 1111 Bishop St; mains $9-16; ⊙ 10am-2pm Mon-Fri) A real find for lunch Downtown. In an older but sparkling open plaza of a commercial building, they cook up so much plate lunch goodness each day. By 1pm things start to run out, so don't dawdle. There are several good casual Asian joints close by.

Marugame Udon UDON $
(Map p90; ☑ 808-545-3000; http://marugameudon.com; 1104 Fort St Mall; mains $6-12; ⊙ 10am-7pm Mon-Sat) Different to Marugame's other location in Waikiki, which caters mainly for tourists, the Downtown store has a different menu, catering to local tastes. There are both hot and cold udon bowls, plus a selection of extras such as fried squid and chicken. The dining area is simple and stylish; place your order at the counter.

'Umeke Market CAFE $
(Map p90; ☑ 808-522-7377; 1001 Bishop St; mains $5-12; ⊙ 7:30am-2:30pm Mon-Fri; ☑) 🍃 Fresh, organic island produce, natural-foods groceries, and a vegetarian- and vegan-friendly takeout deli counter for healthy pick-me-ups such as kale and quinoa salads, hummus

sandwiches, hoisin turkey meatloaf and iced kombucha (effervescent tea). Plenty of seating in its ground-floor location in an office building.

★ **Cafe Julia**   CAFE **$$**

(Map p90; ☑808-533-3334; www.cafejulia hawaii.net; 1040 Richards St; mains $10-26; ☺11am-2pm Mon-Fri) In the charming old YWCA Laniakea building opposite 'Iolani Palace, Cafe Julia is a gem. Named after Julia Morgan, one of America's first female architects, who designed the building, the service and cuisine are superb in an open-air setting. Perfect for *poke* tacos or garlic ahi for lunch.

Pai Honolulu   AMERICAN **$$$**

(Map p90; ☑808-744-2531; www.paihonolulu.com; 55 Merchant St; mains lunch $15-19, dinner $30-40; ☺11am-2pm Wed-Fri, 5-10pm Tue-Sat) Splendid sandwiches top the lunch menu at this full-service, stylish restaurant. People hurry in, take a meeting, close a deal and hurry out. Dinner is a more relaxed affair with complex mains that start with meats and seafood and add a melange of flavors. The open kitchen adds drama. Despite the address, it's in an office tower closer to Bethel St.

✖ Chinatown

Chinese restaurants are plentiful, but the cavalcade doesn't stop there – cuisines from across Asia are also well represented. However, the real stars are the trendy and inventive spots that make Chinatown Honolulu's most exciting dining destination. And don't miss the hole-in-the-wall kitchens, dim-sum palaces and marketplace stalls.

★ **Maguro Brothers**   SEAFOOD **$**

(Map p90; ☑808-259-7100; Kekaulike Market, 1039 Kekaulike St; mains $9-16; ☺9am-3pm Mon-Sat) Buried in Kekaulike Market; you wind your way around vegetable and seafood vendors to this little stall in the back. Everything is spare and sparkling, especially the fish, which could not be fresher. Sashimi comes in many forms atop rice bowls, or opt for the perfectly grilled garlic ahi or teriyaki salmon.

Maunakea Marketplace   ASIAN **$**

(Map p90; ☑808-524-3409; 1120 Maunakea St; mains from $5; ☺5:30am-4pm) In the food court of this marketplace, you'll find over a dozen stalls dishing out hot and wok-fresh Asian fare. Eat at tiny tables in the courtyard or at long plastic tables jammed along the walk-

way inside. Produce and seafood stands, housewares and cheap clothing vendors crowd the dark aisles. Cash only.

Pho To-Chau   VIETNAMESE **$**

(Map p90; ☑808-533-4549; 1007 River St; mains $7-12; ☺8:30am-2:30pm) Always packed, this Vietnamese institution holds fast to its hard-earned reputation for serving top-notch *pho* (Vietnamese noodle soup). With beef, broth and vegetables, the dish is a complete meal in itself. So popular that you may have to queue underneath the battered sign outside to score one of a dozen or so rickety wooden tables. Try *pho* for breakfast.

Bangkok Chef   THAI **$**

(Map p90; ☑808-585-8839; http://bangkok chefexpress.com; 1627 Nu'uanu Ave; mains $8-13; ☺10:30am-9pm) It feels strangely like you're eating out in someone's garage, but who cares when the Thai curries, noodle dishes and savory salads taste exactly like those from a Bangkok street cart? Sit in or take out. There are now several more locations across O'ahu.

Downbeat Diner & Lounge   DINER **$**

(Map p90; ☑808-533-2328; www.downbeat diner.com; 42 N Hotel St; mains from $7; ☺11am-midnight; 🖋🛜) This shiny late-night diner with lipstick-red booths posts a vegetarian- and vegan-friendly menu of salads, sandwiches, grilled burgers and heaping island-style breakfasts such as *loco moco* (rice, fried egg and hamburger patty) and Portuguese sweet-bread French toast. The lounge, running a full bar, features live music five nights a week. On the busiest block of Hotel St.

Royal Kitchen   CHINESE **$**

(Map p90; ☑808-524-4461; http://royalkitchen hawaii.com; Chinatown Cultural Plaza, 100 N Beretania St; snacks from $3; ☺5:30am-4:30pm Mon-Fri, 6:30am-4:30pm Sat, 6:30am-2:30pm Sun) At this humble storefront facing the River St Pedestrian Mall, join the queue for the famous *manapua* (steamed or baked buns) with tantalizing sweet and savory fillings: *char siu* (Chinese barbecue pork), chicken curry, sweet potato, *kalua* pig, black sugar and more. Enjoy your treat on a riverside bench.

★ **Pig & the Lady**   VIETNAMESE **$$**

(Map p90; ☑808-585-8255; http://thepigand thelady.com; 83 N King St; mains $10-30; ☺11am-3pm & 5:30-9:30pm Tue-Sat) This award-winning Vietnamese fusion restaurant is crazy popular. Book well in advance. Imaginative lunch *banh mi* (sandwiches) come with shrimp chips or prime-rib *pho* broth; delicious dinner options include Laotian fried chicken. Can't get a table? There's takeout and you'll spot these guys at Honolulu farmers markets. The tropical-flavored softserve ice cream is a dream.

Little Village Noodle House   CHINESE $$

(Map p90; ☎ 808-545-3008; www.littlevillage hawaii.com; 1113 Smith St; mains $11-20; ⊙10:30am-9:30pm Wed-Mon) If you live for anything fishy in black-bean sauce, this is Honolulu's gold standard. On the eclectic pan-Chinese menu, regional dishes are served up garlicky, fiery or with just the right dose of saltiness. For a cross-cultural combo, fork into sizzling black cod steak or roasted pork with island-grown taro. Reservations recommended for dinner; BYOB.

Rangoon Burmese kitchen   BURMESE $$

(Map p90; ☎808-367-0645; http://rangoon-bur mese-kitchen.business.site; 1131 Nu'uanu Ave; mains $12-20; ⊙11am-2pm, 5-10pm Mon-Sat) This sprightly addition to Chinatown features a high ceiling with a spare yet elegant decor. Paintings of monks cast their serene gazes down upon diners, who enjoy fare such as garlic noodles with organic tofu. Flavors are assertive and the menu is blessedly shorter than many places that misguidedly think 100 choices leads to enlightenment.

Fête   HAWAII REGIONAL $$

(Map p90; ☎808-369-1390; http://fetehawaii .com; 2 N Hotel St,; mains $11-30; ⊙11am-10pm Mon-Thu, to 11pm Fri & Sat) One-page and everchanging, the lunch, dinner and dessert menus reflect the intensely local farm-totable ethos at Fête, run by a talented couple. The food menus may be simple, offering up a good range of takes on seasonal island cuisine, but the cocktails, wine and 'after dessert' menus are extensive. A giant living plant wall adds to the natural charm.

Lucky Belly   ASIAN, FUSION $$

(Map p90; ☎808-531-1888; www.luckybelly .com; 50 N Hotel St; mains $10-25; ⊙11am-2pm & 5pm-midnight Mon-Sat) Sleek bistro tables are packed elbows-to-shoulders at this artsdistrict noodle bar, which crafts hot and spicy Asian-fusion bites, knockout artisanal cocktails and amazingly fresh, almost architectural salads that the whole table can share. A 'Belly Bowl' of ramen soup topped with three kinds of pork is superb, as is the Korean-style brisket. A historical plaque outside notes that this is where the devastating fire of 1886 started.

LEI LOWDOWN

The tradition of lei dates back to the Polynesians, who wore garlands of everyday objects such as flowers and feathers for status, honor and beauty.

The tradition of giving lei to visitors to Hawaii dates to the 19th-century ships that first brought tourists. Passengers were greeted by local vendors who would toss garlands around the necks of *malihini* (newcomers, or foreigners).

During the golden era of steamship travel to the islands from the mainland in the mid-20th century, it was believed that if passengers threw their lei into the sea as their departing ship passed Diamond Head, and the flowers of the lei floated back toward the beach, they'd be guaranteed to return to Hawaii someday. It was a notion that appealed both to wistful departing tourists and local tourism officials anxious for repeat visitors. Given that the prevailing ocean current would drive the lei where everyone wanted it to go, it was a win-win for all.

In the 1970s, when United Airlines led the way in promoting jet tourism to Hawaii, passengers could order their lei in advance, assured that a winsome local would be waiting in the terminal to place it around their necks. And no package tour of the islands was complete without a bullet-pointed 'Lei greeting!' in the brochure.

Today, as the travel industry competes fiercely on cost, operators aren't so free with their lei, but the tradition continues. There is still a signposted row of drive-up lei shops at the airport, so you can stock up on the fragrant symbols before you greet arrivals. Better hotels still honor arriving guests with a lei and a few traditional lei-makers such as Cindy's Lei Shoppe (p128) are still going strong, making and selling hundreds a day.

Given you can get good lei for as little as $10, why not succumb to the gentle caress of the flower petals on your skin while the fragrant floral scent envelopes you? And, yes, they look great in selfies.

LUNCH AT ETHEL'S

Among the several top local food places you'll pass near on the road to the airport, **Ethel's Grill** (Map p86; ☑808-847-6467; 232 Kalihi St, Kalihi; mains $8-12; ⊗8am-2pm Tue-Sat) is a standout and a legend. One of Honolulu's greatest hole-in-the-wall restaurants, Ethel's serves Japanese diner fare with an Okinawan bent and an overlay of Hawaii. This bustling, cash-only place has 24 seats and six parking spots, and all are usually full when Ethel's is open. Ponder photos of sumo wrestlers on the walls while you tuck into garlic ahi, *mochiko* (batter-fried) chicken and miso soup.

Mei Sum   CHINESE $$
(Map p90; ☑808-531-3268; 1170 Nu'uanu Ave; mains $10-20; ⊗8am-9pm Thu-Tue) Where else can you go to satisfy that crazy craving for dim sum in the afternoon or evening (though it may not be as fresh as it is in the morning)? This no-nonsense corner stop with a tree-shaded entry cranks out a multitude of cheap little plates and a full range of Chinese mains.

Duc's Bistro   FUSION $$
(Map p90; ☑808-531-6325; www.ducsbistro.com; 1188 Maunakea St; mains $12-25; ⊗11am-2pm & 5-9pm Mon-Fri, 5-9pm Sat & Sun) Honolulu's bigwigs hang out after work at this swank French-Vietnamese bistro with a tiny bar. Ignore the inauspicious outside appearance and step inside this surprising culinary oasis for buttery escargot, *bánh xèo* (Vietnamese crepes), pan-fried fish with green mango relish, and fire-roasted eggplant. A small jazz combo serenades diners some evenings. Reservations recommended.

JJ Dolan's Pizza Pub   PIZZA $$
(Map p90; ☑808-537-4992; www.jjdolans.com; 1147 Bethel St; pizzas from $16; ⊗11am-2am Mon-Sat) If the neighborhood's superb Asian fare just doesn't appeal, this sociable Irish pub offers excellent NYC-style pizza. The crust is thin and the topping choices myriad (go for the garlic and meatball). It also serves tasty *pupu* (finger food) and pours cold beer while sports games play on big-screen TVs.

★ Senia   HAWAII REGIONAL $$$
(Map p90; ☑808-200-5412; www.restaurant senia.com; 75 N King St; mains $20-35; ⊗11am-

2pm Tue-Fri, 5:30-9:30pm Mon-Sat) Electricity, buzz, whatever, you'll feel the energy as you enter one of the city's most innovative restaurants. It's not big, so book. Once seated you'll get the ever-changing one-sided menu. The food is local, fresh and defines creative. Don't miss seemingly mundane fare such as charred cabbage. The service, cocktails and wine list all excel.

Each night there are eight seats available for the extraordinary chef's table experience ($195, 6:30pm), which includes a kitchen-side perch as the chefs create dishes for you on the spot. Bookings open 60 days in advance and go quick.

Livestock Tavern   AMERICAN $$$
(Map p90; ☑808-537-2577; http://livestocktav ern.com; 49 N Hotel St; mains $18-40; ⊗11am-2pm Mon-Fri, 5-10pm Mon-Sat) At Livestock, the food is like an old pair of khakis, vaguely stylish but very comfortable. There are seasonal variations, but you'll always find sandwiches, pastas and salads for lunch, lamb shanks, smoked prime rib and roast chicken for dinner. The Livestock-original cocktails are winners. The exposed-brick dining room and bar area has high ceilings and an airy vibe.

✕ Kalihi

The industrial and big-box store area near the docks and between downtown and the airport is home to many humble but excellent restaurants and eateries. Stop off at one of these gems tucked here and there for a proper meal before you board the big bird home.

Young's Fish Market   HAWAIIAN $
(Map p86; ☑808-841-4885; www.youngsfish market.com; 1286 Kalani St; mains $8-19; ⊗9:30am-7pm Mon-Fri, 8am-4pm Sat) Seafood yes, but Young's also serves up plenty of locally beloved *kalua* pork, chicken and beef with the popular plate lunches that it's been dishing up since 1951. The meal to try here is the *laulau* plate, a traditional food staple, where meat is wrapped in *kalo* (taro) leaf and steamed. The dining area decor is basic; huge takeout menu.

Kamehameha Bakery   BAKERY $
(Map p86; ☑808-845-5831; www.kamehameha bakeryhi.com; 1284 Kalani St; snacks from $2; ⊗2am-4pm) Get to this beloved bakery well before noon or the long display cases will contain more air than bread. Get here by 2pm and all you might find will be the lost

butt end of banana bread. Hugely popular pastries, rolls, breads and cakes pour forth from the kitchen from before dawn. Try the poi glaze doughnut.

Alicia's Market   MARKET $

(Map p86; ☑808-841-1921; www.facebook.com/AliciasMarket; 267 Mokauea St; mains $8-16; ⊕8am-7pm Mon-Fri, to 6pm Sat) This storefront neighborhood market sells some of the best *poke* and smoked meat on the island. There's plenty of parking out front; head inside to meat-eater and *poke*-lover heaven, with everything on display to tickle your taste buds before you choose. The takeout plate lunches are fantastic – try the roast pork or the roast duck.

Nico's at Pier 38   SEAFOOD $$

(Map p86; ☑808-540-1377; www.nicospier38.com; 1129 N Nimitz Hwy; breakfast & lunch mains $8-16, dinner mains $15-30; ⊕6:30am-9pm Mon-Sat, 10am-9pm Sun) Inside, the dining room is classy; outside, the seating is near the waterfront and Honolulu's fish auction. Chef Nico was inspired by the island-cuisine scene to merge his classical French training with Hawaii's humble plate lunch. Daily seafood specials are listed alongside market-fresh fish sandwiches and local faves, such as *furikake*-crusted ahi and hoisin BBQ chicken. Good bar.

Uncle's Fish Market & Grill   SEAFOOD $$

(Map p86; ☑808-275-0063; www.unclesfishmarket.com; 1135 N Nimitz Hwy; mains $15-35; ⊕10:30am-9pm) Part of the Pier 38 complex, Uncle's serves fabulously fresh seafood. It's known for its Uncle's Original Poke Tower – sushi rice layered with fresh ahi (tuna) *poke*, guacamole, and ahi tartare. Uncle's menu runs from fish and chips to garlic ahi and lobster, all served in a casual, nautical setting, with seating inside and out.

✖ Kaka'ako

Between Ala Moana and Downtown, Kaka'ako is a commercial and retail district that's morphing into a hip urban area with loft condos and a post-industrial vibe, which is spreading east to Ala Moana.

Honolulu Farmers Market   MARKET $

(Map p96; ☑808-848-2074; http://hfbf.org/farmers-markets/oahu; Neal S Blaisdell Center, 777 Ward Ave; ⊕4-7pm Wed; 🅿🚻) 🍴 Honolulu's farmers markets are extraordinary places to browse the island's famed bounty of produce, prepared foods, snacks, craft items

and a lot more. Graze food stalls set up by island chefs, food artisans and Kona coffee roasters. Check the website for other market locations through the week.

Butterfly Ice Cream   ICE CREAM $

(Map p96; ☑808-429-4483; www.butterflycreamery.com; Salt at Our Kaka'ako, 324 Coral St; treats from $4; ⊕11am-9pm) Shave ice is good but sometimes you want the indulgence of rich, creamy ice cream. This cute little shop makes everything on site. The flavor lineup changes regularly, but you can usually count on island-influenced varieties such as Kona coffee, mango delight and honey macadamia nut.

Highway Inn Kaka'ako   HAWAIIAN $

(Map p96; ☑808-954-4955; www.myhighwayinn.com; Salt at Our Kaka'ako, 680 Ala Moana Blvd; mains $6-19; ⊕8:30am-8:30pm Mon-Thu, to 9pm Fri & Sat, 9am-2:30pm Sun) The original Highway Inn opened in Waipahu in 1947, and third-generation owners have opened a modern version in Kaka'ako. They serve the same Hawaiian food as the original, but have added a number of contemporary Hawaii Regional Cuisine dishes that are keeping the hipster locals happy. People crave the Hawaiian-style nachos with sweet-potato chips and smoky *kalua* pig.

Kewalo Basin Foodtrucks   FOOD TRUCK $

(Makers & Tasters; Map p96; 1011 Ala Moana Blvd; mains $6-14; ⊕hours vary) Wandering food trucks gather at the western end of Kewalo Basin. You never know what you'll find, but generally the quality and variety are excellent. This is a great place for lunch or for grabbing picnic fare during a day at the beach at nearby Ala Moana Regional Park or on the waterfront at Kaka'ako Waterfront Park. Some top Honolulu eateries started out as food trucks and moved to permanent premises once their viability was established and reputation built.

Merriman's Honolulu   HAWAII REGIONAL $$$

(Map p96; ☑808-215-0022; www.merrimanshawaii.com; Ward Village, 1108 Auahi St; lunch mains $16-19, dinner mains $22-50; ⊕11am-9pm Sun-Thu, to 9:30pm Fri & Sat) An originator of Hawaii Regional Cuisine, Merriman's serves comfortable fare with island and Asian accents. Dishes are 90% locally sourced. Regular menu stars like the pot pie made with local shellfish are justifiably famous. There's live, jazzy vocalists every night. The corner location in a modern commercial building has a few tables outside on a raised terrace.

Nobu Honolulu
ASIAN $$$

(Map p96; ☎808-237-6999; www.noburestau rants.com; Waiea Tower, 1118 Ala Moana Blvd; mains $25-50; ☺restaurant 5-10pm) Nobu Matsu-hisa's legendary Japanese-fusion restaurant and sushi bar is in the slick Waiea Tower in Ward Village. Nobu's signature dishes such as Black Miso Cod and Yellowtail Jalape-no continue to draw devotees. Service and attention to detail are hallmarks of Nobu, which has spread worldwide. The flavors of both food and drink are surprising, creative and always delightful.

✖ Ala Moana & Around

Mall food courts are common in this neighborhood, but many star-chef's kitchens are spread out along trafficked thoroughfares such as S King St, or on dumpy-looking side streets. And don't overlook the unprepossessing little holes in the wall. Most of this area is an easy walk from Waikiki.

★Epi-Ya Boulangerie & Patisserie
BAKERY $

(Map p96; ☎808-888-8828; 1296 S Beretania St, Makiki; snacks from $2; ☺6am-7pm) Grab a pair of tongs and fill up your platter with pastries, ham rolls and myriad other treats fresh from the oven (we bought a loaf of their superb country-style whole-grain bread and it was literally straight out of the oven and too hot to hold). Master baker Yukikazu Sato's shop is in a supermarket strip mall.

Joy Cup Noodles Mean
SICHUAN $

(Map p96; ☎808-725-2898; 1608 Kalakaua Ave, Ala Moana; mains $12-15; ☺10am-8pm) Sliced beef or ground pork noodles are combined with authentically piquant Sichuan noodles. A range of spices enliven the homemade beef bone soup, which comes with various daily vegetables on top. You can choose your spiciness level. The storefront location shares frontage with a few other top-notch casual Asian eateries.

Kaka'ako Kitchen
HAWAIIAN $

(Map p96; ☎808-596-7488; http://kaka akokitchen.com; Ward Centre, 1200 Ala Moana Blvd, Ala Moana; meals $8-19; ☺10am-9pm Mon-Sat, to 4pm Sun; ⊕) As *ono* (delicious) as always, this popular cafe dishes up healthy plate lunches with brown rice and organic greens. Lots of ethnic options too, including Indian curry, *kalbi* (Korean barbecued ribs) and kimchi. For a local deli twist, get the tempura mahimahi sandwich on a homemade taro bun. Crowded at lunchtime, but great shady lanai.

Jimbo
JAPANESE $

(Map p96; ☎808-947-2211; www.jimbohawaii.com; 1936 S King St, Ala Moana; mains from $10; ☺11am-2:30pm & 5-9:30pm) Honolulu's first udon noodle restaurant debuted in 1994 and has been serving handmade noodles ever since. Always fresh and flavorful, the noodles are made daily using traditional methods, including stomping the dough. Order 'em cooked in hot broth on rainy days or chilled on a summer's afternoon. Other options too. The strip-mall location defines humble.

Purvé
BAKERY $

(Map p96; ☎808-200-3978; www.purvehawaii.com; 1234 Kona St, Ala Moana; doughnuts from $4; ☺6am-2pm Mon-Thu, to 5pm Fri-Sun) Excellent cake doughnuts get elaborate and at times overwhelming toppings created fresh with each order. Some of the extravagant choices include Ala Wai Tea Bag, which has Fruity Pebbles and Kit Kat chunks up top; and the Umpa Lumpa Wet Dreamcicle, which carries creamy orange glaze and a cheese drizzle. It's tucked away off an upper parking deck.

Shirokiya Japan Village Walk
JAPANESE $

(Map p96; ☎808-973-9111; www.japanvillage walk.com; Ala Moana Center, 1450 Ala Moana Blvd, Ala Moana; mains $7-20; ☺10am-10pm) On the 1st-floor Ewa wing of the Ala Moana Shopping Center, visit Japan without leaving Hawaii. Part culinary theme park, part food court, there are 56 different providers, including several table-service bistros, offering a panoply of Japanese fare. It seats 900. 'Beer stations' offer beer from $1 per (small) glass and it's always happy hour.

Honolulu Museum of Art Café
AMERICAN $$

(Map p96; ☎808-532-8734; http://honolulumu seum.org; Honolulu Museum of Art, 900 S Beretania St, Ala Moana; mains $17-26; ☺11am-2pm Tue-Sun) Market-fresh salads and sandwiches made with O'ahu-grown ingredients, a decent selection of wines by the glass and tropically infused desserts make this an indulgent way to support the arts. Open-air tables face the courtyard and soothing fountain with spectacular sculptures by Jun Kaneko. Reservations recommended; last seating at 1:45pm. There is no museum admission charge to dine at the cafe. Parking is diagonally opposite the museum and cafe at 1111 Victoria St (enter off Beretania or Young St), and costs $5. From Waikiki, take bus 2 or 13.

Side Street Inn   HAWAIIAN $$

(Map p96; ☏808-591-0253; http://sidestreet
inn.com; 1225 Hopaka St, Ala Moana; mains $8-30;
⊙2pm-midnight Mon-Thu, to 1am Fri, 1pm-1am Sat,
1pm-midnight Sun) This late-night hub is where
you'll find Honolulu's top chefs hanging out
after hours, along with partying locals who
come for hearty portions of *kalbi,* pan-fried
pork chops and lots of local and mainland
comfort fare. Make reservations and bring
friends, or order a takeout plate lunch. The
kitchen closes two hours before the bar.
There's another location on Kapahulu Ave.

Ichiriki Japanese Nabe   JAPANESE $$

(Map p96; ☏808-589-2299; http://ichirikinabe
.com; 510 Pi'ikoi St, Ala Moana; mains $12-35;
⊙11am-10pm Sun-Thu, to midnight Fri & Sat) Sumo
wrestler–sized Japanese *nabemono* (variety of hot dishes), *shabushabu* (thinly sliced
beef and vegetables) and *sukiyaki* (sim-
mered beef) hot pots. You won't leave hungry! Japanese beer, *shochu* and sake are also
on the menu. Parking is available behind the
tidy white restaurant. Ichiriki also has locations in Kaimuki, Kane'ohe and Aiea.

Shokudo Japanese
Restaurant and Bar   JAPANESE $$

(Map p96; ☏ 808-941-3701; www.shokudojapa
nese.com; 1585 Kapi'olani Blvd, Ala Moana; mains
$8-25; ⊙ 11:30am-1am Sun-Thu, to 2am Fri & Sat)
Knock back lychee sake-tinis at this sleek,
bright red Japanese restaurant (*shokudō*
means 'dining room') that's always filled
to the ceiling (which is the bottom deck
of the parking garage overhead). A mixed-
plate traditional Japanese and island-fusion
menu depicts dozens of dishes, from *mochi*
(rice cake) cheese gratin to lobster dynamite
rolls and more traditional noodles and sushi. Reservations recommended.

Inaba   JAPANESE $$

(Map p96; ☏808-953-2070; http://inabahono
lulu.com; 1610 S King St, Ala Moana; mains $11-
22; ⊙7-10am Thu-Mon, 11:30am-2pm & 5:30-9pm
Thu-Tue) Handmade soba noodles (with soba
flour imported directly from Japan), sushi
and lighter-than-air tempura are superb at
this long-term Japanese favorite. The Inaba
Bento (which changes seasonally) followed by
green-tea ice cream is the way to go. Order
takeout with pick-up at this tiny strip mall.

Thai Lao   ASIAN $$

(Map p96; ☏808-943-4311; McCully Shopping
Center, 1960 Kapi'olani Blvd, Ala Moana; mains
$12-25; ⊙11am-9:30pm) One of several good

restaurants in the McCully Shopping Center,
Thai Lao has statues out front. Inside, the
place is bright with white tablecloths, the
decor authentic and the meals tasty. The
flavors pop on the dishes, which span the
Mekong River on the border of Thailand
and Laos.

★Alan Wong's   HAWAII REGIONAL $$$

(Map p96; ☏808-949-2526; www.alanwongs.com;
1857 S King St, Ala Moana; mains $35-45; ⊙5-
10pm) 🍴 One of O'ahu's big-gun chefs, Alan
Wong offers his creative interpretations of
Hawaii Regional Cuisine with a menu inspired by the state's diverse ethnic cultures.
Emphasis in the open kitchen is on fresh
seafood and local produce. Order Wong's
time-tested signature dishes, such as ginger-
crusted *onaga* (red snapper), steamed shellfish bowl, and twice-cooked *kalbi* (short
ribs). Reserve in advance.

★Sushi Izakaya Gaku   JAPANESE $$$

(Map p96; ☏808-589-1329; 1329 S King St, Ala Moana; shared plates $7-40; ⊙5-10:30pm Mon-Sat)
Known mostly by word of mouth, this in-
siders' *izakaya* (Japanese gastropub) beats
the competition with adherence to tradition
and supremely fresh sushi and sashimi – no
fusion novelty rolls named after caterpillars
or California here. A spread of savory and
sweet, hot and cold dishes include hard-
to-find specialties such as *chazuke* (tea-
soaked rice porridge) and *natto* (fermented
soybeans).

Chef Mavro   FUSION $$$

(Map p96; ☏808-944-4714; www.chefmavro.com;
1969 S King St, Ala Moana; multicourse tasting
menus from $120; ⊙6-8:30pm Tue-Sat) After a
high-profile solo run, maverick chef (and
namesake) George Mavrothalassitis has
paired up with chef Jeremy Shigekane to
continue creating avant-garde dishes, all
paired with Old and New World wines. The
award-winning kitchen matches the produce and flavors of Hawaii with chef Mavro's
homeland of Provence and beyond. Choose
between four- and six-course tasting menus.
Reserve ahead.

Mariposa   BISTRO $$$

(Map p96; ☏808-951-3420; http://neimanmarcus
hawaii.com; Ala Moana Center, 1450 Ala Moana Blvd,
Ala Moana; mains $18-34; ⊙11am-8pm Sun-Thu, to
9pm Fri & Sat) This attractive and airy bistro,
on the 3rd floor of the Nieman Marcus department store at the Ala Moana Shopping
Center, features a fusion of American and

Hawaiian cuisine. There's lanai seating with ocean views out over Ala Moana Regional Park, and impressive lunch and dinner menus with fresh and casual fare. The wine menu is extensive.

Sushi Sasabune JAPANESE $$$
(Map p96; ☑808-947-3800; http://sushisabune.tumblr.com; 1417 S King St, Ala Moana; mains $12-50; ☺noon-2pm Tue-Fri, 5:30-10pm Tue-Sat) *Omakase* (chef's tasting menu) meals are Honolulu's pick for serious sushi aficionados. As at top sushi places in Japan, Sasabune's chefs are fanatical experts who take pride in their presentation. Considered the gold standard for sushi and sashimi, but priced accordingly. Sasabune also has locations in California and New York.

✖ University Area

A gaggle of restaurants cluster south of the UH Manoa campus on the strips around the three-way intersection of University Ave and S King and Beretania Sts. Plenty of veggie and vegan options here, plus great coffee to help UH students keep their minds on the job. This area is more walkable than most.

★Kahai Street Kitchen HAWAIIAN $
(Map p100; ☑808-845-0320; www.kahaistreet-kitchen.com; 946 Coolidge St; plate lunches $11-15; ☺10:30am-7:30pm Tue-Fri, to 2:30pm Sat) This smart-looking corner place has a curving front and is hugely popular with locals. There are four sizable tables out front on Coolidge St, or you can head inside for more seating. The kitchen specializes in gourmet plate lunches, salads and sandwiches. The burgers are great, as is the pork *katsu* (deep-fried fillets), and breakfast includes eggs Benedict.

★Sweet Home Café $
(Map p100; ☑808-947-3707; 2334 S King St; shared dishes $3-18; ☺4-11pm) Expect lines of locals waiting outside this cafe's tiny strip mall location. On wooden family-style tables sit steaming-hot pots; pick your broth, then choose from countless options of all kinds of vegetables, tofu, lamb, chicken or tender beef tongue. Besides the great food and good fun, there is complimentary shave ice for dessert.

Waiola Shave Ice ICE CREAM $
(Map p100; ☑808-949-2269; www.waiolashaveice.com; 2135 Waiola St; treats $3-6; ☺10am-

6pm) The original store of this mini-chain dates to the 1940s – and looks it. The shave ice here is old-style: sliced powder fine, then flavored with an array of syrups. Go local and try the POG (passion fruit, orange, guava) or the luscious banana cream. The unchanged grocery store interior boasts lots of old-timey candy. Seating is limited to a wooden bench out front.

Aloha Vietnamese Food VIETNAMESE $
(Map p100; ☑808-941-1170; 2320 S King St; mains $8-15; ☺5pm-midnight Fri-Wed) This is no-frills family-run Vietnamese at its best. It's a local favorite, so don't be fazed by lines out the door or the lack of decor beyond the various pipes and electrical conduits. The menu is extensive, the service is friendly and the food is superb. Try the brisket and sirloin *pho*.

Yama's Fish Market HAWAIIAN $
(Map p100; ☑808-941-9994; www.yamasfishmarket.com; 2332 Young St; mains $8-14; ☺9am-5pm Wed-Mon) Swing by this side-street seafood market for heaping island-style plate lunches (eg *kalua* pig, *mochiko* chicken, *lomilomi* salmon) and freshly mixed *poke* by the pound with sour poi (fermented taro paste) and sweet *haupia* (coconut pudding) on the side. There are a couple of small tables outside to eat at, but it's really all takeout.

Peace Cafe VEGAN $
(Map p100; ☑808-951-7555; www.peacecafehawaii.com; 2239 S King St; mains $9-14; ☺9am-8pm Mon-Sat, to 3pm Sun; 🖉) Vegan home cooking is the theme at this mellow kitchen, where daily dishes get handwritten on the chalkboard. Pick an avocado or cilantro hummus sandwich to go, or a substantial lunch box with Moroccan stew. *Mochi* and soy ice creams are dairy-free delights.

Down to Earth Natural Foods SUPERMARKET $
(Map p100; ☑808-947-7678; www.downtoearth.org; 2525 S King St; mains $5-8; ☺7am-10pm; 🖉) Organic and natural foods are the draw at this always-busy grocery store. It has a vegetarian- and vegan-friendly salad bar, a deli for sandwiches, a juice and smoothie bar, and a few sidewalk tables for chowing down. Free parking in the rear.

Dagon BURMESE $$
(Map p100; ☑808-947-0088; www.instagram.com/dagonburmesecuisine; 2671 S King St; mains $13-17; ☺11am-2pm & 5-10pm Wed-Mon) The city's top Burmese restaurant may be in a

small space on King St, but it has an authentic atmosphere. The various pork dishes, pineapple curry chicken and tea-leaf salad are carefully garnished, and flavors authentically capture the deep spices of Burmese fare. The unreconstructed storefront recalls Honolulu in the 1930s. There is parking out back. It's BYOB.

Imanas Tei
JAPANESE $$

(Map p100; ☑808-941-2626; 2626 S King St; mains $14-28; ⊙5-11:30pm Mon-Sat) Look for the orange sign well off the street at this long-standing *izakaya* (a casual pub), where staff shout their welcome *('Irrashaimase!')* as you make your way to a tatami-mat booth. Sake fans come here to quench their thirst, then graze their way through a seemingly endless menu of sushi and epicurean and country-style Japanese fare. Reserve ahead or stand in line for open seating after 7pm.

Nook Neighborhood Bistro
BISTRO $$

(Map p100; ☑808-942-2222; www.thenookhonolulu.com; 1035 University Ave #105, University are; mains $13-16; ⊙8am-2pm Tue-Fri, 7am-3pm Sat & Sun) Tucked away (and a tad hard to find) behind a raucous bar, the Nook boasts locally sourced ingredients and an inspiring menu. Equally inspiring is the motto: 'a neighborhood boozy bistro...' Possibly the most laid-back *and* fun place for brunch in town, Nook serves up fresh takes on eggs and other breakfast classics along with plenty of drinks!

✖ Kaimuki

The old neighborhood of Kaimuki bookends Chinatown for creative cuisine. Wander Wai'alae Ave, from the Market City Shopping Center all the way to Koko Head Ave, for a variety of appealing eateries. Prices here are more affordable than other parts of Honolulu. Note that most of the restaurants on Kapahulu Ave (p162) just south in Waikiki are nearby.

★ Cafe Kaila
CAFE $

(Map p86; ☑808-732-3330; www.cafe-kaila-hawaii.com; Market City Shopping Center, 2919 Kapi'olani Blvd; mains $8-12; ⊙7am-6pm Mon-Fri, 7am-3:30pm Sat & Sun) This place at the top of Kapi'olani Blvd racks up best breakfast gold medals in local culinary awards. Expect to queue to get in for the legendary lineup of incredibly well presented breakfast specials.

All the beauty is on the plate (the pancakes!) – the dining room is pure utility.

★ Tamura's Fine Wine & Liquors
SEAFOOD $

(Map p86; ☑808-735-7100; www.tamurasupermarket.com/daily-poke-menu; 3496 Wai'alae Ave; poke $9-12; ⊙9:30am-9pm Mon-Sat, to 8pm Sun) Arguably the best *poke* on the island is in this unpromising-looking liquor store. Just head inside to the *poke* counter in the back and feast your eyes. The 'spicy ahi' and the smoked marlin are simply beautiful and, like the rest of the big selection, super-fresh. Ask for tastes before you buy and take away. Fabulous beer selection too!

Kaimuki Superette
CAFE $

(Map p86; ☑808-734-7800; 3458 Wai'alae Ave; mains $6-15; ⊙7:30am-2:30pm) A diner for the modern age, the Superette has top quality comfort fare. French toast made with bread from famous local bakeries, chia seed pudding made with Manoa honey, a club sandwich with seared ahi and wasabi aioli, you get the point. It's run by neighboring Mud Hen Water (p120), a top local draw.

Juicy Brew
VEGAN $

(Map p86; ☑808-797-9177; www.juicybrewahawaii.com; 3392 Wai'alae Ave; mains $6-11; ⊙9am-6pm Mon-Fri, 9am-2pm Sat & Sun) Beautiful home-cooked food is boxed up and ready to go, or you can enjoy it at one of the small tables. Most everything is sourced locally and includes baked goods, salads and sandwiches. Try the dragon fruit *mochi*.

Donut King
BAKERY $

(Map p86; ☑808-258-4119; http://donutkinghawaii.com; Market City Shopping Center, 2919 Kapi'olani Blv; doughnuts from $1; ⊙6am-5pm Mon-Fri, 7am-5pm Sat, 8am-5pm Sun) Don't expect $4 doughnuts with toppings such as marzipan acai at this splendid little old-school doughnut bakery. Among the dozens of classic flavors is glazed old fashioned. Just try to walk by this supermarket strip-mall location and not buy one – or two.

Gina's Barbecue
KOREAN $

(Map p86; ☑808-735-7964; www.ginasbbq.com; Market City Shopping Center, 2919 Kapi'olani Blvd; mains $10-12; ⊙10am-10pm) The BBQ ribs plate lunch is huge at this unfussy strip mall Korean kitchen. Fast service and tons of parking. The chicken *katsu* is a winner.

FIRST FRIDAYS IN CHINATOWN

Chinatown's somewhat battered and historic Nu'uanu Ave and Hotel St have become the anchors for the monthly evening dose of urban art and culture, socializing and bar-hopping known as First Friday. Check out the excellent maps and monthly schedule at www. firstfridayhawaii.com.

The action starts at 5pm. Many shops and galleries stay open until 9pm, drink specials in bars abound and there are events such as talks by artists. Just a short walk east, the Hawai'i State Art Museum (p88) has lawn concerts starting at 6pm.

Nabeya Maido   JAPANESE $

(Map p86; ☎808-739-7739; Market City Shopping Center, 2919 Kapi'olani Blvd; mains $10-16; ⊗11am-9pm Sun-Thu, to 10pm Fri & Sat) Choose your broth from five different styles at this hot pot storefront, then decide what you want to put into it, including meats, seafood and vegetables. Finally, cook it all up to your liking and plunge into some savory goodness.

W & M Bar-B-Q Burger   BURGERS $

(Map p86; ☎808-734-3350; 3104 Wai'alae Ave; mains $4-7; ⊗10am-4:30pm Wed-Fri, 9am-4:30pm Sat & Sun) This legendary burger spot has stood the test of time since Wilfred and May Kawamura (W & M) kicked it off in 1940 with their own secret sauce. These days, it's onto third-generation owners and the teri burger has become the top draw. Plenty of parking, which is good since your car is also your dining room.

Happy Days Chinese
Seafood Restaurant   CHINESE $

(Map p86; ☎808-738-8666; www.happydayshi.com; 3553 Wai'alae Ave; mains $11-20; ⊗8am-10pm) Locals consider Happy Days to be one of the top casual Chinese restaurants in the city (and possibly the least adorned). The vast menu boats all the standards, plus more esoteric items such as a seafood tofu casserole. But the real stars are the dim sum, offered in myriad variety (from $3 a plate).

★ Mud Hen Water   FUSION $$

(Map p86; ☎808-737-6000; www.mudhenwater.com; 3452 Wai'alae Ave; mains $10-28; ⊗5:30-10pm Tue-Fri, 9:30am-2pm & 5:30-10pm Sat & Sun) Chef Ed Kenney has pulled off a real trick at this comfy corner bistro: he's created a menu of comfort foods drawn from Honolulu's many cultures and he's made it harmonize. One of the city's most lauded restaurants, Mud Hen Water has seating inside or at picnic tables in a cute little side yard.

Enjoy fried chicken with Szechuan salt, mussels with Portuguese sausage, beet *poke*, chicken croquettes and much more. The brunch menu is worth getting up for and the bar brings crafty wit to its cocktails. Be sure to reserve.

Gazen Izakaya   JAPANESE $$

(Map p86; ☎808-737-0230; www.e-k-c.co.jp/gazen/honolulu; 2836 Kapi'olani Blvd; mains $12-25; ⊗4:30-11pm) It might look nondescript from the outside, but Gazen Izakaya seems like little Japan when you walk through the door. There's an authentic and refined yet casual feel, and the menu features everything from fresh sashimi and sushi to flaming teppanyaki and silky smooth homemade tofu (try the sampler for $13). Try the sweet-potato *mochi* for dessert. Plenty of parking.

Himalayan Kitchen   NORTH INDIAN $$

(Map p86; ☎808-735-1122; 1137 11th Ave; mains $11-17; ⊗11am-2pm & 5-10pm Tue-Fri, 5-10pm Sat-Mon; ⊘) Lots of Nepali and Indian favorites on offer in this popular upstairs place with seating both inside and outside on the balcony. Naan and breads are cooked in a traditional tandoori clay oven, and meals are prepared mild, medium, spicy or Nepali Heat. There are many good options for vegetarians.

Mr Ojisan   JAPANESE $$

(Map p86; ☎808-735-4455; http://mrojisan.net; 1016 Kapahulu Ave; mains $15-30; ⊗5-11pm Mon-Sat) At the top of Kapahulu Ave, Mr Ojisan specializes in Japanese *teishoku* (fixed, multicourse) dinners, where you choose a main dish such as *wafu* (Japanese-style) steak, tempura, *tonkatsu* (deep-fried pork) or fish, and it comes as a set with miso soup, pickles and rice. Also on the menu are sashimi and udon noodles. An authentic spot with parking out back.

Surfing Pig   AMERICAN $$$

(Map p86; ☎808-744-1992; https://thesurfingpighawaii.com; 3605 Wai'alae Ave; mains $16-38; ⊗11am-2pm Mon-Fri, 4-10pm daily) This restaurant has a gastropub vibe, but it's definitely a food-first place (although the drinks menu is deep and creative). Mains are a meaty mix of excellent burgers, steaks and seafood, and all dishes have some island accents. There are numerous small plates for those who want more pub in their evening. The brunch menu is more lunch than breakfast.

12th Avenue Grill   BISTRO $$$
(Map p86; ☎808-732-9469; http://12thavegrill.com; 1120 12th Ave; mains $18-38; ☺5:30-9pm) Combining the efforts of an impressive kitchen team and sourcing almost everything locally, this tidy little restaurant turns out refined meals without fuss. The *steak-frites* is an example of the special touch they bring to seemingly simple dishes, and the local beef is seared just so. The dining room is also refined but not ostentatious.

Town   FUSION $$$
(Map p86; ☎808-735-5900; www.townkaimuki.com; 3435 Wai'alae Ave; mains $16-34; ☺5:30-9:30pm Sun-Thu, to 10pm Fri & Sat) 🌿 At this hip bistro hybrid in Kaimuki, the motto is 'local first, organic whenever possible, with aloha always.' On the daily-changing menu of boldly flavored cooking are burgers and steaks made from North Shore free-range cattle and salads that taste as if the ingredients were just plucked from a backyard garden. The pasta's good too.

🍴 Manoa Valley

For a delightful – and edible – surprise, head up into the verdant and affluent Manoa Valley for some top local eats.

★Waioli Kitchen & Bake Shop   CAFE $
(Map p86; ☎888-744-1619; 2950 Manoa Rd; mains $8-12; ☺7:30am-2pm Tue-Sun) Set in a vintage compound amid enormous trees, this little cafe cooks up superb breakfasts and lunches. Sit out on the gracious Craftsman-style 1920s veranda of what was once a girls' orphanage. Today, many of the staffers are troubled locals learning a trade, serving up fantastic macadamia nut pancakes, excellent scones, burgers and more. Excellent coffee too.

**Andy's Sandwiches
& Smoothies**   SANDWICHES $
(Map p86; ☎808-988-6161; www.andyssandwiches.com; 2904 E Manoa Rd; items from $4;

☺7am-5pm Mon-Thu, to 4pm Fri, to 2.30pm Sun) Family-run Andy's anchors Manoa Valley's casual food scene. Next to a Starbucks and across the road from Manoa Marketplace, it can be a squeeze to get in, but it's definitely worth the effort. The sandwiches, smoothies, baked goods and salads are superb, especially the green chili melt sandwich. There's a couple of small tables on the sidewalk.

Serg's Mexican Kitchen   MEXICAN $
(Map p86; ☎808-988-8118; www.facebook.com/SergsMexicanKitchen; 2740 E Manoa Rd; mains $7-15; ☺11am-9pm Mon-Fri, 8am-9pm Sat, 8am-8pm Sun; 🍴) This former gas station has been transformed into a cheery local hangout. Where the pumps stood are now a dozen shady outdoor tables. At the south end of the E Manoa Rd commercial strip, it serves fresh and tasty Mexican classics such as perfectly crispy flautas. Serg also has an outpost at Waimanalo on the Windward Coast.

🍴 Greater Honolulu

Scattered about Honolulu's older neighborhoods are some great little local favorites.

Liliha Bakery   BAKERY $
(Map p86; ☎808-531-1651; www.lilihabakery.com; 515 N Kuakini St; items/mains from $2/6; ☺24hr, 6am Tue to 8pm Sun) A local favorite since 1950, Liliha is not far northwest of Chinatown. This old-school island bakery and diner causes a neighborhood traffic jam for its coco-puff and green-tea cream pastries. Still hungry? Grab a counter seat and order a hamburger steak or other hearty faves in Liliha's retro coffee shop.

There's another location in Kalihi and the baked goods are sold at Macy's in Ala Moana Center (p127).

Govinda's Vegetarian Buffet   VEGETARIAN $
(Map p86; ☎808-595-4913; www.iskconhawaii.com; 51 Coelho Way; suggested donation $13; ☺11am-2pm Mon-Sat; 🍴) Honolulu's Hare Krishna temple has a vegetarian buffet lunch under one of the most spectacular banyan trees on the island. Even if not eating, stop by just to see the tree, which is behind the temple in this residential neighborhood. There's indoor seating if it's raining. People rave about the mostly Indian fare on offer, and seconds are only a $5 donation.

A VETERAN OF VETERANS

In Honolulu's sleepy days before WWII, Hotel St was the center of shore leave for seamen from Pearl Harbor. The crews of the big battleships, which numbered well over 1000 per ship, each had their 'own' bar – a place the men would gather with familiar faces for raucous nights out. This era is entirely gone, with one very notable exception: **Smith's Union Bar** (Smitty's; Map p90; ☑808-538-9145; 19 N Hotel St, Chinatown; ☺8am-2am). Barely changed in decades, it's easy to feel you're in a scene of *From the Here to Eternity*, the classic film about prewar military life on O'ahu. There's the long bar, the narrow space and the ragtag paraphernalia. But much more important is the bar's tie to the Pearl Harbor attack on December 7, 1941: Smith's was the chosen bar of the sailors on the USS *Arizona*, the battleship sunk that day with a loss of more than 1100 men.

Every year, Smith's is a gathering spot for people remembering the Pearl Harbor attack. The rest of the time it's a dive bar in the best sense, with cheap cold beer (even a few craft brews) and a genial crowd of locals, office workers, students and the odd tourist. You can see a reminder of Hotel St's notorious past in the old neon sign hanging over the building next door: 'Club Hubba Bubba Live Nude Shows.'

Natsunoya Tea House
JAPANESE $$

(Map p86; ☑808-595-4488; www.natsunoya hawaii.com; 1935 Makanani Dr; per person from $20; ☺confirm in advance) This traditional family-run Japanese teahouse on a hillside is the very place where a man from the Japanese consulate spied on the US fleet in Pearl Harbor before the attack. Today, it seems little changed from those days. Shoe racks adorn the entrance in abundance. Enjoy a traditional afternoon tea ceremony, but be sure to confirm its hours in advance.

53 By The Sea
SEAFOOD $$$

(Map p96; ☑808-536-5353; http://53bythesea. com; 53 Ahui St; mains $22-58; ☺restaurant 11am-2pm & 5-10pm, bar 11am-11pm) The views here are superb, looking east past Waikiki to Diamond Head. Yet, despite the beauty arrayed in front of diners, many can't take their eyes off the top-end food. Consider the extravagant seafood tower ($72), a stunning erection of shellfish, sashimi, *poke* and more. The bar has an equally indulgent wine list.

Mitch's Fish Market & Sushi Bar
SEAFOOD $$$

(Map p86; ☑808-837-7774; http://mitchssushi. com; 524 Ohohia St; small plates $6-35, set meals $32-42, chef's tasting menu from $90; ☺11:30am-8:30pm) A bare-bones sushi bar near the airport for connoisseurs, who come for the chef's superbly fresh *omakase* and the rarely seen delicacies shipped in from around the globe. Don't let the location put you off. Reservations essential; BYOB.

Drinking & Nightlife

Every self-respecting bar in Honolulu has a *pupu* menu to complement the liquid sustenance, and some bars are as famous for their appetizers as for their good-times atmosphere. A key term to know is *pau hana* (literally 'stop work'), Hawaiian for 'happy hour.'

Gastropubs – mixing craft beers and clever cocktails with excellent casual food – are popular, especially in Kaka'ako and Kaimuki. For the widest assortment of bars with sunset views, head to Waikiki (p164).

Downtown

Workers flee Downtown at the end of the day. On weekdays you can find chain outlets for coffee, but otherwise walk west to the myriad bars of Chinatown or the hipster dens of Kaka'ako.

★ Bar Leather Apron
COCKTAIL BAR

(Map p90; ☑808-524-0808; www.barleather apron.com; 745 Fort St; ☺5pm-midnight Tue-Sat) An old-school bar with serious cocktails crafted by a new school of wizards. It's a casual yet elegant place to try one of four clever takes on the venerable old fashioned (trying all four is *not* recommended). The house mai tai arrives in a tiki-shaped box that's actually smoking. Ingredients include raisin-infused El Dorado Rum, spiced orgeat and ohia blossom honey.

Located on the mezzanine level of the Topa Financial Center.

Brue Bar

COFFEE

(Map p90; ☑ 808-441-4470; www.bruebar.com; 119 Merchant St; ☺ 7am-4pm Mon-Fri) In a gorgeous old building on Merchant St, Brue Bar's passion for quality is keeping both tea lovers and coffee aficionados happy. Order a *cortado*, an uncommon coffee drink created with aplomb here: the shot of espresso and steamed milk is served just right. Find a seat and plan out your day.

Chinatown

Long the center of Honolulu's most raucous nightlife, Chinatown's edgy bar scene revolves around N Hotel St, which was the city's notorious red light district through the 1990s. Today it's almost refined by comparison.

Hank's Cafe

BAR

(Map p90; ☑ 808-526-1410; www.hanktaufaasau.com; 1038 Nu'uanu Ave; ☺ 7am-2am) You can't get more low-key than this neighborhood dive bar. Live music rolls in some nights and the amiable regulars practically call it home as they watch sports on TV. As owner Hank Taufaasau puts it: 'I opened it as an art gallery to showcase my paintings and prints. But I put the bar in to pay the rent. Artists starve!'

Tea at 1024

TEAHOUSE

(Map p90; ☑ 808-521-9596; www.teaat1024.net; 1024 Nu'uanu Ave; ☺ 11am-1pm Wed-Fri, seatings at 11am, 1pm & 3pm Sat & Sun) This retro gem takes you back in time to an era when cutesy sandwiches, scones and cakes were enjoyed in the afternoon and eaten with a pinkie extended. Enjoy your choice of tea as you relax and watch the Chinatown crowd rush by the window. Set afternoon tea menus run from $25 per person; reservations recommended. There are even bonnets for you to don to add to the ambience.

Manifest

BAR

(Map p90; http://manifesthawaii.com; 32 N Hotel St; ☺ 8am-midnight Mon-Thu, to 2am Fri & Sat, 10am-5pm Sun; 🛜) Smack in the middle of the Hotel St nightlife, this lofty space features red-brick walls and provocative photos and paintings. It serves as a serene coffee shop by day and a cocktail bar by night, hosting movie and trivia nights and DJ sets.

Scarlet

GAY & LESBIAN

(Map p90; http://scarlethonolulu.com; 80 S Pau'ahi St; ☺ 8pm-2am Fri & Sat) Drag shows and DJs make this LGBTIQ bar in Chinatown jump. Loosely based on a dollhouse theme, Scarlet has a spacious dance floor flanked by a handful of VIP areas. The Tiki Rooms provide respite for those who need a mood shift from music, videos and corsets.

Bar 35

BAR

(Map p90; ☑ 808-537-3535; www.bar35hawaii.com; 35 N Hotel St ☺ 4pm-2am Mon-Fri, 6pm-2am Sat) This indoor-outdoor watering hole has a big selection of domestic and international beer, bottled and on tap, with fusion pizzas to absorb the suds. There's live music or DJs some weekend nights. It gets very lively at night, with a hard-drinking, young and upscale crowd overseen by Chinatown nightlife impresario Dave Stewart.

Next Door

CLUB

(Map p90; ☑ 808-200-4470; http://nextdoorhi.com; 43 N Hotel St; ☺ 8pm-2am Wed-Sat) This svelte cocktail lounge on the Hotel St strip is a brick-walled retreat with vivid red couches and flickering candles. DJs spin hip-hop, funk, mash-ups and retro sounds, while on other nights local bands play just about anything.

O'Toole's Irish Pub

IRISH PUB

(Map p90; ☑ 808-536-4138; https://irishpubshawaii.com; 902 Nu'uanu Ave; ☺ 10am-2am) Part of a collection of Irish-themed bars on O'ahu that includes Murphy's across the street, this pub doesn't bother with such niceties as food. Live music includes both Irish bands and rock. Needless to say, this corner of Chinatown throbs with green cheer on March 17.

Murphy's Bar & Grill

IRISH PUB

(Map p90; ☑ 808-531-0422; http://murphyshawaii.com; 2 Merchant St; ☺ 11am-2am Mon-Fri, 4pm-2am Sat & Sun) This stock Irish pub is in a lovely 1890 brick building on Merchant St. Yes, Guinness and Kilkenny are on tap. Food options run to familiar bar fare (potato skins, burgers) along with faux Irish classics such as shepherd's pie.

Ala Moana & Kaka'ako

★Honolulu Beerworks

MICROBREWERY

(Map p96; ☑ 808-589-2337; www.honolulubeerworks.com; 328 Cooke St, Kaka'ako; ☺ 11am-10pm Mon-Thu, to midnight Fri & Sat) This corrugated-metal-fronted warehouse microbrewery is one of O'ahu's best brewers. The inside is a cavernous mix of distressed wood and concrete, while outside there's a sweet little beer garden. Besides an ongoing mix of seasonal beers, try the regulars such as the lemony Pia Mahi 'Ai Honey Citrus Saison. Creative pub chow soaks up the suds.

Aloha Beer Co BREWERY

(Map p96; ☑808-544-1605; www.alohabeer. com; 700 Queen St, Kaka'ako; ⊙4-11pm) A big open-fronted brewery with more than a dozen house beers on offer at any time. Choices are edgy – try the Froot Lupes IPA, made with fruity hops and offering plenty of tropical essence offset by a pleasing bitterness. Food options are meaty, with charcuterie boards.

Chez Kenzo Bar And Grill BAR

(Map p96; ☑808-941-2439; www.chezkenzo.net; 1431 S King St, Ala Moana; ⊙5pm-1am) Sake heaven. There are generous pours of house sake, sake cocktails, sake-tinis, sake shots and sake flights, but it's not all sake at this local, sports-bar-style place. Enjoy the international menu as well.

Real Gastropub CRAFT BEER

(Map p96; ☑808-200-2739; www.realgastro pub.com; 506 Keawe St, Kaka'ako; ⊙2pm-11am Mon-Thu, noon-midnight Fri & Sat, noon-9pm Sun) In an industrial-chic space in the ground-floor corner of a modern apartment building, this pub is home to the noted craft brewer, Bent Tail Brewing. In addition to the

LAST OF THE GREAT TIKI BARS

Time warp! Who says all the great tiki bars are gone? Irreverent and kitschy, **La Mariana Sailing Club** (Map p86; ☑808-848-2800; www.lamarianasailing club.com; 50 Sand Island Access Rd, Kalihi; ⊙11am-9pm) is a thatch-walled 1950s joint on the harbor filled with modern-day sailors and bemused locals. Classic mai tais are as killer as the other tropical potions, complete with tiki-head swizzle sticks and tiny umbrellas. Grab a waterfront table and dream of sailing the South Pacific.

Much of the best tiki-themed decor and furniture was rescued by the owners from long lost Waikiki tiki bars, such as Don the Beachcomber. Food here is an afterthought.

house brews, there are numerous other local beers on tap. The menu is an appealing mix of fusion comfort food. Grab some fresh air at the picnic tables out front.

Brewseum BAR

(Map p96; ☑808-396-8112; http://homeofthe bravehawaii.com; 901 Waimanu St, Kaka'ako; ⊙bar 5-10pm Tue-Thu, to 11pm Fri & Sat) Part bar, part brewery, part museum of Hawaii in WWII, the Brewseum wears many hats – or should we say helmets. Military artifacts are jammed into every corner and line every wall. You could spend hours reading the framed mementos, but, fortunately, there's beer. Don't try to understand, just go.

Bevy BAR

(Map p96; ☑808-594-7445; www.bevyhawaii.com; 675 Auahi St, Kaka'ako; ⊙4pm-midnight Mon-Thu, to 2am Fri & Sat) 🍺 The old industrial area of Kaka'ako has become trendy and Bevy is one of the trendiest, offering inventive and classic cocktails in artsy surrounds. There's tasty small-plate food, served on wine-box tables on concrete floors under dangling exposed light bulbs, and an airy terrace.

Amuse Wine Bar WINE BAR

(Map p96; ☑808-237-5428; www.amusewine bar.com; 1250 Kapi'olani Blvd, Ala Moana; ⊙5-10pm Tue-Sat) Amuse, at the Honolulu Design Center, offers over 80 wines that you can pour yourself. Just put some credit on a house card and wander the taps sampling in 2oz tastes. There's also a full bar and upscale food for snacking – cheese plates etc.

District Nightclub CLUB

(Map p96; ☑808-949-1349; www.thedistrict nightclub.com; 1349 Kapi'olani Blvd, Ala Moana; ⊙11pm-4am Wed, 8pm-1am Thu, 10pm-4am Fri & Sat) District features a spacious dance floor, three bars, VIP seating and live DJ performances. Thursday nights are salsa nights. Despite the address being on Kapi'olani Blvd, it's buried in a parking garage off Kona St.

🍷 University Area & Manoa Valley

★**Beer Lab Hawaii** BREWERY

(Map p100; ☑808-888-0913; www.beerlabhi. com; 1010 University Ave, University area; ⊙11am-10pm Mon-Thu, to midnight Fri & Sat, to 7pm Sun) Three nuclear engineers working at Pearl Harbor, who were also beer geeks, opened this brewpub, where they brought a mad-scientist ethos to the beer. The ever-changing tap list easily has Hawaii's most experimental brews – they try all sorts of things with hops, flavorings, malts and techniques. You're welcome to bring in your own food. Two more locations have now opened.

★ Morning Glass Coffee COFFEE
(Map p86; ☑ 808-673-0065; www.morning glasscoffee.com; 2955 E Manoa Rd, Manoa Valley; ☺ 7am-3pm Mon-Fri, 7:30am-3pm Sat) Up the Manoa Valley, Morning Glass is a small, all-open-air coffee bar that serves terrific breakfasts and lunches. Try the hearty macaroni and cheese pancakes or fried rice and sausage omelet for breakfast. It gets busy.

Glazers Coffee CAFE
(Map p100; ☑ 808-391-6548; www.glazerscoffee.com; 2700 S King St, University area; ☺ 7am-10pm Mon-Thu, 7am-9pm Fri, 8am-10pm Sat & Sun; ☎) They're serious about brewing strong espresso drinks and batch-roasted coffee at this UH students' hangout. Kick back on comfy living-room sofas next to jazzy artwork and plentiful electrical outlets.

Pint & Jigger PUB
(Map p96; ☑ 808-744-9593; http://pintand jigger.com; 1936 S King St, University area; ☺ 4:30pm-midnight Mon-Thu, 8am-2am Fri-Sun) Red-brick walls and high-top tables make this gastropub appeal to a hip mix of foodies and beer geeks. It's got a shadowy vibe with stools at tall tables. The menu offers creative pub staples and brunch standbys such as Belgian waffles.

🍴 Kaimuki

Formaggio Wine Bar WINE BAR
(Map p86; ☑ 808-739-7719; www.formaggio honolulu.com; Market City Shopping Center, 2919 Kapi'olani Blvd; ☺ 5:30pm-midnight Mon-Thu, to 1am Fri & Sat) Ignore the grim exterior in this storefront below the Foodland supermarket, there are surprises in this cave-like Italian restaurant. Specifically, you'll be amazed at the wines on offer. The vast and carefully curated list wins popularity contests year-in and year-out. Some come for the pasta, but many more come for the extraordinary choices by the glass.

Brew'd Craft Pub CRAFT BEER
(Map p86; ☑ 808-732-2337; http://brewdcraft pub.com; 3441 Wai'alae Ave; ☺ 4pm-2am Mon-Sat) A neighborhood gastropub with heaps of wood

and stone in its decor. The knowledgeable staff help you sort out the impressively deep beer list and there's a modestly priced menu of pub food, good for snacking or a meal.

Curb COFFEE
(Map p86; ☑ 808-367-0757; https://the curbkaimuki.com; 3408 Wai'alae Ave; ☺ 6:30am-4pm Mon-Fri, 7am-3pm Sat & Sun; ☎) You'll get a buzz just from the coffee smells as you step into this small cafe, where they are passionate about their locally roasted beans. The vibe is modern, the tables small.

☆ Entertainment

The local events calendar is fairly busy. Good online sources for what's on include *Honolulu Star-Advertiser* (www.staradvertiser.com/calendar) and *Honolulu Magazine* (www.honolulumagazine.com), but you're best off checking with specific venues.

Live Music

You can find plenty of tourist-friendly, island-flavored live music in Waikiki (p167). In Honolulu, there are regular performances in a variety of styles in Chinatown and at locations widely scattered around the city.

★ Royal Hawaiian Band LIVE MUSIC
(Map p90; ☑ 808-922-5331; www.rhb-music.com) Founded in 1836 by King Kamehameha III, the Royal Hawaiian Band is the only band in the US with a royal legacy, and is the only full-time municipal band in the country. The band plays all over O'ahu (check out the calendar online), including a free concert most Fridays at noon at 'Iolani Palace (p87).

Dragon Upstairs LIVE MUSIC
(Map p90; ☑ 808-526-1411; 2nd fl, 1038 Nu'uanu Ave, Chinatown; ☺ 8pm-2am Thu-Sat) Right above Hank's Cafe in Chinatown, this laid-back hideaway with a sedate vibe and lots of funky stylized masks on the walls and mirrors hosts a rotating lineup of jazz, blues and folk. Occasional $5 cover charge. Try the specialty drink – the pineapple upside-down cake.

Hawaiian Brian's LIVE PERFORMANCE
(Map p96; ☑ 808-946-1343; http://hbsocial club.com; 2nd fl, 1680 Kapi'olani Blvd, Ala Moana; cover free-$20; ☺ 2pm-2am Mon-Fri, 6am-2am Sat & Sun) The 500-person Crossroads Concert Hall here sees acts of all kinds, especially blues, soul and rock. It's also home to the HawaiiSlam (p126), and there are pool

tables. Although sizable, the club is buried in a parking garage. To reach it from the street, you have to take the stairs through a 24 Fitness health club.

Republik
LIVE MUSIC

(Map p96; ☑ 808-941-7469; http://jointhere publik.com; 1349 Kapi'olani Blvd, Ala Moana; ☺ lounge 6pm-2am on performance nights) Honolulu's most intimate concert hall for touring and local acts – indie rockers, punk and metal bands, even ukulele players – has a graffiti-bomb vibe and backlit black walls that trippily light up. Adjoining the concert space is the Safehouse, a sleek lounge that's a vision in white.

Jazz Minds Art & Café
LIVE MUSIC

(Map p96; ☑ 808-945-0800; http://jazzhonolulu. com; 1661 Kapi'olani Blvd, Ala Moana; ☺ 9pm-2am Mon-Sat) Hidden back off the street, this brick-walled lounge with an almost speakeasy ambience pulls in top island talent – fusion jazz, funk, bebop, hip-hop, surf rock and minimalist acts. Cover charges average $10. This is the state's only dedicated jazz club.

Anna O'Brien's
LIVE MUSIC

(Map p100; ☑ 808-946-5190; http://irishpubs hawaii.com; 2440 S Beretania St, University area; cover free-$10; ☺ 2pm-2am Mon-Fri, from 10am Sat & Sun) A college dive bar, part roadhouse and part art house, this Irish-themed bar has a club upstairs with live music by local bands. Acts include reggae, alt-rock, punk and metal. Also: regular DJs, comedy nights and more.

Performing Arts

Hawaii's capital city is home to a broad array of cultural institutions big and small.

★ Hawaii Theatre
PERFORMING ARTS

(Map p90; ☑ box office 808-528-0506; www.hawaii theatre.com; 1130 Bethel St, Chinatown) Beautifully restored, this architecturally significant historic theater (p94) is a major venue for dance, music and theater. Performances include top Hawaii musicians, contemporary plays, international touring acts and film festivals. The theater also hosts the annual Ka Himeni Ana competition of singers in the traditional *nahenahe* style.

★ Kumu Kahua Theatre
THEATER

(Map p90; ☑ 808-536-4441; www.kumuka hua.org; 46 Merchant St, Chinatown) ⚑ In the restored 1871 Kamehameha V Post Office building, this little 100-seat treasure is dedicated to premiering works by Hawaii's playwrights. Themes focus on contemporary multicultural island life, often richly peppered with Hawaiian pidgin.

Manoa Valley Theatre
THEATER

(Map p86; ☑ 808-988-6131; http://manoaval leytheatre.com; 2833 E Manoa Rd, Manoa Valley) This small community 150-seat theater puts on plays and musicals from mainstream to off-Broadway. It was formed in 1969 by UH Theatre Department grads. The season runs from September to July.

Hawai'i Symphony Orchestra
CLASSICAL MUSIC

(Map p96; ☑ 808-946-8742; http://hawaiisym phonyorchestra.org; Neal S Blaisdell Concert Hall, 777 Ward Ave, Kaka'ako) The second-oldest orchestra in the USA west of the Rocky Mountains, the Hawai'i Symphony Orchestra was founded in 1900. It plays at the Neal S Blaisdell Concert Hall near Ala Moana. Check the website for ticket sources around town that let you avoid excessive Ticketmaster fees.

HawaiiSlam
PERFORMING ARTS

(Map p96; ☑ 808-387-9664; www.hawaiislam.com; Hawaiian Brian's, 1680 Kapi'olani Blvd, Ala Moana; before/after 8:30pm $3/5; ☺ 8:30pm 1st Thu of each month) Founded and hosted by Kealoha (the Poet Laureate of Hawai'i), HawaiiSlam is the largest registered poetry slam in the world. International wordsmiths, artists, musicians, MCs and DJs share the stage, often with over 500 in attendance. For aspiring spoken-word stars, sign-up starts at 7:30pm. Held at Hawaiian Brian's (p125) in the Crossroads Concert Hall.

Arts at Marks Garage
PERFORMING ARTS

(Map p90; ☑ 808-521-2903; www.artsatmarks. com; 1159 Nu'uanu Ave, Downtown; ☺ hours vary) On the cutting edge of the Chinatown arts scene, this artist-run, nonprofit community arts center, gallery and performance space puts on a variety of live shows, from stand-up comedy, burlesque cabaret nights and conversations with island artists to live jazz and Hawaiian music. It has regular special exhibitions by local artists.

Neal S Blaisdell Center
PERFORMING ARTS

(Map p96; ☑ 808-768-5400; www.blaisdell center.com; 777 Ward Ave, Kaka'ako) A cultural linchpin, this modern performing-arts complex stages symphony and chamber-music concerts, opera performances and ballet recitals, prestigious hula competitions and Broadway shows. Big-name pop and rock touring acts also play here.

Ala Moana Center Stage
PERFORMING ARTS

(Map p96; ☑808-955-9517; www.alamoana center.com; ground fl, Center Court, Ala Moana Center, 1450 Ala Moana Blvd, Ala Moana) The mega shopping center's courtyard area is the venue for all sorts of free island entertainment, including music by O'ahu musicians and the Royal Hawaiian Band, Japanese *taiko* drumming and Sunday-afternoon *keiki* (children's) hula shows. Most days there's a hula show at 1pm.

Cinemas

Honolulu has several multiplex cinemas showing the usual latest Hollywood releases.

★ Doris Duke Theatre
CINEMA

(Map p96; ☑box office 808-532-6097; http:// honolulumuseum.org; Honolulu Museum of Art, 900 S Beretania St, Ala Moana; film tickets $12) The Doris Duke Theatre shows an array of experimental, alternative, retro-classic and art-house films, especially groundbreaking documentaries, inside the Honolulu Museum of Art, which has had a lauded film program since the 1930s. The theater also hosts lectures, performances and concerts.

Parking is diagonally opposite the museum and theater at 1111 Victoria St (enter off Beretania or Young St), and costs $5. From Waikiki, take bus 2 or 13.

Movie Museum
CINEMA

(Map p86; ☑808-735-8771; www.kaimukihawaii .com/d/c/movie-museum.html; 3566 Harding Ave, Kaimuki; tickets $5; ☺noon-8pm Thu-Mon) In the Kaimuki neighborhood, east of the UH Manoa campus, watch classics, foreign flicks and indie films – including some Hawaii premieres – in a tiny theater equipped with digital sound and just 20 comfy Barcaloungers. It faces the parking lot behind Harding Ave.

Regal Dole Cannery ScreenX
CINEMA

(Map p86; ☑844-462-7342; www.regmovies.com; 735B Iwilei Rd; ☺11am-11pm) This massive complex in what was the old Dole pineapple canning factory just west of Chinatown features 18 theaters, which play current-release films. Seldom crowded, it has decent seating and a variety of special screens, such as IMAX and RPX. There are shops, eateries and plenty of history in the complex.

Consolidated Theatres Ward
CINEMA

(Map p96; ☑808-594-7044; www.consolidated theatres.com; Ward Centre, 1044 Auahi St, Ala Moana; tickets $10-20; ☺10am-midnight) Part of the Ward Centre, this modern movie theater complex features 16 theaters. Head upstairs to see Hollywood blockbusters and a selection of international films. Among the screens is the enormous 'Titan XC,' which features a deafening sound system.

🛍 Shopping

Honolulu has unique shops and multiple malls offering plenty of local flavor, from traditional flower lei stands and ukulele factories to Hawaiiana souvenir shops, and from contemporary island-style clothing boutiques to vintage and antiques stores. The Ala Moana Center alone has over 340 stores and restaurants in the world's largest open-air shopping center.

Shopping Malls

Ala Moana Center
MALL

(Map p96; ☑808-955-9517; www.alamoana center.com; 1450 Ala Moana Blvd, Ala Moana; ☺9:30am-9pm Mon-Sat, 10am-7pm Sun; 🚗) This vast and bewildering open-air shopping mall and its 340-plus department stores and mostly chain stores draws mobs of locals and tourists. A handful of Hawaii specialty shops are thrown into the mix. Stores tend to be tony, but you'll also find the big-box discounter Target. Note that 'information' counters are often shills for timeshare vendors.

Salt at Our Kaka'ako
MALL

(Map p96; ☑808-260-5692; http://saltatkaka ako.com; 691 Auahi St) This block-sized open-air mall mixes local shops and restaurants with national chains. It matches the neighborhood's postindustrial vibe and has numerous interesting outlets, as well as the hip Bevy (p124) bar. There's a large, mural-covered parking garage buried in the complex.

Ward Centre
MALL

(Map p96; ☑808-591-8411; www.wardvillage shops.com; 1240 Ala Moana Blvd, Ala Moana) Houses a number of restaurants, bars and interesting locally owned shops.

The beaches at Ala Moana Regional Park beckon from just south.

Hawaiiana

★ **Tin Can Mailman** VINTAGE
(Map p90; ☎808-524-3009; http://tincanmail man.net; 1026 Nu'uanu Ave, Chinatown; ☺11am-5pm Mon-Fri, to 4pm Sat) If you're a big fan of vintage tiki wares and 20th-century Ha-waiiana books, you'll fall in love with this little Chinatown vintage collectibles shop. Thoughtfully curated treasures include jewelry and ukuleles, silk aloha shirts, tropical-wood furnishings, vinyl records, rare prints and tourist brochures from the post-WWII tourism boom. Excellent selection of hard-to-find books too.

★ **Cindy's Lei Shoppe** ARTS & CRAFTS
(Map p90; ☎808-536-6538; www.cindysleishop pe.com; 1034 Maunakea St, Chinatown; ☺6am-6pm Mon-Sat, to 5pm Sun) At this inviting little shop, a Chinatown landmark, you can watch aunties craft flower lei made of orchids, plumeria, twining maile, lantern *'ilima* (flowering ground-cover) and ginger for all occasions ($8 to $10). Several other lei shops clustered nearby will also pack lei for you to carry back home. If worried about parking, you can order online and arrange curbside pickup.

Kamaka Hawaii MUSICAL INSTRUMENTS
(Map p96; ☎808-531-3165; www.kamaka hawaii.com; 550 South St, Kaka'ako; ☺8am-4pm Mon-Fri) ✐ Kamaka specializes in gorgeous handcrafted ukuleles made on O'ahu since 1916, with prices starting at around $1000. Call ahead for free 30-minute factory tours, usually starting at 10:30am Tuesday through Friday. There are no retail sales on site, but they can tell you where to purchase both new and secondhand Kamaka ukuleles.

KoAloha Ukulele MUSICAL INSTRUMENTS
(Map p96; ☎808-847-4911; http://koaloha.com; Iolani, 1234 Kona St, Ala Moana; ☺9-11:30am & 12:30-4:30pm Mon-Fri) Hidden off a 2nd-floor parking deck, this small shop modestly proclaims that it's the source of the finest hand-made ukuleles in the world. For once the boast may be true. See for yourself on one of the free weekday tours (1pm) of the on-site factory, where you'll see artisans crafting ukuleles from the finest woods.

Aloha Board Shop SPORTS & OUTDOORS
(Map p100; ☎808-955-6030; www.alohaboard shop.com; 2658 S King St, University area; ☺10am-6pm Mon-Sat, to 5pm Sun) Head here for all your boarding needs, be they surfboards, bodyboards, skateboards or anything associated. There's new and used, all sorts of accessories, knowledgeable and helpful staff, plus parking out back. Plenty of aloha here with a relaxed friendly vibe. Rent a top-quality surfboard (per hour/day $35/70).

Owens & Co HOMEWARES
(Map p90; ☎808-531-4300; http://owens andcompany.com; 1152 Nu'uanu Ave, Chinatown; ☺10am-6pm Mon-Fri, 11am-4pm Sat) All sorts of items for the home from local artisans and companies can be found in this cute corner shop. Handmade tea towels, decorator items, books, kitchen accessories and more.

Hungry Ear Records MUSIC
(Map p96; ☎808-262-2175; http://hungryear.com; Salt at Our Kaka'ako, 675 Auahi St, Suite E3-200, Kaka'ako; ☺10am-6pm) Head here to look for rare Hawaii albums. Recently relocated to the hip Salt at Our Kaka'ako development, you can peruse used and new vinyl and CDs, with plenty of local music up for grabs. The owner offers copious and valuable advice.

Surf 'N Hula VINTAGE
(Map p86; ☎808-428-5518; 3588 Wai'alae Ave, Kaimuki; ☺10:30am-5pm Mon-Sat) One of the pleasures of a Kaimuki stroll is discovering little shops like this one for vintage Hawaii collectibles. The husband and wife owners have a deep knowledge of local history. The shop displays a wealth of everyday items and rarer finds from O'ahu's recent past.

Antique Alley ANTIQUES
(Map p96; ☎808-941-8551; www.portaloha .com/antiquealley; 1030 Queen St, Kaka'ako; ☺noon-5pm Mon, Tue & Thu-Sat) Unbelievably crammed with rare collectibles and other cast-off memorabilia from Hawaii through the decades, this co-op shop, which once cameoed on PBS' *Antiques Roadshow,* sells just about any Hawaiiana that you can imagine buying, from poi pounders and traditional fish hooks to vintage hula dolls and Matson cruise-liner artifacts. Note: upscale developments are looming in from all sides.

Old Ironside Tattoo BODY ART
(Map p90; ☎808-520-0213; www.facebook.com/ oldironsidetattoo; 1033 Smith St, Chinatown; ☺noon-8pm Mon-Sat) Come here for the Hawaiian-style tattoos in Sailor Jerry's old shop. This is where WWII sailors and soldiers fulfilled the third part of their legendary motto: 'stewed, screwed and tattooed.' Back then, a tattoo cost $3; expect to pay

$100 for a deposit these days. A major venue during the Sailor Jerry Festival held in June.

Used Surfboards Hawaii   SPORTS & OUTDOORS
(Map p96; 808-591-9995; www.usedsurf boardshawaii.com; 762a Queen St, Kaka'ako; 10am-6pm Mon-Fri, to 5pm Sat, to 3pm Sun) Why wipe out your budget buying a new surfboard when you can get a used board by a famous shaper for a fraction of the cost? This slick warehouse has hundreds of surfboards on display. Browse dozens of choices for any style and budget. They ship boards worldwide – even ones they didn't sell.

Flowers By Jr Lou & T   GIFTS & SOUVENIRS
(Map p100; 808-941-2022; 2652 S King St, University area; 7:30am-7:30pm) Ignore the name of this open-front store – what you're really here for is displayed in proliferation across the front: bonsai! Hundreds of the miniature living shrubs and trees are arrayed for inspection. Examples of the Japanese bonsai art are affordable: $80 will get you a small bush.

Mālie Organics   COSMETICS
(Map p96; 808-946-2543; www.malie.com; Ala Moana Center, 1450 Ala Moana Blvd, Ala Moana; 9:30am-9pm Mon-Sat, 10am-7pm Sun) Kauai-based Mālie offers all-natural, organic luxury spa and beauty products based on the botanical benefits of Hawaii's fruits and flowers. All ingredients are sustainably grown, and there is an aroma collection, bath and body products and a range of travel goods.

Fabric Mart   TEXTILES
(Map p96; 808-947-4466; http://hawaii fabricmart.com; 1631 Kalakaua Ave, Ala Moana; 9am-7pm Mon-Sat, to 6pm Sun) This fabric store has masses of colorful Hawaiian print materials, which can be used for everything from cushion covers, curtains and dresses to aloha shirts. Buy them at best prices by the yard. The only place on the island with more fabric is the main store (p182) out in 'Aiea.

T&C Surf   SPORTS & OUTDOORS
(Map p96; 808-973-5199; www.tcsurf.com; Ala Moana Center, 1450 Ala Moana Blvd, Ala Moana; 9:30am-9pm Mon-Sat, 10am-7pm Sun) Big international surf design company T&C got its start just west of Honolulu in 1971. Today it's still based in 'Aiea and has shops worldwide. This mall store displays the whole range of surfing accessories, gear and clothing, each

---

SAILOR JERRY TATTOOS

It won't take too many days on the island to figure out that you're in the land of the tattoo. Long before they became part of international pop culture, tattoos were an integral element of Hawaiian and Polynesian culture. The word itself, 'tattoo,' comes from the Polynesian word *tatau*, meaning 'to write.'

During WWII, 'stewed, screwed and tattooed' was the proud motto of sailors and soldiers stationed in Honolulu. Hotel St was lined with brothels, bars and many tattoo parlors, but the legendary guy to get your $3 tattoo from was Norman Collins, aka Sailor Jerry. Collins died in 1973, but his legacy lives on with the annual Sailor Jerry Festival (p109) in Chinatown in June. A number of venues open up with music, stand-up comedy and movies, and you can even get a tattoo or pick up Sailor Jerry memorabilia at his old shop, Old Ironside Tattoo.

---

branded with the distinctive T&C yin-and-yang logo.

Bookstores

The bookstore at the visitor center (p178) of the Pearl Harbor National Memorial has a superb selection of books about the attack as well as Honolulu during the war.

★ Da Shop   BOOKS
(Map p86; 808-421-9460; http://dashophnl.com; 3565 Harding Ave, Kaimuki; 11am-4pm Mon & Sun, 10am-6pm Tue-Sat;) Hidden away on a Kaimuki back street is Honolulu's best bookstore. Run by a local publisher, the carefully curated selection of books includes plenty of staff recommendations and Hawaii titles. There are regular events featuring authors.

Nā Mea Hawaii   BOOKS
(Map p96; 808-596-8885; www.nameahawaii .com; Ward Centre, 1200 Ala Moana Blvd, Ala Moana; 10am-9pm Mon-Sat, to 6pm Sun) So much more than just a bookstore stocking Hawaiiana tomes, CDs and DVDs, this cultural gathering spot also sells beautiful silkscreened fabrics, koa-wood bowls, Hawaiian quilts, fish-hook jewelry and hula supplies. Check for special events, including author readings, live local music and cultural classes (p108).

Hakubundo   BOOKS

(Map p96; ☎808-947-5503; http://hakubundo.
com; Ward Centre, 1200 Ala Moana Blvd, Ala Moana;
⊙10am-9pm Mon-Sat, to 6pm Sun) For over 100
years, Hakubundo has been selling books in
Japanese and books in English about Japan
in Honolulu. Their magazine racks have
been a vital connection to home for generations of people in the local Japanese community. Today, this modern shop still sells
books and magazines, as well as high-quality
Japanese pens and other stationery.

UH Manoa Bookstore   BOOKS

(Map p100; ☎808-956-6884; www.bookstore.ha
waii.edu; Campus Center, 2465 Campus Rd, University area; ⊙8am-6pm Mon-Fri, 9am-12:30pm Sat)
Head to the UH campus bookstore to get all
that cool UH gear that locals wear, including T-shirts, singlets, caps and hoodies. Of
course, there are also books, many of which
are hard-to-find academic titles by UH profs
on myriad Hawaii-related topics.

Galleries

★Honolulu Museum
of Art Shop   ARTS & CRAFTS

(Map p96; ☎808-532-8703; http://honolulu
museum.org; 900 S Beretania St, Ala Moana;
⊙10am-4:30pm Tue-Sun) The shop at the Honolulu Museum of Art provides an opportunity to purchase superb Hawaiian artworks
and crafts. On offer are publications, stationery, prints, posters, and works by Hawaii
artisans and designers that won't be found
outside the islands. No ticket is needed to
visit the shop.

Parking is diagonally opposite the museum at 1111 Victoria St (enter off Beretania or
Young St), and costs $5. From Waikiki, take
bus 2 or 13.

Louis Pohl Gallery   ART

(Map p90; ☎808-521-1812; www.louispohlgallery
.com; 1142 Bethel St, Chinatown; ⊙11am-5pm

> **ℹ CHINATOWN ART
> GALLERIES**
>
> Pick up a free art map from any of
> Chinatown's galleries, most within a few
> blocks of the Hawaii Theatre (p94). You
> can also find good maps online at www.
> firstfridayhawaii.com. And the entire
> area celebrates art on the first Friday of
> every month, at the eponymous festival
> (p120).

Tue-Fri, to 3pm Sat) This gallery in Chinatown
features paintings by contemporary island
artists and works by the former 'living treasure' of Hawaii, Louis Pohl, who died in 1999.
Gallery profits fund programs of the Louis
Pohl Foundation, which focuses on pre-
serving Pohl's artwork and legacy, and promoting Hawaiian artists and art education
programs.

Pegge Hopper Gallery   ART

(Map p90; ☎808-524-1160; www.peggehopper.
com; 1164 Nu'uanu Ave, Chinatown; ⊙11am-4pm
Tue-Fri, to 3pm Sat) Hopper moved to Honolulu in 1963, opened her gallery in 1983,
and has been selling distinctive colorful
prints and paintings depicting island wom-
en ever since. The gallery also hosts special
exhibitions.

Food & Drink

For serious shopping for O'ahu's food bounty with an Asian accent, don't miss Chinatown's markets (p95).

★Lonohana Estate Chocolate   CHOCOLATE

(Map p96; ☎808-286-8531; www.lonohana.
com; Salt at Our Kaka'ako, 324 Coral St, Kaka'ako;
⊙11am-6pm Sun-Thu, to 8pm Fri & Sat) 🌿 All the
cocoa beans used for the chocolate sold in
this exquisite little shop are grown on a 14-
acre plot on O'ahu's North Shore. The brains
behind the operation is Seneca Klassen, who
grows the beans, manufactures the chocolate and creates the treats sold here in his
shop. Sustainability is a core tenet of the
company.

Lin's Hawaiian Snacks   FOOD

(Map p96; ☎808-597-8899; www.linsmarket
hawaii.com; 401 Kamake'e St, Ala Moana;
⊙9:30am-9pm Mon-Sat, 10am-7pm Sun) A crack
seed store for the modern age. Wide and tidy
aisles allow easy access to dozens of containers of the island treats. Also serves tea,
smoothies, milkshakes and, yes, shave ice.

Lion Coffee   COFFEE

(Map p86; ☎808-843-4294; www.lioncoffee.com;
1555 Kalani St, Kalihi; ⊙6am-5pm Mon-Fri, 9am-
3pm Sat; 🛜) In an out-of-the-way warehouse
west of downtown en route to the airport,
this discount grown-in-Hawaii coffee giant
roasts myriad flavors, ranging from straight-
up strong (100% Kona 24-Karat and Diamond Head espresso blend) to outlandishly
wacky (chocolate mac-nut, toasted coconut).
There are 30-minute tours at 10:30am and
12:30pm Monday to Friday, which include

complimentary tastings. There's also a full espresso bar.

Sake Shop
ALCOHOL

(Map p96; ☑ 808-947-7253; http://sakeshop hawaii.com; 575 Cooke St, Kaka'ako; ⊙noon-8pm Mon-Sat, to 5pm Sun) This store is like a gold mine for those interested in Japanese sake. O'ahu's only dedicated sake shop, you'll find everything associated with rice wine here, including sake imported from Japan and sake from various makers on the mainland. The owner and staff offer great advice.

Sun Chong Grocery
FOOD

(Map p90; ☑ 808-537-3525; 127 N Hotel St, Chinatown; ⊙ 7:30am-5pm) Wade into the jammed aisles at Sun Chong's shop to browse for dried, sugared and spiced crack seed (Chinese preserved fruit), from candied ginger and pineapple to dried squash and lotus root. The candied lemon rinds are a treat. You'll also find all manner of piles of dry goods, such as noodles.

Wholesale Unlimited
FOOD

(Map p86; ☑ 808-834-2900; www.wholesaleun limitedhawaii.com; 960 Ahua St, Greater Honolulu; ⊙9am-6pm Mon-Fri, to 4:30pm Sat, 10am-3:30pm Sun) This place will knock your socks off if you are into crack seed, dried fruit, dried veggies, Japanese *sembei* (rice crackers), dried seafood, cookies, jerky, taro chips, sauces, seasonings, nuts, jams, jellies, candies or chocolate. This is the flagship store, but there are several more locations across Honolulu and O'ahu.

Honolulu Cookie Company
FOOD

(Map p96; ☑ 808-945-0787; www.honolulucookie. com; Ala Moana Center, 1450 Ala Moana Blvd, Ala Moana; ⊙9am-9pm Mon-Sat, to 7pm Sun) This place caters to all your cookie needs, be they immediate cravings or beautifully packaged souvenirs to take home. Everything is Hawaii-inspired and packs come in boxes shaped like surfboards and pineapples. Lots of island flavors such as *liliko'i* (passion fruit), mango and macadamia. This shop is in the mall's Makai Market Food Court on the 1st floor.

There are outlets in major resorts across O'ahu and Hawaii.

Local Wear

Kiholo Kai
CLOTHING

(Map p90; ☑ 808-936-9407; http://kiholokai.com; 125 Merchant St, Downtown; ⊙9am-4:30pm) Home to O'ahu's finest Hawaii shirts for

TOP CRACK SEED

Crack seed, the traditional treat loved in Hawaii (p40), confounds visitors. Is it sweet? Sour? Salty? *What* is it? Answers to all these questions can be found at **Kaimukī Crack Seed Store** (Map p86; ☑ 808-737-1022; 1156 Koko Head Ave, Kaimuki; ⊙ 9:30am-5:30pm Mon-Sat; 🖰), a timeless crack seed paradise in Kaimuki. Sample your way through the myriad versions on offer.

This tiny mom-and-pop candy store vends overflowing glass jars of made-from-scratch crack seed, plus addictive frozen slushies spiked with *li hing mui* (dried plums in rock salt). There's a mind-blowing number of edibles in here to choose from. Try the pickled mango.

men, this elegant shop is filled with refined patterns that will work nicely for an afternoon soiree at your waterfront estate. There's a wide range of natural fabrics and sizes – you can get your shirt (they start at $100) in traditional or tailored fit.

Reyn Spooner
CLOTHING

(Map p96; ☑ 808-949-5929; www.reynspooner. com; Ala Moana Center, 1450 Ala Moana Blvd, Ala Moana; ⊙9:30am-9pm Mon-Sat, 10am-7pm Sun) The original Reyn Spooner aloha shirt store opened in the Ala Moana Center in 1962 and the company has never looked back. 'Reverse print' aloha shirts have been the signature product since 1964. Head to the 2nd floor (Macy's end) for a wide selection of classic Hawaiian wear.

Manuheali'i
CLOTHING

(Map p96; ☑ 808-942-9868; www.manuhealii.com; 930 Punahou St, Ala Moana; ⊙ 9:30am-6pm Mon-Fri, 9am-4pm Sat, 10am-3pm Sun) Look to this island-born shop for original and modern designs. Hawaiian musicians often sport Manuheali'i's bold-print silk aloha shirts. Flowing synthetic print and knit dresses and wrap tops take inspiration from the traditional muumuu, but are transformed into spritely contemporary looks. It's in a quiet backstreet location.

Fighting Eel
CLOTHING

(Map p90; ☑ 808-738-9300; www.fightingeel.com; 1133 Bethel St, Chinatown; ⊙10am-6pm Mon-Sat, to 4pm Sun) A one-stop made-in-Hawaii shop for blowsy, draped dresses in modern solids, resort flowers and geometric prints. They're perfect whether you're hitting the beach in girly flip-flops or strapping on heels for an island wedding.

This is the main store in the Downtown area, but Fighting Eel is also in Waikiki and Kahala Mall.

Tori Richard   CLOTHING
(Map p96; ☑ 808-952-9105; www.toririchard. com; Ala Moana Center, 1450 Ala Moana Blvd, Ala Moana; ⊙ 9:30am-9pm Mon-Sat, 10am-7pm Sun) This popular Honolulu-based company has been producing men's and women's resort wear for 60 years. On the 2nd floor of the Ala Moana Center (Macy's end), you'll find one of their bright and breezy stores offering up sophisticated and attractive aloha wear, including shirts for men, dresses for women, and shorts and pants.

Barrio Vintage   CLOTHING
(Map p90; ☑ 808-674-7156; www.barriovintage. com; 1161 Nu'uanu Ave, Chinatown; ⊙ 11am-6pm Mon-Thu, to 7pm Fri, to 5pm Sat) One-of-a-kind fashions from decades past jostle on the racks of this Chinatown secondhand shop, showing off mod dresses and skirts for women, hip jackets and pants for men, designer handbags and glamazon shoes.

T&L Muumuu Factory   CLOTHING
(Map p96; ☑ 808-941-4183; www.muumuu factory.com; 614 Cooke St, Kaka'ako; ⊙ 9am-6pm Mon-Sat, 10am-4pm Sun) So much flammable aloha wear in one space! Bold-print muumuus for women run in sizes from super-model skinny to Polynesian island queen. On the men's side, aloha shirt sizes run from XS up to 6XL, so you know they ca-

ter for everyone. All the garments are designed and made locally at this family-run operation.

Roberta Oaks   CLOTHING
(Map p90; ☑ 808-526-1111; www.robertaoaks.com; 19 N Pau'ahi St, Chinatown; ⊙ 10am-6pm Mon-Fri, to 4am Sat, 11:30am-4pm Sun) The Roberta Oaks men's tailored shirts – aloha-print or *palaka* (plantation-style checkered) – are perhaps even more appealing than the women's strappy sundresses and super-short board shorts. That's not all there is though – there are also bandanas, bags and beach gear.

Island Slipper   SHOES
(Map p96; ☑ 808-947-1222; www.islandslipper. com; Ala Moana Center, 1450 Ala Moana Blvd, Ala Moana; ⊙ 9:30am-9pm Mon-Sat, 10am-7pm Sun) Across Honolulu and Waikiki, scores of stores sell flip-flops (aka 'rubbah slippahs'), but nobody else carries such ultra-comfy suede and leather styles – all made in Hawaii since 1946 – let alone such giant sizes (as one clerk told us, 'We fit *all* the island people.').

Hilo Hattie   CLOTHING
(Map p96; ☑ 808-973-3266; www.hilohattie.com; Ala Moana Center, 1450 Ala Moana Blvd, Ala Moana; ⊙ 9:30am-9pm Mon-Sat, 10am-7pm Sun) While the real Hilo Hattie was a Native Hawaiian singer, hula dancer, actress and comedian who died in 1979, her name lives on in this Ala Moana Center store and in other shops throughout the islands. You'll find all kinds of aloha wear here, including men's, women's and children's clothing, plus plenty of souvenirs and popular chocolate-covered macadamia nuts.

ⓘ PARKING
....
➡ Downtown and Chinatown have on-street metered parking; it's reasonably easy to find an empty space on weekends, but nearly impossible on weekdays. Bring lots of quarters.

➡ Pay parking is also available at municipal and private garages throughout the busier parts of the city.

➡ Most shopping centers, larger stores and some restaurants provide free parking for customers, although the number of spaces can be very limited.

ⓘ Information

ACCESSIBLE TRAVEL
➡ As a city, Honolulu is traveler-friendly to those with disabilities, especially at the large hotels and resorts.

➡ TheBus has disability fares (one-way fare $1) and buses will usually 'kneel' if you are unable to use the steps.

➡ Bring your disability parking placard from home to use designated disabled-parking spaces.

DANGERS & ANNOYANCES
The north side of Chinatown, particularly along Nu'uanu Stream and the River St Pedestrian Mall, should be avoided after dark.

THE TRAIN IS COMING...

Anyone caught in Honolulu's coagulated traffic, both on the freeways like the H-1 and the surface streets, will understand the allure of soaring above it all on a fast train. And that's just what is promised with the Honolulu Authority for Rapid Transit (HART) project. Venture west of the city to the airport, Pearl Harbor and beyond and you'll see the huge concrete viaducts for tracks and stations being built high overhead.

However, there has been nothing but trouble on this ticket to paradise. Waves of missed deadlines have put completion years past what was originally promised, while the budget has soared from $4 billion to over $8 billion to date.

But the promise of zipping from Ala Moana to the airport in 16 minutes or Pearl Harbor in 19 minutes is irresistible and keeps support for the trains solid despite the debacles. Plans call for the 20-mile system to be completed in three stages, of which only the last will benefit most visitors.

Western Half Sometime in 2020 or 2021, the portion of HART from Aloha Stadium through 'Aiea, Waipahu and on to Kapolei will start running. None of this will help tourists much.

Airport Guideway In 2022, trains will reach the airport station at the terminals and continue on to the edge of Kalihi. But this still won't help tourists much, as none of the stops from the airport are close to where most tourists stay.

City Center The final portion of HART will be revolutionary, serving Kalihi, Chinatown, Downtown, Kaka'ako and Ala Moana. It will transform travel for locals and visitors alike. The one catch is that as of 2019, no contracts to build this portion had been signed, so the promised completion date of 2025 is likely illusionary.

There are a lot of homeless people in Honolulu, particularly in Chinatown after dark as well as most of the parks during daylight hours.

MEDIA

Honolulu Magazine (www.honolulumagazine. com) Glossy monthly magazine, website and app covering arts, culture, fashion, shopping, lifestyle and cuisine.

Honolulu Star-Advertiser (www.staradver tiser.com) Honolulu's daily newspaper has an excellent website and app with calendar listings.

KINE 105.1 FM (www.hawaiian105.com) Popular community radio station with Hawaiian music played 24/7.

MEDICAL SERVICES

Queen's Medical Center (☎ 808-691-1000; www.queensmedicalcenter.net; 1301 Punchbowl St, Downtown; ⊙24hr) O'ahu's biggest, best-equipped hospital has a 24-hour emergency room downtown.

ⓘ Getting There & Around

Once you're on O'ahu, getting to Honolulu is easy using either your own rental wheels or TheBus public transportation system.

BICYCLE

Honolulu has a shared bicycle scheme called Biki (http://gobiki.org). There are dozens of stations for the distinctive turquoise bikes all over Honolulu and Waikiki. Like other bike-sharing schemes worldwide, you pick up a bike at one and drop it at another. Pay for the service with a credit card at the station or using the handy app.

Biki rates for non-Hawaii residents are $4 for the first 30 minutes and $4.50 for every 30 minutes thereafter. Or you can buy a total of 300 minutes of use for $25, which can consist of multiple trips – by far the best value.

BUS

Just northwest of Waikiki, the Ala Moana Center mall (p127) is the central transfer point for TheBus (p311), O'ahu's public transportation system. It offers a network of useful services, but the lack of useful overall system maps makes using TheBus a lot harder than it should.

CAR

Major car-rental companies are found at Daniel K Inouye International Airport and in Waikiki.

Traffic jams up during rush hours, roughly from 7am to 9am and 3pm to 6pm weekdays. Expect heavy traffic in both directions on the H-1 Fwy during this time, as well as on the Pali and Likelike Hwys headed into Honolulu in the morning and away from the city in the late afternoon.

ROAD TRIP: PUNCHBOWL, PU'UOHI'A & ROUND TOP DRIVE

Heading up into Honolulu's backdrop of lush green mountains provides a grand break from sand and surf. Few fail to be startled by the prolific tropical vegetation, the elevation gained and the stupendous panoramas on this adventurous drive up Pu'uohi'a, commonly known as Mt Tantalus. Stop midway and wander a hiking trail, or just marvel at the views from Honolulu's highest homes.

➊ Punchbowl

Sitting just to the east of downtown Honolulu, Punchbowl is an extinct volcanic tuff cone.

While Punchbowl is not as distinctive and recognizable as Diamond Head, it is still a standout and obvious geographical landmark in its own right.

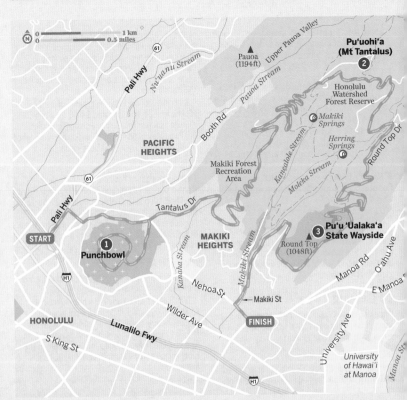

Great for... Outdoors, History & Culture, Families

Best Time to Go Anytime during daylight

If you're coming from Waikiki on the H-1 Fwy, take the Pali Hwy turnoff and be ready to turn right almost immediately and follow the signs to the **National Memorial Cemetery of the Pacific** (p94) in Punchbowl.

Hawaiians called the bowl-like crater Puowaina (Hill of Human Sacrifices). Today the remains of ancient Hawaiians share the crater floor with the bodies of nearly 50,000 soldiers, many of whom were killed in the Pacific during WWII. Even without the dramatic war sights, Punchbowl would be worth the drive up for the plum views of the city and Diamond Head. After entering the cemetery, bear left and go to the top of the hill, where there's a sweeping ocean-view lookout.

Leaving Punchbowl, you'll make a right turn and join Tantalus Dr. The road climbs into hillside Honolulu at first and you pass many suburban houses with enviable views. Gradually the density of housing will reduce until you are on a narrow switchback road that wends its way up into the Makiki forest reserves.

Maximum enjoyment is to be had if you are driving a rental convertible. But watch out for skateboarders and cyclists using the road as a downhill racetrack. Technically, you're passing many a vantage point with sweeping city vistas; if you catch a glimpse of a view, grab it and give thanks to the tourist gods.

② Puʻuohiʻa (Mt Tantalus)

Puʻuohiʻa (2014ft), aka Mt Tantalus, is the heart of what's literally an urban jungle. Just a few minutes ago, you were in the sun-dappled city. Now you're up in the clouds, where rain is either falling or about to fall (OK, maybe you didn't need the convertible). Here, near the top, you'll spot hiking trails leading into the jungle from the many turnouts. Pick one at random and go for a stroll. You'll feel the high humidity and fragrant warmth of the dense living and rotting vegetation in your bones.

The mountain is actually an extinct volcanic cone. If you could see it from above, you'd see a small crater at its very top. All around you are myriad tree species; look for ironwood, pine and guava. If the latter are bearing fruit, it will likely have fallen in profusion and begun fermenting – possibly adding a contact buzz to your sensory overload. Flowering trees such as jacaranda and African tulips add to the visual stimulation.

From its high point, Tantalus Dr turns into Round Top Dr for its descent down the eastern side of the mountain. After your drive up, you'll feel like an old hand with the (slightly) gentler curves heading down.

③ Puʻu ʻUalakaʻa State Wayside Park

One of Oʻahu's underappreciated treasures, **Puʻu ʻUalakaʻa State Wayside Park** (p101) is well worth the stop. Its viewpoint presents sweeping views of Waikiki and Honolulu from Diamond Head in the east around to the Waiʻanae Range in the west. The high-rises of Waikiki jut up like the teeth of an alligator. The many sparkling office towers downtown attest to the city's economic strength. Planes fly overhead on their way to land, while you'll see others banking sharply away from the runway on takeoff.

Back out on Round Top Dr, the views continue as you head down the hill. There are open vistas and fewer clouds, but none compare to those you enjoyed from the lofty heights of Puʻu ʻUalakaʻa. However, the long turnout along the east side of the road is a great place to take in the city lights below and the constellations above.

It's another 2.5 miles down Round Top Dr in ever-increasing suburbia to Makiki St at the foot of the mountain. You may want to head up into the Manoa Valley, which you recently surveyed, to try some of its fine cafes and eateries.

AT A GLANCE

POPULATION
35,000

BEACHSIDE AVENUE
Kalakaua Ave

BEST TIKI BAR
Cuckoo Coconuts
(p166)

BEST SHIRT SHOP
Bailey's Antiques &
Aloha Shirts (p170)

BEST SHAVE ICE
Waiola Shave Ice
(p162)

WHEN TO GO
Sep–Nov Ideal
as the weather is
balmy, plus prices
and visitor numbers
are low.

Dec–Jan Expect an
energetic buzz every-
where, along with big
crowds and prices.

Feb–May Not as
packed but you'll run
into lots of snowbirds
from the mainland.

Waikiki Beach (p139)
MCDOW PHOTO INC / SHUTTERSTOCK ©

Waikiki

Once a Hawaiian royal retreat, Waikiki now revels in its role as a retreat for the masses. This famous strand of sand moves to a rhythm of Hawaiian music at beachfront high-rises and resorts. In this pulsing jungle of modern hotels and malls, you can, surprisingly, still hear whispers of Hawaii's past, from the chanting of hula troupes at Kuhio Beach to the legacy of Olympic gold medalist Duke Kahanamoku.

Take a surfing lesson from a bronzed instructor, then spend a lazy afternoon lying on Waikiki's golden sands. Before the sun sinks below the horizon, hop aboard a catamaran and sail off toward Diamond Head. Sip a sunset mai tai and be hypnotized by the lilting harmonies of slack key guitar, then mingle with the colorful locals, many of whom have made this their lifetime playground, who come here to party after dark, too.

Waikiki Highlights

1 Queen's Surf Beach
(p144) Frolicking on less crowded sand and diving into family-friendly surf.

2 House Without a Key (p167) Enjoying lilting Hawaiian tunes, sunset over the Pacific and the graceful swaying of hula.

3 Queens (p150) Surfing where it all began, right off Waikiki Beach, on a great all-around, year-round wave.

4 Kuhio Beach Torchlighting & Hula Show (p167) Taking in this free show of Hawaiian culture performed by vaunted local talent.

5 Royal Hawaiian Band
(p167) Singing Queen Lili'uokalani's 'Aloha 'Oe' at these performances by O'ahu's oldest band.

6 Moana Surfrider (p156) Quaffing a mai tai at this legendary resort dating to 1901, with a courtyard featuring a huge banyan tree.

History

Looking at Waikiki today, it's hard to imagine that less than 150 years ago this tourist hot spot was almost entirely wetlands filled with fishponds and *lo'i kalo* (taro fields). Fed by mountain streams from the Manoa Valley, Waikiki (Spouting Water) was once one of O'ahu's most fertile farming areas. In 1795 Kamehameha I became the first *ali'i* (chief) to successfully unite the Hawaiian Islands under one sovereign's rule, bringing his royal court to Waikiki.

Later in the 19th century, Queen Kapi'olani had two homes in today's Waikiki. One grander palatial estate was at the southeast end of today's Ala Wai Canal, near where her namesake park is today. Another more modest home was on the waterfront. This was her favorite and she spent her days here writing poetry and working to preserve ancient forms of hula (which missionaries of the day condemned as 'heathen displays').

By the 1880s Honolulu's more well-to-do citizens had started building gingerbread-trimmed cottages along the narrow oceanfront. Tourism started booming in 1901 when Waikiki's first luxury hotel, the Moana, opened its doors on a former royal compound and the one part of the shoreline with an actual beach. Tiring quickly of the pesky mosquitoes that thrived in Waikiki's wetlands, early beachgoers petitioned to have the 'swamps' brought under control. From 1922 to 1927, the Ala Wai Canal was dug to divert the streams that flowed into Waikiki and to dry out the wetlands. Tourists quickly replaced the water buffaloes.

In the 'Roaring '20s' the Royal Hawaiian hotel opened to serve passengers arriving on luxury ocean liners from San Francisco. The Depression and WWII put a damper on tourism, but the Royal Hawaiian was turned into an R&R playground for sailors on shore leave. From 1935 to 1975 the classic radio show *Hawaii Calls,* performed live at the Moana hotel, broadcast dreams of a tropical paradise to the US mainland and the world. As late as 1950 surfers could still drive their cars right up to the beach and park on the sand.

In the 1960s huge megaresorts priced for the masses, such as the Ilikai (which soon gained fame in the opening credits of top-rated TV show *Hawaii Five-O)* and what's now known as the Hilton Hawaiian Village, helped fuel an enormous increase in tourism. Fast jets such as the DC-8 linked the islands to the US mainland in a matter of hours. Later models like the 747 brought thousands of tourists to Hawaii daily. In the 1970s most visitors began and/or ended their holidays on Waikiki, or simply never left at all. A five-decade-long building boom has turned the enclave into one massive tourism machine and continually expanded Waikiki's beach, which originally covered little of the shore.

The process whereby old modest apartment buildings favored by surfers and beach bums of all ages are replaced by resorts, condos (some insist time-share sales were invented here) and upscale malls continues unabated. Even as visitors from all over the world (especially Asia) continue flocking to Waikiki, locals are grappling with issues such as traffic, beach erosion and housing costs.

🐾 Beaches

The 2-mile stretch of white sand that everyone calls Waikiki Beach runs from the Hilton Hawaiian Village (p155) all the way to Kapi'olani Beach Park. Along the way, the beach keeps changing names and personalities. In the early morning, quiet seaside paths belong to walkers and runners, and strolling toward Diamond Head at dawn can be a meditative experience. By midmorning it looks like any resort beach – packed with water-sports concessionaires and lots of tourist bodies. By noon it's a challenge to walk along the full beach without stepping on anyone. (Try Fort DeRussy, Queen's Surf and Kaimana Beaches for less-crowded alternatives.)

If you want to walk the length of the beach, you may find it impossible due to the ongoing problems with beach erosion (p172). Specifically, the sand between the Halekulani hotel and the Royal Hawaiian often vanishes underwater. The alternative, public access along a waterfront walkway, is a challenge as it is very narrow and disconnected (at one point you end up traipsing through the Sheraton Waikiki).

The following listings of Waikiki's individual beaches run from west to east.

Kahanamoku Beach   BEACH
(Paoa Pl; ♿) Fronting the Hilton Hawaiian Village (p155), large Kahanamoku Beach is Waikiki's westernmost beach. It takes its name from Duke Kahanamoku (1890–1968), the legendary Waikiki surfer whose family once owned the land where the resort

Waikiki

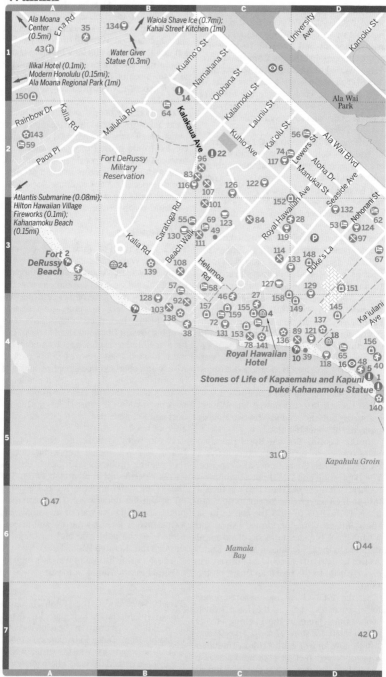

Ala Moana Center (0.5mi)

Ena Rd

35

43

134

Waiola Shave Ice (0.7mi); Kahai Street Kitchen (1mi)

Water Giver Statue (0.3mi)

Ilikai Hotel (0.1mi); Modern Honolulu (0.15mi); Ala Moana Regional Park (1mi)

150

Rainbow Dr

Kalia Rd

143

59

Paoa Pl

Malihia Rd

Kuamo'o St

Namahana St

Olohana St

Kalaimoku St

Launiu St

Kuhio Ave

University Ave

Kamoku St

6

Ala Wai Park

Kalakaua Ave

14

64

22

96

83

116

107

126

122

Kai'olu St

56

74

117

Lewers St

Aloha Dr

Ala Wai Blvd

Manukai St

Seaside Ave

Nohonani St

132

62

Atlantis Submarine (0.08mi); Hilton Hawaiian Village Fireworks (0.1mi); Kahanamoku Beach (0.15mi)

Fort DeRussy Military Reservation

Saratoga Rd

101

55

69

123

130

111

49

84

152

28

119

53

124

97

Royal Hawaiian Ave

Fort DeRussy Beach

2

37

24

139

Kalia Rd

Beach Walk

108

57

58

Helumoa Rd

46

27

114

133

148

Duke's La

129

151

67

145

Ka'iulani Ave

156

7

128

103

138

92

157

155

159

72

131

153

78

141

136

89

121

18

10

39

65

118

16

48

40

5

1

137

149

158

127

71

4

38

Royal Hawaiian Hotel

Stones of Life of Kapaemahu and Kapuni Duke Kahanamoku Statue

140

31

Kapahulu Groin

47

41

Mamala Bay

44

42

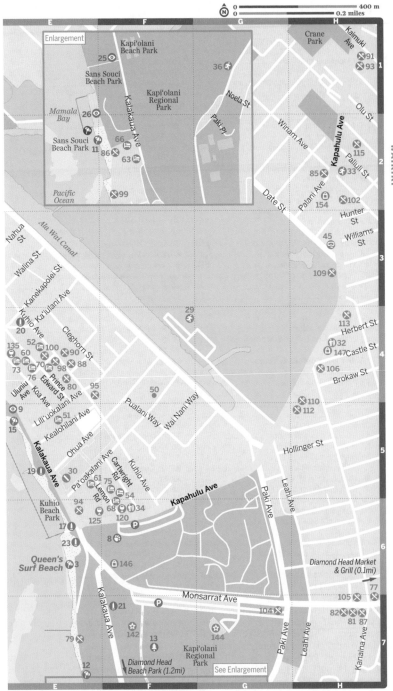

WAIKIKI

Waikiki

now stands. Hawaii's champion surfer and Olympic gold medal winner learned to swim here. The beach offers calm swimming conditions and a gently sloping, if rocky, bottom. Public access is at the end of Paoa Pl, off Kalia Rd, and Holomoana St (where there's easy parking). Behind the

beach, the artificially created **Duke Kahanamoku Lagoon** offers family-friendly placid waters and sand.

★ **Fort DeRussy Beach**   BEACH
(off Kalia Rd; ⓚ) Less crowded than adjoining beaches, this often-overlooked beauty

extends along the shore of its namesake military facility. The water is usually calm and good for swimming, but it's shallow at low tide. When conditions are right, windsurfers, bodyboarders and board surfers all play here. KOA Beach Service (p150) rents bodyboards, kayaks and snorkel sets. A wide, grassy lawn with palm trees offers some sparse shade, an alternative to baking on the sand.

There are shady picnic tables and a snack bar selling drinks and cold beer.

Gray's Beach   BEACH

(off Kalia Rd) Nestled up against the Halekulani luxury resort (p156), Gray's Beach has suffered some of the Waikiki strip's worst erosion. Because the seawall in front of the Halekulani hotel is on the waterline, there's often no sand here at all, though the offshore waters do offer decent swimming conditions. Public access is along a narrow elevated walkway, which is disconnected and can make trying to walk from the Outrigger Reef hotel to the Royal Hawaiian a hassle.

The beach is named after Gray's-by-the-Sea, a 1920s boarding house that stood here.

Kahaloa & Ulukou Beaches   BEACH

(off Kalakaua Ave) The narrow beach between the Royal Hawaiian and Moana Surfrider hotels is Waikiki's busiest section of sand and surf, making it great for people-watching. Most of the beach has a shallow bottom with a gradual slope. The only drawback for swimmers is its popularity with beginner surfers, and the occasional catamaran landing hazard. Queens and Canoes, Waikiki's best-known surf breaks, are just offshore. Paddle further offshore over a lagoon to Populars (aka 'Pops'), a favorite of longboarders.

Kuhio Beach Park   BEACH

(off Kalakaua Ave; 🚻) If you're the kind of person who wants it all, this beach offers everything from protected swimming to outrigger canoe rides, and even a free sunset hula and Hawaiian music show. You'll find restrooms, outdoor showers, a snack bar and beach gear rental stands at **Waikiki Beach Center**, near the police substation. Also here is the Kuhio Beach Surfboard Lockers (p146), an iconic storage area for local surfers. World-famous Canoes (p150) surf break is right offshore – you can spend hours watching surfers of all types riding the curls.

The beach, which does get very crowded, is marked on its opposite end by **Kapahulu Groin**, a walled storm drain with a walkway on top that juts out into the ocean. A low stone breakwater called the Wall runs out from Kapahulu Groin, parallel to the beach. It was built to control sand erosion and, in the process, two nearly enclosed swimming pools were formed.

The pool closest to Kapahulu Groin is best for swimming. However, because circulation is limited, the water gets murky. Kapahulu Groin is one of Waikiki's hottest bodyboarding spots. If the surf's right, you can find a few dozen bodyboarders riding the waves. These experienced local kids ride straight for the groin's cement wall and then veer away at the last moment, thrilling the tourists watching them from the little pier above.

★ Queen's Surf Beach   BEACH

(Wall's; off Kalakaua Ave, Kapi'olani Beach Park; 🚻) Just south of Kuhio Beach, the namesake beach for the famous surf break is a great place for families as the waves are rarely large when they reach shore but they are still large enough for bodyboarding, which means older kids can frolic for hours. Also, there are lifeguards. At the south end of the beach, the area in front of the beach pavilion is popular with the local gay community.

Kapi'olani Beach Park   BEACH

(off Kalakaua Ave, Kap'iolani Regional Park) Where did all the tourists go? From Kapahulu Groin south to the Natatorium, this peaceful stretch of beach, backed by a green space of banyan trees and grassy lawns, offers a relaxing niche with none of the frenzy found on the beaches fronting the Waikiki hotel strip. Facilities include restrooms and outdoor showers. Kapi'olani Beach is a popular weekend picnicking spot for local families, who unload the kids to splash in the ocean while adults fire up the BBQ.

The widest northern end of Kapi'olani Beach is nicknamed Queen's Surf Beach . On a few summer nights, classic movies are shown for free on a huge outdoor screen (www.sunsetonthebeach.net). Right in the middle sits the excellent Barefoot Beach Cafe (p159), reason enough to visit this stretch of the shore.

Kaimana Beach   BEACH

(Sans Souci Beach) At the Diamond Head edge of Waikiki, Kaimana is a prime triangle of sandy stretch of oceanfront that's far from the frenzied tourist scene. It's commonly called Sans Souci Beach for the name of the hotel that once stood near today's **New Otani Kaimana Beach Hotel** (2863 Kalakaua Ave). Local residents come here for their daily swims. A shallow reef close to shore and a breakwater make for wave-free, protected waters and provide good snorkeling. There are lifeguards.

◉ Sights

Yes, the beach is the main sight, but Waikiki also has historic hotels, evocative public art, amazing artifacts of Hawaiian history, and even a zoo and aquarium.

★ Royal Hawaiian Hotel   HISTORIC BUILDING

(📞 808-923-7311; www.royal-hawaiian.com; 2259 Kalakaua Ave; ⊙ tours 1pm Tue & Thu) FREE With its Moorish-style turrets and archways, this gorgeously restored 1927 art deco landmark, dubbed the 'Pink Palace,' is a throwback to the era when Rudolph Valentino was *the* romantic idol and travel to Hawaii was by Matson Navigation luxury liner. Its guest list reads like a who's who of A-list celebrities, from royalty to Rockefellers, along with luminaries such as Charlie Chaplin and Babe Ruth. Today, historic tours explore the architecture and lore of this grande dame.

Don't miss the remarkable painting of Hawaii completed by Ernest Clegg for the hotel's opening. Painted directly on the plaster, it has been a permanent feature outside the elevators in the original building since the hotel opened. The free tours are recommended and no reservations are needed – meet at the bakery off the lobby.

Moana Surfrider Hotel   HISTORIC BUILDING
(☎808-922-3111; www.moana-surfrider.com; 2365 Kalakaua Ave; ⏱tours 11am Wed) **FREE** Christened the Moana Hotel when it opened in 1901, this beaux-arts plantation-style inn was once the haunt of Hollywood movie stars, aristocrats and business tycoons. The historic hotel embraces a seaside courtyard with large banyan trees and a wraparound veranda, where island musicians and hula dancers perform in the evenings.

Upstairs from the lobby you'll find displays of memorabilia from the early days: everything from scripts of the famed *Hawaii Calls* radio show broadcast live from the courtyard here between 1935 and 1975 to woolen bathing suits, historical period photographs and a short video of Waikiki back in the days when the Moana was the only hotel on the oceanfront horizon. Tours are open to anyone – meet on the 2nd floor above the lobby.

Waikiki Aquarium   AQUARIUM
(☎808-923-9741; www.waikikiaquarium.org; 2777 Kalakaua Ave; adult/child $12/5; ⏱9am-5pm, last entry 4:30pm; 🔅) 🖉 Located on Waiki-

ki's shoreline, this university-run aquarium recreates diverse tropical Pacific reef habitats. You'll see rare fish species from the Northwestern Hawaiian Islands, as well as hypnotic moon jellies and flashlight fish that host bioluminescent bacteria. Especially hypnotizing are the Palauan chambered nautiluses with their unique spiral shells – in fact, this is the world's first aquarium to breed these endangered creatures in captivity, a ground-breaking achievement. It's a pleasant 15-minute walk southeast of the main Waikiki beach strip.

An outdoor pool is home to rare and endangered Hawaiian monk seals. A garden with native Hawaiian plants features a self-guided tour. Make reservations for special family-friendly events and fun educational programs for kids, such as a behind the scenes tour (adult/child $16/10, 3pm Wednesday). There's a nice lawn for picnics.

Huge Banyan Tree   LANDMARK
(off Kalakaua Ave, Kuhio Beach Park) Generations of surfers and sunbathers have enjoyed shade under this century-old banyan tree. It's the perfect pictorial backdrop for photos and it serves as a vast natural umbrella when the skies open up.

WAIKIKI'S SACRED STONES

Near the police substation at Waikiki Beach Center, four ordinary-looking volcanic basalt boulders are actually sacred and legendary Hawaiian symbols. The **Stones of Life of Kapaemahu and Kapuni** (Na Pohaku Ola Kapaemahu a Kapuni; off Kalakaua Ave, Kuhio Beach Park) are said to contain the *mana* (spiritual essence) of four wizards who came to O'ahu from Tahiti around AD 400. According to ancient legend, the wizards helped the island residents by healing their maladies, and their fame became widespread. As a tribute when the wizards left, the islanders placed the four boulders where the wizards had lived.

The two heaviest stones weight 8 and 10 tons respectively; how the ancients moved them the 2 miles from a quarry east of Diamond Head is a mystery.

Like the Hawaiian people, the stones suffered many indignities in the 20th century. Archibold Scott Cleghorn, the Scottish husband of Princess Likelike and father of Princess Ka'iulani, discovered them on his Waikiki waterfront property. He had them excavated and stone idols were found with them. The princesses regularly placed seaweed offerings on them. When Cleghorn died in 1910, his will stipulated the stones be protected, which didn't happen.

In 1941 a bowling alley was built on the site and the stones were used in the foundation, despite protests from the local community. After the structure was demolished in 1958, the stones were given some prominence in the newly created Kuhio Beach park. However, more indignities were to come. They were dug up yet again in 1980, so a sewer line and toilet could be built on the spot. Tourists began using them as a towel-drying rack, sparking many Hawaiian community protests. In 1997 the stones were moved yet again to their present spot and fenced off. Look for the sacred *ahu* (altar) that was added.

Kuhio Beach Surfboard Lockers LANDMARK
(off Kalakaua Ave, Kuhio Beach Park) Where most cities have bike racks and others have big parking garages, Waikiki has a public facility that embodies the very spirit of the beach: a huge locker area for surfboards right near the sand. Located next to the police substation, it's the perfect offbeat photo op. Hundreds of boards are stored here by locals in between their time out on the water.

US Army Museum of Hawai'i MUSEUM
(☑808-955-9552; www.hiarmymuseumsoc.org; 2131 Kalia Rd; donations welcome, audio tour $5; ☺10am-5pm Tue-Sat, last entry 4:15pm; 🅿) FREE
At Fort DeRussy, this museum exhibits an almost mind-numbing array of military paraphernalia as it relates to Hawaii's history, starting with shark-tooth clubs that Kamehameha the Great used to win control of the island more than two centuries ago. Old photographs and stories convey an understanding of the influence of the US military presence in Hawaii.

Extensive exhibits include displays on the 442nd, the Japanese American regiment that became the most decorated regiment in WWII, and on Kaua'i-born Eric Shinseki, a retired four-star army general who spoke out against the US invasion of Iraq and who served as Secretary of Veterans Affairs. The building was once the fortified Shore Battery Randolph, which housed large defense guns. It resisted demolition efforts in 1969, so it was converted to today's museum.

Kapi'olani Regional Park PARK
(☑808-768-4623; off Kalakaua & Paki Aves) In its early days, horse racing and band concerts were the biggest attractions at Waikiki's favorite green space. Although the racetrack is long gone, this park named after Queen Kapi'olani, who once lived nearby, is still a beloved outdoor venue for live music and local community gatherings, from farmers markets and arts-and-crafts fairs to festivals and rugby matches. On a stroll, you'll marvel at the many huge, old trees.

The tree-shaded Kapi'olani Bandstand is ideal for catching a concert by the time-honored Royal Hawaiian Band (p167), which performs classics here on many Sunday afternoons.

**Waikiki Natatorium
War Memorial** HISTORIC SITE
(☑808-254-1828; http://natatorium.org; 2815 Kalakaua Ave, Kapi'olani Beach Park) Opened in 1927 as a beaux-arts-style memorial to those who served in WWI, the Natatorium has a saltwater pool that's 100m long and 40m wide. Unfortunately, its current condition is an indictment of bureaucratic neglect: the city and county of Honolulu assumed control of the site in 1949 and allowed it to deteriorate until it was closed in 1961.

The condition of this historically registered landmark has continued to deteriorate in the decades since.

Ala Wai Canal CANAL
The Ala Wai Canal was completed in 1927 to drain the taro fields, marshes and swamps that would become present-day Waikiki. Running from Kapahulu Ave, the waterway runs in a straight line down the back of Waikiki before turning left and out to sea between the Ala Wai Yacht Harbor and Ala Moana Beach Park's (p85) Magic Island. The canal is a popular spot with kayakers and outrigger-canoe teams.

Honolulu Zoo ZOO
(☑808-971-7171; www.honoluluzoo.org; cnr Kapahulu & Kalakaua Aves; adult/child $19/11; ☺9am-4:30pm; 🅿 👶) Honolulu Zoo displays tropical species from around the globe. There are 42 acres of tropical greenery, over 1200 animals and a petting zoo for kids. Hawaii has no endemic land mammals, but in the aviary near the entrance you can see some native birds, including the *nene* (Hawaiian goose) and *'apapane,* a bright-red Hawaiian honeycreeper. Make reservations for family-oriented twilight tours and zoo campouts.

The city-run zoo has struggled through years of challenges. In 2016 it lost its Association of Zoos and Aquariums accreditation over its perennial funding woes. However, voters later approved a dedicated revenue stream, so the zoo hopes to regain its accreditation in 2020. In a positive step forward, it welcomed three new cheetahs in 2019.

Statues
Waikiki's diverse collection of statues all come with plaques with fascinating details on the figure depicted as well as local historical and cultural details.

⭐**Duke Kahanamoku Statue** STATUE
(off Kalakaua Ave, Kuhio Beach Park) On the waterfront on Kalakaua Ave, this imposing statue of Duke Kahanamoku is always draped in colorful lei. The Duke was a true Hawaiian hero, winning numerous Olympic swimming medals, breaking the world record for the 100yd freestyle in his first competitive event,

and becoming known as 'the father of modern surfing.' He even had stints as sheriff of Honolulu and as a Hollywood actor. Duke also pioneered the Waikiki 'beachboys,' teaching visitors how to surf.

Some local surfers have taken issue with the placement of the statue – Duke is standing with his back to the sea, a position they say he never would've taken in real life.

Makua and Kila Statue   STATUE
(off Kalakaua Ave, Kuhio Beach Park) A bronze charmer, this warm-hearted public art sculpture shows a young surfer (Makua) sharing a moment with a monk seal (Kila). It's inspired by the children's book *Makua Lives on the Beach*, a story about Hawaiian values of love and respect.

Princess Kaiulani Statue   STATUE
(off Kuhio Ave) Princess Kaiulani was heir to the throne when the Kingdom of Hawaii was overthrown in 1893. This statue of the princess feeding her beloved peacocks sits in Waikiki's Kaiulani Triangle Park and was unveiled in 1999 on the 124th anniversary of her birth. Known for her beauty, intelligence and determination, the Princess visited President Cleveland in Washington after the overthrow but could not prevent the annexation of Hawaii by the US. She died at the young age of 23.

King David Kalakaua Statue   STATUE
(off Kalakaua Ave) Born in 1836, King Kalakaua ruled Hawaii from 1874 until his death in 1891. With his wife, Queen Kapi'olani, Kalakaua traveled the world extensively. This statue, designed by Native Hawaiian sculptor Sean Browne, greets visitors coming into Waikiki and was donated by the Japanese-American Community of Hawaii to mark 100 years of Japanese immigration in 1985. Kalakaua was instrumental in the signing of a Japan-Hawaii Labor Convention that brought 200,000 Japanese immigrants to Hawaii between 1885 and 1924.

Storyteller Statue   STATUE
(Map p86; off Kalakaua Ave) This bronze statue just off Kalakaua Ave represents 'The Storytellers,' the keepers of Hawaiian culture. For centuries, women have been at the top of Hawaiian oral traditions, and the storytellers preserve the identity of their people and land by reciting poems, songs, chants and genealogies. The Storyteller's companion statue is the Water Giver statue (p98) at the Hawaiian Convention Center.

A FAMILY OF STATUES

The main courtyard at the International Market Place (p170) has three life-size statues of Hawaiian royal family members not found elsewhere. Together the three account for a fairly tragic story.

Kamehameha IV Only king for barely nine years, he died at age 29 in 1863. Born Alexander 'Iolani Liholiho, he contended with American racism and repression for much of his life. As king, he tried to create a health-care system for the islands and expand education.

Queen Emma Wife of Kamehameha IV, she died at age 49 in 1885. She helped fund and establish the Queen's Hospital in Honolulu, which today is the island's premier medical center. She bonded with Queen Victoria of England, a relationship that deepened after both were widows.

Prince Albert Kamehameha The only son of Kamehameha IV and Queen Emma died at age four of what today is thought to have been an appendicitis. The king was inconsolable and died a year later. The Queen rarely left his gravesite at the Royal Mausoleum State Monument (p102) for several years. Albert was Queen Victoria's godson.

Prince Kuhio Statue   STATUE
(off Kalakaua Ave) This statue of Prince Jonah Kuhio Kalaniana'ole fronts Kuhio Beach. It celebrates the man who was prince of the reigning House of Kalakaua when the Kingdom of Hawaii was overthrown in 1893. After Hawaii was annexed as territory of the US, Kuhio was elected as Hawaii's congressional delegate for 10 consecutive terms. Kuhio was often called Ke Ali'i Maka'ainana (Prince of People), and is well known for his efforts to preserve and strengthen the Hawaiian culture.

It's hard not to see the typical film portrayal of Hercule Poirot in this rendition.

Surfer on a Wave Statue   STATUE
(off Kalakaua Ave) Opposite the entrance to Honolulu Zoo (p146) and right on the beach, the *Surfer on a Wave* statue celebrates surfing as a major part of the culture of Waikiki. Cast in bronze by Robert Pasby, it was unveiled in 2003.

Queen Kapi'olani Statue STATUE

(off Kalakaua Ave, Kap'iolani Regional Park) This bronze statue depicts Queen Kapi'olani, the wife of King David Kalakaua – his statue sits at the other end of Waikiki. The Queen was a beloved philanthropist, known as the queen who loved children. Among other accomplishments, she founded a maternity home in 1890 for disadvantaged Hawaiians and today you'll hear her name often – the park, a hospital, a major boulevard and a community college are named for her.

She had two homes near the statue, including her favorite on the waterfront. The near-lifesize statue is always covered with fresh lei.

Activities

Waikiki is good for swimming, bodyboarding, surfing, sailing and other water sports most of the year, and there are lifeguards, restrooms and outdoor showers scattered along the beachfront. Between May and September, summer swells make the water a little rough for swimming, but great for surfing.

Inland, you can run, play tennis, enjoy a round of golf etc.

Ala Wai Golf Course GOLF

(☑reservations 808-296-2000; www.honolulu. gov/des/golf/alawai.html; 404 Kapahulu Ave; green fees $33-66; ☉6am-5:30pm) With views of Diamond Head and the Ko'olau Range, this flat 18-hole, par-70 layout scores a Guinness World Record for being the world's busiest golf course. Local golfers are allowed to book earlier in the week and grab most of the starting times, leaving few for visitors (who may call to reserve up to three days in advance starting at 6:30am).

If you get there early in the day and put yourself on the waiting list – and as long as your entire party waits at the course – you'll probably get to play. Driving range and club rentals available.

Hiking Hawaii HIKING

(☑855-808-4453; http://hikinghawaii808.com; 1956 Ala Moana Blvd; custom hikes from per hr $50) Offers a number of custom hiking options daily across O'ahu, from a Makap'u Lighthouse walk to a hike to Manoa Falls to a full-day trip to the North Shore. Waikiki hotel pickups, transportation and guide are included.

⊀ City Walk
Waikiki Beach

START KAHANAMOKU BEACH
FINISH BAREFOOT BEACH CAFE
LENGTH 1.7 MILES; TWO HOURS

Start your walk at ➊**Kahanamoku Beach** (p139), a large patch of sand that exists thanks to the curving breakwaters. Surfing legend Duke Kahanamoku learned to swim here when his family owned the land under what's now the ➋**Hilton Hawaiian Village** (p155). One of the world's largest resorts (3386 rooms), construction began in 1955 and has never really stopped. The iconic Rainbow Tower opened in 1968 and has the world's largest (again!) ceramic-tile mosaic, a 286ft-tall rainbow. In 1961 Elvis Presley filmed *Blue Hawaii* here.

Follow the beach southeast. The line of beachfront high-rises is broken at usually less-crowded ➌**Fort DeRussy Beach** (p142), the sandy front yard of Fort DeRussy Military Reservation. A leftover from a much earlier time, the 'fort' today is home to some US Army departments, but is mostly green grass.

About 200 yards further on, the ➍**US Army Museum of Hawai'i** (p146) details military paraphernalia as it relates to Hawaii's history, starting with shark-tooth clubs that Kamehameha the Great used to win control of the island more than two centuries ago. It's in the former Shore Battery Randolph, which housed large guns meant to help protect O'ahu from invasion.

At the ➎**Castle Waikiki Shore** condo, with its ugly Subway fast-food joint despoiling the beachfront, hang a left and walk along the grass to Kalia Rd and turn right. Walk past the posh ➏**Halekulani** (p156) and turn left again. Follow a pathway into the gargantuan ➐**Sheraton Waikiki** (2255 Kalakaua Ave) complex. Built in 1971, this 1636-room behemoth dwarfs everything around it. Exit onto the vast courtyard and cross over to the upscale ➑**Royal Hawaiian Center** (p152). If your timing is right you can try free Hawaiian cultural classes and demonstrations.

Cross over the large plaza to the ➒**Royal Hawaiian Resort** (p156). This gorgeous 1927 art deco landmark is dubbed the 'Pink Palace.' Drop inside the

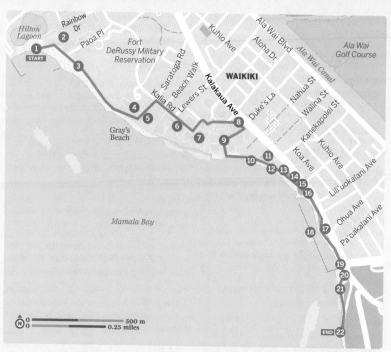

hotel to see the map of Hawaii painted by Ernest Clegg; it's part of the wall outside the elevators in the main building. Wander around and look for historic photos of Waikiki. Exit out to the beach and turn left at the sand. These are **10 Kahaloa and Ulukou Beaches** (p143), the busiest swaths of Waikiki sand. When the huge banyan tree comes into view, step into the open courtyard of the **11 Moana Surfrider Hotel** (p145). Opened in 1901, this plantation-style inn is where local tourism began. Pause for refreshments at the Beach Bar (p164), where you can get a fine mai tai, or take a load off on one of the rocking chairs on the veranda overlooking Kalakaua Ave.

Return to the beach and continue in the direction of Diamond Head. You're entering **12 Kuhio Beach Park** (p144), where beach and surfing culture thrives. Note the local version of bike racks, the **13 Kuhio Beach Surfboard Lockers** (p146). Just south and away from the water, you'll find the **14 Wizard Stones of Kapaemahu** (p145) – no one knows how ancient Hawaiians were able to move them here from elsewhere on Oʻahu.

Next up is the **15 Duke Kahanamoku Statue** (p146), where selfies rule and the outstretched arms of the legendary surfer are

always draped in leis. At the **16 huge banyan tree** (p145), take note of the mound and return at dusk on one of the days when you can witness the excellent free Kuhio Beach Torchlighting & Hula Show (p167).

Continue along to the **17 Prince Kuhio Statue** (p147), honoring the man who was prince when the Kingdom of Hawaii was overthrown in 1893. He later became Hawaii's congressional delegate for 10 consecutive terms. Shift over to the water and **18 Kapahulu Groin**. This pair of breakwaters is a people-watching hot spot.

Where Kalakaua Ave meets Kapahulu Ave, look for two works of public art near the sand. The first is the **19 Makua and Kila Statue** (p147), a sentimental favorite that depicts a young boy and his friend, a seal. It's based on a popular local children's book. Just south, the somewhat less charming **20 Surfer on a Wave Statue** (p147) is just that. You might pause on the sand at **21 Queen's Surf Beach** (p144), one of Waikiki's most pleasant. Or continue along the waterfront walkway (at high tide the sand vanishes for several hundred yards south of Queen's) to the excellent **22 Barefoot Beach Cafe** (p159).

Surfing, Stand-Up Paddleboarding & Bodyboarding

Waikiki has good surfing year-round, with the largest waves rolling in during winter. Gentler summer surf breaks are best for beginners. Surfing lessons and surfboard, stand-up paddleboarding (SUP) and bodyboard rentals can be arranged at the concession stands along the sand at Kuhio Beach Park, near the bodyboarding hot spot of Kapahulu Groin. There are also numerous shops located along the streets.

★ Diamond Head Surfboards
SURFING

(☑ 808-691-9599; https://dhshi.myshopify.com; 525 Kapahulu Ave; surfboard rentals per day from $25; ⊘ 10am-6pm Mon-Thu, to 7pm Fri-Sun) One of the best Waikiki-area shops for board rentals of all kinds, with a huge and affordable range on offer. As well as renting out surfboards, stand up paddleboards and bodyboards by the hour, day or week, it has excellent personalized surfing lessons based out of its well-stocked shop. Its Hawaii Republic T-shirts are popular.

★ Queens
SURFING

The perfect break for beginners who've mastered Canoes, Queens is an all-around great wave. It's a longboard dream and is usually crowded, especially when any of the many surf contests held here are on.

Threes
SURFING

Very reliable at low tide, Threes has a big following with locals, who appreciate its picture-perfect form in almost all conditions (when highest, it forms small barrels). It's a half-mile out, so be ready for a long paddle.

Ala Moana Bowls
SURFING

Literally known for its 'bowls,' this break has barrels you can stand up in when conditions are right. It's near the entrance to Ala Wai Harbor and is a fast hollow left. There's usually a serious crew of locals here.

Quality Surfboards Hawaii
SURFING

(☑ 808-947-7307; www.qualitysurfboardshawaii.com; 1860 Ala Moana Blvd; surfboard/SUP rental per day $20/40; ⊘ 8am-8pm) The name's no lie: hit this local surfer's shop for board, SUP, snorkel, bike and beach-gear rentals. Ask about the rental delivery options. Private lessons also available (per hour $150).

Hawaii Surfboard Rentals
SURFING, SUP

(☑ 808-689-8989; www.hawaiisurfboardrentals.com; surfboard rental minimum 2 days $60; ⊘ 7am-8pm) Has a huge variety of boards to rent. Free surfboard, SUP, bodyboard and car-rack delivery and pickup across Waikiki and much of O'ahu; weekly rates are an especially good deal.

Hans Hedemann Surf
SURFING

(☑ 808-924-7778; www.hhsurf.com; 150 Kapahulu Ave, Queen Kapi'olani Hotel; 2hr group/semiprivate/private lesson $85/130/165; ⊘ 8am-5pm) You can take baby steps and learn to bodyboard, paddle surf or surf at this local pro surfer's well-established school. Although not the cheeriest place, it's conveniently near Queen's Surf Beach.

Canoes
SURFING

(Pops) Not the best but owing to its location right offshore, Canoes is one of the most famous spots and often busy with surfing classes. It's an easygoing mix of left and right breaks with a crowd from around the world enjoying long, consistent rides.

Publics
SURFING

A long left, it breaks over a variety of coral heads. Usually less crowded than the more famous breaks just west.

Populars
SURFING

(Pops) Populars is a favorite of longboarders.

Techniques
SURFING

The name of this break dates to the 1930s when surfers developed hollow boards in order to execute the maneuvers needed to surf these breaks. Previously the cumbersome heavy redwood boards couldn't be used here.

Beach Gear

Outlets for beach gear like chairs, umbrellas, boogie boards and sun lotion dot Waikiki's beaches. Often you'll also find a nearby drinks vendor.

KOA Beach Service
BEACH

(☑ 808-944-1962; https://koabeachservice.com; Fort DeRussy Beach; umbrella & 2 beach loungers all day $50; ⊘ 9am-6pm Jun-Aug, to 5pm Sep-May) Right on the sand, this well-run stand has everything you might want for a fun-filled day on uncrowded Fort DeRussy Beach. Rentals here include several types of chairs and loungers, lockers, SUPs (all day $75), surfboards (all day $50), one-person kayaks (per hour $15) and snorkel sets (all day $20).

WAIKIKI FOR FAMILIES

Waikiki defines family-friendly. Start at the beach. In just an hour or so, the older kids can learn how to stand up on a board and surf, or they can rent a bodyboard and ride on their bellies.

Want to see the world from beneath the waves? Don a snorkel and take a look at the colorful fish at Queen's Surf Beach (p144) or take a ride on the Atlantis Submarine (p153) and see it all through a porthole.

Waikiki Aquarium (p145), with its kaleidoscopic array of tropical fish and reef sharks, has lots of fun just for *na keiki* (children). Check online for the schedule of family programs such as 'Marine Munchies' feedings for ages five and up, or wet-and-wild 'Exploring the Reef at Night' field trips for ages six and up (reservations required).

The small Honolulu Zoo (p146) has a petting zoo – where children can get eye-to-eye with tamer creatures – and weekend 'twilight tours' geared to children aged five and older.

Families sprawl with beach mats on the grass to watch the Kuhio Beach Torchlighting & Hula Show (p167). And then there are Waikiki's luau and dance shows, all with a lively drum beat and hip-shakin' hula and fire dancing. Everyone enjoys the Hilton Hawaiian Village Fireworks (p167) display that's visible from the beach for free.

Many restaurants have kids menus and there are plenty of places such as shave ice shops that delight all ages.

Most bathrooms have changing facilities and the sidewalks are stroller-friendly.

Snorkeling & Scuba Diving

Waikiki's crowded central beaches are not particularly good for snorkeling. Two top choices are Kaimana Beach (p144) and Queen's Surf Beach (p144), where you'll find some live coral and a decent variety of tropical fish. But to really see the gorgeous stuff – coral gardens, manta rays and more exotic fish – head out on a boat. You can easily rent snorkel sets and scuba-diving equipment, or book ahead for boat trips and PADI Open Water certification courses.

★ **O'ahu Diving**   DIVING
(☎ 808-721-4210; www.oahudiving.com; 2-dive trips for beginners $145) Specializes in first-time experiences for beginner divers without certification, as well as deepwater boat dives offshore and PADI refresher classes if you're already certified and have some experience under your diving belt. Trips depart from various locations near Waikiki.

★ **Snorkel Bob's**   SNORKELING
(☎ 808-735-7944; www.snorkelbob.com; 700 Kapahulu Ave; snorkel set rental per week from $9; ⏰ 8am-5pm) A top spot to get your gear. Rates vary depending on the quality of the snorkeling gear and accessories packages, but excellent weekly discounts are available and online reservations taken. You can even rent gear on O'ahu, then return it to a Snorkel Bob's location on another island. Also rents beach gear and wetsuits.

AquaZone   DIVING, SNORKELING
(☎ 808-923-3483; www.aquazonescuba.com; 2552 Kalakaua Ave, Waikiki Beach Marriott Resort; beginner dive 2 tank $155; ⏰ 8am-5pm) Dive shop and tour outfitter in the rear of the Waikiki Beach Marriott (Kuhio Ave entrance). Offers beginner's scuba-diving trips that include orientation in the hotel pool (no PADI certification required) and boat dive, a sea-turtle snorkeling tour or a morning deepwater boat dive, including out to WWII shipwrecks. Rental snorkel and diving gear available.

Kayaking & Windsurfing

Fort DeRussy Beach has fewer swimmers and catamarans to share the water with than Waikiki's central beaches, which makes it a good spot for kayaking. KOA Beach Service rents kayaks here. Most local windsurfers sail near breezy Diamond Head.

★ **Go Bananas Watersports**   WATER SPORTS
(☎ 808-737-9514; https://gobananaskayaks.com; 799 Kapahulu Ave; 1-/2-person kayak per day $35/50; ⏰ 9am-7pm) Everything you need to kayak in the waters off O'ahu is available at this fully stocked shop, including great advice. Rates include everything you need for your adventure, even roof racks for rental cars. They also rent SUPs.

Running

If you're into running, you're in good company: statistics estimate that Honolulu has

BURIAL SITES

When land is developed in Hawaii, more than earth and plants may be disturbed. Construction workers may dig up the *iwi* (bones) and *moepu* (funeral objects) of ancient Hawaiian burial sites. Locals tell 'chicken skin' (goose flesh) stories of machinery breaking down and refusing to operate until the bones are removed and prayers are said. It's common practice for a Hawaiian priest to bless ground-breaking at construction sites.

A memorial in Kapi'olani Regional Park contains the skeletal remains of around 200 Native Hawaiians unearthed over the years by construction projects in Waikiki. Some say that the foundations of all of Waikiki's resort hotels contain *iwi*, simply because the sand used to make the concrete also contained it.

more joggers per capita than any other city on the planet. Two of the best places in Waikiki to break out your running shoes in the early morning or late afternoon are along the Ala Wai Canal (p146) and around Kapi'olani Regional Park (p146).

Honolulu Marathon Clinic RUNNING
(http://honolulumarathonclinic.org; 3833 Paki Ave, Kapi'olani Regional Park; 7:30am Sun mid-Mar–early Dec) **FREE** Free community volunteer-led training runs are open to everyone, with runners joining groups of their own speed.

Tennis

If you've brought your own rackets, the Diamond Head Tennis Center, at the Diamond Head end of Kapi'olani Regional Park, has 10 courts. For night play, go to the **Kapi'olani Regional Park Tennis Courts**, opposite the aquarium; all four courts are lit. All of these public courts are free and first-come, first-served.

Spas

Most of the resorts offer spas for a vacation indulgence.

Abhasa Spa SPA
(808-922-8200; www.abhasa.com; 2259 Kalakaua Ave, Royal Hawaiian Hotel; 50min massage from $165; 9am-9pm) Locally inspired experiences include traditional Hawaiian-style *lomilomi* (loving hands) and *pohaku* (hot

stone) massage, sea-salt scrubs, as well as *kukui* (candlenut), coconut and coffee-oil body treatments. A sister spa to Spa Khakara (p152).

Spa Khakara SPA
(808-685-7600; www.khakara.com; 2255 Kalakaua Ave, Sheraton Waikiki; 50min massage from $140; 9am-9pm) Spa specializing in organic, holistic and natural spa treatments. Afterward, unwind in the contempo relaxation lounge. A sister spa to Abhasa Spa.

Aisawan Thai Spa & Massage SPA
(808-688-7557; www.aisawanspahi.com; 345 Royal Hawaiian Ave Ste 201; 1hr massage from $95; 10am-10pm) Right in the heart of Waikiki, this Thai-style spa offers massages along with various extras such as hot stones and various potions and lotions. It is off a backstreet and the decor is simple, but you'll never notice as you go 'ahhh.' Big local following.

Na Ho'ola Spa SPA
(808-237-6330; www.nahoolaspawaikiki.com; 2424 Kalakaua Ave, Hyatt Regency Waikiki; 50min massage from $200; 8:30am-9pm) At this bi-level spa, *limu* (seaweed) wraps detoxify, *kele-kele* (mud) wraps soothe sore muscles and *ti*-leaf wraps heal sun-ravaged skin, while macadamia-nut oil and fresh pineapple scrubs exfoliate. Ocean views are blissful.

Courses

Royal Hawaiian Center CULTURAL
(schedule information 808-922-2299; www.royalhawaiiancenter.com; 2201 Kalakaua Ave, Guest Services, 1st fl, Building E; classes 9:30am-4pm Mon-Sat) **FREE** Glossy shopping mall that offers free cultural classes and demonstrations that are great introductions to Hawaiian arts and crafts. Try quilting and lei-making, plus hula dancing, ukulele playing and even *lomilomi* traditional body massage.

Waikiki Beach Walk MUSIC
(808-931-3591; www.waikikibeachwalk.com; Lewers St) **FREE** The large block-long open-air mall offers a schedule of free cultural lessons and demonstrations. Look for free ukulele lessons with loaner instruments (10:30am and 4:30pm daily, suite 218) and music.

Waikiki Community Center CULTURAL
(808-923-1802; www.waikikicommunitycenter.org; 310 Pa'oakalani Ave; most classes $5-16; classes at various times 9am-9pm) Try your hand at the ukulele, hula, tai chi or a vari-

ety of island arts and crafts. Instructors at this homespun community center are brimming with aloha. Although most students are locals, visitors are welcome too. Preregistration may be required. Also offers good special interest tours.

Tours

Hop aboard a boat for a jaunt to see the sights above and below the water.

Some surf outfits offer outrigger-canoe rides (from $100 for four people) that take off from the beach and ride the tossin' waves home – kids especially love those thrills.

Several catamaran cruises leave right from Waikiki Beach – just walk down to the sand, step into the surf and hop aboard. There is the option of a 90-minute, all-you-can-drink 'booze cruise.' Reservations are recommended for sunset sails, which sell out quickly.

Holokai Catamaran
CRUISE

(☑ 808-922-2210; https://sailholokai.com; near Outrigger Reef Waikiki Beach Resort, Gray's Beach; catamaran trips $40-80; ⏺) Sporting tall orange and white sails and a white body, this custom-built catamaran offers windy but thrilling high-speed cruises, more relaxed snorkel trips and, of course, a sunset booze cruise departing from Gray's Beach between the Halekulani (p156) resort and the Outrigger Reef Waikiki Beach Resort.

Na Hoku II Catamaran
CRUISE

(☑ 808-336-7422; https://nahoku2.com; near Outrigger Waikiki Beach Resort; 90min catamaran trips $40-45) With its unmistakable yellow-and-red striped sails, this catamaran is a local icon. These hard-drinkin' tours (drinks included in ticket price) set sail four times daily, shoving off from in front of Duke's Waikiki (p165) bar. The sunset sail usually sells out, so book early.

Maita'i Catamaran
CRUISE

(☑ 808-922-5665; http://maitaicatamaran. net; on shore, off Kalakaua Ave; adult/child from $40/20; ⏺) Departing from shore between the Halekulani (p156) and Sheraton Waikiki (p148) hotels, this white catamaran with green sails offers a big variety of boat trips. Reserve ahead for a 90-minute daytime or sunset booze cruise (children allowed; yes, they serve soft drinks as well as mai tais) or a moonlight sail to take in the Hilton Hawaiian Village's Friday fireworks show.

Atlantis Submarine
TOUR

(Map p86; ☑ 800-548-6262; www.atlantissub marines.com; 252 Paoa Pl, Hilton Hawaiian Village; ⏲ 60min tour adult $120, child taller than 36in $60) See the world from a porthole aboard the sub that dives to a depth of 100ft near a reef off Waikiki, offering views of sea life otherwise reserved for divers – though honestly, it's not nearly as exciting as it sounds. There are several sailings daily; you should book ahead online for discounts. Check-in is at the Hilton Hawaiian Village (p155) pier in front of the Ali'i Tower.

Segway Waikiki Tours
TOUR

(☑ 808-941-3151; www.segwayofhawaii.com; 2552 Kalakaua Ave, Waikiki Beach Marriott Resort; 30min per person from $75; ⏲ office 8am-8pm) Buzz around Waikiki and further afield on guided Segway tours. Options include a 30-minute intro tour and a two-hour Sunset to Diamond Head Tour.

Festivals & Events

Waikiki loves to party year-round and there are special events every month. A good source of events info is www.hawaii.com/oahu/events.

Honolulu Festival
ART, CULTURAL

(www.honolulufestival.com; ⏲ Mar) Free Asian and Pacific arts and cultural performances are staged for three days across Honolulu, including Waikiki. On the Sunday, there's a festive parade along Kalakaua Ave followed by a fireworks show in front of Waikiki's beaches.

Waikiki Spam Jam
FOOD & DRINK

(www.spamjamhawaii.com; Kalakaua Ave; ⏲ late Apr or early May; ⏺) Join thousands of Spam aficionados celebrating at this street festival devoted to Hawaii's favorite tinned meat product. The events take over Kalakaua Ave for one Saturday. Vendors offer Spam-themed merchandise and improbable food featuring Spam.

Pan-Pacific Festival
CULTURAL

(www.pan-pacific-festival.com; ⏲ mid-Jun) This Asian and Polynesian cultural festival puts on a performing-arts showcase at various venues, including outdoor hula shows at Kuhio Beach Park, a huge *ho'olaule'a* block party and parade along Kalakaua Ave, dancing at Waikiki Beach Walk and performances at nearby Ala Moana Center.

Duke Kahanamoku Challenge CULTURAL
(www.waikikicommunitycenter.org; Kahanamoku
Beach; ⊙ Jul; 🛶) Outrigger-canoe and stand-
up paddleboarding (SUP) races, island-style
local food, traditional Hawaiian games, arts
and crafts vendors and live entertainment
all happen on a Sunday at Duke Kahanamoku Beach. Note: the event's date can vary
widely year to year.

Ukulele Festival MUSIC
(www.ukulelefestivalhawaii.org; Kapiolani Regional
Park; ⊙ mid-July) Since 1971 this has been one
of the world's premier festivals celebrating
the ukulele. The current explosion in popularity of the diminutive stringed instrument
has made the event a don't-miss celebration.

Nā Hula Festival CULTURAL
(www.facebook.com/NaHulaFestival/; Kapiʻolani
Regional Park; ⊙ early Aug) Local hula *halau*
(schools) gather for two days of music and
dance celebrations at Kapiʻolani Regional
Park.

**Hawaiian Slack Key
Guitar Festival** MUSIC
(www.facebook.com/pg/Hawaiian-Slack-Key-Guitar
-Festival-111570488881029; ⊙ mid-Aug) A day-
long celebration of traditional Hawaiian
slack key guitar and ukulele music with food
vendors and an arts-and-crafts fair. It is often held at the Waikiki Aquarium.

Aloha Festivals CULTURAL
(www.alohafestivals.com; ⊙ Sep) During Hawaii's premier statewide cultural festival,
Waikiki is famous for its royal court ceremonies and also its huge *hoʻolauleʻa* evening
block party and float parade along Kalakaua
Ave, with food vendors, live music and hula
dancers in Kapiʻolani Regional Park.

Na Wahine O Ke Kai SPORTS
(www.nawahineokekai.com; Kahanamoku Beach;
⊙ late Sep) Hawaii's major annual women's
outrigger-canoe race starts at sunrise on the
island of Molokaʻi and ends 41 miles later
at Waikiki's Kahanamoku Beach. Best time
(2008): five hours, 22 minutes, five seconds.

Honolulu Pride CULTURAL
(https://hawaiilgbtlegacyfoundation.com; Kapiʻolani Regional Park; ⊙ Oct) Hawaii's largest LG-
BTIQ event features a huge pride parade
that begins on Magic Island in Ala Moana
Regional Park and follows Kalakaua Ave in
Waikiki to Kapiʻolani Regional Park where
there is music and a festival. There are doz-

ens of additional events in the days before
and after the parade.

Molokaʻi Hoe SPORTS
(www.molokaihoe.com; Kahanamoku Beach;
⊙ mid-Oct) The men's outrigger-canoe world
championship race starts just after sunrise
on Molokaʻi and then finishes 41 miles later
at Waikiki's Kahanamoku Beach. Best time
(2011): four hours, 30 minutes, 54 seconds.

Honolulu Marathon SPORTS
(www.honolulumarathon.org; ⊙ Dec) The USA's
third-largest marathon runs from downtown Honolulu to Diamond Head on the
second Sunday of December.

🛏 Sleeping

Waikiki's main beachfront strip, along Kalakaua Ave, is lined with hotels and sprawling resorts. Some of them are true beauties
with either historic or boutique atmosphere.
Most are aimed at the masses, however.

Further from the sand, look for inviting
small hotels on Waikiki's backstreets. Many
are quite affordable year-round. And don't
forget the hundreds of condos, timeshares
and apartments offered as short-term and
holiday rentals, but know that recent changes in the law (p111) have upended this sector.

🛏 Waikiki Beach Area

Big resorts line Waikiki Beach and parallel
Kalakaua Ave. Some are historic, others are
luxurious (or both) and some simply pack
visitors in by the thousands. Obviously being *on* the beach beats having to cross the
road to get there.

There's a cluster of budget hotels and
hostels in old apartment buildings at the
southeast end of Waikiki on Lemon and
Cartwright Rds, and they have a mere
5-minute walk to the beach. The northwest
end features a cluster of aging high-rises
that feels more Manhattan than beach
paradise.

★ **Beach Waikiki
Boutique Hostel** HOSTEL $
(📞 808-922-9190;   www.thebeachwaikikihostel.
com; 2569 Cartwright Rd; dm/r from $36/85;
🅿 ❄ 🛜) Guest rooms at this sociable hostel
include 4-, 6- and 8-bed dorms plus various
flavors of private rooms. Among the included extras are breakfast, coin laundry, free
pizza nights and a fridge and a microwave
in all rooms. Guests love hanging out on the

roof terrace, which has a kitchen. Several other hostels are nearby.

★ Polynesian Hostel
HOSTEL $

(☎808-922-1340; https://polynesianhostel.com; 2584 Lemon Rd; dm/r from $30/80; ☺reception 24hr; P☂) An older study in concrete block, this converted small apartment complex has had a sprightly renovation and now is a cheery hostel. Rooms have tropical motifs, attractive furniture and wood floors. The long amenities list includes breakfast, beach gear, linens, lockers and luggage storage. There's a big kitchen and they rent surfboards.

Waikiki Beachside Hostel
HOSTEL $

(☎808-923-9566; www.waikikibeachsidehostel.com; 2556 Lemon Rd; dm/r from $30/70; ☺reception 24hr; P☂) This hostel attracts an international party crowd and offers plenty of perks, from a cafe to bed linens. Like most hostels on back-alley Lemon Rd, this one occupies an older apartment complex. Each dorm has its own kitchen and bathroom, most have four to eight beds. Some private rooms have balconies. The cheapest dorms are fan-only, the rest have air-con.

Stay Waikiki
HOTEL $$

(☎808-923-7829; www.stayhotelwaikiki.com; 2424 Koa Ave; r from $165; P☀☂) This mod property (vibrant blues and oranges throughout) on a side street one block from the beach is cheery enough. The 73 rooms are bright and come with amenities such as fridges and microwaves; request one with a balcony. Upper-floor deluxe rooms are roomier. Coin-op laundry on site. The resort fee is $10. Wang Chung's (p165), a delightful karaoke bar, keeps things crooning until late.

Breakers
HOTEL $$

(☎808-923-3181; www.breakers-hawaii.com; 250 Beach Walk; s/d from $150/160; P☀☂☷) Not another high-rise timeshare, this two-story Polynesian-style place is a throwback to another era (one without a 'hospitality' fee...). You'll either love or hate the Breakers' old, creaky facilities and motel-style rooms, all with kitchenettes. Studios on the 2nd floor each have a private lanai and Japanese *shōji* (sliding paper-screen doors). Parking is free but extremely limited. The site is spacious.

Hilton Hawaiian Village
RESORT $$

(☎808-949-4321; www.hiltonhawaiianvillage.com; 2005 Kalia Rd; r from $220; P☀@☂☷) On the Honolulu end of Waikiki, the Hilton is

---

MID-CENTURY DESIGN IN WAIKIKI

Mid-century architecture fans take note: the building boom of the 1960s and 1970s left Waikiki with a plethora of concrete creations that revel in their pastiches of *Jetsons*-International Style designs. Start with the iconic Ilikai Hotel and the Rainbow Tower at Hilton Hawaiian Village. Then head to the backstreets off Kuhio Ave where there are myriad examples big and small. Oh for the era of the decorative concrete block!

Waikiki's largest resort hotel – practically a self-sufficient tourist fortress with 22 acres of towers, restaurants, bars, five pools and myriad franchise shops. It's geared almost entirely to families and package tourists, with 3386 hotel rooms of varying quality, swimming pools and a lagoon, and tons of kid-centric activities by the beach.

Every Friday at 7:45pm the resort stages a spectacular 10-minute fireworks display over Kahanamoku Beach. The hotel's iconic **Rainbow Tower** opened in 1968 and has the world's largest ceramic-tile mosaic – the famous 286ft-tall rainbow. In 1961 Elvis Presley filmed *Blue Hawaii* at the resort.

Hotel Renew
BOUTIQUE HOTEL $$

(☎808-687-7700; www.hotelrenew.com; 129 Pa'oakalani Ave; r from $175; P☀@☂) ✎ Design-savvy, ecofriendly accommodations come with mod platform beds and a color palette that looks like a box of chocolates. Rooms come with either double, king or two beds. Frills include an 'aroma concierge' who will provide a custom room scent (!). Valet-parking only. Ultimately, under the wellness facade, it's a hotel without a pool or balconies.

Ilikai Hotel
HOTEL $$

(☎808-949-3811; www.aquaaston.com/hotels/ilikai-hotel-luxury-suites; 1777 Ala Moana Blvd; studios from $200; P☀☂☷) On the far north side of Waikiki near the Ala Wai Yacht Harbor, this mid-century landmark is walkable distance from both the Ala Moana Center mall and the beach. The spacious high-rise studio and two-bedroom apartments with full kitchens and private lanai are quite comfortable. There is a nightly tiki torch-lighting ceremony.

The 30th floor stars in the opening credits of both the new and old versions of *Hawaii Five-O* as the camera zooms in on Steve McGarrett.

★ Halekulani   RESORT $$$

(☎800-367-2343; www.halekulani.com; 2199 Kalia Rd; r/ste from $530/1100; P✳🅿️🛜🏊) Evincing modern sophistication, this family-owned resort lives up to its name, which means 'House Befitting Heaven.' It's an all-encompassing experience of gracious living. Meditative calm washes over you immediately as you step onto the lobby's cool stone tiles. The design focuses on the blue Pacific, and the hubbub of Waikiki is walled away. There's no resort fee.

Peaceful rooms are equipped with comforts such as hi-tech entertainment centers, as well as deep soaking tubs and expansive lanai. Among the myriad touches, guests receive fruit and chocolates upon arrival. Eclectic luxury suites include one personally designed by Vera Wang. Find ultimate relaxation in the pampering Spa Halekulani. The hotel bar, House Without a Key (p167), is one of Waikiki's best.

★ Moana Surfrider   HISTORIC HOTEL $$$

(☎808-922-3111; www.moana-surfrider.com; 2365 Kalakaua Ave; r from $450; P✳🅿️@🛜🏊) Waikiki's most historic beachfront hotel (parts date to 1901), this grand, colonial-style establishment retains its character. Graceful yet compact guest rooms no longer retain much of their period look, having been upgraded with modern amenities and style.

A line of rocking chairs beckons on the front porch and Hawaiian artwork hangs on the walls, while wedding parties sweep through the bustling lobby every 10 minutes. Its ocean-facing courtyard has a huge and iconic banyan tree and one of Waikiki's best beachfront bars.

Royal Hawaiian Resort   RESORT $$$

(☎808-923-7311; www.royal-hawaiian.com; 2259 Kalakaua Ave; r from $400; P✳🅿️🛜🏊) Waikiki's original luxury hotel, this pink Spanish-Moorish-style landmark is loaded with vintage opulence, which is kept relevant by continuous subtle upgrades. The historic section (p144; 1927) of the aristocratic 'Pink Palace' maintains its classic appeal, although you may prefer the modern high-rise tower for rooms with ocean views and rooms with large windows.

Spa suites are adorned in carved teak, bamboo and mosaic glass, with cabana daybeds on the lanai to help you unwind. The hotel offers free tours of its extensive art collection and historical displays. Enjoy the elegant common areas with their pictures from a time when Waikiki was the height of genteel style. The gardens are a tropical fantasy. One off-note, under management by

---

THE DREADED RESORT FEE

Waikiki is ground zero for the resort fee scam. Never optional, the fees are simply a way for hotels to make their base rates seem smaller than they really are. Resorts will defend those fees and say that they include 'free' wifi, maybe a welcome drink on arrival, a small bottle of water in the room and/or meaningless discounts off affiliated businesses such as 15% off in the hotel's overpriced restaurant.

And just like airlines and baggage fees, hotels have found resort fees (or some other blandly cynical euphemism such as 'convenience fees' or 'hospitality fees') a great way to sneakily increase their profits. The fees have shot up in the last few years and it's not uncommon to see resort fees of $50 a night.

When comparing rates, it's essential to try to figure out the final cost per night. Keep the following in mind as you budget for your Hawaii trip:

➡ Determine if there is a resort fee and the amount per night.

➡ Many Waikiki hotels still don't charge resort fees; the higher the hotel's basic rate, the higher the odds that there is going to be a resort fee.

➡ If you'll need parking, find out the cost. Major resorts charge upwards of $50 a night to park your car. Some places only offer valet parking or they offer cheap, or even free parking.

➡ Add in the tax rate for Honolulu (which includes Waikiki) hotel stays: almost 15%. Note that some hotels levy a 'taxes and fees' charge that's over 15%, which is their way of burying the resort fee.

Marriott, the hotel's extra charges and fees have proliferated (the resort fee is $38, valet parking is $40 etc).

Halepuna Waikiki by Halekulani   BOUTIQUE HOTEL **$$$**

(☑ 808-921-7272; www.halepuna.com; 2233 Helumoa Rd; r from $350; P ✳ 🛜 🏊) This is the slightly edgy, slightly more affordable sibling of the vaunted Halekulani across the street. The highlight is the fab rooftop lounge with a pool oriented at the Pacific between other high-rises, which gives an infinity effect. Service is lavish; rooms higher up the rate chain feature balconies and views. A refreshing change: there are no resort fees.

Modern Honolulu   BOUTIQUE HOTEL **$$$**

(☑ 855-970-4161, 808-450-3379; www.themodernhonolulu.com; 1775 Ala Moana Blvd; r from $290; P ✳ @ 🛜 🏊) Terraced ocean-view rooms and suites are elementally chic, showing off teak doors and marble baths. Not all rooms have balconies and some also lack basics like a fridge. The two deck pools overlook Ala Wai Yacht Harbor and have sensuous loungers and imported sand.

'Alohilani Resort Waikiki Beach   HOTEL **$$$**

(☑ 808-922-1233; www.alohilaniresort.com; 2490 Kalakaua Ave; r from $300; P ✳ 🛜) Opened in 2018, the 'Alohilani is the reimagining of a dour package-tour hotel. The reborn lobby features a two-story aquarium that the hotel modestly calls the 'Oceanarium.' The pool deck is a destination itself, with a saltwater infinity pool and a kid-friendly shallow pool. At night, tiki torches glow and surf videos are projected on the side of the hotel.

Rooms have a pale motif, and those on higher floors in-your-face ocean and Diamond Head views.

Regency on Beachwalk Waikiki   CONDO **$$$**

(☑ 808-922-3871; www.outrigger.com; 255 Beach Walk; r from $250, 2-night minimum; P ✳ @) This modern high-rise has more than respectable 1- and 2-bedroom units, with earth-toned furnishings, marble baths and bold, modern artwork. Spacious condo-style suites have full kitchens and some have private lanai with peek-a-boo ocean views. Beware of the mandatory departure cleaning charge that starts at $250.

Step outside the downstairs lobby and you're right on Waikiki Beach Walk (p152) – then keep walking five minutes to the beach or the off-site swimming pool.

🛏 Kuhio Avenue Area

The area of Waikiki east of Kalakaua Ave is getting evermore large hotels. But in the streets that radiate off Kuhio Ave you can still find lots of older and smaller hotels, many loaded with rugged charm. Here you'll get to rub elbows with the characters and ageless beach bums who still call Waikiki home. Be dubious of any claims for ocean views back here.

★ Waikiki Central Hotel   HOTEL **$**

(☑ 808-922-1544; www.waikikicentral.com; 2431 Prince Edward St; r from $120; P ✳ 🛜) Don't judge this six-story, 1970s-era apartment complex based on its unpromising off-white concrete cover. Inside this standout budget option are 27 compact yet cheery rooms with kitchenettes that feel fresh and modern. All have balconies. There are no resort fees.

Royal Grove Hotel   HOTEL **$**

(☑ 808-923-7691; www.royalgrovehotel.com; 161 Uluniu Ave; r from $95; ✳ 🛜 🏊) No frills – and you're not here for the decor – but plenty of aloha characterize this kitschy, candy-pink, six-story hotel that attracts so many returning snowbirds that you'll need to reserve well in advance. Motel-style rooms in the main wing are basic but do have balconies. Many rooms have kitchenettes. Offers discounted weekly off-season rates. The neon sign is a mid-century classic.

'Ilima Hotel   HOTEL **$**

(☑ 808-923-1877; www.ilima.com; 445 Nohonani St; studios from $140, 1br/2br from $190/250; P ✳ 🛜 🏊) Life feels less hurried at this older, backstreet high-rise hotel. All studios and suites come equipped with full kitchens and balconies. Rooms have tables and desks as well. Book far ahead. Limited free parking is available. The beach is about a 10-minute walk.

HI-Waikiki   HOSTEL **$**

(Hostelling International; ☑ 808-926-8313; www.hostelsaloha.com; 2417 Prince Edward St; dm/r from $36/80; ⊙ reception 7am-midnight; P @ 🛜) Occupying an older converted foam-green, four-story apartment building, this popular hostel is just a few blocks from the beach. Inside are fan-cooled single-sex 6-bed dorms and basic private rooms with bathrooms, a kitchen and coin-op laundry. No alcohol allowed and no daytime lockout or curfew either. Reservations are imperative (seven-night maximum stay). Limited parking ($10 per night).

Surfjack Hotel & Swim Club
BOUTIQUE HOTEL $$

(☎808-923-8882; www.surfjack.com; 412 Lewers St; r from $220; ❄🐾🏊) If your Don Draper fantasy still sizzles years after *Mad Men*, then you'll love this retro-chic 10-story hotel that re-creates a posh early 1960s world that may not have existed but which would have been cool if it had. Rooms in this vintage building encircle a courtyard pool. All have balconies and reimagined mid-century furniture your parents would have thrown out.

There are designer toiletries that go beyond Brylcreem, mini-fridges and high-tech sound systems in every room. Larger rooms have one or two bedrooms. The beach is a hike.

Aqua Ohia Waikiki
HOTEL $$

(☎808-926-6442; www.ohiahotel.com; 2280 Kuhio Ave; r from $135; ❄🐾🏊) Basic rooms in an older high-rise on Waikiki's rear echelon translate into cheap rates. Many have small lanais, small fridges and small bathrooms. All rooms have cooking facilities, and some have full kitchens.

Coconut Waikiki Hotel
HOTEL $$

(☎808-923-8828; http://coconutwaikikihotel.com; 450 Lewers St; r from $180; P❄🐾🏊) The Coconut delivers a splash of mod style for anyone doing Waikiki on a budget. Rooms are not large but all have balconies, wet bars and microwaves. The views are of Waikiki's backside. There's a small pool, a sandbox for the kids (or cats), an included modest breakfast and BBQ grill on the communal terrace.

Aqua Bamboo
HOTEL $$

(☎808-954-7412; www.aquabamboo.com; 2425 Kuhio Ave; studio/1-bedroom ste from $160/240; P❄🐾🏊) Looking for a meditative retreat in Waikiki's concrete jungle? This 12-story hotel with an intimate cabana spa has a small pool. Stylishly minimalist rooms include studios and suites with kitchenettes or full kitchens. Most have lanais or balconies. Rooms are smallish.

Pearl Hotel Hawaii
HOTEL $$

(☎808-922-1616; www.pearlhotelwaikiki.com; 415 Nahua St; r $130-220; P❄🐾) Centrally, this typically bland high-rise hotel on Waikiki's back acre is affordable. Spacious, elementary rooms each have a microwave and mini-fridge. The cheapest rooms lack a balcony, which makes them a bit dire. One-bedroom suites have a full kitchen.

Luana Waikiki Hotel & Suites
HOTEL $$

(☎808-955-6000; www.luanawaikiki.com; 2045 Kalakaua Ave; r from $175; P❄🐾🏊) Studios equipped with kitchenettes and one-bedroom condos with kitchens are the best options at this high-rise hotel, which also has basic hotel rooms. It has a sunny swimming pool and deck. Some units have wide views of Waikiki with a 'glimpse' (as the hotel says) of the Pacific. All have fridges and balconies.

🛏 Kaimana Beach Area

South past Kapi'olani Regional Park is an outcrop of 1960s high-rise hotels and condos that enjoy great views but are removed from Waikiki's hustle and crowds.

Lotus Honolulu
BOUTIQUE HOTEL $$$

(☎808-922-1700; www.lotushonoluluhotel.com; 2885 Kalakaua Ave; r from $300; ❄🐾) This hip boutique hotel is a lovely sanctuary near Kaimana Beach. At the calm southern edge of Waikiki, many rooms have panoramic views of Diamond Head. Mingle with honeymooners looking for a romantic escape or head off on a tour of Waikiki using the hotel's bikes. Rooms have scalloped balconies, fridges and espresso machines. There's a free nightly wine party.

🍴 Eating

Waikiki has a lot of restaurants aimed at the vacationing masses, but amid the overpriced underwhelmers you can find some gems, including a few where a beach view doesn't equal dull food.

Waikiki is close to Honolulu neighborhoods with excellent restaurants, the Ala Moana (p116) area is just west. Kapahulu Ave (p162) stretches north from the east end and offers a pearl necklace of great dining options while the casual enclave of Monsarrat Ave (p163) is just a short walk.

🍴 Waikiki Beach Area

You can have a good meal and a view along Waikiki Beach. Just inland, there are many more decent options. Along Kalakaua Ave, chains overflow with hungry tourists – most of whom can probably find the same chains in their hometowns.

Ramen Nakamura
JAPANESE $

(☎808-922-7960; 2141 Kalakaua Ave; mains $11-23; ☺11am-11:30pm; 🛜🈺) Hit this simple noodle shop at lunchtime and you'll have to strategically elbow aside tourists toting Gucci and Chanel bags just to sit down. Then dig into hearty bowls of oxtail or *tonkatsu* (breaded and fried pork cutlets) or kimchi ramen soup with crunchy fried garlic slices on top. Cash only, although the sign notes 'Yen Accepted.' Much of the menu is in Japanese – always a good sign.

Eggs 'n' Things
BREAKFAST $

(☎808-923-3447; www.eggsnthings.com; 343 Saratoga Rd; mains $9-18; ☺6am-10pm; 🈺) This bustling diner dishes straight-up comfort food: banana macadamia-nut pancakes with tropical syrups (guava, honey or coconut), sugary crepes topped with fresh fruit, or fluffy omelets scrambled with Portuguese sausage. You'll fit right in with the early-morning crowd of jet-lagged tourists lined up outside the door.

Tonkatsu Ginza Bairin
JAPANESE $$

(☎808-926-8082; www.pj-partners.com/bairin; 255 Beach Walk; mains $11-39; ☺11am-9:30pm Sun-Thu, to 10:30pm Fri & Sat) Why go to Tokyo for perfect pork *tonkatsu* when you can enjoy the lightly breaded bits of deep-fried pork goodness right here near Waikiki Beach? The family behind this restaurant has been serving *tonkatsu* at a Ginza restaurant since 1927. At this outpost, nothing has been lost. Besides the namesake, there is great sushi, rice bowls and more.

Waikiki Yokocho
JAPANESE $$

(☎808-926-8093; www.waikiki-yokocho.com; 2250 Kalakaua Ave; mains $7-30; ☺11am-midnight) Ride an escalator down to a perfectly authentic Japanese food court. Try to choose between 16 different stalls and restaurants. Your options range from organic *o-musubi* (rice cakes) to bento (Japanese-style boxed lunch) to tempura and more. Some places are self-serve, while others offer table service. Kids are delighted by the rows of free vintage arcade games.

Sansei Seafood Restaurant & Sushi Bar
JAPANESE $$

(☎808-931-6286; www.sanseihawaii.com; 2552 Kalakaua Ave, 3rd fl, Waikiki Beach Marriott Resort; shared plates $5-20, mains $16-38; ☺5:30-10pm Sun-Thu, to 1am Fri & Sat; 🅿) From the mind of one of Hawaii's top chefs, DK Kodama, this Pacific Rim menu rolls out everything from

WAIKIKI'S BEST BEACH CAFE

Waikiki's best beach cafe, **Barefoot Beach Cafe** (☎808-924-2233; https://barefootbeachcafe.com; 2699 Kalakaua Ave, Queen's Surf Beach; mains $8-15; ☺7am-8:30pm) is just south of the sand at Queen's Beach. Order at the window and grab a shady table close to the water and tuck into island-accented breakfasts, snacks and lunches. The kitchen shows great attention to detail, whether it's eggs Benedict, garlic fries or a plate lunch. There's live music nightly (5:30pm).

Shave ice and smoothies are cooling treats for those on a stroll or lounging on the shore. Extras include free container refills with fruit-accented water.

creatively stylish sushi and sashimi to Dungeness crab ramen with black-truffle broth – all to rave reviews. Tables on the torchlit veranda equal prime sunset views. Free parking with validation.

LuLu's Waikiki
AMERICAN $$

(☎808-926-5222; www.luluswaikiki.com; 2586 Kalakaua Ave, Park Shore Waikiki; mains $7-25; ☺7am-2am; 🈺) Surfboards on the wall and an awesome ocean view set the mood at this cheery open-air restaurant, bar and nightclub. LuLu's filling breakfasts, complete with 'dawn patrol' omelets, eggs Benedict, stuffed French toast, *loco moco* (dish of rice, fried egg and hamburger patty topped with gravy or other condiments) and fruit bowls, are always a hit. Sunset happy hour runs 3pm to 5pm.

Gyū-kaku
JAPANESE $$

(☎808-926-2989; www.gyu-kaku.com; 307 Lewers St; mains $12-24; ☺11:30am-11:30pm) Who doesn't love a grill-it-yourself BBQ joint? Settle in with your entourage at this branch of the local chain for Kobe rib-eye steak, *kalbi* (marinated short ribs), garlic shrimp and enoki mushrooms, served with plentiful sweet and spicy marinades and dips. Show up for happy-hour food and drink specials (before 6:30pm or after 9:30pm).

Hula Grill
HAWAIIAN $$

(☎808-923-4852; www.hulagrillwaikiki.com; 2335 Kalakaua Ave, 2nd fl, Outrigger Waikiki Beach Resort; mains $20-40; ☺6:30am-10pm; 🅿🈺) Come early to the Outrigger Waikiki Beach Resort to score a table overhanging Kahaloa

WAIKIKI'S MYSTERY OBSERVER

Nobody knows his or her name, but on Instagram, @misterver has a huge following thanks to a steady stream of brilliant candid photos shot on Waikiki's streets and beaches. Don't look for glossy tourist moments, instead savor candid sides of a neighborhood more known for its ever-changing flood of visitors. Dogs, decrepit buildings, unguarded moments, artful snaps and idiosyncratic looks are captured anonymously and on the fly.

& Ulukou Beaches and watch the sun set as slack key guitars play. Reward yourself with cheap mai tais, 'wrong island' ice teas and *pupu*-like (appetizer) mango BBQ ribs. Simple à la carte breakfasts bring out some refreshingly healthy options. Happy hour is 3pm to 6pm.

Azure SEAFOOD $$$

(☎808-921-4600; www.azurewaikiki.com; 2259 Kalakaua Ave, Royal Hawaiian Resort; mains from $49-68; ⊘5:30-9pm) Azure is the signature restaurant at the Royal Hawaiian Resort (p156). Seafood fresh from the market is celebrated in the bouillabaisse, and simplicity is the hallmark of the steak and seafood mains. Given the quality, the tasting menu is fine value. The drinks and wine lists will delight. You can dine near the sand under a 'Royal Hawaiian' pink-and-white awning.

You can also opt for a five-course tasting menu (with/without wine $145/105).

Roy's Waikiki HAWAII REGIONAL $$$

(☎808-923-7697; www.royshawaii.com; 226 Lewers St; mains $24-53; ⊘light menu 11am-5pm, dinner 5-9:30pm Mon-Thu, to 10pm Fri-Sun) This contemporary incarnation of Roy Yamaguchi's island-born chain is perfect for a flirty date or just celebrating the good life. The ground-breaking chef's signature *misoyaki* butterfish, blackened ahi (yellowfin tuna) and macadamia-nut-crusted mahimahi are always on the menu. The famous hot chocolate soufflé for dessert is a must. The bar makes great cocktails and there's seating outside under tiki torches.

Orchids BUFFET $$$

(☎808-923-2311; www.halekulani.com; 2199 Kalia Rd, Halekulani; brunch buffet adult/child $76/34, mains other times $16-64; ⊘7:30am-9:30pm Mon-

Sat, 9am-2:30pm Sun) O'ahu's most elegant Sunday brunch spread covers all the bases, with a made-to-order omelet station; a buffet of *poke*, sashimi, sushi and salads; and a decadent dessert bar with coconut pie and homemade Kona coffee ice cream. This indulgence draws acolytes from across O'ahu, reserve ahead.

But don't come just for the food – it's the smashing ocean view, tropical flowers and cheesy harp and flute music that set the honeymoon mood. On other days, the restaurant serves a full menu through the day. At night there's a strict dress code – resort attire required.

La Mer FRENCH $$$

(☎808-923-2311; www.halekulani.com; 2199 Kalia Rd, Halekulani; 3-/4-course prix-fixe dinner menu $125/155; ⊘5:30-9:30pm; P) At the luxury Halekulani (p156) resort, La Mer is rated by traditionalists as Waikiki's top fine-dining destination. A neoclassical French menu puts the emphasis on Provençal cuisine with the addition of fresh Hawaii-grown ingredients such as seafood, including abalone. Wines are perfectly paired; diners are required to have jackets. The beach views are superb.

Valet parking is free for diners.

Okonomiyaki Chibo JAPANESE $$$

(☎808-922-9722; www.chibohawaii.com; 280 Beach Walk; set lunch $14-25, dinner $30-80; ⊘11:30am-2pm & 5-10pm) Showing off a sleek, dark-wood interior, this high-end Japanese teppanyaki grill is a standout for its *okonomiyaki* (savory cabbage pancakes). Go traditional and order one made with *buta* (pork) or *ika* (squid), or splurge on steak, scallops and prawns. Lunch is a simpler affair. Great selection of Japanese whiskeys and sake. Snare a table outside.

✖ Kuhio Avenue Area

Along Kuhio Ave, and the many nearby streets and alleys, are all manner of places to eat, from humble to superb; many are just holes in the wall.

★ Musubi Cafe Iyasume JAPANESE $

(☎808-921-0168; https://iyasumehawaii.com; 2427 Kuhio Ave, Aqua Monarch Hotel; mains $5-9; ⊘6:30am-9pm) This hole-in-the-wall keeps busy making fresh *onigiri* (rice balls) stuffed with seaweed, salmon roe and sour plums. Other specialties include salmon-roe rice bowls, Japanese curry and island-style *mochiko* fried chicken. In a hurry? Grab a *bentō* box to go. The namesake *musubi* is a definitive version with grilled Spam atop a block of white rice wrapped in *nori* (seaweed sheet).

By noon, the lunch lines are long. Mostly takeout (get a beachside picnic table) but there are a couple tables.

★ Marukame Udon   JAPANESE $

(☑ 808-931-6000; www.facebook.com/marukame udon; 2310 Kuhio Ave; mains $4-12; ⊘ 7am-10pm; ♿) Everybody loves this reconstructed Japanese noodle shop, which is so popular there is often a line stretching down the sidewalk. Watch those thick udon noodles get rolled, cut and boiled fresh right in front of you, then stack mini plates of giant tempura and *musubi* (rice balls) stuffed with salmon or a sour plum on your cafeteria tray.

Wash it all down with iced barley or green tea; there's no booze.

Mahiku Farmer's Market   MARKET $

(☑ 808-225-4002; https://mahikufarmersmarket. com; 2155 Kalakaua Ave, Bank of Hawaii Waikiki Center; snacks from $1.50; ⊘ 4-8pm Mon-Tue & Thu) Wrapping around a glassy commercial building, this farmers market attracts dozens of vendors selling produce, prepared foods, artworks and crafts. Sample your way around the myriad mostly Asian-flavored snacks; the fresh banana *lumpias* are extraordinary.

Hula Dog Kuhio   FOOD TRUCK $

(☑ 808-256-7008; www.huladogkuhiohonolulu. com; 206 Kapuni St; mains $7; ⊘ 11am-9pm) Set on a patch of Astroturf with picnic tables fronting Kuhio Ave, this food truck serves one thing: hot dogs. Choose between a Polish sausage or a veggie dog, then pick a bun, add some tropical-accented mustard and then pick the heat level of the topping that sets these wieners apart: garlic-lemon sauce. Wash it all down with lemonade.

Blue Ocean   SEAFOOD $

(☑ 808-542-5587; 2449 Kuhio Ave; mains $8-19; ⊘ 10am-10pm) Shrimp in all forms are the stars at this vibrant blue food truck. The spicy garlic shrimp po' boy is a delight, with succulent little crustaceans spilling out all over. Other treats include some excellent salmon dishes. There's a few rudimentary seats here, otherwise enjoy your feast as takeout. Staff are charmers.

Me BBQ   KOREAN $

(☑ 808-926-9717; 151 Uluniu Ave; mains $8-15; ⊘ 7am-9pm Mon-Sat; ♿) The street-side take-out counter may be a tad short on atmosphere, but there is a fine little side yard with shady plastic tables where you can chow down on Korean standards such as kimchi and *kalbi*. The wall-size picture menu offers a mind-boggling array of mixed-plate combos including chicken *katsu* (batter-fried chicken), Portuguese sausage and eggs, and other only-in-Hawaii tastes.

MAC 24/7   AMERICAN $$

(☑ 808-921-5564; www.mac247waikiki.com; 2500 Kuhio Ave, Hilton Waikiki Beach; mains $9-32; ⊘ 24hr; ♿) If it's 3am and you're famished, skip the temptation for a cold $25 burger from room service (*if* you have room service) and drop by Waikiki's best all-night diner (their slogan: 'We don't close unless it snows.'). The dining room has a bold style palette and by day has a lovely garden view. Food (and prices) are a cut above.

Pancakes are a real specialty here and, if you're up for it, try the famous MAC pancake challenge: eat three huge 14-inch pancakes (total weight 5 pounds) in under 90 minutes and you get your picture on the wall of fame – about one person a month wins.

Mahina & Sun's   AMERICAN $$

(☑ 808-924-5810; http://mahinaandsuns.com; 412 Lewers St, Surfjack Hotel & Swim Club; mains $12-32; ⊘ 6:30am-10pm Sun-Thu, to midnight Fri & Sat) ⊘ Overlooking the stylish pool at the Surfjack Hotel (p158), this open-air bistro has a well-imagined casual and comfortable menu of classics, such as burgers, salads, pizza and seafood (which is sustainably sourced). Most ingredients are organic. Enjoy drinks until late from the creative bar. Up early? Try the banana bread or the avocado toast at breakfast (served till 2pm).

★ Hy's Steakhouse   STEAK $$$

(☑ 808-922-5555; www.hyswaikiki.com; 2440 Kuhio Ave; mains $40-110; ⊘ 5-10pm) Hy's is so old-school that you expect to find inkwells on the tables. This traditional steakhouse has a timeless old leather and wood interior. But ultimately, it's not whether you expect to see Frank and Dean at a back table; rather, it's the steak at Hy's that is superb.

From a glassed-in booth off the dining room, the meat master cooks up an array of succulent cuts of beef. There are plenty of sides and salads you can order – and they're all fine – but really save room (and save some money) for the steaks. The garlic one is highly recommended as is the literally over-the-top, infinitely tender and massive Wagyu Tomahawk cut, the cut favored by cavemen with champagne tastes.

✖ Kaimana Beach Area

You can find some old-style fancy meals in this enclave away from the crowds.

Michel's at Colony Surf   INTERNATIONAL $$$
(📞 808-923-6552;   https://michelshawaii.com; 2895 Kalakaua Ave; mains $40-70, tasting menu $100; ⏰ 5:30-9pm) Michel's opened in 1962 and little seems to have changed since. The beautiful water view out over a small pocket beach, with the heart of Waikiki glowing in the distance, is the same, as is the menu. Old classics like steak Diane are prepared tableside and flambéed. Other dishes served with flourishes include lobster bisque and caviar. Service is formal and valet parking is free.

Think of this place as a destination for an anniversary meal or honeymoon celebration. Book ahead.

Hau Tree Lanai   SEAFOOD $$$
(📞 808-921-7066; www.kaimana.com; 2863 Kalakaua Ave, New Otani Kaimana Beach Hotel; lunch mains $19-25, mains $30-55; ⏰ 7am-9pm) A beautiful beachfront setting under an arbor of three namesake hibiscus trees brings retirees and tourists back to this open-air pink-tablecloth restaurant on Kaimana Beach. Perennially popular mainly for the views; the pricey menu has dashes of Hawaiian flavor from classic breakfasts to casual lunches and onto more formal seafood dinners.

✖ Kapahulu Avenue

On the outskirts of Waikiki, Kapahulu Ave is one of the most interesting streets for dining across Honolulu. The sheer number of creative bistros and cafes rewards anyone hungry out for a stroll. It's an easy walk from Waikiki Beach. Look for standout neighborhood eateries, drive-ins and bakeries, cooking up fare from Hawaiian soul food to Japanese country fare.

★ Waiola Shave Ice   DESSERTS $
(📞 808-949-2269; www.waiolashaveice.com; 3113 Mokihana St; shave ice $3-5; ⏰ 11am-5:30pm; 🅿️ 🚇) This clapboard corner shop has been making the same superfine shave ice since

1940, and we'd argue that it's got the formula exactly right. Get yours doused with 20-plus flavors of syrup and topped by azuki beans, *liliko'i* (passion fruit) cream, condensed milk, Hershey's chocolate syrup or spicy-sweet *li hing mui* (crack seed). Go all Hawaii and get yours POG-flavored (passion-orange-guava). There's an even older location in Honolulu (p118).

It's one building in on Mokihana St and a bit hard to spot from Kapahulu Ave. Look for the picnic tables.

Ono Seafood   SEAFOOD $
(📞 808-732-4806; 747 Kapahulu Ave; mains $7-12; ⏰ 9am-6pm Tue-Sat) Arrive early at this addictive, made-to-order *poke* shop before it runs out of fresh fish marinated in *shōyu* (soy sauce), house-smoked *tako* (octopus), spicy ahi rice bowls or boiled peanuts spiked with star anise. The *shōyu* ahi is beloved by regulars. There are a couple of humble tables outside. Very limited parking.

Haili's Hawaiian Foods   HAWAIIAN $
(📞 808-735-8019; http://hailishawaiianfood.com; 760 Palani Ave; meals $11-16; ⏰ 10am-5pm Tue-Sat, to 2pm Sun; 🚇) Three generations at Haili's have been cooking up homegrown Hawaiian fare since 1950. Locals shoehorn themselves into kid-friendly booths and tables, then dig into heaping plates of *kalua* pig (cooked in an underground pit), *lomilomi* salmon and *laulau* (meat wrapped in taro leaves and steamed) served with poi (mashed taro) or rice.

For a little variety, try the grilled ahi (yellowfin tuna) plate lunches, bowls of tripe stew, *poke* bowls or, yes, raw beef liver poke.

Rainbow Drive-In   HAWAIIAN $
(Map p86; 📞 808-737-0177; www.rainbowdrivein. com; 3308 Kanaina Ave; meals $4-10; ⏰ 7am-9pm; 🅿️ 🚇) This plate-lunch legend draws legions of locals and tourists from Waikiki. Wrapped in rainbow-colored neon, it's a throwback to another era. Construction workers, surfers and gangly teens order down-home favorites such as mixed-plate lunches, *loco moco* and Portuguese sweet-bread French toast. Everything's fresh, although there are better plate-lunch places, such as Kahai Street Kitchen (p118) over by the University of Hawaii.

Started by an island-born US army cook after WWII, Rainbow's regulars have included a teenage Barack Obama (p102), who said he lounged away many a day at the shady picnic tables.

Kono's Northshore
HAWAIIAN $

(☑ 808-892-1088; http://konosnorthshore.com; 945 Kapahulu Ave; mains $10-16; ⊙7am-6:30pm) In a case of the country coming to town, Kono's on Kapahulu is a city outpost for the popular North Shore–based purveyor of 12-hour slow-roasted *kalua* pork. They also serve popular breakfast sandwiches and decent salads. The milkshake menu is even longer than the pork menu; try flavors like key lime and coconut cream pie.

Leonard's
BAKERY $

(☑ 808-737-5591; www.leonardshawaii.com; 933 Kapahulu Ave; snacks from $1.30; ⊙5:30am-10pm Sun-Thu, to 11pm Fri & Sat; P 🅿) It's almost impossible to drive by the Leonard's eye-catching vintage 1950s neon sign without seeing a crowd of tourists. This bakery is famous for its *malasadas* (sweet deep-fried dough rolled in sugar) Portuguese-style – like a doughnut without the hole. Order variations with *haupia* (coconut cream) or guava filling for more flavor. Be sure to get yours hot from the fryer.

Other baked goods like the bland sausage croissants aren't worth the hype. If there's a line, there are displays of logo-emblazoned T-shirts to divert you.

★ Tonkatsu Tamafuji
JAPANESE $$

(☑ 808-922-1212; www.facebook.com/tamafuji honolulu; 449 Kapahulu Ave; mains $16-30; ⊙4-9:30pm Mon & Wed-Fri, 5-9:30pm Sat & Sun) Kat-su, the deep-fried Japanese cooking method that coats meats like pork and chicken in a perfectly crispy exterior made from panko bread crumbs. This bright and cheerful place packs in crowds for some of O'ahu's best. Choose your cut of pork and soon you're enjoying fabulous katsu with unlimited shredded cabbage and rice. Meat options include oysters, chicken and shrimp.

Call ahead to get your name on the waiting list, then walk over.

Side Street Inn Kapahulu
HAWAIIAN $$

(☑808-739-3939; http://sidestreetinn.com; 614 Kapahulu Ave; shared plates $7-15, mains $12-25; ⊙3pm-1am Mon-Fri, 1pm-1am Sat & Sun, kitchen closes at 11:30pm daily; P 🅿) A Hawaiian-style sports bar with meal portions so huge that virtually everyone walks out with a bag containing what they couldn't eat. The good news is that the food is great. Thinly sliced pan-fried pork chops, kimchi fried rice and 'Side' soba are all tops. Enjoy the many draft microbrews while you wait for a table.

Uncle Bo's Pupu Bar & Grill
FUSION $$

(☑808-735-8311; www.unclebosrestaurant.com; 559 Kapahulu Ave; shared plates $8-21, mains $20-39; ⊙5pm-1am, kitchen until 11:45pm) Inside this mustard-yellow storefront, boisterous groups devour the inventive chef's encyclopedic list of fusion *pupu* crafted with island flair, such as *kalua* pig nachos and garlicky spicy shrimp. For dinner, focus on market-fresh seafood such as baked *opah* (moonfish) or pan-roasted shellfish. Reservations recommended. There's a full bar and a cheap late-night menu.

Tokkuri Tei
JAPANESE $$

(☑808-732-6480; www.tokkuritei-hawaii.com; 449 Kapahulu Ave, #201; mains $7-25; ⊙11am-2pm & 5:30pm-midnight Mon-Fri, 5:30pm-midnight Sat, 5-10:30pm Sun) An upbeat neighborhood *izakaya* (Japanese pub) upstairs in a tiny open-air mall offers contemporary versions of Japanese bar-food standards. Paper lanterns hang overhead, fishing nets divide tables, and bookshelves behind the bar hoard customers' private bottles of sake and *shōchū* (potato liquor). Squid pancakes, crispy salmon-skin salad and grilled yellowtail cheek sell out quickly. Reserve ahead.

Get a seat at the counter overlooking the busy chefs.

✖ Monsarrat Avenue

Wander past the zoo and Waikiki School to reach an outcrop of great casual cafes and restaurants on mostly residential Monsarrat Ave, right in the shadow of Diamond Head.

LOCAL KNOWLEDGE

TOP PLATE LUNCHES

The crowds are proof: people love theJapanese-fusion plate lunches at **Pioneer Saloon** (☑808-732-4001; www.pioneer-saloon.net; 3046 Monsarrat Ave; mains $9-16; ⊙11am-8pm), with dozens of choices from grilled ahi to fried baby octopus to *yakisoba* (fried noodles). The fried chicken with garlic sauce and the grilled miso salmon are tops. Look for the potted plants outside; loads of whimsical nonsense decor inside. Don't miss the shave ice.

Note: the 'saloon' in the name is a ruse, there's no booze, but there is a tiny side yard with umbrella-shaded seats.

★**Ars Cafe and Gelato** CAFE $

(☑808-734-7897; http://ars-cafe.com; 3116 Monsarrat Ave; mains $6-12; ☉6:30am-6pm Mon-Sat, 8am-6pm Sun) Avocado toast two cuts above the cliche is but one of the delights at this cafe, which is also a gallery for local artists. Enjoy excellent coffee as mellow, jazzy tunes play gently. Don't miss the ice cream by the wizard of the Mid-Late Summer creamery, Aaron Lopez. His esoteric flavors like burnt milk and marshmallow maple molasses change weekly.

Hawaii Sushi SUSHI $

(☑808-734-6370; 3045 Monsarrat Ave, Suite 1; mains $6-11; ☉10am-8pm) A winner for the Hawaiian-style fresh sushi with rolls and bowls (such as the Spicy Ahi Bowl, made with local ahi); you can't get fresher fish anywhere else in Waikiki. The specials are excellent and change daily. There's some parking outside and a few seats inside.

Diamond Head Market & Grill HAWAIIAN $

(☑808-732-0077; www.diamondheadmarket.com; 3158 Monsarrat Ave; meals $9-18; ☉deli 7am-9pm, kitchen 8am-8pm; ℗) Step inside this fantastic gourmet deli and bakery for take-away roast pork loin and citrus jicama (yam bean) salad, perfect for a beach picnic. Outside at the takeout window, surfers and families order *char siu* (Chinese barbecued pork) plate lunches, portobello mushroom burgers and, at breakfast, tropical-fruit pancakes. Do takeout or eat at the sun-drenched picnic tables.

Bogart's Cafe CAFE $

(☑808-739-0999; www.bogartscafe.com; 3045 Monsarrat Ave, Suite 3; mains $8-18; ☉7am-3pm; ℐ) Regulars crave the taro-banana pancakes at Bogart's, which uses fresh local produce in its full menu of breakfast and lunch items. The avocado-and-spinach Benedict is a tasty winner. There's a few tables out front under a tree. Reserve ahead.

Da Cove Health Bar & Cafe CAFE $

(☑808-732-8744; http://dacove.com; 3045 Monsarrat Ave, #5; mains $6-12; ☉9am-8pm Mon, Wed & Fri, to 11pm Tue & Thu, 8am-8pm Sat & Sun; ℐ) This place specializes in acai bowls, fruit smoothies, healthy wraps, fresh *poke* and sashimi. Chill out with a coconut-husk dose of '*awa* (kava), Polynesia's mildly intoxicating elixir, and enjoy a relaxed vibe on '*awa* nights (Tuesday and Thursday), when local musicians play until late.

People's Open Market MARKET $

(cnr Monsarrat & Paki Aves, Kapi'olani Regional Park; ☉10-11am Wed; ℐ) 🌿 City-sponsored farmers market in Kapi'olani Regional Park that trades in O'ahu's enormous fresh bounty from *mauka* (land) to *makai* (sea). Only a short walk from Waikiki; plenty of parking.

🍷 **Drinking & Nightlife**

If you're looking for a frosty cold beer or a fruity cocktail to help you recover from a day at the beach, there are endless options in Waikiki. Sip a sunset mai tai and be hypnotized by the lilting harmonies of slack key guitars, then mingle with locals who come here to party too.

◉ **Waikiki Beach Area**

★**Hula's Bar & Lei Stand** GAY

(☑808-923-0669; https://hulas.com; 134 Kapahulu Ave, 2nd fl, Waikiki Grand Hotel; ☉10am-2am; 🎤) This friendly, open-air bar is Waikiki's legendary gay venue and a great place to make new friends, boogie and have a few drinks. Hunker down at the pool table, or gaze at the spectacular vista of Diamond Head. The breezy balcony-bar also has views of Queen's Surf Beach, a prime destination for a sun-worshiping LGBTQ+ crowd.

Beach Bar BAR

(☑808-922-3111; www.moana-surfrider.com; 2365 Kalakaua Ave, Moana Surfrider; ☉10:30am-10:30pm) Waikiki's best beach bar is on an atmospheric stretch of Kahaloa & Ulukou Beaches. The atmosphere comes from the historic Moana Surfrider (p145) hotel and its vast banyan tree. The people-watching of passersby, sunbathers and surfers is captivating. On an island of mediocre mai tais, the versions here are some of O'ahu's best (the 'sunset mai tai' is the top choice).

Although it's always busy, turnover is quick so you won't wait long for a table. There's live entertainment (p168) much of the day.

Lulu's Waikiki COCKTAIL BAR

(☑808-926-5222; www.luluswaikiki.com; 2586 Kalakaua Ave, Park Shore Waikiki; ☉7am-2am) Brush off your sandy feet at Kuhio Beach, then step across Kalakaua Ave to this surf-themed open-air bar and grill with 2nd-story lanai (balcony) views of the Pacific Ocean and Diamond Head. Lap up sunset happy hours (3pm to 5pm daily), then chill out to acoustic acts and local bands later most evenings.

Lewers Lounge
LOUNGE
(☑808-923-2311; www.halekulani.com; 2199 Kalia Rd, Halekulani; ⊙7pm-1am) The nostalgic dream of Waikiki as an aristocratic playground is kept alive at this Halekulani hotel bar. We're talking contemporary and classic cocktails, tempting appetizers and desserts, and smooth jazz combos that serenade after 8:30pm nightly. The dress code is the amorphous 'casual elegant.'

Punchbowl Coffee
COFFEE
(https://punchbowlcoffee.com; 234 Beach Walk; ⊙10am-8:30pm) In the back of a parking lot, this truck uses potted palms to create a minute oasis amid the Waikiki buzz. Serves superb hot and cold coffee and tea drinks, plus a few snacks. Grab a spot on a bench and exhale.

Maui Brewing Co
BREWERY
(☑808-843-2739; http://mauibrewingco.com; 2300 Kalakaua Ave, 2nd fl, Holiday Inn Resort Waikiki Beachcomber; ⊙11am-11pm) Hawaii's largest bar features over two dozen of Maui Brewing's microbrews. Under lights made from kegs, you can lounge in the vast, industrial space, enjoying classic beers like Bikini Blonde lager, Coconut Hiwa porter and Pineapple Mana wheat. The large outdoor terrace has views of the resort-filled skyline.

Wang Chung's
KARAOKE
(☑808-921-9176; http://wangchungs.com; 2424 Koa Ave, Stay Waikiki; ⊙5pm-2am; 🎤) Wang Chung's is a happy-go-lucky gay-friendly karaoke bar that's found a retro chic home

in the Stay Waikiki (p155) hotel just a block inland from Kuhio Beach.

Deck
ROOFTOP BAR
(☑808-931-4488; www.deckwaikiki.com; 150 Kapahulu Ave, Queen Kapi'olani Hotel; ⊙6:30am-11pm) Enjoy a sweeping vista from the third-floor pool deck of the Queen Kapi'olani Hotel. There's a standard coffee-shop menu of breakfasts and burgers etc but the real reason to settle into a lounge chair here is the long list of drinks and cocktails and the view as the setting sun casts a rosy glow on verdant Diamond Head.

RumFire
BAR
(☑808-922-4422; www.rumfirewaikiki.com; 2255 Kalakaua Ave, Sheraton Waikiki; ⊙11:30am-midnight Sun-Thu, to 1:30am Fri & Sat) The collection of vintage rum is mighty tempting at this lively and huge hotel bar, with fire pits looking out onto the beach and live contemporary Hawaiian music or the tunes of resident DJ Taco. Wander over to the resort's cabana-like Edge of Waikiki Bar for knockout views, designer cocktails and more live Hawaiian and pop-rock music poolside.

Duke's Waikiki
BAR
(☑808-922-2268; www.dukeswaikiki.com; 2335 Kalakaua Ave, Outrigger Waikiki Beach Resort; ⊙7am-midnight) It's a raucous scene, especially when weekend concerts spill onto the beach. Taking its name from Duke Kahanamoku, the surfing theme prevails throughout this carousing landmark where selfies and holiday camaraderie are encouraged. Upstairs, the tiki torchlit veranda at the Hula Grill (p159) has a more soothing live

WAIKIKI DRINKING & NIGHTLIFE

LGBTIQ WAIKIKI

Waikiki's LGBTIQ community is tightly knit, but full of aloha for visitors. Start off at friendly, open-air Hula's Bar & Lei Stand, which has ocean views of Diamond Head. Stop by for drinks and to meet a variety of new faces, play pool and boogie. More svelte and classy Bacchus Waikiki (p166) is an intimate wine bar and cocktail lounge with happy-hour specials, shirtless bartenders and Sunday-afternoon parties on the terrace. For nonstop singalongs, hit Wang Chung's, a living-room-sized karaoke bar.

Tiki-themed Tapa's Restaurant & Lanai Bar (p167) is a bigger chill-out spot with cheery bartenders, pool tables, a jukebox and karaoke nights. Hidden up an alley a few blocks away, In Between (p166), a laid-back neighborhood bar, attracts an older crowd for 'the happiest of happy hours.'

By day, have fun in the sun at Queen's Surf Beach (p144) and (illegally clothing optional) Diamond Head Beach Park (p199).

October is a good reason to visit O'ahu as it's Honolulu Pride (p154), with weeks of parties and events culminating in a huge parade followed by concerts.

Hawaiian soundtrack several nights a week. Skip the food.

Top of Waikiki
BAR

(☑ 808-923-3877; www.topofwaikiki.com; Waikiki Business Plaza, 2270 Kalakaua Ave, 18th fl; ☺5-9:30pm) Rotating lazily at one revolution per hour, this decidedly retro tower-top restaurant takes in a 360-degree view. There's purportedly food involved, but the novelty is the slow-motion sit-and-spin with sunset cocktails at the bar; the food is pure afterthought. In fact, the closing time keeps creeping back to just after dusk – there is a dress code, no shorts etc.

🍸 Kuhio Avenue Area

★ Cuckoo Coconuts
LOUNGE

(☑ 808-926-1620; www.cuckoococonutswaikiki. com; 333 Royal Hawaiian Ave; ☺11am-midnight) Mismatched wobbly tables under a canopy of canvas and ragged umbrellas, plus a menagerie of aging potted tropical plants, give this bar a carefree, unpretentious vibe. Every night there's a hard-working lineup of musicians with a familiar list of croon-worthy classics and time-tested patter. Settle back, have some sort of deep-fried treat, enjoy a cheap drink and get carried away.

Gorilla in the Cafe
CAFE

(☑ 808-922-2055; www.facebook.com/gorillahawaii; 2155 Kalakaua Ave; ☺6:30am-9pm Mon-Fri, 7am-10pm Sat & Sun) Owned by Korean TV star Bae Yong-joon, this artisan coffee bar brews Waikiki's biggest selection of 100% Hawaii-grown beans from independent farms all around the islands. Handmade pourovers are worth the extra wait, or just grab a fast, hot espresso or creamy frozen coffee concoction blended with banana. It has a little circle of tables outside.

Bacchus Waikiki
GAY

(☑ 808-926-4167; www.bacchus-waikiki.com; 408 Lewers St, 2nd fl; ☺noon-2am) Intimate 2nd-floor wine-bar cocktail lounge, with happy-hour specials and a Sunday-afternoon beer bust. It's got a more upscale vibe than most. Great mix of locals and tourists.

In Between
GAY

(☑ 808-926-7060; www.inbetweenwaikiki.com; 2155 Lau'ula St; ☺noon-2am) A rubbah-slippah (flip-flops) neighborhood bar that attracts a merry local crowd with 'the happiest of happy hours.' The bartenders welcome tourists

with cheap drinks, Jello shots (!) and good fun. Find it down a covered alley.

Waikiki Brewing
BREWERY

(☑ 808-946-6590; www.waikikibrewing.com; 1945 Kalakaua Ave; ☺11am-midnight) Big, open-air and set back from the street behind tropical plants, Waikiki's namesake brewery has an industrial-chic setting where you can enjoy the nine in-house brews. The Hana Hou Hefe includes the essence of orange peels and strawberries. Food choices are unsurprising: burgers and pizza.

Genius Lounge
LOUNGE

(☑ 808-626-5362; www.geniusloungehawaii.com; 346 Lewers St, 3rd fl; ☺6pm-2am, kitchen to 1am) Like a Japanese speakeasy, this glowing candlelit hideaway is a chill retreat for attitudy hipsters and lovebird couples. East-West tapas bites let you nibble on squid tempura, *loco moco* or banana cake while you sip made-in-Japan sake brews, and retro jazz or cutting-edge electronica tickles your ears. The canvas-topped lanai is a delight.

Honolulu Tavern
BAR

(☑ 808-922-5539; www.facebook.com/honolulutavern808; 417 Nohonani St; ☺11am-2am) Waikiki's dive bars are a dwindling lot as the blocks towards the canal fall to the wrecking ball ahead of a glossier future. So the timeless Honolulu Tavern draws an ever-larger crowd of regulars with its long bar, thatched walls, fruity cocktails, inside jokes and popular pool tables.

Arnold's Beach Bar & Grill
BAR

(☑ 808-924-6887; www.facebook.com/Arnoldswaikiki; 339 Saratoga Rd; ☺10am-2am) The antidote to soulless hotel bars, this grass-shack dive bar with a smoky patio lures beach bums who knock back cheap microbrews in the middle of a sunny afternoon. Down a stiff 'Tiki Tea' while pretending the bar's naked mannequins don't freak you out. It's down an alley; follow the sounds of live music 5pm to 8pm.

Island Vintage Coffee
CAFE

(☑ 808-926-5662; www.islandvintagecoffee.com; Royal Hawaiian Center, 2301 Kalakaua Ave, 2nd fl, building C; ☺6am-11pm; 🛜) If you prefer your [pricey] latte sweetened with Hawaiian honey, or an iced mocha tricked out with macadamia nuts and coconut drizzle, get in line behind all of the other tourists at this cutesy upstairs coffee shop, with lanai table seating.

Tapa's Restaurant & Lanai Bar

GAY

(📞 808-921-2288; www.tapaswaikiki.com; 407 Seaside Ave, 2nd fl; ⏰ 2pm-2am Mon-Fri, from 9am Sat & Sun; 🕿) Tiki-themed Tapa's Restaurant & Lanai Bar is a laid-back spot, with a welcoming vibe, pool tables, a jukebox and a karaoke machine (which blessedly is in its own room). The cheap Sunday brunch is a huge draw, especially the banana pancakes. There's good bar food other times and a fine lanai all the time.

☆ Entertainment

On any given night Waikiki offers first-rate live Hawaiian music and hula dancing. You can enjoy much of it for free or the price of a drink.

Good online sources for what's on – especially special events – include Honolulu Star-Advertiser (www.staradvertiser.com/calendar) and Honolulu Magazine (www.honolulumagazine.com). But you're best off checking with specific venues.

★ Hilton Hawaiian Village Fireworks

FIREWORKS

(Kahanamoku Beach; ⏰ 7:45pm Fri) **FREE** Every Friday night, the Hilton Hawaiian Village (p155) stages a booming 10-minute fireworks show. Although it's done in conjunction with a touristy luau (Hawaiian feast) near one of the pools, the actual show is over the water in front of Kahanamoku Beach and can be seen from across Waikiki. For the best views, join the locals and tourists on Fort DeRussy Beach (p142).

Blue Note Hawaii

LIVE MUSIC

(📞 808-777-4890; www.bluenotehawaii.com; 2335 Kalakaua Ave, Outrigger Waikiki Beach Resort; ticket price varies; ⏰ showtimes vary) A sophisticated music venue that draws top acts performing blues, jazz, pop, rock, reggae and Hawaiian. There's a dinner option that includes banquet fare (mains $25 to $34).

Hawaiian Music & Hula

Traditional and contemporary Hawaiian music calls all up and down the beach in Waikiki, from the rhythmic drums and *ipu* (gourds) accompanying hula dancers to mellow duos or trios playing slack key guitars and ukuleles and singing with *leo ki'eki'e* (male) or *ha'i* (female) high falsetto voices. Most performances are free.

★ Kuhio Beach Torchlighting & Hula Show

LIVE MUSIC, HULA

(📞 808-843-8002; www.waikikiimprovement.com; Kuhio Beach Park; ⏰ 6:30-7:30pm Tue, Thu & Sat Feb-Oct, 6-7pm Nov-Jan) **FREE** It all begins at the Duke Kahanamoku statue (p146) with the sounding of a conch shell and the lighting of torches after sunset. At the nearby hula mound, enjoy a truly authentic Hawaiian music and dance show. This is no bit of tourist fluff either, as top talent regularly performs, including much-lauded hula experts from the University of Hawai'i.

★ Royal Hawaiian Band

LIVE MUSIC

(📞 808-786-6677; www.rhb-music.com; Kapi'olani Park Bandstand, 2686-2882 Kalakaua Ave, Kapi'olani Regional Park; ⏰ 2pm Sun) The Kapi'olani Park Bandstand is the perfect venue for this time-honored troupe that performs classics from the Hawaiian monarchy era. It's a quintessential island scene that caps off with the audience joining hands and singing Queen Lili'uokalani's 'Aloha 'Oe' in Hawaiian. Check their website for details on performances at special events and festivals. They also perform at 'Iolani Palace (p125).

House Without a Key

LIVE MUSIC

(📞 808-923-2311; www.halekulani.com; 2199 Kalia Rd, Halekulani; ⏰ 7-9pm) Named after a 1925 Charlie Chan novel set in Honolulu, this genteel open-air hotel lounge sprawls beneath a waterfront century-old kiawe tree (that's clearly barely hanging on as the sea level rises). A genteel crowd gathers here for sunset cocktails, excellent Hawaiian music and solo hula dancing by former Miss Hawaii pageant winners. Panoramic ocean views are as intoxicating as the tropical cocktails.

Kani Ka Pila Grille

LIVE MUSIC

(📞 808-924-4990; www.outriggerreef.com; 2169 Kalia Rd, Outrigger Reef Waikiki Beach Resort; ⏰ 11am-10pm, live music 6-9pm) Once happy hour ends, the Outrigger's poolside bar sets the scene for some of the most laid-back live-music shows of any of Waikiki's beachfront hotels, with traditional and contemporary Hawaiian musicians playing familiar tunes amid a patter of jokes.

Tapa Bar

LIVE MUSIC

(📞 808-949-4321; www.hiltonhawaiianvillage.com; 2005 Kalia Rd, ground fl, Tapa Tower, Hilton Hawaiian Village; ⏰ 10am-11pm, live music from 7:30-8pm) **FREE** It's worth navigating through the

WAIKIKI ENTERTAINMENT

gargantuan Hilton resort complex to this Polynesian-themed open-air bar just to see some of the best traditional and contemporary Hawaiian groups performing on Oʻahu today. Head over on Friday and Saturday nights to catch longtime favorite Olomana, an acoustic trio. There is also live entertainment many nights in the hotel's Tropics cafe; famed singer Henry Kapono performs Saturdays.

Beach Bar   LIVE MUSIC

(☑ 808-922-3111;   www.moana-surfrider.com; 2365 Kalakaua Ave, Moana Surfrider; ☉ 10:30am-10:30pm) Inside this historic beachfront hotel bar, soak up the sounds of classical and contemporary Hawaiian musicians playing underneath the old banyan tree where the *Hawaii Calls* radio program was broadcast nationwide during the mid-20th century. Live-music schedules vary, but hula soloists dance from 6pm to 8pm most nights. Expect mellow tunes at lunch and through the evening.

Royal Grove   LIVE MUSIC

(☑ 808-922-2299; www.royalhawaiiancenter.com/events; Royal Hawaiian Center, 2201 Kalakaua Ave, ground fl; ☉ 6-7pm Tue-Sat) **FREE** This shopping mall's open-air stage may lack oceanfront views, but Hawaiian music and hula performances by top island talent happen here most evenings. Watch for various traditional music special events.

Waikiki Shell   LIVE MUSIC

(www.blaisdellcenter.com/venues/waikiki-shell; Kapiʻolani Regional Park, 2805 Monsarrat Ave) With Diamond Head as a backdrop, this outdoor amphitheater in Kapiʻolani Regional Park sporadically stages hula troupes and twilight shows by megastars such as ukulele-playin' rocker Jake Shimabukuro. Other concerts feature classical and contemporary Hawaiian musicians. Check the website for details.

Moana Terrace   LIVE MUSIC

(☑ 808-922-6611; 2552 Kalakaua Ave, 2nd fl, Waikiki Beach Marriott Resort; ☉ 11am-11pm, entertainment from 6pm; ▣) **FREE** If you're in a mellow mood, come for sunset happy-hour drinks at this family-friendly, poolside bar, just a lei's throw from Kuhio Beach. Slack key guitarists, ukulele players and *haʻi* falsetto singers perform nightly.

Mai Tai Bar   LIVE MUSIC, HULA

(☑ 808-923-7311; www.royal-hawaiian.com; 2259 Kalakaua Ave, Royal Hawaiian; ☉ 10am-11:30pm, entertainment from 6pm Tue-Wed & Fri-Sun, 8pm Mon & Thu) At the Royal Hawaiian's beach bar, you can catch some great acoustic island-music acts and graceful solo hula dancers some nights. However, the namesake cocktail here is mediocre at best and the experience seems designed to be little more than a tourist tick mark.

Luaus

ʻAha ʻAina   LUAU

(☑ 808-921-4600; http://royal-hawaiianluau.com; Royal Hawaiian Resort, 2259 Kalakaua Ave; adult/child 5-12yr from $180/100; ☉ 5-8pm Mon & Thu) This oceanfront dinner show is like a three-act musical play narrating the history of Hawaiian *mele* (songs) and hula. The buffet features good renditions of traditional Hawaiian and Polynesian fare, and unlimited drinks. There are cultural demonstrations, such as making cloth from bark. The literal highlight is the fire dancing.

Seating is at long tables; request to be near the stage when you book.

Waikiki Starlight Luau   LUAU

(☑ 808-947-2607; www.hiltonhawaiianvillage.com/luau; 2005 Kalia Rd, Hilton Hawaiian Village; adult/child 4-11yr from $111/71; ☉ 5:30-8pm Sun-Thu, weather permitting; ▣) Enthusiastic pan-Polynesian show, with buffet meal, outdoor seating at a rooftop venue, Samoan fire dancing and *hapa haole* (literally, 'half foreign') hula. Like other resort luaus, there are pricey options that allow guests to cut the long food lines.

🛍 Shopping

Amid the chains dotting Waikiki's upscale malls and resorts, you can find excellent local boutiques with island designs and creations.

For mundane needs, you won't be able to miss the ubiquitous ABC Stores, convenient places to pick up essentials such as beach mats, sunblock, snacks, cold beer, macadamia-nut candy and sundries, not to mention 'I got leiʻd in Hawaii' T-shirts and bobbing, grass-skirted hula girls for the dashboard of your car.

Newt at the Royal   CLOTHING

(☑ 808-922-0062; www.newtattheroyal.com; 2259 Kalakaua Ave, Royal Hawaiian Resort; ☉ 9am-9pm) With stylish flair and panache, Newt specializes in Montecristi Panama hats – classic men's fedoras, plantation-style hats and women's *fino*. It also has fine reproductions of aloha shirts using 1940s and '50s designs. This shop was a classic *before* Panama hats became a hipster cliche.

Fighting Eel   CLOTHING
(☑808-738-9295; www.fightingeel.com; 2233 Kalakaua Ave, building B, Royal Hawaiian Center; ☻10am-10pm) Hawaii-designed fashionable wear is the hallmark of local designers Rona Bennett and Lan Chung. Also: swimsuits, children's clothing, jewelry and accessories.

Malie Organics   COSMETICS
(☑808-922-2216; www.malie.com; 2259 Kalakaua Ave, Royal Hawaiian Resort; ☻9am-9pm) Beauty oils, creams, perfumes and more are sold in this shop that looks as good as it smells. Everything is locally made from organic and natural ingredients, mostly derived from native Hawaii plants and flowers.

Angels by the Sea Hawaii   CLOTHING
(☑808-921-9747; http://angelsbytheseahawaii. com; 2348 Kalakaua Ave, Sheraton Princess Kaiulani Resort; ☻9am-10:30pm) Inside a mega chain hotel, this airy boutique owned by a Vietnamese fashion designer (who was once crowned Ms Waikiki) is a gem for handmade beaded jewelry and bags, effortlessly beautiful resort-style dresses, tunic tops and aloha shirts in tropical prints of silk and linen.

Nohea Gallery   ARTS & CRAFTS
(☑808-596-0074; www.noheagallery.com; 2424 Kalakaua Ave, Hyatt Regency Waikiki Beach Resort; ☻9am-10pm) This high-end gallery sells original paintings, *gyotaku* fish prints (rubbings of freshly caught fish), handcrafted jewelry, glassware, pottery and woodwork, all of it made in Hawaii. Local artisans occasionally give demonstrations of their crafts on the sidewalk outside.

Ukulele PuaPua   MUSICAL INSTRUMENTS
(☑808-923-9977; www.hawaiianukuleleonline. com; 2255 Kalakaua Ave #13, Sheraton Waikiki; ☻8am-10:30pm) Avoid those flimsy souvenir ukuleles and head to this serious little shop to find the real thing. Try a free group beginner lesson (4pm daily).

Art on the Zoo Fence   ARTS & CRAFTS
(☑808-372-9578; www.artonthezoofence.com; Monsarrat Ave, opposite Kapi'olani Regional Park; ☻9am-4pm Sat & Sun) Dozens of artists hang their works along the fence on the south side

---

WORTH A TRIP

HAWAIIAN FEATHER LEI

Aunty Mary Louise Kaleonahenahe Kekuewa and her daughter Paulette cowrote Hawaii's celebrated handbook *Feather Lei as an Art*, which encouraged a revival of this indigenous art starting in the late 1970s. That was the heyday of the Hawaiian Renaissance, when indigenous arts, culture and language were being reborn. Although Aunty has since passed away, Paulette and her own daughter and granddaughter keep alive the ancient Hawaiian craft of feather lei-making at **Na Lima Mili Hulu No'eau** (☑808-732-0865; www.feather legacy.com; 762 Kapahulu Ave; ☻usually 9am-4pm Mon-Sat) ✍. This homespun little shop's name translates as 'the skilled hands that touch the feathers.' It can take days to produce a single lei, which are prized by collectors. Make an appointment for a personalized lei-making lesson.

---

of the Honolulu Zoo (p146) every weekend, weather permitting. Browse the contemporary watercolor, acrylic and oil paintings and colorful island photography as you chat with the artists themselves.

Honolua Surf Co   CLOTHING
(☑808-947-1570; www.honoluasurf.com; 2005 Kalia Road, Rainbow Bazaar, Hilton Hawaiian Village; ☻9am-11pm) Named after the bay of monster waves off Maui's northern shore where brave surfers prove their worth, this O'ahu outpost of the Maui surfwear shop sells board shorts, hoodies, T-shirts and knit coverups that will last you just as long as an endless summer.

Loco Boutique   CLOTHING
(☑808-926-7131; www.locoboutique.com; 358 Royal Hawaiian Ave, Outrigger Ohana Malia Hotel; ☻9am-11pm) If you realize that your old swimsuit from the mainland just doesn't measure up to what island folks wear, comb the racks of this locally owned swimwear shop. Hundreds of mix-and-match bikinis, tankinis, board shorts, rash guards, rompers and more come in a rainbow of colors and retro, island-print, sexy and splashy styles. There's another location in Ala Moana Center.

Royal Hawaiian Center   MALL
(☑ 808-922-2299; www.royalhawaiiancenter.com; 2201 Kalakaua Ave; ⊙ 10am-10pm; 🛜) Not to be confused with the Royal Hawaiian Resort hotel next door, this upscale shopping center has four levels and houses more than 80 top-end stores; some local such as Fighting Eel (p169), some chains such as Apple. It hosts many free activities and performances.

Reyn Spooner   CLOTHING
(☑ 808-275-4491; www.reynspooner.com; 2255 Kalakaua Ave, #9, Sheraton Waikiki; ⊙ 8am-10:30pm) Reyn Spooner's subtly designed, reverse-print preppy aloha shirts have been the standard for Honolulu's businessmen, political power brokers and social movers and shakers since 1956.

Muse Hawaii   CLOTHING
(☑ 808-926-9777; https://musebyrimo.com; 2259 Kalakaua Ave, Royal Hawaiian Resort; ⊙ 10am-11pm) Blowsy, breezy feminine fashions are what's sewn by this mainland designer from LA, whose Waikiki Beach shop is a serious addiction for jet-setting girls from Tokyo. Take your pick of cotton-candy tissue tanks, lighter-than-air sundresses, flowing maxi dresses, floppy hats or beaded sandals.

Duke's Marketplace   GIFTS & SOUVENIRS
(5 Dukes Ln; ⊙ 9am-11pm) Over 50 open-air stalls are strung along a back alley in the glossiest quarter of Waikiki. Come here for the tackiest (but at times irresistible) souvenirs – think plastic hula dancers holding signs reading 'Welcome to the Man Cave.' Look for a panoply of stuff you'll never find in the chain stores filling nearby malls.

BROWSE 15,000 ALOHA SHIRTS

Unremarkable outside, **Bailey's Antiques & Aloha Shirts** (☑ 808-734-7628; http://alohashirts.com; 517 Kapahulu Ave; ⊙ 10am-6pm) has the finest aloha-shirt collection on O'ahu, possibly the world! Racks are crammed with thousands of collector-worthy vintage aloha shirts in every conceivable color and style, from 1920s kimono-silk classics to 1970s polyester specials to modern offerings. Prices vary from 10 bucks to several thousand dollars.

International Market Place   GIFTS & SOUVENIRS
(☑ 808-931-6105; www.shopinternationalmarket-place.com; 2330 Kalakaua Ave; ⊙ 10am-10pm; 🛜) Forget the old International Market Place, the beloved 1950s assemblage of tourist stores. This glossy block-filling replacement is a three-level extravaganza of chain stores. It does preserve the main feature of the old market worth saving: the huge 100-year-old banyan tree. There's a public performance space and some excellent public art. Look for the rocking chairs scattered about.

ⓘ Information

MEDICAL SERVICES

Docs on Call (☑ 808-971-6000; www.hawaii pacifichealth.org/straub/patient-visitors/doc tors-on-call; 2255 Kalakaua Ave, Sheraton Waikiki; ⊙ 7am-11pm) operates a nonemergency walk-in clinic. There is also a second **Waikiki location** (☑ 808-973-5250; www.hawaiipacific health.org/straub/patient-visitors/doctors-on-call; Rainbow Bazaar, 2005 Kalia Rd, 2nd fl, Hilton Hawaiian Village; ⊙ 8am-4:30pm Mon-Fri). Otherwise Queen's Medical Center (p133) in downtown Honolulu has a full ER.

POLICE

Waikiki Police Substation (☑ 808-723-8562; www.honolulupd.org; 2425 Kalakaua Ave; ⊙ 24hr) If you need nonemergency help, or just friendly directions, stop here next to Kuhio Beach Park.

ⓘ Getting There & Away

Waikiki is a district of the city of Honolulu, so much of the transport information applies to both.

AIR

Daniel K Inouye International Airport (p309) is about 9 miles northwest of Waikiki.

BUS

Waikiki is well linked to the rest of Honolulu by the public-transit system, TheBus (p311).

CAR

From the airport, the easiest and most atmospheric driving route to Waikiki is via the Nimitz Hwy (Hwy 92), which becomes Ala Moana Blvd. Alternatively, take the H1 (Lunalilo) Fwy eastbound, then follow signs to Waikiki. The drive between the airport and Waikiki takes about 30 minutes without traffic; allow at least 45 minutes during weekday rush hours.

❶ Getting Around

TO/FROM THE AIRPORT

From the airport, reach Waikiki via TheBus (p311) routes 19 or 20. Buses run every 20 minutes from 6am to 11pm daily. Luggage is restricted to what you can hold on your lap or stow under the seat (maximum size 22in x 14in x 9in). Both routes run along Kuhio Ave.

Taxis from the airport to Waikiki cost $35 to $45.

Express Shuttle (☎ 808-439-8800; www. airportshuttlehawaii.com; fare to Waikiki 1 way $17), run by Roberts Hawaii, operates shuttle buses from Daniel K Inouye International Airport to Waikiki's hotels, departing every 20 to 60 minutes. Transport time varies depending on the number of stops. There are surcharges for large luggage like surfboards. Note that groups of three or more will save money using a taxi or rideshare.

BICYCLE

Honolulu's shared bicycle scheme called Biki (p133) has rental stations all over Waikiki.
Hawaiian Style Rentals (☎ 866-916-6733; www.hawaiibikes.com; 2556 Lemon Rd, Waikiki Beachside Hostel; rental per day from $25; ⊙ 8:30am-5pm) Rents a large range of bikes; half-day, daily and weekly rates available. Rates include helmets, locks and gear. An excellent source of O'ahu cycling info at the shop and online.

BUS

Most stops for TheBus in Waikiki are found inland along Kuhio Ave. The Ala Moana Center mall, just northwest of Waikiki, is the island's main bus-transfer point.

Bus 13 is handy: it runs down Kuhio Ave and Kapahulu Ave and operates every 15 to 30 minutes from 5am to 11:30pm. It serves Chinatown and Downtown in the west and the University of Hawaii in the north.

CAR & MOTORCYCLE

Major car-rental companies have branches in Waikiki.
808 Smart Cars Rentals (☎ 808-735-5000; https://808smartcar.com; 444 Niu St, Hawai-

❶ PARKING

Most hotels charge $15 to $50 per night for either valet or self-parking. Rates are similar at public garages. Most hotels offer free parking if you're eating in their restaurants.

Many streets have metered parking. Meters are old-school and only take quarters. At the less-trafficked southeast end of Waikiki, there's a free parking lot along Monsarrat Ave beside Kapi'olani Regional Park with no time limit.

ian Monarch Hotel; rental per day from $60; ⊙ 9am-5pm) Rents Smart cars (some with convertible roofs) that get almost 40mpg on island highways; being smaller, they're also easier to park.
Chase Hawaii Rentals (☎ 808-942-4273; www.chasehawaiirentals.com; 355 Royal Hawaiian Ave; rental per day from $160; ⊙ 8am-6pm) Rents Kawasaki, Indian, Triumph, Harley-Davidson and Honda motorcycles.
Cruzin Hawaii (☎ 808-945-9595, 877-945-9595; http://cruzinhawaii.com; 1980 Kalakaua Ave; moped/motorcycle rental per day from $50/110) Rents mostly Harley-Davidson motorcycles; also mopeds and bikes. Has two other Waikiki locations.

TAXI

Taxi stands are found at Waikiki's bigger resort hotels and shopping malls. Uber, Lyft etc are available.

TROLLEY

The Waikiki Trolley runs six color-coded lines designed for tourists. Routes cover Waikiki, Diamond Head, Honolulu and Pearl Harbor. The passes – good for unlimited use – aren't cheap but can be purchased from hotel activity desks or online. Not actually a trolley, a few are double-deck buses, most are trucks with a crude 'trolley' disguise.

CYCLING TOUR: WAIKIKI BEACH BY BICYCLE

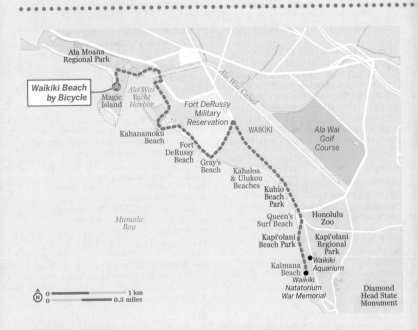

WAIKIKI BEACH

As you cycle along Waikiki's beaches, it may be surprising to note that originally there was very little beach in Waikiki. Until the late 1800s, the shore was mostly rocks and shallow mud that oozed out from the taro fields inland. Landowners began haphazardly constructing seawalls and offshore barriers (called groins) to protect their properties. This caused a few small beaches to form but it also caused the currents to remove sand from where it already existed – a situation that continues to today.

Photos from the 1920s show Waikiki Beach as being very small. About the only place with naturally occuring sand was in front of the Royal Hawaiian and Moana Surfrider resorts, which is why those hotels were built where they are.

Huge beach construction campaigns beginning in the 1950s created Kuhio and Kahanamoku Beaches and most of the others. Some of the sand was barged in from Papohaku Beach on the island of Moloka'i. After that practice was outlawed, sand was pumped in from offshore and pretty much anyplace else it could be found.

The $2 billion in tourism Waikiki generates each year – and surveys which show that 60% of Waikiki visitors wouldn't bother visiting if there was no beach – keeps commercial and government sand-pumping efforts alive to the tune of several million dollars a year.

THE RIDE

START MAGIC ISLAND
END KAIMANA BEACH
DISTANCE 3.5 MILES
DURATION ONE TO TWO HOURS

Begin your ride on **Magic Island**, the peninsula jutting from the southeast side of **Ala Moana Beach Park** (p85). You can warm up riding around this large expanse, which is usually sparsely crowded, especially on weekdays. Gaze out at the unhindered

Explore the intriguing highlights of Waikiki on this ride heading 'Diamond Head,' from Magic Island down to Kaimana Beach, almost at the foot of O'ahu's most famous landmark.

Duke Kahanamoku statue (p146), Kuhio Beach Park

views of Waikiki and Diamond Head, with planes carrying tourists to and fro passing overhead.

Pedal northeast through to the main park entrance and turn right onto Ala Moana Blvd, crossing over the **Ala Wai Canal** (p146). This channel was created in 1922 to drain the mosquito-filled rice paddies, marshes and swamps that would become present-day Waikiki. Look for kayakers and outrigger canoe teams.

Immediately over the bridge, turn right onto quieter Holomoana St. Sailboats bob in **Ala Wai Yacht Harbor**, a major point of departure for yachts on long trans-Pacific voyages. Ride two blocks south until you see the imposing Y-shaped **Ilikai Hotel** (p155). On the 30th floor, two generations of Steve McGarretts have posed manfully as the camera zooms in during the opening credits of *Hawaii Five-O*.

Keep following Holomoana St, past the gentle waters of **Duke Kahanamoku Lagoon**, and hook around to **Kahanamoku Beach** (p139). You may see oceangoing outrigger-canoe teams practicing here. Ride along the beach path southeast past **Hilton Hawaiian Village** (p155) and along **Fort DeRussy Beach** (p142), then cut over along the path to Saratoga Rd and turn right onto busy Kalakaua Ave. Many of the points of interest here in the heart of Waikiki are on the walking tour (p148), especially as you ride past **Kuhio Beach Park** (p144).

As you enter **Kapi'olani Regional Park** (p146), veer over to the path along the sand at **Kapi'olani Beach Park** (p144). If it's near sunset, pause for the view from **Queen's Surf Beach** (p144). Otherwise continue south until you see the **Waikiki Aquarium** (p145). Turn left on the path right before it and then turn right on Kalakaua Ave. Edge right again after the aquarium and pause in front of the crumbling **Waikiki Natatorium War Memorial** (p146), a once-grand erection that's crumbling due to bureaucratic inaction.

Finish your ride at the welcoming sand of **Kaimana Beach** (p144), a favorite with locals.

AT A GLANCE

POPULATION
140,000

LANDMARK ATTRACTION
Pearl Harbor National Memorial (p177)

BEST MARKET
Aloha Stadium Swap Meet & Marketplace (p182)

BEST CAFE
Kahumana Cafe (p191)

BEST LUAU
Paradise Cove (p187)

WHEN TO GO
Jan–Apr Surfers enjoy huge waves on the Leeward Coast, plus the chance of spotting whales.

Jun–Aug Calm conditions on leeward beaches make this the best time for swimming.

Dec Lots of events around the anniversary of the December 7 Pearl Harbor attacks.

USS Arizona Memorial (p177)

Pearl Harbor & Leeward Oʻahu

Pearl Harbor has a resonance for all Americans. The site of the December 7, 1941 attack that brought the US into WWII is accessible, evocative and moving. It's the top site for visitors to Hawaii. Nearby ʻAiea is a slice of modern island life with excellent yet modest restaurants, and the town offers a gateway to Oʻahu's green interior.

Just west, Waipahu gives a glimpse of old Oʻahu. Suburban Kapolei boasts a few family-friendly attractions and Ko Olina seems set to continue growing as a compound of huge high-end resorts. The intrepid traveler venturing further north in Leeward Oʻahu along the untouristy Waiʻanae Coast will find undeveloped beaches and unvarnished communities. Cultural pride is alive here, as more Native Hawaiians live on the Waiʻanae Coast than anyplace else island-wide. Near the island's tip at Kaʻena Point, habitation gives way to green-velvet-tufted mountains and rocky coastal ledges.

INCLUDES

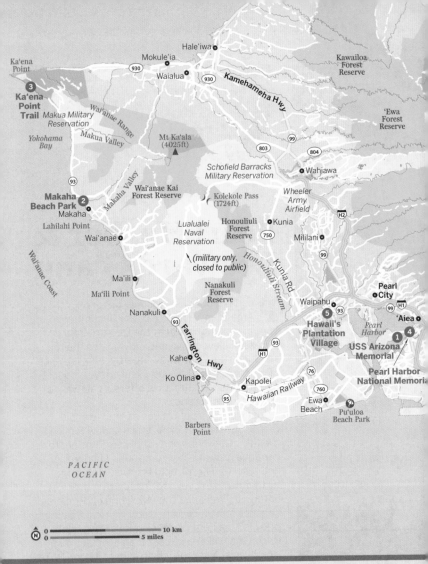

Pearl Harbor & Leeward Oʻahu Highlights

1 USS Arizona Memorial
(p177) Pausing to honor more than 1100 sailors who lost their lives on this sunken battleship during the Pearl Harbor attack.

2 Makaha Beach Park
(p191) Surfing the towering waves in winter; snorkeling and swimming in summer.

3 Kaʻena Point Trail
(p195) Hiking an easy trail to see the Pacific Ocean at its wildest and visiting the furthest western point on Oʻahu.

4 Pearl Harbor National Memorial (p177) Immersing yourself in the dramas of WWII

at the superb museum of the main visitor center for the Pearl Harbor historic sites.

5 Hawaii's Plantation Village (p183) Seeing the villages where the multicultural workers lived when Oʻahu was home to myriad sugar plantations.

Pearl Harbor

The WWII-era rallying cry 'Remember Pearl Harbor!' that once mobilized an entire nation resonates on O'ahu. It was here that the surprise Japanese attack on December 7, 1941, hurtled the US into war in the Pacific. Every year about 1.6 million tourists visit Pearl Harbor's unique collection of war memorials and museums. The iconic offshore shrine at the sunken USS *Arizona* doesn't tell the only story. Nearby are two other historical sites: the USS *Bowfin* submarine, aka the 'Pearl Harbor Avenger,' and the battleship USS *Missouri*, where General Douglas MacArthur accepted the Japanese surrender at the end of WWII. Together, these military sites represent the beginning, middle and end of the war for the US. To visit all three, as well as the Pearl Harbor Aviation Museum, dedicate at least a day. Historic Ford Island, in the middle of the harbor, can only be visited via the official buses to the USS Missouri and the Pearl Harbor Aviation Museum. The rest of the island is off-limits to tourists.

◉ Sights

★**Pearl Harbor National Memorial** PARK
(☑808-422-3399; www.nps.gov/valr; 1 Arizona Memorial Pl; ☺ visitor center 7am-5pm) FREE One of the USA's most significant WWII sites, this National Park Service (NPS) monument narrates the history of the Pearl Harbor attack and commemorates fallen service members. The memorial is entirely wheelchair accessible. The visitor center at the main entrance is the hub for visits to Pearl Harbor's other parks and museums.

The memorial grounds are much more than just a boat dock for the USS Arizona Memorial. Be sure to stop at the two superb **museums**, where multimedia and interactive displays bring to life the Road to War and the Attack & Aftermath through historic photos, films, illustrated graphics and taped oral histories. A shoreside walk passes signs illustrating how the attack unfolded in the now-peaceful harbor.

The bookstore sells many books and movies about the Pearl Harbor attack and WWII's Pacific theater, as well as informative illustrated maps of the battle. If you're lucky, one of the few remaining, 95-plus-year-old Pearl Harbor veterans who volunteer might be out front signing autographs and answering questions.

Various ticket packages are available for the three attractions that have admission fees. The best deal is a seven-day pass that includes admission to all. Tickets are sold online at www.pearlharborhistoricsites.org, at the visitor center ticket counter, and at each attraction. A virtual reality attraction allows visitors to don headsets ($5, 8am to 3pm) and walk the decks of the prewar USS *Arizona*, experience the Pearl Harbor attack and visit the USS Arizona Memorial (good for people who can't get a ticket).

★**USS Arizona Memorial** MUSEUM, MEMORIAL
(☑808-422-3399; www.nps.gov/valr; 1 Arizona Memorial Pl; free, boat-tour reservation fee $1; ☺7am-5pm, boat tours 7:30am-3pm) FREE This somber memorial is one of the USA's most significant WWII sites, commemorating the Pearl Harbor attack and its fallen service members with an iconic offshore monument reachable by boat.

A SURPRISE ATTACK

December 7, 1941 – 'a date which will live in infamy,' President Franklin D Roosevelt later said – began at 7:55am with a wave of more than 350 Japanese planes swooping over the Ko'olau Range, headed toward the unsuspecting US Pacific Fleet in Pearl Harbor. The battleship USS *Arizona* took a direct hit and sank in less than nine minutes, with most of its men killed in the explosion that destroyed the ship. The average age of the 1177 enlisted men who died in the attack on the ship was just 19 years. It wasn't until 15 minutes after the bombing started that American antiaircraft guns began to shoot back at the Japanese warplanes. Twenty other US military ships were sunk or seriously damaged and 347 airplanes were destroyed during the two-hour attack.

Ultimately, the greatest cost of the Pearl Harbor attack was human. Except for three ships sunk that day – the *Arizona*, the USS *Oklahoma* and the USS *Utah* – almost all the rest of the navy ships damaged were repaired and fought in WWII. And while the destruction and damage of the US battleships was massive, events soon proved that such vessels were already obsolete. The war in the Pacific was fought by aircraft carriers, none of which were in Pearl Harbor during the attack.

The memorial was built over the midsection of the sunken USS *Arizona*, with deliberate geometry to represent initial defeat, ultimate victory and eternal serenity. In the furthest of three chambers inside the shrine, the names of crewmen killed in the attack are engraved onto a marble wall. In the central section are cutaways that allow visitors to see the skeletal remains of the ship, which even now oozes about a quart of oil each day into the ocean. In its rush to recover from the attack and prepare for war, the US Navy exercised its option to leave over 900 servicemen inside the sunken ship; they remain entombed in its hull.

Free boat tours to the shrine depart every 15 minutes from 7:30am until 3pm (weather permitting) from the **NPS Visitor Center & Museum** (☎808-422-3399; www.nps.gov/valr; 1 Arizona Memorial Pl; ⊙7am-5pm). The 75-minute tour program includes a 23-minute documentary film about the attack. Make reservations for the tour online at www.recreation.

gov up to 60 days before your visit. You can also try to secure tickets on the website the day before your visit, beginning at 7am Hawaii time – but these are very limited. Some 1300 tickets are available in person on the day of your visit at the visitor center's Aloha Court. However, during peak seasons (summer and Christmas), when more than 4000 people take the tour daily, the entire day's allotment of tickets is often gone by 10am and waits of a few hours are not uncommon, so arrive early, or better yet: reserve in advance. Note that private tours of the memorial only pass by on boats and don't dock.

Battleship Missouri Memorial   MUSEUM, MEMORIAL
(☎877-644-4896; www.ussmissouri.com; 63 Cowpens St, Ford Island; admission incl tour adult/child from $29/13; ⊙8am-4pm) The last battleship built by the US (it was launched in 1944), the USS *Missouri* provides a unique historical 'bookend' to the US campaign in the Pacific during WWII. Nicknamed the 'Mighty Mo,'

Pearl Harbor

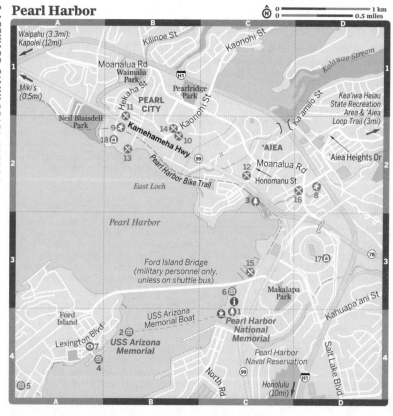

this decommissioned battleship saw action during the decisive late WWII battles of Iwo Jima and Okinawa.

The USS *Missouri* is now docked on Ford Island, just a few hundred yards from the sunken remains of the USS *Arizona*. During a self-guided audio tour, you can explore the officers' quarters, browse exhibits on the ship's history and stride across the deck where General MacArthur accepted the Japanese surrender on September 2, 1945. The huge ship was decommissioned in 1955, but was heavily modified and put back into service in the 1980s during the military build-up near the end of the Cold War.

Guided tours, which are sometimes led by knowledgeable US military veterans, are worth the extra time and expense. To visit the memorial, board the mandatory Ford Island visitor shuttle bus (bring photo ID) at the NPS Visitor Center & Museum (p178).

Pearl Harbor Aviation Museum MUSEUM
(☑808-441-1000; www.pearlharboraviationmuseum.org; 319 Lexington Blvd, Ford Island; adult/child $25/12, incl guided tour $35/12; ☉9am-5pm, last entry 4pm) This military aircraft museum cov-

ers WWII and the conflicts in Korea, Vietnam and beyond. The first aircraft hangar, number 37, features exhibits on the Pearl Harbor attack, the Doolittle Raid on mainland Japan in 1942 and the pivotal Battle of Midway, when the tides of WWII in the Pacific turned in favor of the Allies. Restored planes on display here include a Japanese Zero and a Dauntless navy dive bomber – the single-engined star of 2019's big-budget film *Midway*.

Walk next door to explore the MiG Alley Korean War exhibit, or take a guided tour to look behind the scenes at restoration work in Hangar 79's WWII-era maintenance shop, where you can see ongoing work on a B-17 and other planes. Out on the tarmac, in the shadow of the famous old control tower, you can imagine what it was like in this same spot on December 7, 1941. To visit the museum, board the mandatory Ford Island visitor shuttle bus (bring photo ID) outside the visitor center's Aloha Court. You'll need to ride the shuttle between the museum and the nearby USS *Missouri*, as pedestrians are subject to arrest by navy police.

USS Bowfin Submarine Museum & Park MUSEUM
(☑808-423-1341; www.bowfin.org; 11 Arizona Memorial Dr; self-guided tour $15/7; ☉7am-5pm, last entry 4:30pm) Adjacent to the visitor center for the Pearl Harbor historic sites, this park harbors the moored WWII-era submarine USS *Bowfin*, which you can explore on a self-guided tour. A museum that traces the development of submarines from their origins to the nuclear age and details their use during WWII was reconstructed in 2020. The park has waterside exhibits on every US submarine lost during the war.

Launched on December 7, 1942, one year after the Pearl Harbor attack, the USS *Bowfin* sank 44 enemy ships in the Pacific by the end of WWII. The US undersea war against Japan was a major contribution to winning the war in the Pacific and is often overlooked. Crewed by less than 2% of the Navy's personnel, the subs sank over 55% of all Japanese ships sunk during the war. A self-guided audio tour explores the life of the crew – watch your head below deck. Children under age four are not allowed aboard.

USS Oklahoma Memorial MEMORIAL
(www.nps.gov/valr; cnr Cowpens St & Langley Ave, Ford Island; ☉memorial 24hr, shuttle bus 8am-5pm) FREE After the USS *Arizona*, the second-largest number of lives lost on December 7, 1941 was aboard the battleship

PEARL HARBOR IN FILM

The attack on Pearl Harbor has been the subject of many movies. The following are four notable ones:

Tora Tora Tora (1970) This American-Japanese production keeps getting better with age. It is highly accurate and presents the attack from both sides. It doesn't fake drama but instead lets the incredible events around December 7 drive the story. How the US continually missed clear indications that an attack was coming are still relevant today; George Macready (playing Secretary of State Cordell Hull) is memorable as he excoriates the Japanese ambassador.

From Here to Eternity (1953) Set on O'ahu just before the Pearl Harbor attack, the film evocatively captures the languor of prewar life. The drama is moving and includes the oft-parodied scene – shot at Halona Cove (p210) in southeast O'ahu – of Burt Lancaster and Deborah Kerr getting it on in the surf. It also made a young Frank Sinatra a film star.

Pearl Harbor (2001) The movie *not* to watch. The overwrought script is cringeworthy, the digital effects have not aged well, and the script shows little regard for historical accuracy.

Midway (2019) The effects are suitably eye-popping in this big-budget thriller. It starts with the Pearl Harbor attacks and ends with the eponymous battle just six months later, which was a sweeping American victory that changed the course of the war.

USS *Oklahoma*. Numerous Japanese torpedoes struck the ship early in the attack and it capsized at dock, trapping hundreds of men below decks. Ultimately, 429 of the crew died during the attack and afterwards (some while still trapped below decks). This open-air memorial is close to the USS *Missouri* and can be reached on the same shuttle buses from the NPS Visitor Center (p178). The *Oklahoma* was eventually salvaged and towed away. Many of her dead were buried in mass graves at the Punchbowl, the National Memorial Cemetery of the Pacific (p94). The memorial has full details about the ship and one thin white marble column for each man who died.

Tours

Private tours of Pearl Harbor don't add much to the experience of visiting the memorials and museums. Tourist boats aren't allowed to disembark at the USS Arizona Memorial.

Pearl Harbor Historic Sites   HISTORY
(☑808-453-0686; www.pearlharborhistoricsites.org; 11 Arizona Memorial Dr, NPS Visitor Center; ⊗8am-5pm) Pearl Harbor Historic Sites, a private nonprofit adjunct of the NPS, offers narrated tours of the main sites. It has a desk inside the visitor center and sells various combined tickets to the main attractions. A Passport to Pearl Harbor ticket includes tours of all the main sites and costs adult/child $72/35.

Festivals & Events

Memorial Day   COMMEMORATION
(⊗May) On the last Monday in May, this national public holiday honors military personnel killed in battle. The USS Arizona Memorial, dedicated on Memorial Day in 1962, has a special ceremony.

Veterans Day   COMMEMORATION
(⊗Nov 11) This national public holiday honors US military veterans; the USS *Missouri* hosts a sunset ceremony and tribute.

Pearl Harbor Day   COMMEMORATION
(⊗Dec 7) Ceremonies at Pearl Harbor include a Hawaiian blessing and heartfelt accounts from survivors of the 1941 Japanese attack. Other events take place in the days before and after.

Eating

All four sights have concession stands or snack shops. The Laniākea Café at the Pearl Harbor Aviation Museum has the best selection, although it's rather gloomy. There are some excellent lunch choices in nearby 'Aiwa and Pearl City, while the bounty of Honolulu is not far.

Restaurant 604   AMERICAN $$
(☑808-888-7616; www.restaurant604.com; 57 Arizona Memorial Dr; mains $12-25; ⊗10:30am-10pm Mon-Fri, from 9:30am Sat & Sun) A fine alternative to the ho-hum cafes within the Pearl Harbor historic sites, this waterfront restaurant has outdoor tables and views over a yacht marina. The menu teems with comfort food: great burgers, steaks, salads, plate lunches etc. Weekend brunch is popular. It's a 10-minute walk north under the Ford Island Bridge from the Pearl Harbor visitor center.

❶ Information

NPS Visitor Center & Museum (p178) is the main visitor center of the Pearl Harbor National Memorial, with an excellent museum and bookstore. The boats to the USS Arizona Memorial leave from here, as do the buses for the Ford Island sites. Strict security measures mean you are not allowed to bring in any items that allow concealment (eg purses, camera bags, fanny packs, backpacks, diaper bags etc). Personal-sized phones, cameras and camcorders are allowed. There is a storage facility ($5 per item) to the right of the main visitor-center entrance.

❶ Getting There & Away

The entrance to the Pearl Harbor National Memorial and the other Pearl Harbor historic sites is off the Kamehameha Hwy (Hwy 99), southwest of Aloha Stadium. From Honolulu or Waikiki, take H-1 west to exit 15A (Arizona Memorial/Stadium), then follow the highway signs for the memorial, not the signs for Pearl Harbor (which lead onto the US Navy base). There's plenty of free parking.

From Waikiki, bus 20 and bus 42 are the most direct, running regularly between 6am and 3pm, taking just over an hour each way. The 'Arizona Memorial' stops are at the NPS Visitor Center entrance and right outside the main entrance to the NPS site. Check to see where your bus stops. On the free Ford Island shuttle buses, sit on the left side for the best views as you head to the island.

'Aiea

POP 9400

North of Pearl Harbor lies the town of 'Aiea. Beyond Aloha Stadium and its famous flea market, the crowded old community climbs the hill to a historic *heiau* (stone temple). To the west is strip-mall-filled Pearl City.

◎ Sights & Activities

Kea'iwa Heiau State
Recreation Area   PARK

(📞808-483-2511; http://dlnr.hawaii.gov/dsp/parks/oahu; 99-1849 'Aiea Heights Dr; ⊙7am-7:45pm Apr-1st Mon in Sep, to 6:45pm 1st Tue in Sep-Mar) FREE In the mountains north of Pearl Harbor, this state park protects Kea'i-wa Heiau, an ancient *ho'ola* (healing or medicinal) temple. Today, people wishing to be cured may still place offerings here. The 4ft-high terraces are made of stacked rocks that enclose an approximately 16,000-sq-ft platform; the construction may date to the 16th century. The park includes the splendid 'Aiea Loop Trail (p194), which has

lush views across O'ahu. To get here by car from Honolulu, take exit 13A 'Aiea off Hwy 78. Join 'Aiea Heights Dr, which winds up through a residential area for over 2.5 miles to the park. From downtown Honolulu, bus 74 ('Aiea Heights; hourly) stops about 1 mile downhill from the park entrance.

'Aiea Bay State Recreation Area   PARK

(Kamehameha Hwy; ⊙7am-5:30pm) Hidden on a small access road road off the Kamehameha Hwy, this small waterfront park has views of Pearl Harbor along with shady picnic tables and wide lawns. It's on the east end of the Pearl Harbor Bike Path.

Pearl Harbor Bike Path   CYCLING

A fascinating 5.2-mile bike path that stretches from Waipahu Depot St in the west to 'Aiea Bay State Recreation Area in the east. Along the way it curves around various inlets along the shore of Pearl Harbor. Besides the watery views, there are sections past industrial parks, a few small farms and humble waterfront residences. There are good places to stop for a meal.

Bike Shop   CYCLING

(📞808-487-3615; www.bikeshophawaii.com; 98-019 Kamehameha Hwy; bike rental per day from $20; ⊙9am-8pm Mon-Fri, to 5pm Sat & Sun) An excellent bike shop that offers rentals for riding the Pearl Harbor Bike Path. Staff are knowledgeable and offer excellent advice. The bike selection is large, and you must reserve at least 24 hours in advance.

'Aiea Bowl   BOWLING

(📞808-488-6854; http://aieabowl.com; 99-115 'Aiea Heights Dr, 'Aiea Shopping Center; lane rental per hr $30, shoe rental $4; ⊙9am-midnight Sun-Wed, to 2am Thu-Sat) Lively bowling alley with lots of special events and an excellent restaurant and bar, the Alley Restaurant. There are lots of arcade games for non-bowlers.

✗ Eating

'Aiea is a center for great – and cheap – Asian meals. Kamehameha Hwy has numerous hole-in-the-wall and ethnic eateries. There are also a few fine options amid the chains in neighboring Pearl City.

★ Alley Restaurant
at 'Aiea Bowl   HAWAIIAN $

(📞808-488-6854; www.aieabowl.com; 99-115 'Aiea Heights Dr, 'Aiea Shopping Center; mains $9-25; ⊙7am-9:30pm Sun-Wed, to 10pm Thu-Sat) A bowling-alley-attached restaurant seems an unlikely place to get great food, but not at

LOCAL KNOWLEDGE

CLASSIC DINER

Many fans consider the 30-minute drive to **Anna Miller's** (✆808-487-2421; http://annamillersrestaurant.com; 98-115 Kaonohi S, 'Aiea; mains $6-15; ⊗24hr) coffee shop from Waikiki to be an essential part of their holiday. Classic diner fare is served by waitresses right out of central casting in surroundings that have an authentic 1970s-chic vibe. Breakfast is always served, and a display of over 30 pies greets you at the door. Don't miss the banana cream.

this fabulous diner. Dig into a scrumptious *furikake* ahi (yellowfin tuna) sandwich with super-crispy fries, or Asian braised pork with brown rice, while you listen to strikes in the nearby lanes. Breakfast is served until 10am and it has a full bar.

★**Kehau's Kitchen** HAWAIIAN $
(✆808-487-2220; http://kehauskitchenrestaurant. com; 98-150 Kaonohi St, Pearl City; mains $6-18; ⊗10am-7pm Mon & Sun, to 8pm Wed & Thu, to 9pm Fri & Sat) In an architecturally troubled strip mall, the plate lunches at this simple storefront are superb. *Kalua* pork, *lomilomi* salmon (minced, salted salmon, diced tomato and green onion) and other classics are made in-house with obvious love. The dining area is spartan at best, but you won't notice once you tuck into the excellent fare.

Sushi Spot SUSHI $
(✆808-485-2255; 99-209 Moanalua Rd; mains $6-15; ⊗11am-3pm & 5-9pm Tue-Sat) Ignore the typical 'Aiea strip-mall setting for what's inside this family-run storefront: great custom hand rolls (over 40 choices) and sushi that are impeccably fresh and well prepared. Great bowls, shrimp tempura and more.

Ige's Lunchwagon HAWAIIAN $
(✆808-486-8728; 98-025 Hekaha St, No 16; mains $10; ⊗10am-1pm Tue-Fri) This family-run legend hidden deep in a commercial complex turns out memorable Hawaiian food, including pork teriyaki, beef curry, Korean fried chicken and savory *laulau* (pork steamed in taro leaves). It's all takeout; get there by noon before the specials sell out. Convenient for the Pearl Harbor Bike Path (p181).

Miki's HAWAIIAN $
(✆808-455-1668; 1001 Lehua Ave, Pearl City; mains $6-12; ⊗9pm-4am) For many late-night

denizens, the teri meatballs (flavored with teriyaki) at this literal hole-in-the-wall are an essential part of a night out carousing. The menu changes daily – check the whiteboard – but it usually includes filling options such as *kalua* pork and meatloaf. A couple of battered picnic tables are outside.

Forty Niner Restaurant DINER $
(✆808-484-1940; 98-110 Honomanu St; mains $6-14; ⊗7am-8pm Mon-Thu, to 9pm Fri & Sat, to 2pm Sun) This little diner from 1947 has a tidy building that's on the old historical register. Its old-fashioned saimin (local-style noodle soup) is made with a secret-recipe broth, while the garlic chicken and hamburgers show the same care in the kitchen. This is a great place for breakfast (excellent waffles) before visiting Pearl Harbor, with outdoor picnic tables under umbrellas.

Chun Wah Kam Noodle Factory ASIAN $
(✆808-485-1107; www.chunwahkam.com; 98-040 Kamehameha Hwy, Waimalu Shopping Center; snacks from $2.50, mains $8-13; ⊗7:30am-7pm Mon-Sat, 8am-4pm Sun) Fans of this mini-chain line up for *manapua* (Hawaii version of Chinese-style steamed or baked buns) stuffed with anything from *char siu* (Chinese barbecued pork) or guava BBQ pork to purple sweet potatoes. It's been run by the same family since 1942. This mini-mall is chockablock with many more Asian and local joints.

🛍 Shopping

Aloha Stadium Swap
Meet & Marketplace MARKET
(✆808-486-6704; www.alohastadiumswapmeet. net; 99-500 Salt Lake Blvd, Aloha Stadium; adult/child $1/free; ⊗8am-3pm Wed & Sat, from 6:30am Sun) Hundreds of vendors encircle Aloha Stadium at this famous market. Your eyes will soon cross at the plethora of gaudy souvenirs, cheap T-shirts ($7!), loudly patterned clothes in unnatural fibers, plastic orchids, phone cases and fad foods (think turmeric). Amid it all are interesting handmade items and fresh fruit vendors. Bus 42 passes close by from Waikiki. Despite the posted hours, many vendors don't get set up until after 9am.

Fabric Mart TEXTILES
(✆808-488-8882; http://hawaiifabricmart.com; 98-023 Hekaha St; ⊗9am-6pm Mon-Sat, to 5pm Sun) This fabric mega-mart is the jackpot on O'ahu in terms of the fun and tropical prints that you might need to sew your own quilts or aloha wear. You'll need a car to get here. There's a smaller branch in Honolulu (p129).

❶ Getting There & Away

Several bus routes from Honolulu serve the main roads of 'Aiea, including 40, 42 and 54. The HART train (p133) may start running here by 2021.

Waipahu

POP 38,400

You can see it from any place in town: the 170ft-tall brick smokestack that was once a belching symbol of the O'ahu Sugar Company, the cane-growing industrial giant that dominated life in this part of the island.

Waipahu retains the look of the company town it was from when the sugar mill opened in 1898 to its closure in 1995. More than half the population has roots in the Philippines – a legacy of the ethnic makeup of the plantation workforce in later years. The old center of town radiating from the intersection of Farrington Hwy and Waipahu Depot St is worth a stroll for a glimpse into O'ahu's past. But don't delay, as Honolulu's HART train (p133) will stop here and big changes are planned, including a lot of new development.

◎ Sights & Activities

★ **Hawaii's Plantation Village**   MUSEUM
(Haunted Village; ☑808-677-0110; www.hawaii plantationvillage.org; 94-695 Waipahu St, Waipahu Cultural Garden Park; adult/child $15/6; ⊘tours on the hour 10am-2pm Mon-Sat) Waipahu was one of O'ahu's last sugarcane plantation towns and this outdoor museum tells the story of life on the plantations, especially the local O'ahu Sugar Company. Though the village is definitely showing its age, you can still learn plenty about the lives of plantation workers. The setting is evocative: a fertile little valley surrounded by working-class neighborhoods.

The 90-minute tours start on the hour and take in buildings typical of an early 20th-century plantation: a Chinese cookhouse, a Japanese shrine and replicated homes of the seven ethnic groups – Hawaiian, Japanese, Chinese, Korean, Portuguese, Puerto Rican and Filipino – that worked the fields.

West Loch Municipal Golf Course   GOLF
(☑808-675-6076; www.honolulu.gov/des/golf/west loch; 91-1126 Okupe St, 'Ewa Beach; 18 holes $66; ⊘6am-5:30pm) There are great views of Pearl Harbor's West Loch throughout and nice wide fairways to keep the ball in play at this casual public course. No pro shop, restaurant or club rental. Hit the links by 12:30pm to ensure you get to play a full round. It's on the west side of Waipahu.

✖ Eating

★ **Tanioka's Seafoods & Catering**   HAWAIIAN $
(☑808-671-3779; http://taniokas.com; 94-903 Farrington Hwy; mains $9-12; ⊘9am-3pm) It's all here and it's all good: *poke* bowls, plate lunches, *bentō* (Japanese-style box lunches), legendary garlic ahi and more. The classics of modern Hawaii cuisine are displayed in gleaming cases at this beloved Waipahu institution. Get there early, because when the day's bounty is gone, it's gone. Takeout only.

Rocky's Coffee Shop   BREAKFAST
(☑808-677-3842; 94-316 Waipahu Depot St; ⊘4:30am-noon Fri-Wed) The banana pancakes at this diner are worth getting out of bed for. Amid vintage photos and family memorabilia that make Rocky's a de facto local history museum, you can enjoy excellent egg dishes, fried rice, Spam specials and other treats that fueled generations of plantation workers.

❶ Getting There & Away

Buses 42 and W1 serve Waipahu center from Waikiki.

Leeward O'ahu

O'ahu's west side is full of contradictions. Those looking for upscale packaged holidays enjoy the resorts in the gated enclave of Ko Olina. Inland, this side of O'ahu can feel like one vast housing development, accented by strip malls. But diversions abound, including the beaches in the south at 'Ewa.

On the isolated Wai'anae Coast, there is a collective feeling of the forgotten, with Honolulu feeling more than an island away. Few islanders, let alone visitors, round the corner and follow the Farrington Hwy (Hwy 93) north to Makaha and beyond.

You'll find more Native Hawaiians leeward than anyplace else on the island, and cultural pride is alive.

Kapolei Area

The southwestern corner of O'ahu has few traces of the sugarcane plantations and US Navy facilities once found here. Today these dry plains are an unending series of developments. Amid this, there are some sights, activities and beaches worth seeking out.

◎ Sights & Activities

Hawaiian Railway   HISTORIC SITE
(☑808-681-5461; www.hawaiianrailway.com; 91-1001 Renton Rd, 'Ewa; adult/child $15/10; ⊘3pm Sat,

Kapolei & Ko Olina Areas

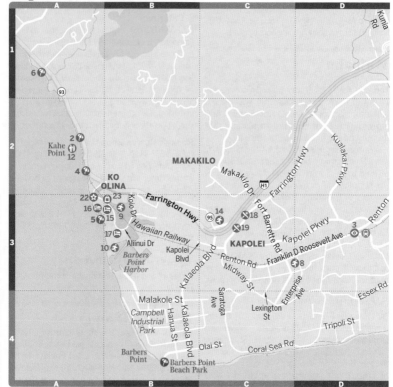

1pm & 3pm Sun) For half a century from 1890 to 1940, a railroad carried sugarcane and passengers from Honolulu all the way around the coast through to Kahuku. The railway closed and the tracks were torn up after WWII and the automobile boom in Hawaii. Thanks to the historical society, trains run again along a segment of restored track between 'Ewa and beachfront Kahe Point. The 90-minute round trip chugs along through sometimes pastoral, sometimes industrial scenery. The yard is a vast junkyard of rusty railway debris and includes the coal engine that pulled the first O'ahu Railway and Land Company train in 1889. The 3pm trains make a popular stop at a Ko Olina ice-cream parlor. There are shady picnic tables at the depot.

Wet 'n' Wild Hawaii   AMUSEMENT PARK
(☎808-674-9283; www.wetnwildhawaii.com; 400 Farrington Hwy, Kapolei; adult/child $50/38; ⊙10:30am-3:30pm Mon, Thu & Fri, to 4pm Sat & Sun, longer hrs Jun-Sep) Every temperament is served at this 25-acre water park. Float on a lazy river or brave a seven-story waterslide and the football-field-sized wave pool. The hillside Tornado offers superb views across O'ahu before guests are shot through a series of watery tubes and slides. Some activities cost extra and parking is $8. Various reserved seating areas and cabanas cost extra too. Bus 40 takes 1¼ hours to get here from the Ala Moana Center in Honolulu; it runs every half-hour between 8:30am and 6:30pm.

Coral Crater
Adventure Park   ADVENTURE SPORTS
(☎808-626-5773; http://coralcrater.com; 91-1780 Midway St, Kapolei; admission from $140; ⊙9am-5pm) On a large, naturalistic plot of land – with plenty of palm trees – this adventure park specializes in ziplines. Six routes pass through palms and other tropical foliage, connected by tall towers. Other activities include all-terrain vehicle (ATV) and horse rides and a climbing wall. Various packages are available; always book in advance. Shoes with closed toes are mandatory.

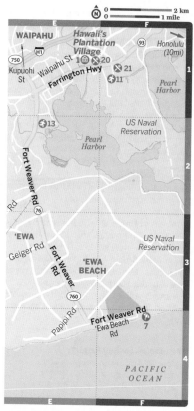

✗ Eating

Along Farrington Hwy (Hwy 93) there are numerous hole-in-the-wall Asian food eateries, strip-mall restaurants and supermarkets. For the best choices head to Waipahu or 'Aiea.

Pho & Company   VIETNAMESE $
(☑ 808-692-9833; http://phoandcompany.com; 890 Kamokila Blvd, Kapolei; mains $7-15; ☺ 10am-9pm Mon-Fri, 11am-9pm Sat, 11am-7pm Sun) Don't miss the pho (beef noodle soup) at this strip-mall storefront also serving spring rolls, rice plates, crunchy banh mi sandwiches and bubble tea. Happy diners praise the house-made broth. It's next to a multiplex cinema.

Kapolei Korean BBQ   KOREAN $
(☑ 808-674-8822; 590 Farrington Hwy, Kapolei; mains $8-10; ☺ 10am-9pm Thu-Tue) Expect good-sized portions of Korean standards such as marinated *galbi* (short ribs) and beef barbecue. The barbecue chicken, pork and beef draw fans from across Leeward O'ahu to the busy strip mall setting.

❶ Getting There & Away

The scattered sites of this region are mostly best reached with your own wheels.

Ko Olina

POP 1800

Don't have a beach? No problem. All it takes is a couple thousand tons of imported sand. In exchange for public beach access, the developers of Ko Olina were allowed to carve out four mushroom-shaped lagoons from the coastline and line them with soft white sand. The golf course, resorts and swaths of condos have a generic upscale atmosphere that could be, well, anywhere. Here, the concept of escape is more important than the destination.

BEACH ESCAPE

A huge grassy lawn and sizable pavilion attract large Hawaiian families to **Pu'uloa Beach Park** ('Ewa Beach Park; ☑ 808-675-6030; www.honolulu.gov/ parks; 91-027 Fort Weaver Rd, 'Ewa Beach; ⊙ 5am-8pm), a hidden gem of a beach, on weekends. There's always a spare table or two for a picnic, and a good view of Honolulu from the long ribbon of pearlescent south-facing sand that extends well beyond the park. On weekdays this park is the perfect escape for the crowd-phobic.

The **surf break** here known as 'Ewa Beach is a long paddle out through the alluring turquoise water to a sandbar. In good conditions, there are rights and lefts, from 2ft to 4ft. Local surfers are at times unwelcoming. That boom you hear may be live-fire training at the military facility immediately east.

◉ Sights

Ko Olina Lagoons BEACH
(www.koolina.com; off Ali'inui Dr, Kapolei; ⊙ sunrise-sunset; ⊕) FREE Ko Olina's four artificial lagoons and beaches have calm waters that are perfect for kids, although the current picks up near the opening to the ocean. A wide, paved recreational path is ideal for a sunset stroll. Extremely limited but free public beach-access parking can be found by each lagoon, off Ali'inui Dr inside the resort area.

Rent snorkel sets and beach gear at Koholā, the biggest and northernmost lagoon, to peer at rainbow-colored tropical fish. Fewer crowds visit the southernmost lagoon (Nai'a).

🏃 Activities

Though most facilities are reserved for guests, hotel grounds are open to the public during the daytime. Exploring around the lush landscaping of Aulani or checking out the saltwater marine-life pools at the Four Seasons is interesting.

The resorts also have activities desks offering a full range of things to do in the lagoons, at the golf course, on the reefs and beyond.

Ko Olina Marina CRUISE
(☑ 808-679-1050; www.koolinamarina.com; 92-100 Waipahe Pl, Kapolei; sunset cruises adult/child from $89/79; ⊙ 8:30am-5pm) The marina will hook you up with snorkeling tours, sunset cruises, scuba diving, whale-watching (December through March) and sport-fishing charters.

Ko Olina Golf Club GOLF
(☑ 808-676-5300; www.koolinagolf.com; 92-1220 Ali'inui Dr, Kapolei; green fees $160-225; ⊙ by reservation only) Both the Ladies Professional Golf Association (LPGA) and the senior PGA tour have held tournaments at this acclaimed course. Mere duffers can also enjoy the landscaped oasis of green among the barren brown hills. Check online for special rates and packages.

🛏 Sleeping

Stay in Ko Olina if you want isolation, as you're far from other parts of O'ahu.

Besides the three large resorts, there are hundreds of time-shares, condos and apartments. Vacation rentals around Ko Olina are generally not small studios; they include villas, multi-bedroom beachfront condos, and golf-course homes. A two-bedroom place runs between $300 and $600 per night.

Disney's Aulani resort with its fanatical focus on families is very popular. There are plans for an opulent and over-the-top Atlantis Resort.

★ **Aulani, A Disney Resort** RESORT $$$
(☑ 866-443-4763; www.disneyaulani.com; 92-1185 Ali'inui Dr, Kapolei; r from $500; ❄@☎☲) The daily activity list at Aulani is mind-boggling. Tone up at beach-body boot camp, take a Hawaiian craft class or hula the day away. All the while, the little ones will be listening to Hawaiian tales at the free Aunty's House kids club and the older kids will be off on a treasure hunt or enjoying fun food at the teen spa.

In the evening you can attend a free Hawaiian dance and music revue, or listen to island music in a lounge, as the teens and tweens karaoke. That's not to mention the stingray interactive experience, character meet-and-greets, the water-park-like pools – and oh, yeah, the beach. You might even appreciate that the Hawaii-inspired, casually luxe rooms are uncharacteristically understated (no giant Mickeys here). Note that most are reserved for Disney time-share patrons. Extra charges abound: a pool cabana costs over $300 a day.

**Four Seasons Resort
Oahu at Ko Olina** RESORT $$$
(☑ 808-679-0079; www.fourseasons.com; 92-1001 Olani St, Kapolei; r from $500; ❄@☎☲) The Four Seasons resort is right on the beach

and is popular with those wanting to avoid the Waikiki scene, but still have all the trappings of top-end luxury. Most of the 371 very large rooms have large ocean-view lanais (terraces). The gardens are a verdant fantasy.

Marriott Ko Olina
Beach Club RESORT **$$$**
(☎808-679-4700; www.marriott.com; 92-161 Waipahe Pl, Kapolei; r from $360; ✿ @ 🛜 🗷) On one of the smaller lagoons, this vacation-club property is less expensive than its neighbors. Plus you get a full kitchen in every room, so you can prepare your own meals and enjoy them on your lanai. It's an easy walk to the other resorts.

Eating

The resorts have a full range of restaurants and most people wander between them. The restaurants in the Ko Olina Center shopping area are mostly unimpressive and pricey, although there is a good supermarket with prepared foods.

Pizza Corner PIZZA **$$**
(☎808-380-4626; http://pizzacornerhawaii.com; 92-1047 Olani St, Ko Olina Center; mains $10-30; ⊙11am-9pm) Creates pizzas with both familiar and island flavors, such as Poke pizza with spicy ahi and *lomilomi* on a thin-crust hand-tossed base, and the Kalua Pork pizza with mango salsa and chutney. There's takeout and they deliver within Ko Olina.

★ Monkeypod Kitchen AMERICAN **$$$**
(☎808-380-4086; www.monkeypodkitchen.com; 92-1047 Olani St, Ko Olina Center; mains $18-42; ⊙11am-11pm) A casual restaurant concept originated by locally renowned chef Peter Merriman. Upscale comfort fare (burgers, sandwiches, seafood, pizza) is sourced locally. Many dishes are pure Modern Hawaii cuisine, with fresh flavors and Asian influences.

The bar offers over 30 craft beers on tap. There's a mimosa-fueled brunch at weekends and quiet tables outside.

Roy's Ko Olina HAWAII REGIONAL **$$$**
(☎808-676-7697; www.royyamaguchi.com; 92-1220 Ali'inui Dr, Ko Olina Golf Club; mains $30-60; ⊙11am-2pm & 5:30-9:30pm) Roy's is located in the clubhouse area of the Ko Olina Golf Club (p186). His famous Modern Hawaii food fusion is creative as always, although not for the faint of wallet ($50 for a Hawaii-style mixed plate etc). There is a very long list of appetizers and shared plates designed to go

with drinks – the perfect accompaniment for telling golf stories.

Drinking & Nightlife

The resorts all have a variety of bars, most with ocean views that glow at sunset. Expect mellow Hawaii tunes in the evenings.

☆ Entertainment

Live music is occasionally staged at the hotel bars.

Paradise Cove LUAU
(☎808-842-5911; www.paradisecove.com; 92-1089 Ali'inui Dr, Ko Olina; adult/child from $107/84; ⊙5-9pm; 🚼) Pre-buffet activities include Hawaiian games and a *hukilau* (net-fishing) party, adding an interactivity that kids love at this luau. The much-hyped dinner show features dances from across Polynesia. It's just north of the resort area, about 30 miles west of Waikiki. Like other luaus, there are extra charges for seating closer to the performers.

Fia Fia Polynesian
Dinner Show LUAU
(☎808-679-4728; 92-161 Waipahe Pl, Marriott Ko Olina Beach Club; adult/child from $125/60; ⊙from 4pm Tue; 🚼) These Polynesian performances lean heavily toward the Samoan, and feature an entertaining 'chief.' Kids love the preshow games and the fire and knife dances (get there by 4pm for these). The buffet has all the usuals, although many complain about the long lines to be seated, get food etc. Valet parking is included in the price for non-resort guests.

🛍 Shopping

Ko Olina Center SHOPPING CENTER
(http://koolina.com/experiences/shopping; 92-1047 Olani St; ⊙hours vary) Two blocks of upscale shops and restaurants that cater to those staying in the Ko Olina resorts.

ℹ Getting There & Around

The H-1 Fwy is often clogged with traffic heading to/from Honolulu. During the day, the 30-mile drive to Waikiki can easily take well over an hour. There is no convenient bus service for the resorts.

The resorts have paid valet parking, but will validate if you spend a set amount at one of their restaurants – easy to do. There is limited free parking on the streets around the resorts, lagoons and beaches. A signboard at the entrance shows how many spaces are free at each location.

Wai'anae Coast

Beyond Ko Olina's artificial enclave of luxury resorts, the stop-and-go Farrington Hwy (Hwy 93) runs the length of the Wai'anae Coast, rolling past working-class neighborhoods and strip malls on one side and inviting white-sand beaches on the other. Human habitation eventually gives way to velvet-tufted mountains and rocky coastal ledges near Ka'ena Point.

Interesting dining options outside the Ko Olina resort area are sparse. If you are touring the coast on a day trip, you might want to bring a picnic for the beach. Note that many of the beaches have long-term residents who are otherwise homeless.

🛈 Getting There & Away

The drive along the Wai'anae Coast, where the Farrington Hwy (Hwy 93) turns north up the coast near Ko Olina, is 19 miles. It's a busy road through Makaha and it slows considerably during rush hour.

Bus routes C and 40 provide frequent service daily up the coast as far north as Makaha, but getting here from Waikiki would take at least two hours. You'll be happiest exploring the area with your own wheels. Note that car break-ins are a problem all along the coast. Leave nothing visible in a parked car.

Wai'anae Coast

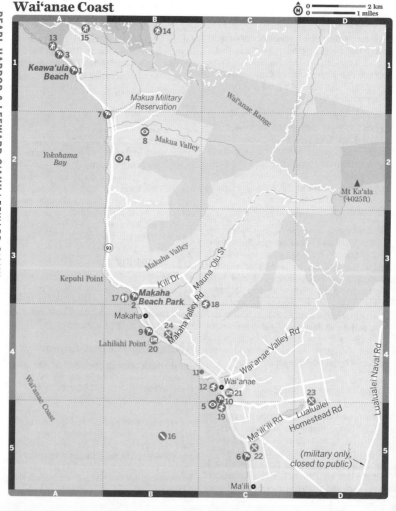

KAHE & NANAKULI

These small towns are notable mostly for their beach parks. Nanakuli has services and places for refreshments. The parks are a bit scruffy and can get very windy, but they are seldom crowded and the raw views over the Pacific are unparalleled.

 Beaches

Kahe Point Beach Park BEACH
(☑808-696-4481; 92-301 Farrington Hwy, Kahe; ⊙6am-10pm) At a rocky point that's popular with snorkelers and anglers. Great coastal views, as well as water, picnic tables and restrooms. This is the end point for the weekend runs of the Hawaiian Railway (p183).

Hawaiian Electric Beach Park BEACH
(Tracks Beach Park; ☑808-768-3003; off Farrington Hwy,Kahe; ⊙5am-10pm) This spot is sometimes called Tracks Beach Park; this is where the weekend beach train once ran before WWII. The sandy strip is good for swimming, bodysurfing and bodyboarding. If you can ignore the smokestacks *mauka* (inland), the beach here is rarely crowded. It was a popular prewar weekend destination for islanders, who rode out on the old plantation railway. It's just north of Kahe Point Beach Park. **Tracks**, named after the beach, is a gentle break that is good much of the year. Reliable swells also mean it's good for bodyboarding.

Nanakuli Beach Park BEACH
(89-269 Farrington Hwy, Nanakuli; ⊙ sunrise-sunset) This beach park lines the south end of Nanakuli in a broad, sandy stretch that offers swimming, snorkeling and diving during the summer. In winter, high surf can

PROUDLY HAWAIIAN

The Wai'anae Coast of Leeward O'ahu is a stronghold of Hawaiian culture with a proud history of resisting change from the outside. When Kamehameha the Great invaded O'ahu in 1795, this area became a refuge for resisters, and when Christian missionaries arrived in O'ahu 25 years later, Wai'anae folks shut them out by blocking the Kolekole Pass that connected Wai'anae to the rest of the island. Even today Wai'anae stands apart, with the largest Native Hawaiian population on O'ahu and a deep sense of connection to the land.

create rip currents and dangerous shorebreaks. The park has a simple playground and ragtag beach facilities. The adjoining town of Nanakuli is a short walk and has fast-food joints and supermarkets.

WAI'ANAE

POP 13,200

Backed by deeply eroded volcanic cliffs covered in a lush green blanket, Wai'anae is this coast's hub for everyday services. Strung out along the highway, the town has stores, a commercial boat harbor and a well-used beach park. IJust south, the adjoining village of Ma'ili has a bit more of the same.

 Beaches

Poka'i Bay Beach Park BEACH
(85-037 Wai'anae Valley Rd) Protected by Kane'ilio Point and a long breakwater, the beach is in need of some maintenance,

Wai'anae Coast

HOMELESS IN PARADISE

You'll see many people living along the beach as you travel the Wai'anae Coast. Estimates indicate that about 4400 homeless people live on O'ahu, with about 2400 being unsheltered (as opposed to living in shelters run by organizations). People can be found living in and out of shelters island-wide, but a big concentration – almost 600 people – live unsheltered on leeward O'ahu. Locals say this is because there are fewer affluent residents and tourists to make a fuss and that there is less of a not-in-my-backyard mentality compared to other parts of the island.

Like elsewhere in the US, the homeless issue in Hawaii is a complex one. The state has a long-term goal of ending homelessness, but despite increasing budgets for housing and services, the number remains at over 5000 statewide each year. Polls show that almost 75% of locals consider homelessness the top problem on O'ahu. Each year new programs are announced to address the problem, while laws have been passed criminalizing people who try to live in parks, all with mixed success. Beginning in 2019, the City of Honolulu and the Hawaii Tourism Authority began installing almost 200 security cameras at O'ahu parks and beaches.

although the luminescent beauty of the sand is undimmed. Waves seldom break inside the bay, and the sandy beach slopes gently. Calm, year-round swimming conditions make it perfect for children, as evidenced by the number of local families here on weekends. The shabby park has showers, restrooms and picnic tables. The walk out to Ku'ililoa Heiau has sweeping coastal views.

Ma'ili Beach Park   BEACH
(87-021 Farrington Hwy; ☺ sunrise-sunset) This attractive beach has the distinction of being one of the longest stretches of white sand on the island. The grassy park that sits adjacent to the beach is popular with families for weekend barbecues. Like other places on the Wai'anae Coast, the water conditions are often treacherous in winter but usually calm enough for swimming in summer. The park is a bit shabby, with a playground, beach facilities and a few coconut palms that provide very limited shade.

⊙ Sights & Activities

Ku'ililoa Heiau   TEMPLE
(off Farrington Hwy) Along the south side of the bay, Kane'ilio Point is the site of a terraced-stone platform temple, partly destroyed by the army during WWII, then later reconstructed by local conservationists. The site was used in part as a teaching and blessing place for navigation and fishing. Wai'anae was one of the last places on the island to accept Christianity, and the heiau (ancient stone temple) continued to be used after the ancient *kapu* (taboo) system was overthrown in 1819. Today, the area around the terraces still affords superb coastal views all the way north to Makaha. To get here, start at the parking lot of Poka'i Bay Beach Park, walk straight across the lawn with the outrigger canoes at your right and take the path half a mile out to the point.

West O'ahu SUP   WATER SPORTS
(☎ 808-425-5818; www.westoahusup.com; 85-979 Farrington Hwy, Suite F; surfboard rental per day $45; ☺ 9am-5pm) The center for ocean activities on the Wai'anae Coast. Rents SUPs, surfboards and other gear. Offers excellent advice and arranges scuba and snorkeling trips.

Hale Nalu Surf & Bike   WATER SPORTS
(☎ 808-696-5897; www.halenalu.com; 85-876 Farrington Hwy; surfboard rental per day from $35; ☺ 10am-6pm Tue-Fri, to 5pm Sat) This sports shop sells and rents mountain bikes, surfboards, snorkel sets and bodysurfing boards.

Mahi Wreck   DIVE SITE
(⌖) A 15-minute boat ride from the Wai'anae Boat Harbor, the *Mahi* is one of O'ahu's most popular dive sites. The former minesweeper was sunk in 1982 as an artificial-reef project. Divers are advised to remain on the outside of the wreck, as the bridge collapsed in a hurricane years ago. The site has a lot of rays.

☞ Tours

★ Wild Side Specialty Tours   WHALE WATCHING
(☎ 808-306-7273; http://sailhawaii.com; 85-371 Farrington Hwy, Wai'anae Small Boat Harbor; tours adult/child from $175/145; ⌖) Recognized by the Hawaii Ecotourism Association, Wild Side caters to the naturalist in you. It takes people to see whales, sea turtles and dolphins in the wild and visits excellent places for snorkeling that other tours rarely include. Tours are limited to six to 10 people.

Hawaii Nautical   BOATING
(☎ 808-234-7245; www.hawaiinautical.com; 85-491 Farrington Hwy, Wai'anae Small Boat Harbor;

tours from adult/child $60/45) Set sail on a deluxe catamaran to look at marine life and go snorkeling on the southwest coast. You can either upgrade to snuba (a hybrid of scuba and snorkeling) or opt for a full-on scuba-dive trip. Also offers whale- and dolphin-watching cruises. There are shuttle rides available from Ko Olina for some trips.

Dolphin Excursions WILDLIFE
(☑808-239-5579; www.dolphinexcursions.com; 85-491 Farrington Hwy, Wai'anae Small Boat Harbor; 3hr tour adult/child from $140/95; ⊞) Snorkeling and spinner-dolphin-watching cruises run year-round, usually in the morning. From December to March, there are whale-watching trips to see humpbacks.

✕ Eating

Wai'anae is your best lunch bet if you're on a day trip and didn't bring a picnic. Amid the fast-food outlets along Farrington Hwy (Hwy 93), there are a couple worthy restaurant options, and lunchtime food trucks.

★Countryside Cafe AMERICAN $
(☑808-888-5448; www.countrysidecafe808.net; 87-070 Farrington Hwy, Ma'ili; mains $7-15; ⊙7am-2pm Mon-Sat, to 1pm Sun) Well-prepared diner fare with an island accent: omelet with *kalua* pork, Hawaii-style hash, passion-fruit biscuits and more. It's at the very south end of Wai'anae and is also right across from the northern end of Ma'ili Beach Park. There are tables outside the storefront location where you can hear the surf.

Coquitos Latin Cuisine LATIN AMERICAN $
(☑808-888-4082; 85-773 Farrington Hwy; mains $8-20; ⊙11am-9pm Tue-Sun) Inside a small, breezy green plantation-style house surrounded by fast-food joints, this cafe looks like it belongs in the Caribbean or Key West. The Puerto Rican kitchen prepares classic dishes such as *mofongo* (mashed plantains with garlic and bacon), grilled Cuban sandwiches, shredded beef empanadas, and tall *tres leches* (sponge cake) for dessert. There is lanai seating.

★Kahumana Cafe HEALTH FOOD $$
(☑808-696-8844; www.kahumana.org; 86-660 Lualualei Homestead Rd; mains $12-21; ⊙11:30am-2:30pm & 6-8pm Tue-Sat; ⊞) ✿ Way off the beaten track, this organic farm's cafe inhabits a cool, tranquil hardwood-floored dining room with green-field views. Fork into fresh daily specials, bountiful salads and sandwiches or macadamia-nut pesto pasta with fish or fowl. Don't forget the homemade *liliko'i* (passion fruit) and mango cheesecake.

The cafe is about 2 miles inland from Farrington Hwy via Ma'ili'ili Rd.

You can tour the organic farms that supply much of the cafe's food by booking in advance. The farmers answer questions and show off the gardens, crops, orchards and animals. The price (adult/child $80/50) includes a three-course meal after the tour.

MAKAHA
POP 8300

Relatively free of tourists even today, this is where big-wave surfing got its start in the 1950s. Makaha means 'ferocious,' and long ago the valley behind the beach was notorious for bandits, but the word could just as easily describe the stark, rugged landscape.

Makaha is known for excellent beaches and pounding surf. It also has some serviceable accommodation.

☂ Beaches

★Makaha Beach Park BEACH
(84-369 Farrington Hwy) This beautifully arching beach invites you to spread out your towel and spend the day. Except for weekends and big surf days, you'll likely have the place to yourself. Snorkeling is good during the calmer summer months. There are showers and restrooms, and lifeguards on duty daily. Winter brings big swells that preclude swimming but are beautiful to photograph – or surf.

Papaoneone Beach BEACH
(Turtle Beach; off Farrington Hwy) This beautiful, mostly deserted half-mile of sand is backed by a few aging condo buildings, including the Hawaiian Princess (p192). If you're lucky, you may see green sea turtles in the surf early mornings or late evenings. There are sea caves and rocks they use as a cleaning station offshore. Though the area is protected somewhat by Lahilahi Point to the south,

PEARL HARBOR & LEEWARD O'AHU LEEWARD O'AHU

OFF THE BEATEN TRACK

MAKAHA'S BIG WAVES

In December 1969, legendary surfer Greg Noll rode what was thought to be the biggest wave in surfing history (to that point) at Makaha. Speculation still rages as to exactly how big the monster wave was, but it is commonly accepted that it was at least a 30ft face – a mountain of water for the era. The long point break at Makaha still produces waves that inspire big-wave surfers.

ⓘ BEACH CONDITIONS

It's a good idea to check the beach and water conditions before you make plans to visit the Wai'anae Coast. The open ocean can deliver some strong waves and currents. Also, winds fresh from the open Pacific Ocean can get extreme. The website, http://hawaiibeachsafety. com/oahu, has island-wide coastal conditions and links to further reports for the entire state.

this beach gets excellent surf near the shore, good for bodysurfers, bad for kids.

🏃 Activities

Surfing the Makaha break is the main activity. Out where the waves break furthest offshore are the popular leeward diving spots. **Mahaka Caverns** has underwater caves at depths of 30ft to 50ft. Divers will also delight in going down onto the wreck of the *Mahi* (p190), a classic dive.

Makaha   SURFING
This legendary surf break preceded the North Shore in fame as a big-wave destination. In winter the break is typically 6ft to 15ft and attracts all types of surfers. Over 15ft and the wave breaks over a treacherous reef. Note: locals boast about making visitors unwelcome.

Makaha Valley Country Club   GOLF
(☑808-695-9578; www.makahavalleycc.com; 84-627 Makaha Valley Rd; 18 holes from $37) A relaxed course tucked right up against the Wai'anae Range with great ocean views. The wide fairways and sand-encrusted greens get popular on the weekends. There's a driving range, and club rental is available.

🛏 Sleeping

Most of the relatively few visitors to the Wai'anae Coast are day-trippers. However, some do spend the night, drawn by the quiet and virtual absence of any nightlife. There are no hotels north of Ko Olina. Makaha has the majority of the coast's vacation rentals; most are in aging beachfront condo buildings (one-bedroom condos start at $100, two bedrooms from $175). Besides the major websites, there are local agents for the vacation rentals, such as **Inga's Realty** (☑808-696-1616; www.in gasrealtyinc.com; 85-910 Farrington Hwy, Wai'anae). Three- to seven-night minimums are common. You should be wary of house rentals on

the *mauka* (inland) side of the highway, as they could be in rough neighborhoods.

Hawaiian Princess   CONDO $$
(☑808-696-1234; www.hawaiianprincessmakaha. com; 84-1021 Lahilahi St; 1 bedroom from $140; P) One of the less attractive condo buildings in Makaha (but there are worse, and when you're inside you can't see it!). Right on Papaoneone Beach, the one- and two-bedroom units in this high-rise are large and have good lanais. Decor and amenities vary widely. You can book through the condo website, local agents or major websites.

🍴 Eating

Most places to eat at are both basic and 2 miles south in Wai'anae.

Mountain Magic Shave Ice   ICE CREAM $
(☑808-681-9582; 84-1170 Farrington Hwy; treats from $4; ⊙11am-6pm) After coastal hikes or lazy days on the beach, cool off with the delicious shave ice treats from this storefront shop. There are dozens of colorful flavors, many with island flair.

MAKAHA TO KA'ENA POINT

As you travel north of Makaha, you leave almost all development behind. Inland, there are a series of military reservations, some of which are still used for training. Along the ocean, white sand alternates with scruffy rocky points and shrubby flatlands.

🏖 Beaches

Makua Beach   BEACH
(Farrington Hwy) Way back in the day, this beach was a canoe-landing site for interisland travelers. In the late '60s it was used as the backdrop for the movie *Hawaii*. Today there is little here beyond a golden stretch of sand, shrubs and trees opposite the Makua Military Reservation. Look for dirt lanes off the main road. It's rarely crowded during the week; gates are often open.

⊙ Sights

Kaneana Cave   HISTORIC SITE
(Farrington Hwy) The waves that created this giant stone amphitheater receded long ago. Now the highway passes right outside the cave, 3 miles north of Makaha Beach. Kahuna (priests) performed rituals inside the inner chamber, the legendary abode of a vicious shark-man, a shape-shifter who lured human victims into the cave before devouring them. Hawaiians consider it a sacred place and

won't enter for fear that it's haunted by the spirits of deceased chiefs. Driving north, it's easy to miss the cave entrance. Look for the parking area on the west side of the road.

Makua Valley
LANDMARK

Makua Valley is wide and grassy near the shore and narrows into a fan of sharply fluted mountains. It's used as a training area for the Makua Military Reservation. The seaside road opposite the southern end of the reservation leads to a little graveyard that's shaded by yellow-flowered be-still trees. This site is all that remains of the valley community that was forced to evacuate during WWII, when the US military took over the entire area.

Eating

Bring a picnic to these deserted beaches, as there are no places for food or drink north of Makaha.

ⓘ Getting There & Away

There is no public transportation north of Makaha, and the roads become rougher.

KA'ENA POINT STATE PARK

You don't have to be well versed in Hawaiian legends to know that something mystical occurs at this dramatic convergence of land and sea in the northwestern corner of the island.

Running along both sides of the westernmost point of O'ahu, this state park is an undeveloped coastal strip with a few beaches. Until the mid-1940s, the O'ahu Railway ran up here from Honolulu. Now the railbed serves as the excellent Ka'ena Point hiking trail. White-sand beaches and aqua-blue waters are the highlights of the park. Car-parking areas can be rough; car break-ins are a problem. There is no source of water.

The giant white spheres perched on the hillsides above the park belong to the US military's Ka'ena Point Satellite Tracking Station.

🏖 Beaches

★ Keawa'ula Beach
BEACH

(Yokohama Bay; Farrington Hwy/Hwy 930; ⊙sunrise-sunset) Some say this is the best sunset spot on the island. It certainly has the right west-facing orientation and a blissfully scenic mile-long sandy beach. You'll find restrooms and showers (but no drinking water) at the park's southern end. Swimming is limited to the summer and then only when calm. When the water's flat, it's also possible to snorkel. Winter brings huge, pounding waves. **Yokohama** is a popular seasonal surfing and body-

surfing spot that's best left to the experts, due to submerged rocks, strong rips and a dangerous shorebreak.

◉ Sights & Activities

Ka'ena Point
LANDMARK

The westernmost point on O'ahu is reached by 2.5-mile-long trails from the south and east. Waves up to 50ft break here in winter. It's a desolate spot with windblown views.

★ Ka'ena Point Trailhead
HIKING

(http://dlnr.hawaii.gov/dsp/hiking/oahu/kaenapoint-trail; end of Farrington Hwy/Hwy 930) An extremely winding, mostly level coastal trail (p195) runs along the old railbed for 2.5 miles from Keawa'ula Beach to Ka'ena Point, then continues another 2.5 miles around the point to the North Shore trailhead at the end of Hwy 930. Most hikers take the trail from the end of the paved road at Yokohama Bay as far as the point, then return the same way.

Kuaokala Trail
HIKING

(☏trail status 808-697-4311; http://hawaiitrails.eha waii.gov) The 2.5-mile, one-way Kuaokala Trail brings hikers to a celebrated ridgetop viewpoint over the Makua Valley and Wai'anae Range. From a dirt parking lot, the dusty trail climbs a high ridge into Mokule'ia Forest Reserve. On a clear day you can see Mt Ka'ala (4025ft), O'ahu's highest peak. Hawaii's Division of Forestry & Wildlife issues permits for the hiking and mountain-biking trail system – including the Kuaokala Trail – surrounding Ka'ena Point's satellite-tracking station. See the website for details on the permit process. Be sure to call and check the trail's status, as it's closed at various times of the year. Check in with your permit at the station guardhouse opposite Yokohama Bay. Without a permit, the Kuaokala Trail can still be accessed via the Kealia Trail (p268), starting from the North Shore's Dillingham Airfield.

WANDERING SOULS

Ancient Hawaiians believed that when people went into a deep sleep or lost consciousness, their souls would wander. Souls that wandered too far were drawn west to Ka'ena Point. If they were lucky, they were met here by their 'aumakua (guardian spirit), who led their soul back to their body. If unattended, their soul would be forced to leap from Ka'ena Point into the endless night.

HIKING AROUND LEEWARD OʻAHU

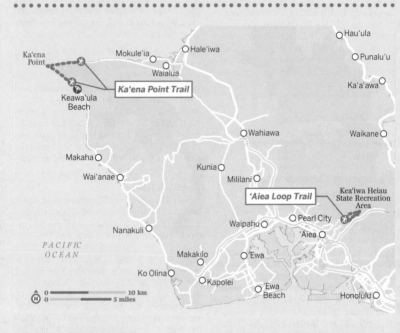

Ka'ena Point
Keawa'ula Beach

Mokule'ia
Waialua

Hale'iwa

Hau'ula

Punalu'u

Ka'a'awa

Waikane

Ka'ena Point Trail

Wahiawa

Makaha
Wai'anae

Kunia
Mililani

'Aiea Loop Trail

Kea'iwa Heiau State Recreation Area

Waipahu
'Aiea
Pearl City

PACIFIC OCEAN

Nanakuli

Makakilo

Ko Olina
Kapolei

'Ewa

'Ewa Beach

Honolulu

0 — 10 km
0 — 5 miles

'AIEA LOOP TRAIL

START/END KEA'IWA HEIAU STATE RECREATION AREA
DURATION 2½ HOURS
DISTANCE LOOP 4.8 MILES

The scenic 'Aiea Loop Trail offers a lush visual feast, including sweeping vistas of Pearl Harbor, Diamond Head and the Ko'olau Range. The park has picnic tables, covered pavilions with barbecue grills, restrooms and drinking water. For the walk, bring waterproof gear; rain is frequent at this elevation. It's also critical to have solid hiking shoes that can deal with the muddy red dirt. Expect mosquitoes, too. Despite these hardships, children who have hiked before usually enjoy the walk.

The hike start point is at the top of the-paved loop road of the **Kea'iwa Heiau State Recreation Area** (p181). Set out amid lemon eucalyptus trees, which give the air a lem-

ony scent. There are also Norfolk pines, with their strange otherworldly appearance. Look for a plaque honoring the crew of a B-24 bomber that crashed near the walk in 1944.

A little over a mile into the walk, you'll see a small side trail; just past this you'll have a sweeping view of the H-3 Hwy majestically curving through the vibrant green mountain valleys from Pearl Harbor to Kane'ohe. You'll get frequent glimpses of this concrete ribbon throughout the second half of the walk.

One of the nice things about this walk is that there are benches and logs you can sit on scattered along the path. These are perfect places for a picnic (which you can pick up in 'Aiea). You also might be able to snack your way along the trail, as there is a lot of fruit growing wild. Look for tiny strawberry guava, passion fruit and more. If you're feeling all foodie, make a salad from the plethora of fern shoots.

A couple of contrasting walks for hikers: the 'Aiea Loop Trail heads up into the verdant mountains, offering magnificent views, while the Ka'ena Point Trail is a coastal walk to O'ahu's westernmost point.

About midway is **Pu'u Uau**, the highest point on the trail (1656ft). Beginning about 500yd beyond here, keep a sharp eye out for scattered pieces of the crashed bomber. The greenish aluminum blends in with the forest. One of the best features of the walk is at first the least noticeable: the silence.

There are some steep, sometimes muddy switchbacks near the end of the hike, which has its finish point at the lower car park on the loop road.

KA'ENA POINT TRAIL

START KEAWA'ULA BEACH
END TRAILHEAD/END HWY 930
DURATION TWO HOURS
DISTANCE ONE WAY 5 MILES

The Ka'ena Point hike offers extraordinary views the entire way, with the ocean on one side and craggy cliffs on the other. You can do it in either direction, starting from either Keawa'ula Beach in the south or at the trailhead at the end of Hwy 930 in the north. You'll have to arrange a pick-up if you don't want to do a 10-mile round trip. Driving between the two trailheads, via Ko Olina, Pearl City and Dillingham Airfield, is a whopping 51 miles.

The trail is extremely exposed and lacks any shade, so take sunscreen and plenty of water and hike during the cooler parts of the day. Be cautious near the shoreline as there are strong currents, and rogue waves can reach extreme heights.

From the south, start at **Keawa'ula Beach**, where you'll find the last real restrooms and a small car park. (The advice to leave nothing of value in your car applies double here.)

As you start walking from the **Ka'ena Point Trailhead** (p193), you'll see traces of the original use of this trail: the railway that hauled sugarcane all the way from the North Shore to Honolulu, which is why the path is so level and easy to walk. Look for tide pools, sea arches and blowholes that occasionally come to life on high surf days. In addition to native and migratory seabirds, you might spot Hawaiian monk seals hauled out on the rocks or the sand – don't disturb these endangered creatures.

At various places you may find that landslides have blocked parts of the trail; simply climb up and over to continue your journey.

At the halfway mark of the hike is **Ka'ena Point** (p193), which has remarkable views out over the white-capped Pacific. Here at the westernmost point on O'ahu, winter waves can reach 50ft.

Assuming you've found an obliging person to give you a lift from the end of the trail, continue east to the north trailhead. Look for whales in winter navigating the rough, storm-tossed ocean. Many of these swells started in Alaska and beyond. At any time, you may see albatrosses overhead.

AT A GLANCE

POPULATION
110,000

TOP LANDMARK
Diamond Head
(p199)

BEST FARMERS MARKET
KCC Farmers Market
(p202)

BEST SHAVE ICE
Kokonuts Shave Ice
& Snacks (p206)

BEST BREWHOUSE
Kona Brewing
Company (p207)

WHEN TO GO
Sep–Oct Enjoy top
sights like Hanauma
Bay and Shangri La
during low season,
without the crowds.

Jun–Aug Swim at
gorgeous beaches
with relatively calm
surf.

Dec–Jan Big, dra-
matic surf and the
chance of spotting
whales offshore.

Diamond Head (p199)
ART WAGER / GETTY IMAGES ©

Southeast O'ahu

Imagine starring in your own TV show or Hollywood blockbuster on O'ahu's most storied stretch of coastline. It looks a lot like Beverly Hills by the beach, with cherry-red convertibles cruising past private mansions that boast drop-dead ocean views. But you'll also find more natural thrills that are open to the public on these scenic shores: the snorkeling hot spot of Hanauma Bay, hiking trails to the top of Diamond Head and the wind-blown lighthouse at Makapu'u Point; plus, O'ahu's most famous bodysurfing and bodyboarding beaches are all just a short ride east of Waikiki.

As you near Makapu'u Point, the road undulates up, down and around spectacular scenery and beaches. Although Southeast O'ahu looks small on the map, its beaches and activities can easily fill a day or more. Many people start here expecting to drive right on to the Windward Coast and never quite get there.

Southeast Oʻahu Highlights

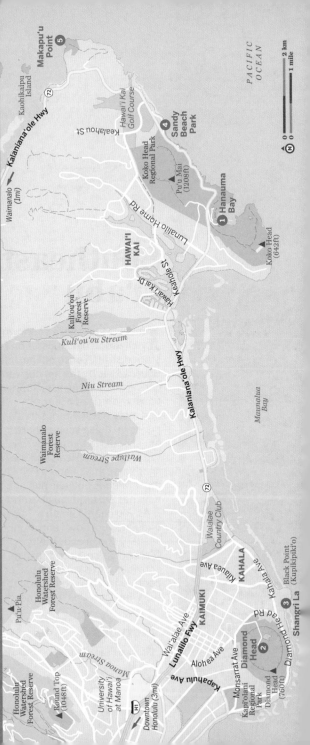

1 Hanauma Bay (p207)
Snorkeling in beautiful waters in a perfect cove with one of Hawaii's best beaches – the fish are extraordinary.

2 Diamond Head (p203)
Climbing the inside of Oʻahu's icon and thrilling to amazing views from the top of this ancient volcanic crater.

3 Shangri La (p201)
Immersing yourself in Doris Duke's stunning array of Islamic art at her beautiful home.

4 Sandy Beach Park (p209) Witnessing the extraordinary feats of bodysurfers from the beautiful sand at the main beach of Koko Head Regional Park.

5 Makapuʻu Point (p211)
Hiking a great trail to a historic lighthouse where you might be able to see other islands and, in winter, whales.

Diamond Head

A dramatic backdrop for Waikiki Beach, Diamond Head is one of the best-known landmarks in Hawaii. Ancient Hawaiians called it Le'ahi, and at its summit they built a *luakini* heiau, a temple dedicated to the war god Ku and used for human sacrifices.

Ever since 1825, when British sailors found calcite crystals sparkling in the sun and mistakenly thought they'd struck it rich, the sacred peak has been called Diamond Head.

The coast is an easy walk from Waikiki and there are some good beaches below the cliffside road and viewpoints.

Beaches

Diamond Head Beach Park BEACH
(3300 Diamond Head Rd) Bordering the lighthouse, this rocky beach occasionally draws surfers, snorkelers and tide-poolers, plus a few picnickers. The narrow strand nicknamed Lighthouse Beach is popular with gay men, who pull off Diamond Head Rd onto short, dead-end Beach Rd, then walk east along the shore to find a little seclusion and (illegally) sunbathe au naturel.

Kuilei Cliffs Beach Park BEACH
(3450 Diamond Head Rd) In the shadow of Diamond Head, this strand of sandy beach draws experienced windsurfers when the trade winds are blowing. The popular Diamond Head Cliffs surf breaks are right offshore. The little beach has outdoor showers but no other facilities. You'll find paved parking lots off Diamond Head Rd, just east of the lighthouse, and a concrete path leading down to the beach.

◉ Sights & Activities

⭐ **Diamond Head Lookout** VIEWPOINT
(3483 Diamond Head Rd) From this small parking area there are fine views over Kuilei Cliffs Beach Park and up the coast toward Kahala. On the east side of the parking area, look for the Amelia Earhart Marker, which recalls her 1935 solo flight from Hawaii to California. It's an enjoyable 1.4-mile walk beyond Kaimana Beach (p144) in Waikiki.

⭐ **Diamond Head
State Monument** STATE PARK
(☑800-464-2924; www.hawaiistateparks.org; per pedestrian/car $1/5; ⊘6am-6pm, last trail entry

4:30pm; 🚻) The extinct crater of Diamond Head is now a state monument, with picnic tables and a spectacular hiking trail (p203) up to the 760ft-high summit. The trail was built in 1908 to service military observation stations located along the crater rim.

Inside the crater rim, the park has information and historical displays, restrooms, drinking fountains and a picnic area. From Waikiki, catch bus 23 or 24; from the closest bus stop, it's about a 20-minute walk to the trailhead. By car, take Monsarrat Ave to Diamond Head Rd and turn right immediately after passing Kapi'olani Community College (KCC). Enter the park through Kahala Tunnel.

Diamond Head Cliffs SURFING
This is one of a series of breaks along the cliffs below Diamond Head. It gets surf from both the east and the south, which makes it very reliable. It's offshore from Kuilei Cliffs Beach Park. In strong winds it does blow out.

☆ Entertainment

Diamond Head Theatre THEATER
(☑box office 808-733-0274; www.diamond headtheatre.com; 520 Makapu'u Ave; ⊘box office 8:30am-4:30pm Mon-Fri, plus 8:30am-1pm some Sat) Opened in 1915 and known as 'the Broadway of the Pacific,' this lovely old theater is the third-oldest continuously running community theater in the USA. It hosts a variety of familiar, high-quality shows throughout the year, with everything from *Billy Elliot* to *South Pacific*. Also runs acting, dancing and singing classes.

❶ Getting There & Away

The Diamond Head area is a pretty 2-mile walk from Waikiki.

Bus routes 14 and 22 follow Diamond Head Rd along the beaches and coast, and then continue along Kahala Ave.

Kahala

The affluent seaside suburb of Kahala is home to many of Honolulu's wealthiest residents, the island's most exclusive resort hotel and the Waialae Country Club, a PGA tournament golf course. The coastal road, Kahala Ave, is lined with expensive waterfront homes that block out virtually any ocean views. In between the mansions, a

SOUTHEAST O'AHU DIAMOND HEAD

Around Diamond Head

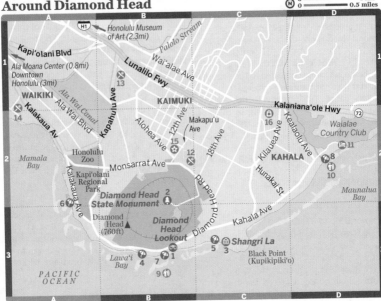

Around Diamond Head

few shoreline access points provide public rights-of-way to the beach, where the swimming is mostly shallow and rocky.

The tiny peninsula of Black Point (Kupikipiki'o) is home to one of O'ahu's top attractions: Shangri La.

Beaches

Wai'alae Beach Park   BEACH
(4925 Kahala Ave; ⊙5am-10pm) At this picturesque sandy beach, a gentle stream meets the sea. Local surfers challenge Razors, a

break off the channel's west side. Swimming conditions are usually calm, though not the best due to the shallow reef. A favorite of wedding parties, the beach park has shady picnic tables, restrooms and outdoor showers. The small parking lot is often full even when the beach itself is uncrowded.

Ka'alawai Beach   BEACH
Play in the lap of luxury at this little gem of a beach between Diamond Head and Black Point, though it's not the best for swimming. Normally uncrowded, it provides a glimpse

of Doris Duke's Shangri La estate. From the intersection of Diamond Head Rd and Kahala Ave, turn *makai* (seaward) onto Kulamanu St, then Kulamanu Pl heads off right down toward the beach. There's limited parking on Kulamanu St.

⊙ Sights & Activities

★ **Shangri La**   HISTORIC BUILDING
(☑ 808-532-3853; www.shangrilahawaii.org; 2½hr tour incl transportation $25, online booking $1.50; ⊙ tours 9am, 10:30am, noon & 1:30pm Wed-Sat, closed early Sep-early Oct) Celebrity Doris Duke had a lifelong passion for Islamic art and architecture, inspired by a visit to the Taj Mahal during her honeymoon at the age of 23. During that same honeymoon in 1935, she stopped at O'ahu, fell in love with the island and decided to build Shangri La, her seasonal residence, on Black Point in the shadow of Diamond Head. You can visit this extraordinary home as part of a tour, but you must book well in advance.

For over 60 years Duke traveled the globe from Indonesia to Istanbul, collecting priceless Islamic art objects. Duke appreciated the spirit more than the grand scale of the world wonders she had seen, and she made Shangri La into an intimate sanctuary rather than an ostentatious mansion. One of the true beauties of the place is the way it harmonizes with the natural environment. Finely crafted interiors open to embrace gardens and the ocean, and one glass wall of the living room looks out at Diamond Head. Throughout the estate, courtyard fountains spritz. Duke's extensive collection of Islamic art includes vivid gemstone-studded enamels, glazed ceramic paintings and silk *suzanis* (intricate needlework tapestries). Art often blends with architecture to represent a theme or region, as in the **Damascus Room**, the restored interior of an 18th-century Syrian merchant's house.

Shangri La can only be visited on a guided tour departing from downtown's Honolulu Museum of Art (p96), where you'll watch a brief background video first, then travel as a group by minibus to the estate. Tours often sell out weeks ahead of time. Children under eight are not allowed.

Razors   SURFING
A small surf break that's popular with locals when the sets are really rolling in. To the west of Wai'alae Beach Park and the channel through the reef.

🍴 Sleeping & Eating

There are fewer choices for eating here than you'd expect. You can assemble picnics and enjoy upscale fast food at the Kahala Mall, and there are some great casual restaurants and cafes just northwest on Wai'alae Ave in Honolulu.

★ **Kahala Hotel & Resort**   RESORT $$$
(☑ 808-739-8888; www.kahalaresort.com; 5000 Kahala Ave; r from $450; ▣ ✳ @ ⎈ ⛱) Facing a lovely beach, this luxury resort is a favorite of celebs, royalty and other rich-and-famous types who crave Kahala's paparazzi-free seclusion. The grande dame still maintains an appealing island-style casualness: staff who have been working here for decades and guests who return every year know each

SOUTHEAST O'AHU KAHALA

DORIS DUKE

Shangri La is captivating not just for its collection but also for the unique glimpse it provides into the life of tobacco heiress Doris Duke (1912–93), once nicknamed 'the richest little girl in the world.' Like her contemporary Howard Hughes, she was eccentric, reclusive and absolutely fascinating.

Duke's immense fortune, which she inherited after her father died in 1925, when she was just 12 years old, granted her freedom to do as she pleased. Among other things, that meant two very public divorces and a scandalous marriage to an international playboy. While living in Hawaii, she became the first white woman to surf competitively and, naturally, she learned from the best: Olympic gold medalist Duke Kahanamoku and his brothers.

Curious to know more? Watch the HBO movie *Bernard and Doris* (2006), starring Susan Sarandon as Doris Duke and Ralph Fiennes as her butler, Bernard Lafferty. Upon her death, Doris appointed her butler as the sole executor of her fortune. She directed that it to be used to further her philanthropic projects, including in support of the arts and against cruelty to children and animals.

WORTH A TRIP

TOP FARMERS MARKET

At **KCC Farmers Market** (www.kapi olani.hawaii.edu/project/farmers-market; parking lot C, Kapiʻolani Community College, 4303 Diamond Head Rd; ⊙ 7:30-11am Sat, 4-7pm Tue; ⊘), Oʻahu's premier gathering of farmers and their fans, everything sold is locally made or grown and has a loyal following, from Nalo greens to Kahuku shrimp and corn. Restaurants and vendors sell all kinds of tasty takeout meals, with Hawaii coffee brewed fresh and cold coconuts cracked open on demand. Get there early for the best of everything.

other by name, and it's that intimacy that really separates it from the Waikiki pack.

Enjoy complimentary use of bicycles and a free surf or SUP lesson. You can expect good views from many (but not all) of the rooms, and there are six cafe and restaurant dining options on-site.

Whole Foods　　　　SUPERMARKET $
(☑ 808-738-0820; www.wholefoodsmarket.com; Kahala Mall, 4211 Waiʻalae Ave; meals from $6; ⊙ 7am-10pm; ⊘) 🍴 Fill your picnic basket with organic produce and locally made specialty foods, hot and cold deli items, takeout sushi and salads, made-to-order hot pizzas, and top-quality beer and wines.

⭐**Hoku's**　　　　　　FUSION $$$
(☑ 808-739-8760; www.kahalaresort.com; Kahala Hotel & Resort, 5000 Kahala Ave; Sun brunch adult/child $78/39, dinner mains $30-60; ⊙ 5:30-9:30pm daily, brunch 9am-3pm Sun) The Kahala Hotel & Resort's top restaurant scoops accolades and awards annually and is revered for its elegant East-West creations. The Sunday brunch buffet stars a seafood bar stacked with delicious sushi and *poke,* including Maine lobster. Topping it all off are superb ocean views. Make reservations; smart-casual attire is required.

☆ Entertainment

Consolidated Kahala Theatre　　CINEMA
(☑ 808-733-6243; www.consolidatedtheatres. com/kahala; Kahala Mall, 4211 Waiʻalae Ave; adult/child $12.50/9) Eight-screen multiplex frequently showing independent, art-house and foreign films.

Shopping

Kahala Mall　　　　　　　MALL
(www.kahalamallcenter.com; 4211 Waiʻalae Ave; ⊙ 10am-9pm Mon-Sat, to 6pm Sun) It's not quite the Ala Moana Center (p127), but this large east-side mall has a noteworthy mix of only-in-Hawaii shops, including Cinnamon Girl clothing boutique, Reyn Spooner and Rix Island Wear for aloha shirts, the Compleat Kitchen, and Sanrio Surprises, selling collectible, hard-to-find imported Hello Kitty toys and logo gear.

ℹ Getting There & Away

Bus routes 14 and 22 follow Diamond Head Rd beside the beaches and coast, and then continue along Kahala Ave.

Hawai'i Kai

With its yacht-filled marina and breezy canals surrounded by mountains, bays and gentle beach parks, this meticulously planned suburb designed by the late steel tycoon Henry J Kaiser (he's the Kai in Hawai'i Kai) offers a pleasant suburban scene. All the action revolves around three shopping centers, where you can try water sports and enjoy a snack or a meal. Hawai'i Kai Towne Center, based around Costco, and Hawai'i Kai Shopping Center, based around Safeway, are entered off Keahole St, while Koko Marina Center is on the coastal Kalanianaʻole Hwy.

⊙ Sights

⭐**Spitting Cave**　　　　VIEWPOINT
This impressive, little-known viewpoint is at the end of Lumahai St in Portlock, *makai* (toward the sea) from the traffic lights at the Koko Marina Center. It's a tad hard to find but well worth the effort for the spectacular views, the pounding surf on layered volcanic rock and an enthralling cave that spits waves back out at the ocean. Take care getting down to the best viewing spots, where whale-watchers often set up to take whale-count surveys in winter.

Cliff jumping is not advised, but thrill-seeking locals and experts can sometimes be seen making the 70ft leap from here into the sea.

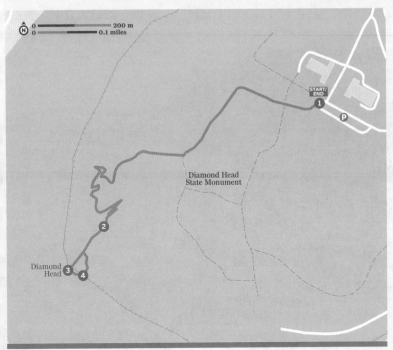

Walking Tour
Climbing Diamond Head

START DIAMOND HEAD STATE MONUMENT
END DIAMOND HEAD STATE MONUMENT
LENGTH 1.6 MILES; ONE TO 1½ HOURS

One of O'ahu's top hikes, the 0.8-mile climb one way to the windy summit of Diamond Head affords fantastic 360-degree views of the southeast coast to Koko Head and the Leeward Coast to the Wai'anae Range. It's a fairly steep trail (you climb 560ft) and has enough thrills that it can feel like a roller coaster on foot. Plenty of people of all ages make the hike. It passes through several tunnels and up head-spinning, claustrophobic staircases, although it's mostly open and hot. The sun-drenched landscape you climb through is more yellow and brown than green inside the crater. Wear a hat and sunscreen and bring plenty of water.

Begin at the ❶ **monument parking lot** (p199) by following the signposted trail. The first set of 74 ❷ **concrete steps** is followed by a lighted 225ft-long tunnel. Next up is a set of 99 steep steps, then entry to the lowest level of the Fire Control Station. The station was built to direct artillery fire from batteries at Fort DeRussy in Waikiki and Fort Ruger outside Diamond Head crater. Inside, climb a lighted spiral staircase until you exit to the exterior of the crater. Finally, a set of 54 metal stairs takes you to the ❸ **crater summit** and the uppermost level of the Fire Control Station (761ft). Enjoy the view!

Don't head back down the way you came. From the summit, follow the trail along the rim and descend the 82 metal steps to the lower trail. The bunkers along the crater rim were built in 1915. Don't miss the ❹ **lookout** (p199), which has impressive views of the Southeast O'ahu coastline towards Koko Head. On a clear day you may even spot the islands of Moloka'i, Maui and Lana'i. If it's winter, watch for passing whales.

To finish, head down the short trail inside the crater rim, which will take you back to the top of the tunnel you went through earlier. From here, continue on to the parking lot.

Makapu'u Beach Park (p211) 2. Sailing off the southeast coast (p206) 3. *Malasadas*

Lazy Days in Southeast O'ahu

Soooo much to do in this part of the island. If you're into activities then the choices are endless. Picture-perfect beaches, stunning views and plenty of places to recover, whether that be with a shave ice or with an ice-cold beer.

Beaches

There are some fabulous beaches to capture your time. You could easily spend a day at Hanauma Bay (p207) eyeballing Technicolor fish, or hitting Sandy Beach (p209) or Makapu'u Beach Park (p211) for bodyboarding. Kuilei Cliffs Beach Park (p199) has top surfing, while Alan Davis Beach (p211) offers respite from crowds.

Panoramic Views

Some stunners! Stop at the Spitting Cave (p202), Lana'i Lookout (p210), Halona Blowhole (p210) and Makapu'u Point lookout (p211) while driving, or hike up Diamond Head (p199), Koko Crater (p206) or out to Makapu'u Point Lighthouse (p211) – and don't forget to look inland at O'ahu's magnificent Ko'olau range of mountains.

Activities

We've mentioned the snorkeling, bodyboarding, surfing and hiking...but that's not the end of it. Operators at Hawai'i Kai (p206) offer up everything from diving, kayaking, parasailing, Jet Skis, waterskiing and sailing to banana boats and jet packs. Try it all!

Refreshments

Great spots to prepare for more time in the outdoors. Koko Marina is replete with choice. Grab a shave ice at Kokonuts (p206) or a *malasada* (custard-filled fried doughnut) or two at Leonard's (p206). Fatboy's (p207) has you covered for a plate lunch, while Kona Brewing (p207) has beer for later in the day.

Activities

Diving

Island Divers DIVING
(☎808-423-8222; www.oahuscubadiving.com; Hawai'i Kai Shopping Center, 377 Keahole St; 2 dives from $130; ⊙7am-7pm) Five-star PADI operation at Hawai'i Kai Shopping Center runs boat dives for all levels, including expert-level wreck dives. Novices can try intro dives in calm waters. Snorkelers can ride along on the dive boats, which visit all sides of the island.

Reef Pirates Diving DIVING
(☎808-348-2700; www.reefpirates.com; Koko Marina Center, 7192 Kalaniana'ole Hwy; 2 dives from $135; ⊙9am-5pm) This outfit at the Koko Marina Center offers beginner trips that, with no certification required, include two shallow reef dives for $135. It also has longer trips for certified divers and runs PADI certification courses. Trips include transportation from Waikiki hotels.

Golf

Hawai'i Kai Golf Course GOLF
(☎808-395-2358; www.hawaiikaigolf.com; 8902 Kalaniana'ole Hwy; green fees incl electric-cart rental from $110, par-3 course from $50; ⊙7am-5pm) About 4 miles east of Hawai'i Kai township, this 18-hole championship course sports Koko Head views; there's also a smaller par-3 executive course designed by Robert Trent Jones Sr in the 1960s. Beginners are welcome and club rentals are available. Call ahead for tee-time reservations.

Hiking

★Kuli'ou'ou Ridge Trail HIKING
(https://hawaiitrails.ehawaii.gov; Kala'au Pl) West of town, this 4-mile round-trip route is open to both hikers and mountain bikers. The trail winds up forest switchbacks before making a stiff but ultimately satisfying 1800ft climb along a ridgeline to a windy summit offering 360-degree views of Koko Head, Makapu'u Point, the Windward Coast, Diamond Head and downtown Honolulu.

The trail is not always well maintained and may be partly overgrown with vegetation. Start from the Na Ala Hele trailhead sign at the end of Kala'au Pl, which branches right off Kuli'ou'ou Rd, just over 1 mile north of the Kalaniana'ole Hwy (Hwy 72).

Koko Crater Trail HIKING
(7604 Koko Head Park Rd; ⊙dawn-dusk) This 1.8-mile round-trip trail is not for anyone with a fear of heights. The fully exposed route leads for almost a mile along an abandoned wooden-tie rail bed to reach the summit of Pu'u Mai (1206ft). There's no shade, but the panoramic views from atop the extinct crater's rim are worth the effort.

Turn north off the Kalaniana'ole Hwy (Hwy 72) onto Lunalilo Home Rd, which borders the east side of Koko Marina Center, then turn right onto Anapalau St, which leads into the community park where you'll find the trailhead.

Water Sports

Hawaii Watersports WATER SPORTS
(☎808-395-3773; www.hawaiiwatersportscenter.com; Koko Marina Center, 7192 Kalaniana'ole Hwy; banana-boat ride $39; ⊙8:30am-5pm) Offers everything from surfing lessons to parasailing to wakeboarding, snorkeling and water-skiing. Many of the thrill rides, such as banana-boat rides, take place at Koko Marina.

H₂O Sports Hawaii WATER SPORTS
(☎808-396-0100; www.h2osportshawaii.com; Hawai'i Kai Shopping Center, 377 Keahole St; 15min jet pack $200; ⊙8:30am-3:30pm) Based at Hawai'i Kai Shopping Center, and offering thrill rides with jet packs, water skis, banana boats, bumper tubes, parasailing trips, wakeboarding, scuba dives, speed sailing – whatever gets your adrenaline pumping. Check online for advance-booking discounts.

Eating

Hawai'i Kai has a number of good eateries, especially at the Koko Marina Center.

★Kokonuts Shave Ice & Snacks SWEETS $
(☎808-396-8809; Koko Marina Center, 7192 Kalaniana'ole Hwy; ⊙10:30am-7:30pm Sun-Thu, to 8pm Fri & Sat) After a tough day at Hanauma Bay, do as former president Obama has done (attested to by photos of him modeling a Kokonuts Shave Ice T-shirt) and drop into Kokonuts at Koko Marina for some tasty refreshment. The acai and pitaya bowls are top notch, the shave ice really hits the spot, and the welcome is friendly.

Leonard's Malasadamobile SWEETS $
(www.leonardshawaii.com/malasadamobile; Koko Marina Center, 7192 Kalaniana'ole Hwy; malasadas $1.30; ⊙7am-5pm) The legend that is Leonard's (p163) on Kapahulu Ave in Waikiki now has a popular food-truck outpost at the Koko Marina Shopping Center. Join the lines to get your incredibly tasty *mala-*

sada, a Portuguese-style custard-filled fried doughnut, in Hawai'i Kai.

Moena Cafe
CAFE $

(☑808-888-7716; www.moenacafe.com; Koko Marina Center, 7192 Kalaniana'ole Hwy; mains from $10; ⊗7am-2:30pm) Farm-fresh salads, grilled panini and all-day breakfasts of crepes, crab eggs Benedict and short-rib *loco moco* (rice, fried egg and meat topped with gravy) bring hungry crowds of locals back to this simple storefront kitchen. It's almost always worth the wait for a table just to taste the cafe's island-style recipes.

Island Brew Coffeehouse
CAFE $

(☑808-394-8770; www.islandbrewcoffeehouse. com; Hawai'i Kai Shopping Center, 377 Keahole St; ⊗6am-6pm; 🐾) With umbrella-shaded tables gazing out at the marina, this unhurried hangout individually brews cups of Hawaii-grown coffee – try richly roasted 100% Kona, Ka'u or Maui Mokka. Thai ice tea, espresso drinks, baked goodies, acai fruit bowls and sandwiches round out the menu. A great break after a Koko Head hike or before a snorkel at Hanauma Bay.

Fatboy's
HAWAIIAN $

(☑808-394-2373; www.fatboyshawaii.com; Koko Marina Center, 7192 Kalaniana'ole Hwy; mains from $8; ⊗9am-8pm Mon-Fri, from 8am Sat & Sun) It may be slightly indelicately named, but if you're into Hawaiian-style plate lunches then the O'ahu mini chain Fatboy's ticks all the boxes. The garlic chicken gets rave reviews, but it's the Fatboy's bento that sells best with locals. Enjoy your meal at tables inside or out.

Sophie's Gourmet Hawaiian Pizzeria
PIZZA $$

(☑808-892-4121; www.sophiespizzeria.com; Koko Marina Center, 7192 Kalaniana'ole Hwy; pizzas from $13; ⊗11am-8pm Wed-Mon; 🐾) Create the pizza of your dreams from the myriad options at this hip pizza place, whose ingredients are sourced from top local produce. Some of the more exotic options include guava-infused dough, zesty sriracha red sauce, arugula and Thai curry chicken. You can sit outside and enjoy marina views.

★ Roy's Hawai'i Kai
HAWAIIAN $$$

(☑808-396-7697; www.royshawaii.com; Hawai'i Kai Towne Center, 6600 Kalaniana'ole Hwy; mains from $38; ⊗5-9:30pm Sun-Thu, to 10pm Fri & Sat) Roy Yamaguchi is one of the driving forces behind Hawaii Regional Cuisine, emphasizing fresh local ingredients with artfully blended European, Asian and Pacific Rim influences. A pilgrimage to the chef's original outpost in Hawai'i Kai rarely disappoints. Classics such as braised short ribs and chocolate soufflé star on the menu, but it's not as glitzy as Roy's Waikiki (p160).

DON'T MISS

ISLAND-STYLE BREWS & EATS

Big Island import **Kona Brewing Company** (☑808-396-5662; www. konabrewingco.com; Koko Marina Center, 7192 Kalaniana'ole Hwy; mains from $12; ⊗11am-10pm; 🐾) is known for its microbrewed beers, especially the Longboard Lager, the Pipeline Porter and the Big Wave Golden Ale. There's live Hawaiian music some nights, and the brewpub's island-style *pupu* (appetizers), woodfired pizzas, burgers, seafood and salads are tasty. Grab a seat outside and let the balmy breezes caress you.

❶ Getting There & Away

From Waikiki, bus 22 stops at Koko Marina Center en route to Hanauma Bay and beyond. Bus 23 from the Ala Moana Center turns inland at Keahole St, stopping near the Hawai'i Kai Towne Center and Hawai'i Kai Shopping Center.

Bus 1 operates daily and offers frequent service along the main southeast road, the Kalaniana'ole Hwy (Hwy 72), linking Honolulu with Hawai'i Kai.

Hanauma Bay

This wide, curved bay of turquoise waters protected by a coral reef and backed by palm trees is a gem, especially for snorkelers. You come here for the scenery, you come here for the beach, but above all you come here to snorkel – and if you've never been snorkeling before, it's a perfect place to start.

The bay is a park and a nature preserve. It's hugely popular; to beat the crowds, arrive as soon as the park opens.

🏖 Beaches

★ Hanauma Bay Nature Preserve
PARK

(☑808-396-4229; www.honolulu.gov/parks-hbay/ home; 100 Hanauma Bay Rd; adult/child under 13yr $7.50/free, parking $1; ⊗6am-6pm Wed-Mon Nov-Mar, to 7pm Wed-Mon Apr-Oct; ⚿) From an overlook you can peer into the translucent

SAVING HANAUMA BAY

Once a favorite Hawaiian fishing spot, Hanauma Bay saw its fish populations nearly depleted by the time it was designated a marine-life conservation district in 1967. After they were protected instead of being hunted, fish swarmed back by the thousands – and the bay's ecological balance went topsy-turvy. Compounding the problem, as many as 10,000 snorkelers started arriving at Hanauma Bay each day, many trampling on the coral and leaving human waste behind them. Snorkelers feeding the fish led to a burst in fish populations beyond naturally sustainable levels and radically altered the variety of species. Now here's the good news: since 1990, scientific ecology-management programs have begun to bring the bay's natural balance back.

waters and see the outline of the 7000-year-old coral reef that stretches across the width of the bay. You're bound to see schools of glittering silver fish, the bright-blue flash of parrotfish and perhaps sea turtles so used to snorkelers they're ready to go eyeball-to-mask with you. Feeding the fish is strictly prohibited, to preserve the delicate ecological balance of the bay.

All built park facilities are wheelchair accessible. Beach wheelchairs for visitors with mobility issues are available free of charge from the information kiosk between 8am and 4pm on a first-come, first-served basis.

Despite its protected status as a marine-life conservation district, this beloved bay is still a threatened ecosystem, constantly in danger of being loved to death.

◉ Sights & Activities

At beach level there are lockers, lifeguards and restrooms, plus concessions renting snorkeling equipment and beach gear.

The bay is well protected from the vast ocean by various reefs and the inlet's natural curve, making conditions favorable for **snorkeling** year-round. The fringing reef closest to shore has a large, sandy opening known as the Keyhole Lagoon, which is the best place for novice snorkelers. It's also the most crowded part of the bay and later in the day visibility can be poor. The deepest

water is 10ft, though it's very shallow over the coral. Be careful not to step on the coral or to accidentally knock it with your fins.

For confident snorkelers and strong swimmers, it's better on the outside of the reef, where there are large coral heads, bigger fish and fewer people; to get there follow the directions on the signboards or ask the lifeguard at the southern end of the beach. Because of the channel currents on either side of the bay, it's generally easier getting outside the reef than it is getting back in. Don't attempt to swim outside the reef when the water is rough: not only are the channel currents too strong but the sand will be stirred up and visibility poor.

If you're **scuba diving** you'll have the whole bay to play in, with crystal-clear water, coral gardens and sea turtles. Beware of currents when the surf is up, especially those surges near the shark-infested **Witches Brew**, on the bay's right-hand side, and the prophetically named **Moloka'i Express**, a treacherous current on the left-hand side of the bay's mouth.

Marine Educational Center MUSEUM
(☎ 808-397-5840; http://hbep.seagrant.soest.hawaii.edu; 100 Hanauma Bay Rd; ☺ 8am-4pm Wed-Mon; ⊕) ✔ Past the park's ticket windows is an excellent educational center run by the University of Hawai'i. Interactive, family-friendly displays teach visitors about the unique geology and ecology of the bay. Everyone should watch the informative 12-minute video about environmental precautions before snorkeling. Visit the website for links to a great app that covers snorkeling in the bay.

❶ Getting There & Away

BUS
Bus 22 runs between Waikiki and Hanauma Bay.
Shuttle buses and tours to the bay are also heavily marketed to tourists.

CAR
Hanauma Bay is about 10 miles east of Waikiki via the Kalaniana'ole Hwy (Hwy 72). Self-parking costs $1. As soon as the parking lot fills (sometimes before 8am!), drivers will simply be turned away, so get there early or, better, take the bus.

Koko Head District Park

With volcanic rock walls on one side and a sea edged by bays and beaches on the other, the drive along this coast rates among Hawaii's best.

The highway rises and falls as it winds around towards the eastern tip of the Ko'olau Range, looking down on stratified rocks, lava sea cliffs, other fascinating geological formations, a famous beach and even a blowhole.

Beaches

★ **Sandy Beach Park**   BEACH
(8800 Kalaniana'ole Hwy; ⏰6am-10pm) Here the ocean usually heaves and thrashes like a furious beast. This is one of O'ahu's most challenging beaches, with a punishing shore break, a powerful backwash and strong rip currents. Expert bodysurfers and

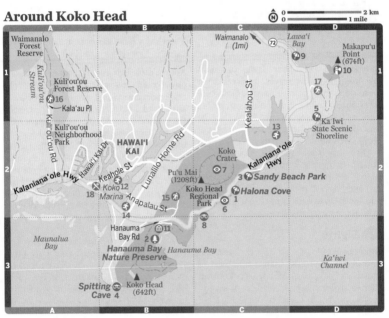

Around Koko Head

SOUTHEAST O'AHU KOKO HEAD DISTRICT PARK

ROMANTIC COVE

Take your lover down for a roll in the sand at sweet pocket **Halona Cove**, made famous in the legendary wave-tossed scene between Burt Lancaster and Deborah Kerr in the 1953 movie *From Here to Eternity*. You can peer down at the cove from the Halona Blowhole parking lot, from where you'll just be able to make out a path leading down to the beach. Head in for a swim if conditions are suitable.

bodyboarders spend hours trying to mount the often pounding waves. Just watching these daredevils being tossed around and occasionally nailing it is a huge attraction. The beach itself is lovely; just know that the water isn't for the inexperienced – dozens of people are injured every year.

There are some narrow areas for advanced swimmers watched over by lifeguards. The best sand is at the west end; the east end has lava rocks and very interesting tide pools. On weekdays you can usually find parking; there are drink vendors.

◉ Sights

Lana'i Lookout   VIEWPOINT
(Kalaniana'ole Hwy) Less than a mile east of Hanauma Bay, roadside Lana'i Lookout offers a panorama on clear days of several Hawaiian islands: Lana'i to the right, Maui in the middle and Moloka'i to the left. If things are a bit hazy and you can only see one island, chances are that it's Moloka'i, the closest at 22 miles away. This is also a good vantage point for getting a look at lava-rock formations that form the sea cliffs along this coast.

Fishing Shrine   SHRINE
(Kalaniana'ole Hwy) As you drive east, keep your eyes toward the ocean. At the highest point you'll spot a volcanic-rock obelisk, dedicated to fishers who have drowned, swept away by unexpected waves while casting off the rocks below. Originally erected by members of the Honolulu Japanese Fishing Club in the 1930s, the present rock features a carving of Jizō, a Buddhist deity and a guardian of fishers. The little roadside pull-off is about a half mile east of the Lana'i Lookout.

Make sure to look east for views down into Halona Cove and further to Sandy Beach.

Halona Blowhole   VIEWPOINT
Here, ocean waves surge through a submerged tunnel in the rock and spout up through a hole in the ledge. The spout is preceded by a gushing sound – the air that's being forced out of the tunnel by rushing water. The action depends on water conditions: sometimes it's barely discernible, while at others it's a real showstopper. There's a sizable car park from where you can also look down into Halona Cove.

Koko Crater Botanical Garden   GARDENS
(www.honolulu.gov/parks/hbg.html; 7491 Kokonani St; ⊙ dawn-dusk) FREE According to Hawaiian legend, Koko Crater is the imprint left by the magical flying vagina of Kapo, sent from the Big Island to lure the pig god Kamapua'a away from her sister Pele, the Hawaiian goddess of fire and volcanoes. Inside the crater today is a quiet, county-run botanical garden abloom with flowering aloe plants and *wiliwili* trees, fragrant plumeria, spiny cacti and other native and exotic dryland species. Connecting loop trails lead through the lonely garden.

To get here, turn *mauka* (inland) on Kealahou St off the Kalaniana'ole Hwy (Hwy 72), opposite Sandy Beach. After about 0.5 miles, turn left onto Kokonani St. From Waikiki, bus 23 stops every hour or so near the intersection of Kealahou and Kokonani Sts, just over 0.3 miles from the garden entrance.

❶ Getting There & Away

From Waikiki, bus 22 heads along the scenic coast en route to Sea Life Park. Bus 23 from the Ala Moana Center takes an inland route from Hawai'i Kai to Sandy Beach Park on its way to Sea Life Park (opposite Makapu'u Beach Park).

Makapu'u Point

Makapu'u Point and its coastal lighthouse mark the easternmost point of O'ahu. On the north side of the point, a roadside **lookout** gives you an exhilarating view down onto Makapu'u Beach Park, its aqua-blue waters outlined by diamond-white sand and jet-black lava. It's an even more spectacular sight when hang gliders or paragliders take off from the cliffs above.

Two islands, the larger of which is **Manana Island** (aka Rabbit Island), can be seen offshore. Once populated by feral rabbits, this aging volcanic crater now harbors burrowing wedge-tailed shearwaters. Curiously, it looks vaguely like the head of a rabbit with its ears folded back. In front is smaller, flat **Kaohikaipu Island**, another seabird sanctuary.

Beaches

Makapu'u Beach Park   BEACH
(41-095 Kalaniana'ole Hwy) Makapu'u Beach is one of O'ahu's top bodyboarding and bodysurfing spots, but as with Sandy Beach Park, Makapu'u is strictly the domain of experts who can handle rough water and dangerous currents. In summer, when the wave action disappears, calmer waters allow swimming. The beach park has restrooms, outdoor showers, drinking water and lifeguards, and the beach is a short walk from the car park.

**Alan Davis Beach
& Pele's Chair**   BEACH
It's an easy, flattish 15-minute walk on the Ka'iwi Shoreline Trail from the parking area for the Makapu'u Lighthouse Trail out to secluded little Alan Davis Beach and its accompanying throne-shaped volcanic rock formation, known as Pele's Chair. This is believed in Hawaiian legend to be the last place the fire goddess sat before she departed the island of O'ahu. There are no facilities, but this is a good excursion for families and a way to escape the crowds.

◉ Sights & Activities

Makapu'u Point Lighthouse   LIGHTHOUSE
(Makapu'u Lighthouse Rd; ⊙7am-6:45pm) O'ahu's easternmost point was the landfall for all ships from the American west coast to Honolulu. The lighthouse dates to 1909, when it was finally built after two decades of petitioning and planning. The 46ft white cylindrical tower sports a red lantern roof and is still an active aid to navigation.

★**Makapu'u Point
Lighthouse Trail**   HIKING
(http://dlnr.hawaii.gov/dsp/hiking/oahu/makapuu-point-lighthouse-trail; ⊙7am-7:45pm Apr-1st Mon Sep, to 6:45pm 1st Tue Sep-Mar) FREE South of the lookout on the *makai* (seaward) side of the road, a well-maintained, paved service road climbs toward the red-roofed Makapu'u Point Lighthouse. Although not difficult, the uphill walk can be hot and extremely windy – take drinks. The views out to sea are sweeping; the landscape is mostly rolling, barren brown hills. The walk is a 2-mile round trip.

Along the way, stop to take in the stellar coastal views of Koko Head and Hanauma Bay and, in winter, look for migrating whales that might be swimming by. The trail is part of the Ka'iwi Shoreline Trail. You can park in the lot just off the Kalaniana'ole Hwy.

ℹ Getting There & Away

The parking lot at Sea Life Park is where three bus routes converge: bus 22 from Waikiki and bus 23 from the Ala Moana Center both follow the Kalaniana'ole Hwy (Hwy 72); bus 57 runs from the Ala Moana Center, along the Pali Hwy to Kailua, then down the coast to Sea Life Park.

SOUTHEAST O'AHU MAKAPU'U POINT

ROAD TRIP: DIAMOND HEAD TO MAKAPU'U BEACH

This drive takes in the real thrill of Southeast O'ahu: the exhilarating drive along the Kalaniana'ole Hwy (Hwy 72). Expect volcanic cones and landscapes, pounding surf on sandy beaches, blowholes, stunning views out to other islands and a whole lot of fun and intrigue.

❶ Diamond Head Lookout

Barely a mile from Waikiki, **Diamond Head Lookout** (p199) has views of the dramatic coast you'll be driving. Head east on Diamond Head Rd, curving around its namesake icon. You can detour through the Kahala Tunnel into **Diamond Head State Mon-** ument (p199) for the incredible hike to the top, or just keep going, taking Kilauea Ave to reach the Kalaniana'ole Hwy at Kahala Mall.

❷ Kahala Mall

Kahala Mall (p202) is an optional stop to assemble a picnic at Whole Foods. Just be-

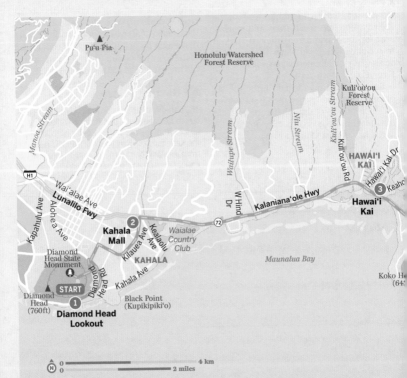

yond, on your right, is the exclusive Waialae Country Club, which opened in 1927.

➌ Hawai'i Kai

Hawai'i Kai is a good place for breakfast or lunch, with some great options, such as **Kokonuts Shave Ice & Snacks** (p206) and **Moena Cafe** (p207), both at the Koko Marina Center. Enjoy views of the marina and the Ko'olau Range. Gird yourself, as the next stop is a big one.

➍ Hanauma Bay

Gorgeous crescent-shaped **Hanauma Bay** (p207) is a place of tropical fishbowl waters and coral kingdoms. There's no better spot

to break out your mask, snorkel and flippers. Get here early or hope for an opportunity later in the day, as parking can be tight.

➎ Halona Coast

As you hit the coastal road, there's a staccato burst of visual pleasure. Less than a mile east of Hanauma Bay, **Lana'i Lookout** (p210) lets you spot up to three neighboring islands: Moloka'i, the closest, Maui and Lana'i. Next, keep your gaze up and look for the rock obelisk that is the **Fishing Shrine** (p210), dedicated to the protection of fishers. There may be brave souls casting off on the rocks below.

Halona Cove (p210) and its **blowhole** (p210) are just a bit further on. The short cliffside trek down to Halona Cove is worth the scramble: this gorgeous pocket of sand cameoed in the steamy love scene involving Burt Lancaster and Deborah Kerr in the classic 1953 movie *From Here to Eternity*.

➏ Sandy Beach Park

After the twists and turns you just navigated, the highway settles down along the coast at **Sandy Beach Park** (p209), where bodysurfers and bodyboarders put on a show for onlookers on the lovely beach. It's worth the stop, but use your common sense when it comes to entering the water, as Sandy Beach's pounding surf results in more injuries than that of any other beach on the island.

➐ Makapu'u

The road winds back into the hills. You'll see a parking area for the easy hike to the **Makapu'u Point Lighthouse** (p211) and its panorama. If you'd like to head off the beaten path even more, wander 15 minutes down to **Alan Davis Beach & Pele's Chair** (p211) from the same car park. Just a little further on up the main road is the spectacular roadside Makapu'u Lookout, where you can gaze down at **Makapu'u Beach Park** (p211), Manana Island (aka Rabbit Island) and Kaohikaipu Island, and out to Waimanalo Bay and up the Windward Coast. If you've got time for a swim, head down to the beach park and contemplate the beauty of Southeast O'ahu.

Kalaniana'ole Hwy

Kaohikaipu Island

72 **Makapu'u** — Makapu'u Point Lighthouse

FINISH ➐

Kealahou St

Hawai'i Kai Golf Course — Alan Davis Beach & Pele's Chair

nalilo Home Rd

Koko Head Regional Park

Pu'u Mai (1206ft) ➏ **Sandy Beach Park**

Halona Cove

Fishing Shrine

➎ Lana'i Lookout

➍ **Halona Coast**

anauma Bay

PACIFIC OCEAN

AT A GLANCE

POPULATION
120,000

LARGEST TOWN
Kailua (p219)

BEST TAKEOUT
Kalapawai Market
(p224)

**BEST KAHUKU
SHRIMP**
Fumi's Kahuku
Shrimp (p240)

BEST ART STUDIO
Gyotaku by Naoki
(p229)

WHEN TO GO
May–Jun Good
weather and fewer
visitors make this a
great time to visit.

Aug–Sep Rainfall is
low on the rainiest
coast and beach
temperatures peak.

Dec–Jan Hawaii's
busy tourist months
are also the
Windward Coast's
rainiest.

Ho'omaluhia Botanical Garden (p228)
SHANE MYERS PHOTOGRAPHY/SHUTTERSTOCK ©

Windward Coast

Welcome to O'ahu's lushest, most verdant coast, where turquoise waters and light-sand beaches share the dramatic backdrop of misty cliffs in the Ko'olau Range. Cruise over the *pali* (mountains) from Honolulu (only 20 minutes) and you first reach Kailua, a pleasant place with an extraordinary beach.

Many repeat visitors make this laid-back community their island base, whether they intend to kayak, stand-up paddle (SUP), snorkel, dive, drive around the island or just laze on the sand. To the south, more beautiful beaches (and good food) await in Waimanalo. North up the coast, the Kamehameha Hwy narrows into a winding two-lane road with a dramatic oceanfront on one side and farms, towns and frequent sheer cliffs on the other.

The coast is the main part of the round-island drive that also circles through the North Shore. Don't be surprised if you want to hit the brakes and stay awhile.

Kahuku
Point

0 — 10 km
0 — 5 miles

3 Kahuku
Mākahoa Point
Moku'auia
(Goat Island)
La'ie • — La'ie Point

KO'OLAU RANGE

Kahuku
Forest
Reserve

Pu'u
Ka'inapua'a
(2361ft)

Hau'ula

Kaipapa'u
Forest
Reserve

Kawailoa
Forest
Reserve

*Sacred
Falls*

• Punalu'u

*Kahana
Bay*

Opaeula Stream

Hau'ula
Forest
Reserve

'Ewa
Forest
Reserve

Swanzy
7 Beach Park
Ka'a'awa

Ahupua'a
o Kahana
State Park

**Kamehameha
Hwy**

Pu'u
Ka'aumakua
(2681ft)

Schofield Barracks
Military Reservation

4 Kualoa Regional Park
Mokoli'i Island
(Chinaman's Hat)

Kipapa Stream

• Waikane

• Waiahole

Wailau Point

*Kapapa
Island*

*Moku
Manu*

Waiahole
Forest
Reserve

KO'OLAU RANGE

83 • Kahalu'u

• 'Ahuimanu

*Kane'ohe
Bay*

Mokapu
Peninsula

He'eia

Kane'ohe
Marine Corps
Base Hawaii
(MCBH)

Mokapu
Point

H2

'Ewa Forest
Reserve

Pu'u
Kawipo'o
(2441ft)

Kahekili Hwy

Kapoho
Point

*Kailua
Bay*

**Pearl
City**

H1

H3

• Kane'ohe

Kailua

**Kailua
1 Beach Park**

• Lanikai

• 'Aiea

*Pearl
Harbor*

Ford
Island

Honolulu
Watershed
Forest Reserve

99

78

63

Likelike Hwy

Pali Hwy

H1

Puuohia
(Mt Tantalus)
(2013ft)

Olomana

61

5
**Maunawili
Trail**

*Bellows
Air Force
Station*

72

Waimanalo

**Waimanalo Bay
Beach Park 2**

*Waimanalo
Bay*

PACIFIC
OCEAN

Windward Coast Highlights

1 Kailua Beach Park (p221)
Thrilling to this 4-mile-long
beach perfect for swimming
year-round, then windsurfing,
kitesurfing, kayaking or stand-
up paddleboarding on the bay.

**2 Waimanalo Bay Beach
Park** (p217) Curling your
toes in the sand at one of
the world's most stunning

beaches, while the water
beckons.

3 Kahuku's shrimp trucks
(p240) Letting the juices
tickle your taste buds as you
savor shrimp at one of these
roadside purveyors.

**4 Driving the Windward
Coast** (p244) Stopping at
Kualoa Regional Park, on

O'ahu's best drive for beaches,
lush tropical scenery and
dramatically carved cliff faces.

5 Maunawili Trail (p242)
Stepping back to a pre-contact
Hawaii on this hike along
rainforest-covered mountain
ridges; there's an optional
detour to Maunawili Falls.

ℹ Getting There & Away

Gorgeous two-lane Hwy 83 runs right on the coast north from Kailua all the way over to the North Shore. South from Kailua, Hwy 72 has a shorter but equally scenic run to Southeast Oʻahu. There are three options for linking Kailua with Honolulu: the speedy H-3 Fwy, and the older Hwys 61 and 63, which get you closer to the lush mountains you pass through.

Bus service is good. Route 57 connects Honolulu's Ala Moana Center to downtown Kailua. Some buses continue south on Hwy 72 to Sea Life Park, where you can connect to routes 22 and 23 to travel around Southeast Oʻahu. Route 55 follows Hwy 83 to the North Shore.

Waimanalo

POP 5500

The proudly Hawaiian community of Waimanalo sprawls alongside Oʻahu's longest beach, where the white sands stretch for miles, within view of offshore islands and a coral reef that keeps breaking waves at a comfortable distance. Small hillside farms in 'Nalo, as it's often called, grow many of the fresh leafy greens served in Honolulu's top restaurants.

🏖 Beaches

⭐ **Waimanalo Bay Beach Park**　　BEACH
(Map p230; https://camping.honolulu.gov; 41-43 Aliloi St; ☺6am-7:45pm) Also known as Sherwood Forest, as a gang likening themselves to Robin Hood and his merry men operated here in the 1960s, this spectacular broad sandy beach backed by ironwood trees is popular with surfers and bodyboarders. Countless weddings take place on the enchanting strand. There are lifeguards, campsites and restrooms. Entrance is opposite the Honolulu Polo Club. At research time Native Hawaiian protests against planned development were taking place (p218), but access to the beach park was not disrupted.

Bellows Field Beach Park　　BEACH
(Map p230; 220 Tinker Rd; ☺public access noon Fri-midnight Sun) An extenuation of stunning Waimanalo Beach, this beach park is only open to civilians on weekends (and national holidays), as it fronts Bellows Air Force Station. Lifeguards, showers, restrooms, drinking water and camping are all on-site. The entrance is just north of Waimanalo Bay Beach Park; you can walk along the sand to Bellows Field Beach even when the vehicle entrance is closed.

The first Japanese POW of WWII was captured here the day after the Pearl Harbor attack when his midget submarine ran aground on coral in Waimanalo Bay.

Waimanalo Beach Park　　BEACH
(Map p230; 41-741 Kalanianaʻole Hwy; ☺7am-9pm) By the side of the roadway south of the main business area, this sloping strip of soft white sand has little puppy waves that are excellent for swimming. Manana Island and Makapuʻu Point are visible to the south. The facilities include a huge grassy picnic area, restrooms, ball-sports courts, a playground and an unappealing campground. Lifeguards are on duty here.

Activities

Olomana Golf Links　　GOLF
(Map p230; ☎808-259-7926; www.olomanalinks.com; 41-1801 Kalanianaʻole Hwy; green fees $40-105; ☺6:30am-6:30pm) LPGA star Michelle Wie got her start here: a regulation 18-hole, par-72 course beneath the dramatic backdrop of the Koʻolau Range. The facilities include a driving range and a restaurant.

🛏 Sleeping

⭐ **Bellows Field Beach Park**　　CAMPGROUND $
(Map p230; https://camping.honolulu.gov; 41-043 Kalanianaʻole Hwy; 3-day camping permit $32; ☺noon Fri-midnight Sun, gates closed 8pm-6am) The nearby military-base guard shack makes this the area's most secure campground. Some of the 50 sites are beneath the ironwood trees, some by the beach. Barbecue grills, showers and restrooms are available. Note that buses stop in front of the entrance road, about 1.5 miles from the beach itself.

Waimanalo Bay Beach Park　　CAMPGROUND $
(Map p230; https://camping.honolulu.gov; 41-043 Aliloi St; 5-day camping permit $52; ☺6am-7:45pm) The 10 tree-shaded sites here, just back from the beach, are a good choice. The beach park has barbecue grills and restrooms with showers.

Beach House Hawaii　　ACCOMMODATION SERVICES $$
(☎808-224-6213; www.beachhousehawaii.com) Has a number of properties in Waimanalo ranging from studios to five-bedroom estates.

HAWAIIAN HOMELAND WAIMANALO

Waimanalo is an area set aside in 1920 for the 'homesteading' of Native Hawaiians and it remains a staunch and proud Hawaiian community to this day. As such, it is a focal point for Native Hawaiian protests against perceived injustices, mistreatment, inequality and lack of consultation on a number of issues. Visitors passing through Waimanalo will see plenty of upside-down state flags (signaling distress), Hawaiian royal flags and Kanaka Maoli, the red, green and yellow flag popular among Hawaiian activists.

At research time there was an ongoing local protest movement against the development of Sherwood Forest, part of Waimanalo Bay Beach Park, which had resulted in a number of arrests. The plight of Native Hawaiians could clearly be seen by the tent city of homeless along the highway outside the beach park.

Eating

Waimanalo town is small, but it does have some good eats. Watch for food trucks parked near the beaches and the convenience store, on the *mauka* (inland) side of the road.

★ Ono Steaks & Shrimp Shack
HAWAIIAN $

(Map p230; ☑ 808-259-0808; 41-037 Wailea St; mains from $8; ⊙ 10:30am-8pm Mon-Sat) Superb plate lunches can be enjoyed at tables inside and out at this super-casual (but not shack-like) local eatery. The beach is a short walk away; get your meal to go and have a picnic on the shore. The garlic shrimp is worth the billing it gets in this restaurant's name.

★ Ai Love Nalo
HAWAIIAN $

(Map p230; ☑ 808-888-9102; www.ailovenalo.com; 41-1025 Kalaniana'ole Hwy; mains from $10; ⊙ 10:30am-3pm Mon-Fri, to 5pm Sat & Sun; ☑) ✔ Vegan meets Hawaiian at this Waimanalo sensation, where you can savor back-to-the-earth farm goodness from a family kitchen. Dishes such as the roasted-veg plate are revelations of the delights possible from the earth's bounty. Sandwiches based on portobello mushrooms or avocados are simply superb. Enjoy smoothies and/or soft-serve 'ice cream' made with a banana-coconut base.

And yes, the building used to be a gas station.

Hawaiian Island Cafe
CAFE $

(Map p230; ☑ 808-312-4006; Waimanalo Town Shopping Center, 41-1537 Kalaniana'ole Hwy; ⊙ 8am-4.30pm Tue-Sat) Eclectic comfort food keeps the regulars happy and entices newcomers at this popular cafe, now at the Waimanalo Center. Pizza, sandwiches, acai bowls and various breakfast items plus daily specials are all expertly prepared and boast island accents.

Shopping

East Honolulu Clothing Company
CLOTHING

(Map p230; ☑ 808-259-7677; www.doublepawswear.com; Waimanalo Town Shopping Center, 41-1537 Kalaniana'ole Hwy; ⊙ 9am-5pm) The striking, graphic one-color tropical prints on the clothing here are all designed and silk-screened in-house. This company provides many local hula schools with their costumes. There's plenty of local artwork to peruse as well.

Waimanalo Market Co-op
MARKET

(Map p230; ☑ 808-690-0390; www.waimanalomarket.com; 41-1029 Kalaniana'ole Hwy; ⊙ 10am-6pm Wed-Sat, to 5pm Sun) A local cooperative selling everything from art to kitchenware to fruit and vegetables.

❶ Getting There & Away

Waimanalo is only 10 minutes (6 miles) down the coast from Kailua.

Bus 57 travels between Honolulu's Ala Moana Center and Waimanalo via Kailua. It makes stops along the Kalaniana'ole Hwy (Hwy 72) through town, ending at Sea Life Park.

Maunawili

Maunawili covers a large area of the emerald Ko'olau Range and includes a namesake valley. Slicing through this verdant expanse, the Pali Hwy (Hwy 61) runs between Honolulu and Kailua. If it's been raining heavily, every fold and crevice in the jagged cliffs will have a fairyland waterfall streaming down it.

Once upon a time, an ancient Hawaiian footpath wound its way perilously over these cliffs. In 1845 the path was widened into a horse trail and later into a cobblestone carriage road. In 1898 the Old Pali Hwy (as it's now called) was built along the same route, but it was abandoned in the 1950s after tunnels were blasted through the Ko'olau Range.

◉ Sights & Activities

★ Nu'uanu Pali State Wayside   VIEWPOINT

(Map p230; www.hawaiistateparks.org; per car $3; ☉sunrise-sunset) About 5 miles northeast of Honolulu, turn as indicated to the popular ridgetop lookout with a sweeping vista of Windward O'ahu from a height of 1200ft. As you stand at the edge, Kane'ohe lies below straight ahead, Kailua to the right, Mokoli'i Island and the coastal fishpond at Kualoa Point to the far left. The winds that funnel through the *pali* (cliffs) here are so strong you can sometimes lean against them; it's usually so cool that you'll want a jacket.

This is where more than 500 O'ahuan warriors plunged to their deaths when chased by the forces of Kamehameha the Great in 1795.

Old Pali Hwy   HISTORIC SITE

(Nu'uanu Pali Dr; Map p230) On the Honolulu side of the island, you can make a scenic side trip along a remnant of the Old Pali Hwy, now called Nu'uanu Pali Dr. The road runs through lush vegetation and a cathedral of trees draped with hanging vines and philodendrons. You can make this interesting detour heading in either direction when traveling over the modern Pali Hwy. Look out for Nu'uanu Pali Dr road signs pointing east of the new Pali Hwy.

★ Maunawili Falls Trail   HIKING

(Map p230; www.maunawilifalls.com) The most popular, and populated, trail on Windward O'ahu ascends and descends flights of wooden stairs and crosses a stream several times before reaching the small, pooling Maunawili Falls amid tropical vegetation. When the trail forks, veer left; straight ahead is the connector to the much longer Maunawili Trail (p242).

Even with the moderate elevation change, this 2.5-mile round trip is kid-friendly, and you'll see lots of families on the trail on weekends. Just be prepared, as the way can be muddy and mosquitoes are omnipresent.

To reach the trailhead, driving east on the Pali Hwy from Honolulu, take the second right-hand exit onto A'uloa Rd. At the first fork, veer left onto Maunawili Rd, which ends in a residential subdivision; look for a gated trailhead-access road on the left. Note that this road is accessible only to pedestrians (and by residents' vehicles); non-residents may not drive or park along this road. Instead, park along nearby residential streets that aren't gated.

Kailua

POP 42,500

A long, graceful bay protected by a coral reef is Kailua's delight. The nearly 4-mile-long stretch of ivory sand is made for strolling, and the weather and wave conditions can be just about perfect for swimming, kayaking, windsurfing and kitesurfing. None of this has gone unnoticed. Decades ago expatriates from the mainland bought up

WINDWARD COAST KAILUA

THE BATTLE OF NU'UANU

O'ahu was the linchpin conquered by Kamehameha the Great during his campaign to unite the Hawaiian Islands under his rule. In 1795, on the quiet beaches of Waikiki, Kamehameha landed his fearsome fleet of canoes to battle Kalanikupule, the *mo'i* (king) of O'ahu.

Heavy fighting started around Puowaina ('Hill of Sacrifice,' now nicknamed Punchbowl), and continued up the Nu'uanu Valley. O'ahu's spear-and-stone warriors were no match for Kamehameha's troops, which included a handful of Western sharpshooters. O'ahu's defenders made their last stand at the narrow ledge near the current-day Nu'uanu Pali lookout. Hundreds were driven over the top to their deaths. A century later, during the construction of the Old Pali Hwy, more than 500 skulls were found at the base of the cliffs.

Some O'ahu warriors, including their king, escaped into the forest. When Kalanikupule surfaced a few months later, he was sacrificed by Kamehameha to the war god Ku. Kamehameha's taking of O'ahu marked the last battle ever fought between Hawaiian warriors.

Kailua

Kailua

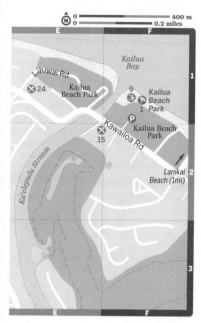

This is the place to be at sunset, when it seems as though half the community gathers on the small dunes to watch the reflected glow in the sky.

Lanikai Beach
BEACH

(Map p230) Just southeast of Kailua, Lanikai is an exclusive residential neighborhood fronting a gorgeous stretch of powdery white sand overlooking two postcard-perfect islands, known locally as the Mokes. Today the beach is shrinking: nearly half the sand has washed away as a result of retaining walls built to protect the neighborhood's multimillion-dollar mansions. There are 11 narrow public beach-access walkways off Mokulua Dr. No bathrooms, no lifeguards.

Kalama Beach Park
BEACH

(Map p230; 248 N Kalaheo Ave) Kalama Beach Park, 1 mile north of Kailua Beach Park on Kalaheo Ave, is the best place to park for a great walk. Climb over the grassy lawn to a much more residential stretch of sand. Weekdays there's hardly a soul besides locals walking their dogs and the occasional group of parents with infants. Restrooms and outdoor shower available. No lifeguards.

◉ Sights

Amid the suburban sprawl, there are some important old Hawaiian sites. Note that sights in the nearby Kaneʻohe Bay area are also easily accessible.

Ulupo Heiau State Monument
TEMPLE

(Map p230; http://dlnr.hawaii.gov/dsp/parks/oahu/ulupo-heiau-state-historic-site; 635 Manu Oo St; ☉sunrise-sunset) 🚶 **FREE** Rich in stream-fed agricultural land, fishing grounds and protected canoe landings, Kailua was an ancient economic center that supported at least three temples. Ulupo – once bordered by 400 acres of cultivated fishponds and taro fields, which are now encompassed by Kawai Nui Marsh – is the only heiau (ancient stone temple) left to visit here. It measures 140ft by 180ft, with walls up to 30ft high.

Construction of this imposing platform temple was traditionally attributed to *menehune,* the 'little people' who legend says created much of Hawaii's impressive stonework, finishing each project in one night. It's thought the temple's final use may have been as a *luakini,* a place for human

cottages crowded into the little neighborly lanes; the ones near the beachfront were often replaced with megahouses. South along the shore lies the exclusive enclave of Lanikai, with million-dollar views – and mansions to match.

In ancient times Kailua (meaning 'Two Seas') was a home to Hawaiian chiefs, including, briefly, Kamehameha the Great after he conquered Oʻahu. Today it's the Windward Coast's largest town, where you'll find the vast majority of the coast's restaurants and retail. This is the place for a day trip from Waikiki or a weeklong idyll.

☂ Beaches

★ Kailua Beach Park
BEACH

(Map p220; 526 Kawailoa Rd) A wide arc of sand drapes around the jewel-colored waters of Kailua Bay, bookended by formidable volcanic headlands and with interesting little islands rising offshore. It's ideal for long, leisurely walks, family outings and all kinds of aquatic activities such as kitesurfing and windsurfing. The beach has a gently sloping sandy bottom with usually calm waters; it's excellent for swimming year-round, especially in the morning. The wind can blow any time but generally kicks up in the afternoon.

sacrifice dedicated to the war god Ku. Good interpretive panels provide an artist's rendition of the site as it probably looked in the 18th century. The tiny, tree-shaded parking area feels suitably hidden and melancholy. The heiau is a mile southwest of downtown Kailua, tucked away behind the YMCA at 1200 Kailua Rd. Use the access road off the main highway.

Kawai Nui Marsh
PARK

(Map p230; http://dlnr.hawaii.gov; ⊙7am-7pm) **FREE** One of Hawaii's largest freshwater marshes, Kawai Nui provides flood protection for the town and a habitat for endangered waterbirds, and is also one of the largest remaining fishponds once used by ancient Hawaiians. You may see rare birds, including the *koloa maoli* (Hawaiian duck), *ae'o* (Hawaiian black-necked stilt), *'alae kea* (Hawaiian coot) and *kolea* (Pacific golden plover). Several local groups work to preserve and restore the marsh.

To access the area, park in the lot at the end of Kaha St, off Oneawa St, just over a mile northwest of Kailua Rd. It's a very historical spot: for over a thousand years it was a fishpond fed by copious amounts of freshwater. In the 1800s it was partly filled to allow the farming of taro and rice.

Hamakua Marsh Wildlife Sanctuary
WILDLIFE RESERVE

(Map p220; ⊙sunrise-sunset) **FREE** Downstream from Kawai Nui Marsh, this tiny nature preserve provides more habitat for rare waterbirds, including the *koloa maoli* (Hawaiian duck), *ae'o* (Hawaiian black-necked stilt), *'alae kea* (Hawaiian coot) and *'alae 'ula* (Hawaiian moorhen). Bird-watching is best after heavy rains. To keep these endangered birds wild, do not feed them. Park off Hamakua Dr, behind Down to Earth natural-foods store.

🏃 Activities

There are a handful of water-sports outfitters with in-town shops where you can arrange activities or rent gear. Many more operators bring in groups from Waikiki for a day of frolicking at the beach.

Ka'iwa Ridge (Lanikai Pillboxes) Trail
HIKING

(Map p230; 265 Ka'elepulu Dr; ⊙6am-8pm) Though officially named for Ka'iwa Ridge, this 1.25-mile (one way), half-hour trek is better known for the several WWII 'pill-boxes,' aka concrete bunkers, it passes. The barren trail is steep and often slippery. Make it to the top and you'll be rewarded with head-spinning views of the Mokulua Islands in Kailua Bay, Lanikai and the Ko'olau Range.

Blue Lotus Kailua
YOGA

(Map p230; ☎808-772-3520; www.bluelotus kailua.com; 38 Kane'ohe Bay Dr; classes $10; ⊙hours vary) This yoga *kula* offers classes in a range of yoga styles (vinyasa, flow, gentle, Ashtanga) at two locations, several times a day Monday through Saturday. Also has a branch in Pali.

Lomilomi Hana Lima
MASSAGE

(Map p220; ☎808-263-0303; www.lomilomi hanalima.com; 315 Uluniu St, 2nd fl, Kailua Sq; 1hr massage from $90; ⊙9am-5pm Mon-Sat) 🖐 Give your body a holiday with a traditional Hawaiian *lomilomi* massage and an island-grown organic body wrap.

Water Sports

⭐ We Go Island Canoe
CANOEING

(Map p220; ☎808-238-1368; www.wegoislandca noe.com; Kailua Beach Park; per person from $150) Visit the Mokulua Islands off Kailua Beach and learn how to paddle a traditional outrigger canoe. The three-hour tour includes time on the islands, some snorkeling in a cove and, if conditions permit, a thrilling ride back through the surf. Drinks and snacks provided. Confirm the meeting place when you book.

⭐ Kailua Beach Adventures
WATER SPORTS

(Map p220; ☎808-262-2555; www.kailuasail boards.com; Kailua Beach Center, 130 Kailua Rd; kayak rental per half/full day $59/74, SUP lesson from $139; ⊙8am-5pm) Good all-purpose outfitter with energetic staff and great kayak tours, near the beach. Lots of options such as kayaking, stand-up paddleboarding (SUP), surfing and kitesurfing. Free parking, showers, lockers and dressing room on-site. Offers discounts online.

⭐ Naish Hawaii
WINDSURFING

(Map p220; ☎808-262-6068; www.naish.com; 155c Hamakua Dr; windsurf rental per half/full day from $60/80; ⊙9am-5:30pm) Owned by the family of one of the sport's local pioneers, Robbie Naish, this is *the* place to go for windsurfing. In addition to windsurfing and kitesurfing lessons, it also has the gear for rent. Check out the Naish foiling wing-surfer.

Hawaiian Watersports
WATER SPORTS

(Map p220; ☑ 808-262-5483; www.hawaiian watersports.com; 171 Hamakua Dr; SUP lesson $164, kayak rental per day $59; ☺9am-5pm) Focuses on the many wind-based local water sports. Gives discounts for online bookings at least 24 hours in advance, especially kayak, stand-up paddleboard and surfboard rentals. Also does windsurfing and kiteboarding.

Twogood Kayaks Hawaii
KAYAKING

(Map p220; ☑ 808-261-3111; www.twogoodkay aks.com; 134b Hamakua Dr; tours adult/child from $115/81; ☺8am-6pm) Focusing on kayaks: take a tour, rent your own or book an advanced lesson and learn to surf the waves or race in the craft. Snorkel gear and stand-up paddleboards also available.

Kailua Ocean Adventures
CANOEING

(Map p220; ☑ 808-518-1284; 348 Hahani St; rates vary; ☺7am-6pm Mon-Sat; ⊞) Paddling trips aboard Hawaiian outrigger canoes on Kailua Bay and to offshore islands are conducted by enthusiastic guides. Fun for both adults and children.

Flat Island
SURFING

(Popoia; Map p230) This surf break is right by its namesake island. The swells are slow, which suits beginner surfers. On days when the wind is making the kitesurfers gleeful, you'll be much grimmer as you try to paddle out to the break.

Tours

Segway Hawaii-Kailua
TOURS

(Map p220; ☑ 808-262-5511; www.segwayofhawaii -kailua.com; Kailua Beach Center, 130 Kailua Rd; tours from $89; ☺8:30am-5:30pm) Take a Segway tour along Kailua Beach (p221), into Lanikai, out to Ulupo Heiau (p221) or through Kawai Nui Marsh.

⭐ Festivals & Events

'I Love Kailua' Town Party
CULTURAL

(www.lkoc.org/town-party.html; Kailua Rd; ☺Apr) One Sunday in April the whole community turns out for a giant block party, with hula schools and bands performing, local artists selling wares and local restaurants feeding the masses.

WINDWARD COAST KAILUA

OFF THE BEATEN TRACK

LIKEKE FALLS

Ready for a hidden waterfall, and maybe even being lucky enough to have it to yourself? The family-friendly **Likeke Falls Trail** (Map p230; off Kionaole Rd; ⊞) winds through a forest of native and exotic trees into the lush Ko'olau Range. It starts out unspectacularly, uphill along a paved maintenance road. Veering left before a water tank, the trail enters the forest, ascending a set of steps alternating with moss-covered rocks and gnarled tree roots. This shady path eventually emerges briefly onto a cobblestone road (part of the Old Pali Hwy) that continues climbing. Keep a sharp eye out for the (often muddy) side trail leading to the right toward the waterfall. You'll do some more forest climbing before you reach the lacy 15ft-high cascade, where often the only sounds are of tumbling water and tropical birdsong. The water is too shallow to take a dip, but you can get your feet wet. Be sure to continue up the short hill past the falls to see some great valley views. You can keep going for about another mile, but you'll have to turn around to return. The 2-mile round trip to the falls takes about an hour.

Do not attempt this hike if dark clouds are in the sky and rain is forecast: there is the danger of flash floods along the stream. Be aware that this trail accesses a frequently used but informal right of way on private land. While there were no 'Kapu' (No Trespassing) signs posted at the time of writing, these could appear at any time. If so, then consider this trail closed to the public. It is illegal (not to mention unsafe) to trespass in Hawaii.

To get to the trailhead en route from Kailua to Kane'ohe, turn off on Kionaole Rd, just west of Kamehameha Hwy (Hwy 83) near the H-3 Fwy junction. The trail starts past a chain-link gate at the uphill end of the Ko'olau Golf Club parking lot, in the furthest corner from the clubhouse.

🛏 Sleeping

Kailua isn't hotel or motel country, but vacation rentals abound, some on or near the beach. Besides the major websites, check out Lanikai Beach Rentals (www.lanikaibeach rentals.com) and Kailua Beach Properties (www.patskailua.com).

Kailua Guesthouse   APARTMENT **$$**

(Map p220; ☑ 808-375-3304; www.kailuaguest house.com; 345 Wana'ao Rd; rates vary; ☎) Not far from downtown, two large apartment studio-style suites feel bright and breezy. Helpful amenities include digital in-room safes and shared washer and dryer access. The owner is an excellent source of local lore. It's a healthy 10-minute walk to the beach. Has 30-night-minimum-stay specials and a $75 cleaning fee.

Manu Mele
Bed & Breakfast   APARTMENT **$$**

(Map p230; ☑ 808-262-0016; www.manumele. net; 153 Kailuana Pl; d from $140; ❄ ☎ ⛱) Close to the beach, Manu Mele enjoys a peaceful location west of town. The simple, island-contemporary guest rooms feel light and bright. Comforts include private entrances, Hawaiian quilts, and a pool available for guest use. Includes beach accessories and complimentary baked goods and fruit on your first morning.

Papaya Paradise
Bed & Breakfast   APARTMENT **$$**

(Map p220; ☑ 808-261-0316; www.kailuaoahu hawaii.com; 395 Auwinala Rd; r from $100; ❄ ☎ ⛱) The giant covered patio with comfortable sofas, reading nook and dining table is more like a living room than a lanai – with views of Mt Olomana. The quiet atmosphere here is best suited to more mature travelers. Rooms are simple and come with supplies for a self-catered breakfast. Shared kitchen available. There's a $25 'departure' fee.

Sheffield House   APARTMENT **$$**

(Map p220; ☑ 808-262-0721; www.hawaiishef fieldhouse.com; 131 Ku'ulei Rd; r from $135; ☎) Bring the family: the two private-entrance apartment suites here welcome kids. The beach is an easy, 10-house walk down the road. And the suitably cottagey decor fits right in with the lush tropical gardens created by landscape designer and architect owners.

🍴 Eating

Given that virtually all of Kailua's accommodations are self-catering, it's good that the town has three large supermarkets. There are quite a few excellent breakfast and lunch places, but more limited dinner options. The bay may be beautiful, but there's nowhere to dine by the waterfront.

★ Moké's Bread & Breakfast   CAFE **$**

(Map p220; ☑ 808-261-5565; https://mokesha waii.com; 27 Ho'olai St; breakfast & lunch from $8; ⏰ 6:30am-2pm Wed-Mon) Locals reading the paper or petting their dogs at the blue-checker-clothed tables are the norm at this legendary cafe. The famous *liliko'i* (passion fruit) pancakes and fresh-veggie frittatas are mighty fine. It has proper hash browns. Breakfast served until 1pm.

★ Over Easy   HAWAIIAN **$**

(Map p220; ☑ 808-260-1732; www.overeasy hi.com; 418 Ku'ulei Rd, No 103; mains from $11; ⏰ 7am-1pm Tue-Fri, to 1:30pm Sat & Sun) It's a little hard to spot from the street, but you'll be glad you made the effort at Kailua's favorite breakfast, brunch and lunch spot. A fave is the Kalua Pig Hash ($15), featuring two sunny-side-up eggs, delicious *kalua* (pit-oven-roasted) pulled pork and Okinawan sweet potatoes. The Custard French Toast is also popular. Sit inside or out.

Tamura's Poke   SEAFOOD **$**

(Map p230; ☑ 808-254-2000; www.tamuras finewine.com; 25 Kane'ohe Bay Dr; per pound from $7; ⏰ 9:30am-9pm Mon-Sat, to 8pm Sun) The wine is fine, but you're really here for the *poke*. Tucked into the back of Tamura's Fine Wines & Liquors at the Aikahi Park Shopping Center on Kane'ohe Bay Dr is a deli with a top *poke* selection. It's strictly takeout; get some on the way to the beach.

Kalapawai Market   DELI **$**

(Map p220; ☑ 808-262-4359; www.kalapawai market.com; 306 S Kalaheo Ave; meals from $6; ⏰ 6am-9pm) A 1930s landmark market near the beach that sells picnic supplies, convenience foods, made-to-order sandwiches and market-fresh salads. Good coffee, too. Take out and stroll down to Kailua Beach Park.

Hibachi   HAWAIIAN **$**

(Map p220; ☑ 808-263-7980; www.thehibachi hawaii.net; 515 Kailua Rd; mains from $7; ⏰ 10am-8pm Sun-Thu, to 9pm Fri & Sat) Super-casual *poke* place renowned for the freshness of its seafood. Watch the chefs hard at work. The choices change daily; enjoy them to go or at one of the tables inside and out. It also has warm dishes such as chicken and rice. Marinated meats are sold ready for you to grill.

Rai Rai Ramen
JAPANESE $

(Map p220; ☑ 808-230-8208; www.rairaira menkailua.com; 124 Oneawa St; mains from $10; ⊙ 11am-8:30pm Wed-Mon) Look for the red-and-white banner written in kanji outside this brightly lit noodle shop. The menu of ramen styles ranges from Sapporo south to Hakata, all with rich broth and topped with tender pork, if you like. The *gyōza* (dumplings) are grilled or steamed bundles of heaven.

Cinnamon's Restaurant
BREAKFAST $

(Map p220; ☑ 808-261-8724; www.cinna mons808.com; 315 Uluniu St, Kailua Sq; mains from $7; ⊙ 7am-2pm; 🔊) Locals pack this family cafe for the airy chiffon pancakes drowning in guava syrup, red-velvet pancakes (yum!), Portuguese-sweet-bread French toast, eggs Benedict, mahimahi (with proper hash browns), curried-chicken-and-papaya salad, and Hawaiian plate lunches. Waits are long on weekends; only the breakfast menu is available on Sunday. Get a mac-nut cinnamon roll to go.

Bob's Pizzeria
PIZZA $

(Map p220; ☑ 808-263-7757; Kailua Beach Center, 130 Kailua Rd; slices from $6; ⊙ 11am-8pm) Authentic flat-crusted pizzas. Buy by the slice or by the pie. Close to the beach, it has a fine terrace with tables under umbrellas. Does a huge takeout business with locals.

Tokoname Sushi Bar & Restaurant
JAPANESE $

(Map p220; ☑ 808-262-8656; www.tokoname hawaii.com; 442 Uluniu St; sushi from $5, dinner mains from $13; ⊙ 4-10pm) Pretty good sushi in a non-central location. Daily early-bird and late-night (9pm to 10pm) specials help keep the costs down. Presentation is stylish; the dining room is spare and simple.

Lemongrass
SOUTHEAST ASIAN $

(Map p220; ☑ 808-261-0222; www.lemon grassoahu.com; 20 Kainehe St; mains from $8; ⊙ 11am-3pm & 5-9pm Tue-Sun) This Thai-Vietnamese joint will soothe your soul with its earth-toned decor, avocado-colored bar and tropical-flower prints on the wall. The *pho* (Vietnamese noodle soup) and Thai noodle and curry dishes are mildly spiced, but it's all fresh. Takeout is popular.

★ Kalapawai Cafe & Deli
BISTRO $$

(Map p220; ☑ 808-262-3354; www.kalapawai market.com; 750 Kailua Rd; dinner mains from $16; ⊙ 6am-9pm Mon-Fri, from 7am Sat & Sun) An excellent gourmet, self-serve deli by day, Kalapawai transforms after 5pm into an inviting, eclectic bistro. The eggplant bruschetta and other share dishes are excellent paired with a wine flight (a series of tasting-size pours). But it's hard to resist the creative, locally sourced mains. Dine street side on the lanai or in the intimate candlelit dining room.

Uahi Island Grill
HAWAIIAN $$

(Map p220; ☑ 808-266-4646; www.uahiisland grill.com; 33 Aulike St; dishes from $8; ⊙ 11am-9pm Mon-Fri, from 9am Sat & Sun) Get your fresh and flavorful plate-lunch fix: *furikake*-crusted grilled tofu, red seafood curry, *kalua* pork with kale, garlic ahi (yellowfin tuna) and chicken in many forms. Dine outside along this quiet commercial street. The grill has a full bar and a large selection of iced teas.

Formaggio Grill
ITALIAN $$

(Map p220; ☑ 808-263-2633; www.formag gio808.com; 305 Hahani St; mains from $13; ⊙ 5-9pm Mon-Thu, to 10:30pm Fri & Sat, 4:30-9pm Sun) Dozens of wines by the glass; convivially large, high dining tables with stools; and hearty dishes (braised lamb, large burgers, myriad pastas) help ensure this place is always buzzing. It has a nice mood-lit vibe.

Baci Bistro
ITALIAN $$

(Map p220; ☑ 808-262-7555; www.bacibistro.com; 30 Aulike St; dinner from $17; ⊙ 11:30am-2pm & 5:30-9pm Mon-Fri, 5:30-9pm Sat & Sun) Home-style Italian cooking is on offer here, where the owner knows most patrons by name. Don't miss the white-chocolate and mascarpone cheesecake. The ravioli is made fresh daily. Tables in the cute, small dining room have white tablecloths. Located on a quiet side street.

Buzz's Original Steakhouse
STEAK $$$

(Map p220; ☑ 808-261-4661; www.buzzs originalsteakhouse.com; 413 Kawailoa Rd; mains lunch from $12, dinner from $19; ⊙ 11am-3pm & 3-9:30pm) This is one of the only options to dine near the gorgeous beach, and even then you can hear the surf way more than you can see it. Buzz's has been here forever – since

WINDWARD COAST KAILUA

1962. The old-school island decor is kitschy, the surf'n'turf menu (with throwback salad bar that does have fresh avocado) is so-so and the mai tais are watery.

Supermarkets

Whole Foods SUPERMARKET $
(Map p220; ☑808-263-6800; www.wholefoods market.com/stores/kailua; Kailua Town Center, 629 Kailua Rd; ⊙7am-10pm; 🄿) 🌿 This chain supermarket offers high-end foods at high-end prices. It has a very large selection of organic fare and lots of prepared meats and seafood ready for the grill. There's a vast hot-meal and salad bar. The deli offers sandwiches, barbecue meats, pizza, *poke,* sushi and more.

Very unusually for a Whole Foods, this one has a popular bar with happy-hour drinks, appetizers, and sports on TV.

Down to Earth Organic & Natural SUPERMARKET $
(Map p220; ☑808-262-3838; www.downtoearth. org; 573 Kailua Rd; ⊙6:30am-10pm; 🄿) 🌿 Part of the O'ahu-wide chain, this large natural-foods store with a takeout deli and hot-and-cold meal bar has moved into a massive space on Kailua Rd. There is a large area of tables inside and free wi-fi.

Foodland SUPERMARKET $
(Map p220; ☑808-261-3211; www.foodland.com; 108 Hekili St; ⊙5am-midnight) This large super-market has the lowest prices locally.

Farmers Markets

★ Kailua Town Farmers' Market MARKET $
(Map p220; ☑808-388-9696; www.farmlovers markets.com; Pali Lanes parking lot, 120 Hekili St; ⊙8am-noon Sun) An excellent addition to the line-up of local farmers markets, this one lasts all morning. Wake up with local cof-

fee and browse fresh foods, prepared foods, crafts and more. There's live music, and breakfasts from vendors.

Kailua Farmers Market MARKET $
(Map p220; www.hfbf.org; Kailua Town Center, 609 Kailua Rd; ⊙5-7:30pm Thu; 🄿) 🌿 Artisan breads, organic fruit and veggies, and fill-ing plate meals, from island-style barbecue to Filipino stew, are sold by vendors in the large parking areas behind Longs Drugs.

Kailua People's Open Market MARKET $
(Map p220; ☑808-522-7088; www.local-farm-ers-markets.com; 21 S Kainalu Dr; ⊙9-10am Thu) Get here early; locals line up for the freshest papayas, mangoes and pink-ginger flowers around.

Drinking & Nightlife

★ Grace in Growlers BEER HALL
(Map p220; ☑808-975-9317; www.facebook.com/ graceingrowlers; 143 Hekili St; ⊙noon-9pm Mon-Thu, to 10pm Fri & Sat, to 8pm Sun) With only a few years under its belt, this beer bar is already a Kailua institution. It's a real com-munity gathering spot and has an innova-tive concept: you choose from a huge variety of excellent microbrews and pour your own glass, running your own tab. The owners are charmers, and the industrial-chic atmos-phere is appealing.

★ Maui Brewing Co. SPORTS BAR
(Map p220; ☑808-518-2739; www.mbcrestau rants.com/kailua; 573 Kailua Rd; ⊙11am-10:30pm Sun-Thu, to 11pm Fri & Sat) These guys have opened a large bar and restaurant on Kail-ua Rd, adding immensely to Kailua's drink-ing options. Expect island-inspired cuisine, more than 30 beers on tap and screens for sports viewing. Some interesting craft beers, including Maui Brewing's Bikini Blonde La-ger, Big Swell IPA and Pau Hana Pilsener, are on the drinks card.

Happy hour is 3:30pm to 5:30pm and 9:30pm to close daily.

Kailua Town Pub & Grill PUB
(Map p220; ☑808-230-8444; www.kailua townpub.com; 26 Ho'olai St; ⊙11am-2am Mon-Fri, 9am-2am Sat & Sun; 🄰) This sports pub stays open late by local standards. It has a friend-ly mixed-age crowd of regulars. Decent bar food includes burgers, fish and chips, na-chos and other standards. The woodsy inte-rior complements the creative cocktails and the microbrews on tap.

Lanikai Juice   JUICE BAR
(Map p220;   ☑ 808-262-2383; www.lanikai
juice.com; Kailua Shopping Center, 600 Kailua
Rd; ⊙ 6am-8pm Mon-Sat, 7am-7pm Sun) With
fresh fruit gathered from local farmers, this
brightly lit, fruit-colored juice bar blends a
tantalizing assortment of smoothies with
names such as Ginger 'Ono and Kailua
Monkey. Hang out at sunny sidewalk tables
with big bowls of granola topped with acai
berries, bananas, blueberries and grated
coconut.

ChadLou's Coffee & Tea   CAFE
(Map p220; ☑ 808-263-7930; www.facebook.com/
chadlouscoffee; 45 Kihapai St; snacks & drinks $2-
8; ⊙ 7am-7pm Mon-Fri, to 6pm Sat & Sun; 🛜) This
laid-back coffee shop with comfy sofas and
chairs is where friends chat over espresso
drinks, blended frozen coffees and ice-cream
floats or cookie sandwiches. Peruse locally
made jewelry, art and souvenirs while you
wait.

Morning Brew Coffee
House & Bistro   CAFE
(Map p220; ☑ 808-262-7770; www.morningbrew
hawaii.com; Kailua Shopping Center, 600 Kailua Rd;
⊙ 6am-6pm; 🛜) Baristas at this pleasant cafe
cup everything from chai to 'Funky Monkey'
mochas with banana syrup. It has a long
breakfast menu as well as baked goods,
sandwiches, wraps, salads, bagels and more
later in the day. There are tables outside.

🛍 Shopping

Kailua at first doesn't exude retail charm,
given that most stores are in strip malls of
varying sizes. But look a little longer and
you'll find an exceptional assortment of locally owned boutiques and producers.

★ Lanikai Bath & Body   COSMETICS
(Map p220; ☑ 808-262-3260; http://lanikai
bathandbody.com; Kailua Shopping Center, 600 Kailua Rd; ⊙ 10am-6pm Mon-Fri, to 5pm Sat, to 4pm
Sun) Locally produced tropically scented
lotions and soaps. Anything accented with
plumeria is addictive. Great for gifts.

★ Bookends   BOOKS
(Map p220; ☑ 808-261-1996; Kailua Shopping
Center, 600 Kailua Rd; ⊙ 9am-8pm Mon-Sat, to
5pm Sun) This fabulous and small indie book-
shop has a great selection of used and new
books, including a lot of Hawaiiana. Staff are
great with recommendations.

Manuheali'i   CLOTHING
(Map p220; ☑ 808-261-9865; www.manuhealii.
com; 5 Ho'olai St; ⊙ 9:30am-6pm Mon-Fri, 9am-
4pm Sat, 10am-3pm Sun) Looking for aloha
wear? Don't settle for less than one of the
modern designs at the Kailua shop of this
Honolulu artist.

Ali'i Antiques II   ANTIQUES
(Map p220; ☑ 808-261-1705; www.aliiantiques.
com; 28 Oneawa St; ⊙ 10:30am-4:30pm Mon-Sat)
Search the stacks (and more stacks) and you
may find a treasure among the mishmash of
Hawaiiana and junk – a vintage postcard or
print, a feather lei or tiki barware, maybe.

Under a Hula Moon   GIFTS & SOUVENIRS
(Map p220; ☑ 808-261-4252; www.shophula
moon.com; Kailua Shopping Center, 600 Kailua Rd;
⊙ 9:30am-6pm Mon-Sat, 10am-5pm Sun) Bring
a piece of Hawaii home in the form of is-
land-made or inspired art, jewelry, stationery or home goods.

Coconut Grove Music   MUSIC
(Map p220; ☑ 808-262-9977; www.coconutgrove
music.com; 167 Hamakua Dr; ⊙ 10am-6pm Mon-
Sat, 11am-4pm Sun) Great guitar shop carrying
name-brand ukuleles – including Kamaka,
handmade in Honolulu – and vintage ukes
from the early 20th century. Upstairs on
Hamakua Dr.

Fighting Eel   CLOTHING
(Map p220; ☑ 808-738-9301; www.fightingeel.com;
Kailua Town Center, 629 Kailua Rd; ⊙ 10am-7pm
Mon-Fri, to 6pm Sat, to 4pm Sun) A fashion-sav-
vy import from over the *pali* in Waikiki and
Honolulu. The stylish goods are designed
and made on O'ahu.

Sand People   TOYS
(Map p220; ☑ 808-261-8878; www.sandpeo
ple.com; Kailua Shopping Center, 600 Kailua Rd;
⊙ 9:30am-6pm Mon-Sat, 10am-5pm Sun) Beachy
Hawaiian-style home accents, tote bags, souvenirs and gifts. Part of a local chain. Sand
Kids, with goodies for children, is right next
door.

Manoa Chocolate   FOOD
(Map p220; ☑ 808-262-6789; http://manoachoc
olate.com; 333 Uluniu St; ⊙ 9am-5pm Mon-Sat,
to 2pm Sun) Expensive but utterly delicious
handmade chocolate gets processed from
cacao bean to foil-wrapped bar inside this
workshop. Sample the goat's-milk, pineapple, Hawaiian-sea-salt, or chili-pepper

flavors. These tasty treats are sold in gourmet shops across O'ahu.

Muse Room CLOTHING
(Map p220; ☑ 808-261-0202; www.musebyrimo.com; 330 Uluniu St; ☺10am-5pm) Beachy and grown-up girly styles inspired by dreamy fantasies. The little shop is as cute as Barbie's Dream House.

❶ Getting There & Around

BICYCLE
Avoid parking headaches by cycling around town.

Bike Shop (☑ 808-261-1553; www.bikeshophawaii.com; 767 Kailua Rd; rentals per day/week from $20/100; ☺9am-8pm Mon-Fri, to 5pm Sat, 10am-5pm Sun) Large, full-service sales, rental and repair shop. In addition to cruisers, it rents performance street and mountain bikes ($40 to $85 per day).

BUS
Though having a car is most convenient, especially if you're visiting the rest of the Windward Coast, riding buses to, and around, Kailua is possible. Useful routes:

Routes 56 and 57 Honolulu's Ala Moana Center to downtown Kailua (corner Kailua Rd and Oneawa St, 45 to 60 minutes, every 15 minutes). Route 57 continues to Waimanalo (25 minutes), and some go on to Sea Life Park (30 minutes), where you can connect to routes 22 and 23 to continue around Southeast O'ahu. Routes 56 and 57 connect with route 55, which goes north along the coast just west of Kailua.

Route 70 Downtown Kailua to Kailua Beach Park (five minutes) and Lanikai (15 minutes).

CAR & MOTORCYCLE
Outside the morning and evening commutes, it's normally a 30-minute drive between Waikiki and Kailua along the Pali Hwy (Hwy 61), and about the same from the airport via the H-3 Fwy.

SHUTTLE
SpeediShuttle (☑ 877-242-5777; www.speedishuttle.com; per person from $30) Offers a shared-ride service from Honolulu airport.

Kane'ohe Bay Area

The state's largest bay and reef-sheltered lagoon, Kane'ohe Bay is largely silted and not great for swimming. The town itself is a marine-base suburb, populated by chain restaurants and stores. It doesn't boast the beaches, rentals and restaurants of neighboring Kailua, which is only 6 miles south.

GILLIGAN'S COCONUT ISLAND

Offshore in Kane'ohe Bay, **Moku o Lo'e** (Coconut Island), southeast of He'eia State Park (p229), was a royal playground, named for the coconut trees planted there in the mid-19th century by Princess Bernice Pauahi Bishop. During WWII the US military used it for R&R. Today the Hawai'i Institute of Marine Biology occupies much of the island, which you might recognize from the opening credits of *Gilligan's Island*.

Kane'ohe is all about Marine Corps Base Hawaii (MCBH), which occupies the Mokapu peninsula to the northeast of town. Naval Air Station Kane'ohe Bay saw the first action in WWII in the Pacific when it was attacked nine minutes before the attack on Pearl Harbor in 1941. MCBH is connected with Pearl Harbor by the remarkable 15-mile H-3 Fwy. Completed in 1997 after 20 years of wrangling, it was exempted from most environmental laws over the protests of Native Hawaiians and paid for by the Department of Defense.

◉ Sights

★**Ho'omaluhia**
Botanical Garden GARDENS
(Map p230; ☑ 808-233-7323; www.honolulu.gov/parks/hbg.html; 45-680 Luluku Rd; ☺9am-4pm) **FREE** The dramatic ridged cliffs of the Ko'olau Range are arrayed in front of you like an Imax screen at O'ahu's largest botanical garden. It encompasses 400 acres of trees and flowers from around the world. Plants are arranged in six regionally themed areas accessible by car. Pick up a map at the small visitor center, located at the far end of Luluku Rd, over 1 mile *mauka* (inland) from the Kamehameha Hwy.

The garden and lake were designed and built by the US Army Corps of Engineers to provide flood protection for Kane'ohe.

Valley of the Temples & Byōdō-In TEMPLE
(Map p230; www.byodo-in.com; 47-200 Kahekili Hwy; temple adult/child $5/2; ☺8:30am-5pm) It's so peaceful and parklike that it might take you a minute to realize that Valley of the Temples is an interdenominational cemetery. Up at the base of the Ko'olau mountains' verdant fluted cliffs sits Byōdō-In, a replica of a 900-year-old temple in Uji,

Japan. The symmetry is a classic example of Japanese Heian architecture, with rich vermillion walls. The 3-ton brass bell is said to bring peace and good fortune to anyone who rings it.

Bus 65 stops near the cemetery on Kahekili Hwy, but from there it's a winding 0.7-mile hike up to the temple.

He'eia Pier
HARBOR

(Map p230) Just north of He'eia State Park, off the Kamehameha Hwy, is one of the Windward Coast's only small-boat harbors. Watch the comings and goings of local boat owners; on weekends they head out to the 'sandbar,' a raised spit in the bay that becomes a mooring place for people to cut loose and party.

He'eia State Park
STATE PARK

(Map p230; ☑808-235-6509; www.heeia statepark.org; 46-465 Kamehameha Hwy; ⊙7am-7pm) FREE This park on Kealohi Point has picnic potential and views of He'eia Fishpond to the south. This location was sacred to ancient Hawaiians as a place of final judgment at life's end. Some believe that there is still a portal to the spirit world here, but the heiau (temple) on this site was destroyed in the 1800s and the park office and community hall were subsequently built over it.

🎿 Activities

Kama'aina Kayak and Snorkel Eco-Ventures
KAYAKING

(Map p230; ☑808-781-4773; www.kamaaina kidskayaking.org; He'eia State Park, 46-465 Kamehameha Hwy; self-guided tour from $109; ⊙8am-4pm Mon-Sat) Reserve ahead for a four-hour self-guided kayak and snorkel adventure on Kane'ohe Bay from He'eia State Park; the tour includes round-trip transportation from Waikiki if required. It also operates catamaran sailing and stand-up paddleboarding and has kayak rentals.

Ko'olau Golf Club
GOLF

(Map p230; ☑808-236-4653; www.koolaugolf club.com; 45-550 Kionaole Rd; green fees from $95; ⊙7:30am-6pm) Considered the toughest golf course on O'ahu and also one of the most picturesque, this tournament course has a modest clubhouse and is scenically nestled beneath the Ko'olau Range. For practice, there's a driving range and both chipping and putting greens.

Pali Golf Course
GOLF

(Map p230; ☑info 808-266-7612, reservations 808-296-2000; www.honolulu.gov/des/golf/pali. html; 45-050 Kamehameha Hwy; green fees resident/nonresident from $22/66; ⊙6am-5:30pm) This municipal 18-hole hillside course has stunning mountain views stretching across to Kane'ohe Bay. Club and cart rentals are available. Reserve tee times in advance.

👉 Tours

Captain Bob's Picnic Sail
BOATING

(Map p230; ☑808-942-5077; www.captain bobpicnicsail.com; He'eia Pier; 4hr cruise adult/child $137/116; ⊙cruises Mon-Sat, office 8:30am-5:30pm) Captain Bob's catamaran tour launches at He'eia Pier and stops at the sandbar for aquatic frolicking, as well as for reef snorkeling and lunch. Transportation from Waikiki is included.

🛏 Sleeping & Eating

Excepting a couple of restaurants, the nearby town of Kailua is the better place to eat – unless you crave generic fast food.

Ho'omaluhia Botanical Garden
CAMPGROUND $

(Kahua Nui-Makai Campsites; Map p230; ☑808-233-7323; https://camping.honolulu.gov; 45-680 Luluku Rd; 3-night campsite permit $32; ⊙office

---

OFF THE BEATEN TRACK

FABULOUS FISH PRINTS

You'll probably have seen Naoki's magnificent *gyotaku* (Japanese-style fish prints) all over O'ahu in galleries, restaurants and bars, but there's nothing like watching him print up a freshly caught fish in his own studio, **Gyotaku by Naoki** (Map p230; ☑808-330-2823; www.gyotaku.com; 46-020 Alaloa St, Unit D, Kane'ohe; ⊙by appointment). All the fish he prints are eaten later and the spectacular art on hand is for sale. If you've been out fishing and have a trophy you'd like him to print, get in touch before you eat it!

Call ahead to check the studio is open because Naoki is often out fishing or at local schools teaching the kids about marine conservation. His studio is a little hard to find, but well worth the effort.

Greater Kailua, Kane'ohe & Waimanalo

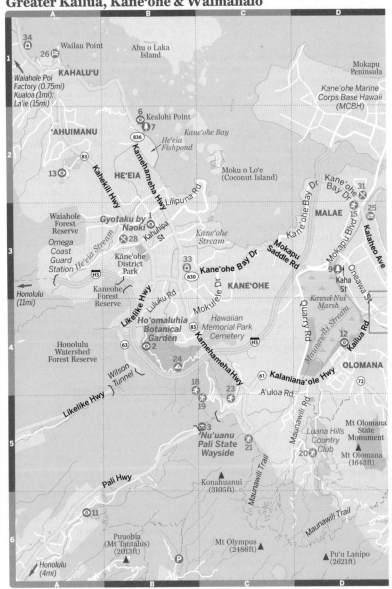

Waiahole Poi
Factory (0.75mi);
Kualoa (1mi);
La'ie (15mi);

KAHALU'U

Wailau Point

Ahu o Laka
Island

Mokapu
Peninsula

Kane'ohe Marine
Corps Base Hawaii
(MCBH)

'AHUIMANU

Kealohi Point

Kane'ohe Bay

He'eia
Fishpond

Kamehameha Hwy

HE'EIA

Kahekili Hwy

Moku o Lo'e
(Coconut Island)

Kane'ohe
Bay Dr

Kane'ohe
Bay Dr

MALAE

Waiahole
Forest
Reserve

Gyotaku by
Naoki

He'eia Stream

Kahuhipa
St

Lilipuna Rd

Kane'ohe
Stream

Kane'ohe
Bay Dr

Mokapu
Saddle Rd

Mokapu Blvd

Kalaheo Ave

Omega
Coast
Guard
Station

Kāne'ohe
District
Park

Kane'ohe Bay Dr

Kaha
St

Oneawa St

Honolulu
(11mi)

Kaneohe
Forest
Reserve

Luluku Rd

Mokulele Dr

KANE'OHE

Kawai Nui
Marsh

Maunawili Stream

Kailua Rd

Likelike Hwy

Ho'omaluhia
Botanical
Garden

Hawaiian
Memorial Park
Cemetery

Quarry Rd

OLOMANA

Honolulu
Watershed
Forest
Reserve

Kamehameha Hwy

Wilson
Tunnel

Likelike Hwy

Kalaniana'ole Hwy

A'uloa Rd

Maunawili Rd

Mt Olomana
State
Monument

Mt Olomana
(1643ft)

Nu'uanu
Pali State
Wayside

Luana Hills
Country
Club

Maunawili Trail

Pali Hwy

Konahuanui
(3105ft)

Honolulu
(4mi)

Puuohia
(Mt Tantalus)
(2013ft)

Mt Olympus
(2486ft)

Maunawili Trail

Pu'u Lanipo
(2621ft)

8am-4pm Mon-Fri; P) The grassy, botanical-garden-surrounded tent sites at the base of the Ko'olau Range are cool and green, fed by frequent mists. With an overnight guard and gates that close, it's among O'ahu's most petty-theft-free campgrounds. Reserve your permit for one of 15 campsites online. There are two other smaller campgrounds, Kahua Kuou and Kahua Lehua, nearby.

Hale'iwa Joe's   HAWAIIAN $$

(Map p230; ☑808-247-6671; www.haleiwajoes. com; 46-336 Haiku Rd; mains from $12; ⊙4:30-9pm Sun-Thu, to 10pm Fri & Sat; 🐾) The view of

N
0 — 2 km
0 — 1 mile

Mokapu
Point

*PACIFIC
OCEAN*

Kapoho
Point

*Kailua
Bay*

8

Popoi'a Island
(Flat Island)

16

See Kailua
Map (p220)

KAILUA

10

Mokulua
Islands

Moku
Nui

17

Moku
Iki

*Ka'elepulu
Pond*

Wailea
Point

Keolu Dr

Bellows
Air Force
Station

22

5

29 32

Waimanalo Bay
Beach Park

Kalaniana'ole Hwy

WAIMANALO

4

27

30 14

the lushly green Haiku Gardens valley dropping off from the open-air dining room here is a stunner that's worth the trip. You can enjoy coconut shrimp, prime rib or *poke* while overlooking a lily pond beneath the Ko'olau Range. Reservations are not needed; arrive early and get a table on the lanai.

Shopping

Fabric Mart   TEXTILES
(Map p230; ☑808-234-6604; www.hawaiifab
ricmart.com; 45-681 Kamehameha Hwy; ⊙9am-
6pm) Colorful Hawaiian-print fabric is for
sale at this friendly Windward Coast outlet
of Fabric Mart, also to be found in Honolulu
and 'Aiea. Make your own muumuu, aloha
shirt or cushion cover at the best prices.

❶ Getting There & Away

Two highways run north–south through Kane'o-
he. The slower but more scenic Kamehameha
Hwy (Hwy 830) hugs the coast. Further inland,
the Kahekili Hwy (Hwy 83) intersects with the
Likelike Hwy (Hwy 63) and continues north past
the Valley of the Temples.

Bus route 55 runs from Honolulu's Ala Moana
Center to downtown Kane'ohe, then continues
along Kamehameha Hwy to the North Shore.
Route 56 connects Kailua and Kane'ohe.

Kahulu'u & Waiahole

Driving north along the Kamehameha
Hwy, you'll cross a bridge near Kahulu'u's
Hygienic Store (formerly owned by the Hygienic Dairy Company). There you'll make
a physical and cultural departure from the
gravitational pull of Honolulu. Now you've
officially crossed into 'the country,' where
the highway becomes a two-laner and the
ocean shares the shoulder.

★**Sunshine Arts Gallery**   ART
(Map p230; ☑808-239-2992; www.sunshinearts.
net; 47-653 Kamehameha Hwy; ⊙9am-5:30pm)
Tropical murals emblazon the exterior of
this place, but that's nothing compared to
the riot of creativity inside. A rotating array
of the work of more than 100 island artists is
displayed at the coast's largest gallery. Most
are works by modern and traditional painters, printmakers and photographers, but
there's also some impressive blown glass,
carved koa wood and jewelry.

Paradise Bay Resort   HOTEL **$$$**
(Map p230; ☑808-239-5711; www.paradise
bayresorthawaii.com; 47-039 Lihikai Dr; studios/
1 bedrooms from $316/376; ❋ 🛜 ☀) On the
point next to Kahulu'u Fishpond, the Wind-
ward Coast's only resort property is an al-
ternative to the myriad area rentals. Casual,
earth-tone contemporary rooms with kitch-
enettes are just the beginning. Here, kayak,
SUP and snorkel gear are included. There

Greater Kailua, Kane'ohe & Waimanalo

are often substantial rate reductions on the website.

★ **Waiahole Poi Factory** HAWAIIAN $
(Map p236; ☎808-239-2222; www.waiaholepoifactory.com; 48-140 Kamehameha Hwy, Waiahole; meals from $8; ⊙10am-6pm) 𝄐 This family-owned roadside landmark sells *'ono* (delicious) traditional Hawaiian plate lunches, baked *laulau* (bundle made of pork or chicken with salted butterfish wrapped in taro and *ti* leaves and steamed) and squid, freshly pounded poi and seafood *poke* by the pound, and homemade *haupia* (coconut pudding) for dessert. Get here early at lunchtime, as food sells out fast.

It sometimes holds events such as the Hawaiian Nose Flute Workshop or the Poi and Hawaiian Food Demonstration and Tasting. Check availability online.

Kualoa

Although nowadays there's not a lot of evidence of it, in ancient times Kualoa was one of the most sacred places on O'ahu. When a chief stood on Kualoa Point, passing canoes lowered their sails in respect.

🏖 **Beaches**

★ **Kualoa Regional Park** BEACH
(Map p236; ☎808-237-8525; https://camping.honolulu.gov; 49-479 Kamehameha Hwy; camping 3-day permit $32; ⊙7am-8pm) Huge extended-family groups gather for weekend picnics on the wide, grassy field that fronts the narrow white-sand beach here. There's good swimming, with magnificent mountain scenery as a backdrop and Mokoli'i Island offshore to delight. Stroll south along the beach to **'Apua Pond**, a 3-acre salt marsh on Kualoa Point that's a nesting area for the endangered *ae'o* (Hawaiian stilt). Many bus tours stop here for comfort breaks. During WWII Kualoa Park Dr was part of an airfield runway.

◉ **Sights**

Mokoli'i Island ISLAND
(Map p236) That eye-catching islet you see offshore from Kualoa Regional Park is called Mokoli'i (Little Lizard). In ancient Hawaiian legend, it's said to be the tail of a *mo'o* (lizard spirit) slain by the goddess Hi'iaka and thrown into the ocean. Following the immigration of Chinese laborers to Hawaii, this cone-shaped island also came to be called Chinaman's Hat, a nickname that pre-

dominates today, regardless of the political incorrectness.

Tours

Tropical Farms   TOURS
(Map p236; ☑808-237-1960; www.macnutfarm. com; 49-227 Kamehameha Hwy; ⊙9:30am-5pm) Sure, it's a bit of a kitschy tourist trap, but everything for sale at this family-owned business is homegrown Hawaiian. The open-air store overflows with various flavored macadamia nuts, coffee, local jams and sauces, natural remedies and arts and crafts. Free samples, too – right near the cash registers.

Eating

Aunty Pat's Café   CAFE $
(Map p236; ☑800-231-7321; www.kualoa.com/eatshop/auntypats; Kualoa Ranch, 49-560 Kamehameha Hwy; meals from $8, lunch buffet adult/child $18/14; ⊙cafe 7:30am-3:30pm, snacks to 6pm; ♿) At the Kualoa Ranch visitor center, this cafeteria lays out a filling midday buffet with staples such as *kalua* pork. Banana pancakes for breakfast and grass-fed beef burgers for lunch are cooked to order.

Ka'a'awa

POP 1350

Here the road tightly hugs the coast and the *pali* (cliffs) move right on in, with barely enough space to squeeze a few houses between the base of the sheer cliffs and the highway. If you needed an excuse to spring for the rental convertible, these dramatic vertical sights are it.

Beaches

Swanzy Beach Park   BEACH
(Map p236; 51-369 Kamehameha Hwy; ⊙7am-10pm) Fronted by a shore wall, this narrow neighborhood beach is used mainly by fishers. You'll see kids splashing around and local families picnicking and camping here on weekends. Roadside camping is permitted on weekends, but the sites are noisy and not the best.

Sights

Crouching Lion   MOUNTAIN
(Map p236) The Crouching Lion is a landmark rock formation just north of mile marker 27 on the Kamehameha Hwy. According to legend, the rock is a demigod from Tahiti who was cemented to the mountain during a jealous struggle between the volcano goddess Pele and her sister Hi'iaka. When he tried to free himself by crouching, he was turned to stone.

Eating

Uncle Bobo's   HAWAIIAN $
(Map p236; ☑808-237-1000; www.unclebobos. com; 51-480 Kamehameha Hwy; mains from $7; ⊙11am-3pm Wed-Fri, to 4pm Sat & Sun) You don't usually find buns baked from scratch at a Hawaiian barbecue joint, but here a local family does it right, dishing up smoked brisket and ribs, mahimahi tacos and other island faves. They also make their own original Uncle Bobo's BBQ Sauce.

Kahana Valley

In ancient Hawai'i, all of the islands were divided into *ahupua'a* (wedge-shaped land

WINDWARD COAST KA'A'AWA

SEEN THOSE MOUNTAINS BEFORE?

In the 1800s the Judd family purchased the roughly 4000 acres that make up today's **Kualoa Ranch** (Map 236; ☑808-231-7321; www.kualoa.com; 49-560 Kamehameha Hwy; tours adult/child from $48/37; ⊙tours 8:45am-3pm; ♿) from Kamehameha III and Queen Kalama. It's still O'ahu's largest cattle ranch (with 1500 head), but the family's descendants expanded the business into a slick tourist sight to help support the land.

If you want to see where Godzilla left his footprints and the *Jurassic Park* kids hid from dinosaurs, take the movie tour that covers the many films and TV shows shot in the Ka'a'awa Valley. ATV and horseback rides also mosey along in this busy area. Go a bit more off the beaten trail with the recommended 6WD jungle tour into Hakipu'u Valley's steep slopes, which are covered with tropical vegetation. Hakipu'u is also where most of the ranch's ancient sites are located. There are 12 tour options; check it all out online. Return transfers from Waikiki hotels are available. There's a cafe on-site. Don't expect much solitude!

divisions that ran from the mountains to the sea), providing everything Hawaiians needed for subsistence. Modern subdivisions and town boundaries have erased this traditional organization almost everywhere except here, O'ahu's last publicly owned *ahupua'a*.

Before Westerners arrived, the Kahana Valley was planted with wetland taro, which thrived in the rainy climate. Archaeologists have identified the remnants of more than 120 agricultural terraces and irrigation canals, as well as the remains of a heiau (stone temple), fishing shrines and numerous *hale* (house) sites.

In the early 20th century the lower valley was planted with sugarcane, which was hauled north to Kahuku via a small railroad. During WWII the upper valley was taken over by the US military and used to train soldiers in jungle warfare.

The entire area makes a good pause to savor some Hawaiian culture on your driving adventure.

🏖 Beaches

Kahana Bay   BEACH
(Map p236; www.hawaiistateparks.org; Kamehameha Hwy) The beach here offers mostly safe swimming with a gently sloping sandy bottom. Watch out for the riptide near the bay's southern reef break. There are restrooms, outdoor showers, picnic tables and drinking water.

WHOSE LAND IS IT, ANYWAY?

Not everything on the Windward Coast is as peaceful as the *lo'i kalo* (taro fields) seen alongside the Kamehameha Hwy. Large tracts of these rural valleys were taken over by the US military during WWII for training and target practice, which continued into the 1970s. After decades of pressure from locals, cleanup of ordnance and chemicals by the military is slowly progressing. Not surprisingly, you'll encounter many Hawaiian sovereignty activists here. Spray-painted political banners and signs, Hawaii's state flag flown upside down (a sign of distress) and bumper stickers with antidevelopment slogans such as 'Keep the Country Country' are commonly seen.

⊙ Sights & Activities

Huilua Fishpond   LANDMARK
(Map p236; www.nps.gov/places/huilua-fishpond. htm; Kamehameha Hwy) FREE Although many of Kahana's archaeological sites are inaccessibly deep in the valley, impressive Huilua Fishpond is visible from the highway and can be visited simply by walking down to the beach at Kahana Bay. It's one of only six remaining ancient fishponds (there were once 97). It dates to sometime between the 13th and 16th centuries.

Ahupua'a o Kahana State Park   PARK
(Map p236; ☑808-237-7766; www.hawaii stateparks.org; 55-222 Kamehameha Hwy; ⊙sunrise-sunset) FREE In spite of over 40 years of political controversy and failed plans for a living-history village, this park is currently still open to visitors.

Starting near the community center, the gentle, 1.2-mile round-trip **Kapa'ele'ele Trail** runs along a former railbed and visits a fishing shrine and a bay-view lookout, then follows the highway back to the park entrance.

Park before the private residential neighborhood, then walk 0.6 miles further up the valley road to the start of the **Nakoa Trail**, a 3.5-mile rainforest loop that confusingly crisscrosses Kahana Stream and bushwhacks through thick vegetation.

Both of these trails can be very slippery and muddy when wet. Don't attempt the Nakoa Trail if any rain is forecast or dark clouds are visible in the sky, due to the danger of flash floods.

The signposted park entrance is a mile north of Crouching Lion Inn. Turn *mauka* (inland) past the picnic tables and drive up the valley road to an unstaffed orientation center, where hiking pamphlets with trail maps are available outside by the educational boards.

Punalu'u

POP 1200

This sleepy seaside community consists of a long string of houses and businesses lining the highway, plus two surprisingly large condominium complexes. There are intermittent ribbons of sand that are good places for a picnic or even a quick dip. Otherwise, there's little reason to pause in your looping explorations.

🏖 Beaches

Punalu'u Beach Park BEACH
(Map p236; 53-378 Kamehameha Hwy) At this long, narrow swimming beach, an offshore reef protects the shallow waters in all but stormy weather. Be cautious of strong currents near the mouth of the stream and in the channel leading out from it, especially during high surf. The roadside park has restrooms, outdoor showers and picnic tables.

🛏 Sleeping & Eating

Hanohano Hale CONDO $$
(Map p236; ☑808-293-1062; 53-549 Kamehameha Hwy; P❄🖥) On the low-key, low-rise Windward Coast, this aging seven-story high-rise condo built right on the sand is a bit jarring. Many of the units here are vacation rentals, and the usual cautionary advice about the decorative whims of individual owners fully applies. Units can be found on major rental websites as well as through Paul Comeau Condos (www.pauls punaluucondos.com).

★Shrimp Shack SEAFOOD $
(Map p236; ☑808-256-5589; www.shrimpshack oahu.com; 53-360 Kamehameha Hwy; meals from $10.75; ⊙10am-5pm) The shrimp are fried in garlic and dipped in butter, or you could order mussels or crab legs at this legendary sunny, yellow-painted food truck parked beside Ching's general store. You can't miss it roadside – the menu is on a yellow surfboard. The spicy shrimp come in three levels of heat. A picnic-worthy beach is just across the road.

Ching's MARKET $
(Map p236; ☑808-237-7017; 53-360 Kamehameha Hwy; snacks from $2; ⊙8am-7pm) This general store has changed little in the 70 years since it opened (OK, now there are blue M&Ms...). Locally made snacks include boiled peanuts, *poke*, various *musubi* (rice balls) and rolls, and ice cream.

Keneke's Grill HAWAIIAN $
(Map p236; ☑808-237-1010; www.kenekes.net; 53-138 Kamehameha Hwy; mains from $4; ⊙8am-7:30pm) Right on the road, Keneke's comes complete with Christian sayings and word games on the wall. Hawaiian plate lunches, such as *loco moco* (rice, fried egg and a hamburger patty topped with gravy) and teriyaki steak, plus burgers and daily specials, fill the menu. Don't miss having shave ice or Dave's

ice cream for dessert. Great outdoor seating with mountain views. There's plenty of parking out front.

Hau'ula
POP 3500

A small coastal town sitting against a scenic backdrop of hills and majestic Norfolk pines, Hau'ula has a main drag with not much more than a general store and a modern strip mall. But you can head to the inviting beaches, or to the hills for good hiking.

🏖 Beaches

Hau'ula Beach Park BEACH
(Map p236; Kamehameha Hwy) Right along the highway in the middle of town, this narrow, ironwood-shaded beach has a shallow, rocky bottom that isn't too appealing for swimming but does attract snorkelers. It occasionally gets waves big enough for local kids to ride. The grassy lawn is popular for family picnics on weekends.

🍴 Eating

Papa Ole's Kitchen HAWAIIAN $
(Map p236; ☑808-293-2292; www.facebook.com/ Papa-Oles-Kitchen-LLC-229628883748553; Hau'ula Shopping Center, 54-316 Kamehameha Hwy; mains from $7; ⊙7am-9pm Thu-Sun, to 3pm Mon & Tue) When it bills itself as 'da original, with *'ono grinds*' (good eats), Papa Ole's doesn't lie. Opt for sauteed veggies or a green salad instead of macaroni and you've made your Hawaiian plate lunch a tiny bit healthier. Dine inside the small cafe, outside at strip-mall picnic tables or, better, take it 'to go' to the beach park.

Tamura's Market MARKET $
(Map p236; ☑808-232-2332; www.tamurasmarket. com; Hau'ula Shopping Center, 54-316 Kamehameha Hwy; ⊙8am-9pm) Tamura's is Hau'ula's main supermarket and sells something that can't be bought up the road in Mormon-influenced La'ie: alcohol! It's also open on Sunday and, as with Tamura outlets island-wide, sells some of the best *poke* you'll find on O'ahu.

North Shore Tacos MEXICAN $
(Map p236; ☑808-293-4440; www.northshore-tacos.com; 54-296 Kamehameha Hwy; tacos from $4.75; ⊙8am-9pm) This is the restaurant base in Hau'ula for North Shore Tacos – it

North Windward Coast

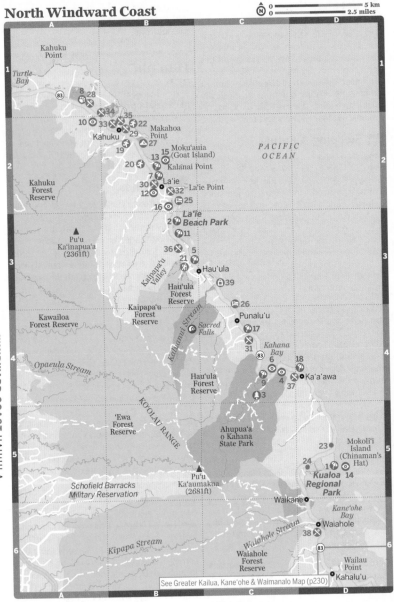

also has a food truck in Pupukea. Nothing fancy, but tasty Baja-style Mexican with award-winning fresh fish tacos and pineapple tiki drinks. Eat inside, outside at shaded tables or take away.

🛍 Shopping

Fairly's Fine Art   ART
(Map p236; ☎808-232-8842; www.lancefairly.
com; 53-839 Kamehameha Hwy; ⊙10am-5pm
Mon-Sat) Dreamlike paintings and prints
here explore the color, light and grandeur

North Windward Coast

of Hawaii. You can put your vacation fantasy on your wall back home. Lance has also written and illustrated his first children's book, *Fly High, Little Honu*. The shop can be found on the ocean side of the Kamehameha Hwy.

La'ie

POP 6200

Bustling and busy, La'ie is quite a contrast to its rural neighbors. This is the center of the Mormon community in Hawaii, so you're just as likely to see white-collared shirts as board shorts in town. Life here revolves around the resident Brigham Young University (BYU) Hawaii, where scholarship programs recruit students from islands throughout the Pacific.

Many students help pay for their living expenses by working at the Polynesian Cultural Center (PCC), the huge tourist complex that draws legions of visitors each year (it's second only to Pearl Harbor among O'ahu's attractions). In keeping with the religion, much is closed locally on Sunday, including some beaches.

🏊 Beaches

★ La'ie Beach Park   BEACH
(Map p236; Pounders Beach; 55-205 Kamehameha Hwy) A half-mile south of the Polynesian Cultural Center (PCC) main entrance, this is an excellent bodysurfing beach, but the shore break can be brutal, thus its nickname, Pounders Beach. Around the corner at the northern end you'll find **Bathtub Beach**, a perfect playground for families with small children as a stretch of beach is protected by a shelf of limestone about 50ft offshore at lower tide times, creating a 'bathtub' of shallow water in which to wallow.

Kokololio Beach Park   BEACH
(Map p236; 55-017 Kamehameha Hwy) A wide patch of sand, good surf and decent parking make this a great beach to pause for a picnic and a splash. There's a wide lawn, picnic tables and shade-giving trees.

Hukilau Beach   BEACH
(Map p236; 55-692 Kamehameha Hwy; ⏰7am-8pm Mon-Sat) North of La'ie Shopping Center is a crescent of white sand that's a leisurely place for swimming when summer waters are calm. Just beware any time the surf's up.

◉ Sights & Activities

Polynesian
Cultural Center   CULTURAL CENTER
(Map p236; PCC; ☑ 808-293-3333; www.polynesia.
com; 55-370 Kamehameha Hwy; adult/child from
$65/52; ⊘noon-9pm Mon-Sat; ▣) A cultural
park owned by the Mormon Church, the
PCC revolves around Polynesian-themed 'villages' representing Hawaii, Samoa, Aotearoa
(New Zealand), Fiji, Tahiti and Tonga. The
admission price is steep, but this includes
frequent village shows and a park-wide boat
parade showcasing native dances.

Brigham Young University (BYU) students dressed in native garb demonstrate
poi pounding, coconut-frond weaving, handicrafts, music and games. The evening Ali'i
Luau show and buffet, an add-on, is a real
spectacle, with some authentic Hawaiian
dances and foods. Afterwards you can see
Ha: Breath of Life, a Polynesian song-and-
dance revue that's partly authentic, partly
Bollywood-style extravaganza.

Check online for ticket packages; advance
discounts are sometimes offered. Numerous
bus tours come here from Waikiki.

Gunstock Ranch   HORSEBACK RIDING
(Map p236; ☑ 808-341-3995; www.gunstock
ranch.com; 56-250 Kamahameha Hwy; trail rides
from $82; ⊘Mon-Sat; ▣) Take a small-group
horseback ride across a working ranch at
the base of the Ko'olau mountains. Options

MORMON TOWN
....
La'ie is thought to have been the site
of an ancient Hawaiian *pu'uhonua* – a
place where *kapu* (taboo) breakers
could escape being put to death. It was
a refuge for Mormon missionaries as
well; after an attempt to create a 'City
of Joseph' on Lana'i failed, the church
purchased a 6000-acre plantation here
in 1865. In 1919 construction began on
a smaller version of the Salt Lake City,
UT, temple at the foot of the Ko'olau
Range. This dazzling, formal white
edifice (Map p236; ☑808-293-9298;
www.ldschurchtemples.com/laie; 55-600
Naniloa Loop; ⊘9am-8pm) – open only
to practicing Latter Day Saint (LDS,
also known as Mormon) church members – stands at the end of a wide
boulevard and may be one of the most
incongruous sights on O'ahu.

---

include scenic mosey-alongs, advanced gid-
dyaps, and picnic and moonlight trail rides.
A kids' experience (ages two to seven; $45)
includes a 30-minute guide-led ride. UTV
tours are also available.

🛏 Sleeping & Eating

In keeping with La'ie's Mormon influences,
you're not going to find anything open on
Sunday. If you're drooling for an ice-cold
beer, forget it.

Courtyard by Marriott
Oahu North Shore   HOTEL $$
(Map p236; ☑ 808-293-4900; www.marriott.
com; 55-400 Kamehameha Hwy; r from $220;
▣❋⊛⊜) The first major new hotel built
in this corner of O'ahu lacks balconies or
lanais. Take a few Hawaiian details off the
facade and it looks bland – probably fitting,
as many of the guests have business at adjoining Brigham Young University and the
Polynesian Cultural Center.

Hukilau Marketplace   MARKET $
(Map p236; ☑ 808-293-3142; www.hukilaumarket
place.com; 55-370 Kamehameha Hwy; ⊘11am-
9:30pm Mon-Sat) The Polynesian Cultural
Center has several eateries and food trucks
in its Hukilau Marketplace, which doesn't
require an admission ticket. You'll find
Pounders Restaurant (named after Pound-
ers Beach, just down the road), Guadalaja-
ra Grill Mexican, Tita's Grill, Aunt Emily's
Bakery, Penny's Malasadas, Elephant Shack
Thai, Kiwi Style Fish 'n Chips, Hale Pops
Gourmet Hotdogs, Beach Side Shave Ice and
Elsie's Smoothie Shack.

There are also some souvenir shops here.
Expect busloads of visitors from Waikiki hotels milling around on their way in or out
of the PCC.

La'ie Shopping Center   SUPERMARKET $
(Map p236; 55-510 Kamehameha Hwy; ⊘Foodland
5am-midnight Mon-Sat) Fast-food restaurants,
shops and services cluster in this mini mall,
about a half mile north of the Polynesian
Cultural Center. Foodland supermarket has
a takeout deli and bakery, but it doesn't sell
alcohol and it's closed on Sunday out of respect for the town's Mormons.

Angel's Ice Cream   DESSERTS $
(Map p236; ☑ 808-293-8260; La'ie Shopping
Center, 55-510 Kamehameha Hwy; snacks from
$4; ⊘10am-10pm Mon-Sat; ▣) Cool off with
an 'Angel's Halo' shave ice or a real-fruit
smoothie next to Foodland at La'ie Shopping

Center. The soft-serve ice cream also has its fans.

Hukilau Cafe
HAWAIIAN $

(Map p236; ☑ 808-293-8616; www.facebook.com/Hukilau-Cafe-359828366472; 55-662 Wahinepe'e St; mains from $6; ⊙ 6am-2pm Tue-Fri, 7-11:30am Sat) In a backstreet north of La'ie Shopping Center, this small cafe is the kind of place locals would rather keep to themselves. Local *grinds* (food) – such as Portuguese sweetbread French toast and a teriyaki-burger lunch – are right on. In case you're wondering, this isn't the restaurant featured in the movie *50 First Dates,* though it's said to be the inspiration for it.

Malaekahana State Recreation Area

Just north of La'ie, a long, narrow strip of appealing sand stretches between Makahoa Point to the north and Kalanai Point to the south, with a thick inland barrier of ironwoods.

🏖 Beaches

Malaekahana State Recreation Area
BEACH

(Map p236; ☑ 808-587-0300; www.hawaiistateparks.org; 56-075 Kamehameha Hwy; ⊙ 7am-7:45pm Apr-early Sep, to 6:45pm early Sep-Mar; ♿) **FREE** The long, relatively uncrowded beach with buff-colored sand is popular with families. Swimming is generally good here year-round, although there are occasionally strong currents in winter. Bodyboarding, surfing and windsurfing are also possible. Weekday visitors may find it hard to believe that the enormous parking lot fills up on weekends, but it often does.

Moku'auia
ISLAND

(Map p236; Goat Island) When the tide is low you can wade from Malaekahana State Recreation Area's southern Kalanai Point to Moku'auia, a state bird sanctuary about 250yd offshore. The island has two attractive beaches that are perfect crescents of sand. The one on the northern side is good for swimming and snorkeling, and there's a good chance you'll have it to yourself. Use common sense when wading across to the island and don't go if conditions are unsuitable.

Consider wearing reef shoes and taking a flotation device for this adventure.

WORTH A TRIP

LA'IE POINT

Crashing surf, a lava arch and a slice of Hawaiian folk history await at the lookout at La'ie Point. The nearshore island with the hole in it is Kukuiho'olua (Puka Rock). In Hawaiian legend, this island was once part of a giant lizard chopped into pieces by a demigod to stop its deadly attack on O'ahu. From Kamehameha Hwy, head *makai* (seaward) on Anemoku St, opposite La'ie Shopping Center, then turn right onto Naupaka St. There's limited parking at the end of the street.

🛏 Sleeping

⭐ Malaekahana Beach Campground
CAMPGROUND $

(Map p236; ☑ 808-674-7715; www.malaekahana.net; 56-335 Kamehameha Hwy; tent sites per son $10, rental units from $60; ⊙ gates 7am-7pm, office 8:30am-4:30pm; 🅿🛜) 🍃 Let the surf be your lullaby and the roosters your wake-up call at Makahoa Point, about 0.7 miles north of the park's main entrance. This family- and community-friendly operation maintains tent sites by the beach, spots for 'vehicle camping,' small, rustic cabins and private rooms. There's a camp store, plus kayak, SUP and surfboard rentals and lessons.

Kalanai Point Campground
CAMPGROUND $

(Map p236; ☑ 808-293-1736; www.hawaiistateparks.org; 56-075 Kamehameha Hwy, Malaekahana State Recreation Area; tent sites from $12; ⊙ 7am-7:45pm Apr-early Sep, to 6:45pm early Sep-Mar; 🅿) Kalanai Point, the main section of Malaekahana park at the beach's southern end, is less than a mile north of La'ie. It has picnic tables, barbecue grills, restrooms, showers and good public camping – advance permits are required.

Kahuku

POP 2700

Kahuku is a former sugar-plantation town. Much of the old sugar mill that operated here until 1996 was knocked down, but the remnants of the smokestack and the old iron gears can be seen behind the post office. The rest of the former mill grounds have been transformed into a small, faded

CONTROVERSIAL WIND FARMS

The North Shore and upper Windward Coast are home to O'ahu's wind-power generation, and while it's agreed that the island needs an increase in renewable energy, locals in Kahuku are angry at the proposed expansion of a wind-farm project that would increase the number of turbines from 12 to 20. They've got precedent on their side after seeing what happened on the North Shore.

The Kawailoa wind-farm project there produced 30 turbines that many locals consider to be an eyesore and an affront to Native Hawaiian sacred lands. If you drive into the Waimea Valley – 'Valley of the Priests' and a sacred site for over 700 years – you're bound to be surprised by the intrusiveness of the massive white turbines. They stretch across the hills of the North Shore and can be seen from parts of Hale'iwa, Wailua, and out to Dillingham Airfield, even though locals say that they were assured that the project would be much less visible.

In 2018 the Kahuku and Kawailoa wind farms generated approximately 3% of O'ahu's energy needs.

shopping center containing the town's bank, grocery store and eateries.

Relics of the cane era aside, the real reason to plan a stop in Kahuku is for its remarkable collection of food trucks and cafes. Kahuku is a favorite lunch stop on circle-island road trips. Shrimp ponds on the north side of town supply O'ahu's top restaurants, while colorful food trucks that cook up the crustaceans are thick along the highway.

⊙ Sights & Activities

Kahuku Farms FARM
(Map p236; ☑ 808-628-0639; www.kahukufarms. com; 56-800 Kamehameha Hwy; tours adult/child $32/22, shop free; ☺ cafe 11am-4pm Wed-Mon; ♿) 🌿 Take a tractor-pulled wagon tour through the taro patch and fruit orchards at this family farm – sampling included. Then stop at the gift shop for bath products and foodstuffs made from the farm's bounty. The cafe has many vegetarian options, such as 'super kale' smoothies. Book the farm tours online.

James Campbell
National Wildlife Refuge WILDLIFE RESERVE
(Map p236; ☑ 808-637-6330; www.fws.gov/james campbell; 56-795 Kamehameha Hwy; ☺ tours by reservation only) 🌿 FREE A few miles northwest of Kahuku town heading toward Turtle Bay, this rare freshwater wetland provides habitat for four of Hawaii's six endangered waterbirds: the 'alae kea (Hawaiian coot), ae'o (Hawaiian black-necked stilt), koloa maoli (Hawaiian duck) and 'alae 'ula (Hawaiian moorhen). During stilt nesting season, usually mid-February through mid-October, the refuge is off-limits to visitors, but there are free guided tours the rest of the year. Check the website for details.

★ CLIMB Works Keana Farms ZIPLINE
(Map p236; ☑ 808-626-5260; www.oahuzipline. com; 1 Enos Rd; tours from $169; ☺ 7am-3:20pm Mon-Sat; ♿) Great fun for all on O'ahu's longest and tallest dual ziplines just southeast of Kahuku. This ecofriendly operation receives rave reviews for its three-hour tour that, besides providing a thrill in a gorgeous environment, educates visitors about a working farm and the rich culture and history of the region. Great for families.

Kahuku Golf Course GOLF
(Map p236; ☑ 808-293-5842; www.honolulu.gov/ des/golf/kahuku.html; 56-701 Kamehameha Hwy; locals/visitors from $18/44; ☺ 6am-5:30pm) Surprisingly for an island like O'ahu, this is the only seaside links course you'll find. It's a sporty little public nine-holer that can get pretty tough when the winds blow. Nothing fancy – bring your own snacks and drinks and make use of the picnic tables. Club and handcart rental available.

✗ Eating

The food-truck scene in Kahuku has expanded exponentially in recent years and you'll find a lot more than just shrimp. Most places have seating and shade. Look out for Nelly's Tacos Mexicano, Thong's Thai, Kalbi on Fire, Cheesus Crust (pizza), Lani's Funnel Cakes and Ono Yo Frozen Yogurt and Acai, among others.

★ Fumi's Kahuku Shrimp SEAFOOD $
(Map p236; ☑ 808-232-8881; www.facebook.com/ Fumis-Kahuku-Shrimp-163293257105870; 56-777 Kamehameha Hwy; plates from $10; ☺ 10am-7:30pm) Just north of town, shrimp is sold from this roadside place with shaded

picnic tables. Menu options include tempura shrimp, fried fish and burgers. Locals fiercely debate whether the shrimp here are just a bit juicier than elsewhere.

Giovanni's Aloha Shrimp SEAFOOD $
(Map p236; ☎808-213-1839; www.giovannis shrimptruck.com; 56-505 Kamehameha Hwy; plates from $13; ☺10:30am-6:30pm) No longer a lonely little vehicle, graffiti-covered Giovanni's is flanked by a covered patio and surrounded by a veritable fleet of other food trucks. With all the great competition, feel free to *not* follow the hordes here, although the garlicky shrimp scampi still pack a punch. Dealing with the shells, however, is a pain.

Mike's Huli Chicken FOOD TRUCK $
(☎808-277-6720; www.mikeshulichicken.com; 56-565 Kamehameha Hwy; meals from $9; ☺10:30am-7pm) Mike and his legendary yellow food truck have moved up the coast to Kahuku. You can't miss the vehicle, emblazoned with the words 'Winna Winna Chicken Dinna.' Mike's has risen above others thanks to his rotisserie (*huli* is Hawaiian for 'turn') chicken, prepared with its own housemade hot sauce. Other options include Hawaiian menu stalwart *kalua* pork.

Seven Brothers
at the Mill AMERICAN $
(Map p236; ☎808-852-0040; www.sevenbrothers burgers.com; 55-565 Kamehameha Hwy; burgers from $6.50; ☺11am-9pm Mon-Sat; 🖪) Serving from a window in one of the old sugar-mill buildings near the center of town, this place specializes in burgers such as the Paniolo (Hawaiian Cowboy) Burger and the Teri Samoa. You won't leave hungry if their fries are involved. Eat at a picnic table or take out.

Romy's Kahuku
Prawns & Shrimp SEAFOOD $$
(Map p236; ☎808-232-2202; www.romyskahuku-prawns.org; 56-781 Kamehameha Hwy; plates from $12; ☺10am-6pm) A fire-engine-red hut with tables under an awning a tad north of town. Eat overlooking the aquaculture farm where your giant prawns are raised. Steamed shrimp and whole fish available, too. Try the *pani popo* (Samoan coconut buns) for dessert. Expect long waits and a need to peel the buttery shrimp.

HIKING ON THE WINDWARD COAST

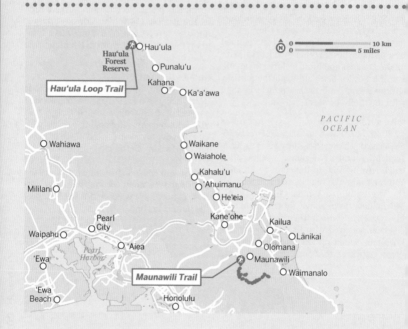

MAUNAWILI TRAIL

START PALI HWY TRAILHEAD
END WAIKUPANAHA ST, WAIMANALO
DURATION/DISTANCE THREE TO SIX HOURS; 9.5 MILES
DIFFICULTY MODERATE

Winding down the coast, this scenic 9.5-mile one-way **hiking trail** (Map p230; http://hawaiitrails.ehawaii.gov) winds along the back side of Maunawili Valley, following the base of the lofty Ko'olau Range. It clambers up and down gulches, across streams and along ridges, awarding panoramic views of mountains and the sea.

Hiking the Maunawili Trail in an easterly direction is least strenuous, as you will be trekking from the mountains down to the coast at Waimanalo. Follow the entire route and you will need to leave one car at the trail start and a second car quite a distance away where the trail ends (in an insecure parking area) or return to your car from the trail's end via services such as Uber or Lyft (about $30 for up to four people).

The **Pali Highway Trailhead** is on the south side of the road and can only be accessed from the eastbound lane. About a mile northeast of the Nu'uanu Pali State Wayside, pull off right at the 'scenic point' turnout at the hairpin turn just before the 7-mile marker. Walk through the break in the guardrail, where a footbridge takes you to the trail.

The first 2 miles of the trail are fairly easy thanks to your start high up the mountain. There's a succession of good views down to the coast or of various lush valleys. At a junction, a nearly mile-long **connector trail** goes steeply downhill (elevation loss: 500ft) to **Maunawili Falls**, where it connects to the Maunawili Falls Trail (p219). Continuing down this 1.25-mile trail means you could create a 3.25-mile hike. In that case, get a ride back to your car from the trailhead.

There's some marvellous hiking to be had on the windward side of the Koʻolau Range that splits Oʻahu. It can get wet and blustery over here facing the trade winds, so come prepared.

The next 7 miles of the trail are simply idyllic. Any evidence of humans other than the physical trail vanishes. Bird calls dominate your ears, myriad forms of green fill your eyes, and scents of wild fruits and flowers tickle your nose. The **trail endpoint** is at Waikupanaha St, where you can retrieve your second car or get your ride.

HAUʻULA LOOP TRAIL

START HAUʻULA LOOP TRAILHEAD
END HAUʻULA LOOP TRAILHEAD
DURATION/DISTANCE 1½ TO TWO HOURS; 2.5 MILES
DIFFICULTY MODERATE

The **Hauʻula Loop Trail** (https://hawaiitrails. hawaii.gov; Maʻakua Rd; ☉ sunrise-sunset) is a scenic 2.5-mile hike that makes a couple of gulch crossings and climbs along a ridge with broad views of the forested interior, the ocean and the town of Hauʻula. This trail passes through a variety of native vegetation and offers good bird-watching.

The signposted **Hauʻula Loop Trailhead** appears on Maʻakua Rd, just beyond a sharp bend in Hauʻula Homestead Rd above the Kamehameha Hwy, north of Hauʻula Beach Park. Trailhead parking is unsafe due to vehicle break-ins, so leave your car by the beach and instead walk a quarter mile from the highway. Note that the 7-mile Hauʻula Uka Loop Trail, which also starts here, is closed due to landslides.

The trail rises quickly through a forest of ohia and hala (screwpine) trees, as well as sweet-smelling guava and bizarre octopus trees, with their spreading tentacle-like branches of pink to reddish flowers. Birds fly about and ocean vistas open up as the trail climbs through shaggy ironwood trees, then splits into a loop about half a mile in.

By going left, the trail remains easier to follow and more clearly laid out. Under ironwoods and towering Norfolk pines, the shady trail switchbacks up and over a ridge into Waipilopilo Gulch, passing rare endemic flora, such as *aʻaliʻi* plants with red seedpods, *ʻakia* shrubs and *lama* (Hawaiian persimmon). The trail crosses a streambed and muddily climbs out of the gulch to fine overlooks of Kaipapaʻu Valley.

As the footpath rolls up and down along the ridge, there are even more spectacular views into the valley. Eventually the trail descends back into ironwood trees, Norfolk pines and Hawaiian ferns, all displaying infinite shades of green. The trail crosses a streambed, then ascends again and levels out into a wide forest path with views of Hauʻula, beaches and offshore islets. Contouring around the ridge, which drops off steeply, the trail starts descending. Keep a sharp eye out for any obscure turnings in the switchbacks. Turn left at the loop-trail junction to reach the trailhead and the paved road.

ROAD TRIP: DRIVING UP THE COAST

The magnificent drive up the length of the Windward Coast is likely to be a highlight of any trip to O'ahu. From sandy beaches to craggy mountains and laid-back locals, this is the other side of the island, the one facing the trade winds. If you think Waikiki is what O'ahu is all about, come over here and take a look.

❶ Waimanalo

Start at **Waimanalo Bay Beach Park** (p217), 2.5 miles northwest of Sea Life Park and 17 miles from Waikiki, both via coastal Hwy 72. The beach here is a real Hawaii fantasy, with surging waves, creamy sand and a string of palm trees. Hungry? You'll find some excellent eats, including typical plate lunches at **Ono Steaks & Shrimp Shack** (p218).

❷ Ulupo Heiau State Monument

Drive the Kalaniana'ole Hwy almost 6 miles northwest until you get to Kailua Rd, turn

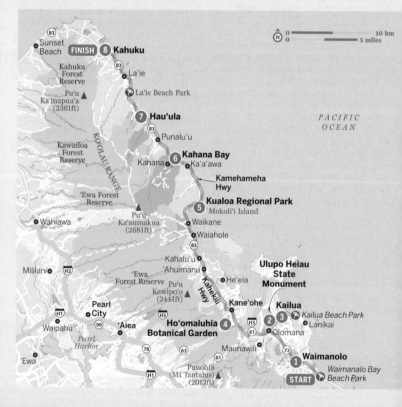

3–6 hours 40 miles / 64km

Great for... Outdoors; Families

Best Time to Go Any time of the year

right and make an immediate left on Uluoa St. Wind back behind the YMCA and you'll find the **Ulupo Heiau State Monument** (p221). In a serene, lonely setting, this is a well-preserved original stone temple. Look beyond to the **Kawai Nui Marsh** (p222), which was an important fishpond until the 1800s.

❸ Kailua

Back on Kailua Rd, find your way out to much-loved **Kailua Beach Park** (p221). Watch windsurfers, kitesurfers and other daredevils out on the water and pause for a dip in the turquoise surf.

Heading back into Kailua township, look on your right for **Island Snow Hawaii** (p226), where you can enjoy a superb shave ice (Barack Obama loved this place during his annual Kailua vacations when he was president). Continue on Kailua Rd and follow it as it makes a sharp right turn. Look for the small strip mall **Kailua Shopping Center** (Map p220; 600 Kailua Rd) on your right; it has a great collection of locally owned shops and boutiques.

❹ Ho'omaluhia Botanical Garden

The next stop is via a series of roads that changes names often, but it's worth it. Take Kailua Rd southwest and continue as it turns into Hwy 61 for a total of 3 miles. Turn right on Hwy 83 and go north for 2.1 miles. Turn left on Luluku Rd and after about half a mile you'll come to **Ho'omaluhia Botanical Garden** (p228). Besides thousands of tropical plants from around Hawaii and the Pacific (and many engrossing displays), there are cinematic views of the looming cliff faces. If you sprang for the convertible, you're happy now.

❺ Kualoa Regional Park

Back on Hwy 83, continue north for 11 miles through the often damp, green scenery until the ocean view opens up on the right and you see **Kualoa Regional Park** (p232). Stop off in this popular park for the views of **Mokoli'i Island** (p232), which still carries the archaic moniker 'Chinaman's Hat.'

❻ Kahana Bay

For the rest of your drive, the Kamehameha Hwy (as Hwy 83 is now known) stays close to the shore, running through tiny towns and open land, punctuated by the occasional mellow attraction aimed at day-tripping tourists (such as kitschy Tropical Farms just before Kualoa Regional Park). At mile marker 27 you can't miss the **Crouching Lion** (p233), a huge rock formation with Polynesian lore. A tad further on, the road turns left along a broad bay. This is the base of the Kahana Valley, an important ancient site. Look right and you'll see the **Huilua Fishpond** (p234), where fish were trapped and caught. It could date back as far as the 13th century. Access it from the beach at **Kahana Bay** (p234).

❼ Hau'ula

Five miles more of beautiful coast driving brings you to barely there Hau'ula. If you have the time, turn west on Hau'ula Homestead Rd and after a sharp bend follow Ma'akua Rd (a combined half mile) to the start of the **Hau'ula Loop Trail** (p243). In only 90 minutes you can get out into the O'ahu countryside and climb up to bluffs for some spectacular coastal views.

If you've resisted the pleasures of the myriad beaches that line this route, be sure to stop at **La'ie Beach Park** (p237) and wander around to wallow in Bathtub Beach. It's at the south end of La'ie, also home to the Polynesian Cultural Center, which is a trip in itself.

❽ Kahuku

Worked up an appetite? Five miles further on you'll love Kahuku. This small town is famous for its food trucks, which dish up all manner of locally farmed shrimp in dishes that are invariably redolent with garlic. Choose from trucks such as **Giovanni's** (p241) or head a tad north of town to **Fumi's** (p240).

From here you can loop through the North Shore along Hwy 83 and reach Waikiki after 47 miles.

Waimea Bay (p253)
ANTHONY QUINTANO / SHUTTERSTOCK ©

North Shore & Central O'ahu

Pipeline, Sunset, Waimea... You don't have to be a surfer to have heard of the North Shore; the epic breaks here are known worldwide. Sure, winter brings giant swells that can reach 15ft to 40ft in height, but there's more to this coast than monster waves. The beaches are gorgeous year-round and perfect for swimming in summer. And there are so many activities besides surfing. Try stand-up paddleboarding (SUP) or kayaking, take a snorkeling or whale-watching tour, go hiking or horseback riding – jump out of an airplane, even.

The laid-back communities here are committed to keeping life low-key and rural – and if that's what you're after, do some exploring among the pineapple and coffee plantations of Central O'ahu. Slow down. Spend the day cruising and don't forget to stop at Green World Coffee Farm for a local brew or at Ted's Bakery for chocolate-*haupia* (coconut pudding) cream pie.

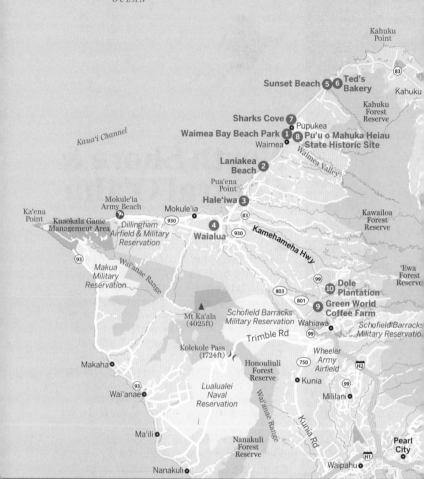

North Shore & Central Oʻahu Highlights

1 Waimea Bay Beach Park (p253) Admiring this picture-perfect beach.

2 Laniakea Beach (p254) Seeing the *honu* (green sea turtles) relaxing on the shore.

3 Haleʻiwa (p260) Enjoying the area's only real town.

4 Waialua Sugar Mill (p266) Exploring the stores

and businesses of this cleverly redeveloped area.

5 Sunset Beach (p253) Surfing the waves in winter; swimming in summer.

6 Ted's Bakery (p255) Tucking into a chocolate-*haupia* (coconut pudding) pie.

7 Sharks Cove (p256) Snorkeling in the cove.

8 Puʻu o Mahuka Heiau State Historic Site (p254) Visiting Oʻahu's largest ancient temple.

9 Green World Coffee Farm (p269) Trying the local brews and soaking up the vibe.

10 Dole Plantation (p270) Learning everything about the pineapple.

❶ Getting There & Away

BUS

Bus route 52 runs between Honolulu and Haleʻiwa via Mililani and Wahiawa. Route 55 runs from Honolulu to Kaneʻohe, then up the Windward Coast, stopping at Turtle Bay on the way to Haleʻiwa. Using both buses, it's possible to go right around Oʻahu, but it's nowhere near as convenient as using a car.

CAR

Getting to the North Shore is easy by car, and Waikiki is only an hour's drive away by the H-1 and H-2 freeways.

From the H-1, there are three potential routes to Wahiawa, the main town in Central Oʻahu. The H-2 is the fastest and most direct; further west, the Kamehameha Hwy winds its way north; still further west is Kunia Rd.

From Wahiawa, the Kamehameha Hwy heads directly to Haleʻiwa, while Kaukonahua Rd, with less traffic, heads to Waialua.

Those on an anticlockwise round-the-island drive will arrive at the North Shore after driving up the Windward Coast and getting to Turtle Bay.

Keep in mind that the North Shore's population seems to double in the winter surf season, and drivers watching waves and surfers can cause some horrendous traffic jams.

Turtle Bay

POP 400

Idyllic coves and coastal rock beds define the island's northeast tip, where the North Shore and the Windward Coast meet. Dominating the area is Turtle Bay Resort, with its low-key, view-perfect hotel and restaurants, golf courses, condo village and public access to nearby beaches. So far, it's the only large-scale tourist development on this side of the island, and locals have fought to keep it that way.

🏖 Beaches

Kuilima Cove   BEACH

(🏖) Just east of Turtle Bay Resort is beautiful little Kuilima Cove with its perfect, protected **Bayview Beach**. On the bay's right-hand side is an outer reef that not only knocks down the waves but facilitates great snorkeling in summer – and, in winter, some moderate surf. Resort guests go swimming here, but the beach is also open to the public. Rent bodyboards, snorkel sets and beach gear on-site. Lots of parking.

Turtle Bay Beach   BEACH

Immediately west of Turtle Bay Resort, Turtle Bay was named because of the green sea turtles that used to lay their eggs on the beach. Not any more, unfortunately. The beach is sandy, but offshore the bottom is rocky, making for poor swimming. This is a popular surf spot, however, and guests at the resort sometimes learn here.

Kaihalulu Beach   BEACH

A short walk along the beach east of Kuilima Cove is this beautiful, curved, white-sand beach backed by ironwoods. The rocky bottom means it's not great for swimming, but the shoreline attracts morning beachcombers. Continue another mile east, detouring up onto the bluff by the golf course, to reach scenic **Kahuku Point**, where fishers cast throw-nets and pole-fish from the rocks. This is Oʻahu's northernmost point.

★ Kawela Bay   BEACH

West of Turtle Bay Resort, a 1.5-mile shoreline trail runs over to Kawela Bay. In winter you might spy whales cavorting offshore. After walking round **Protection Point**, named for its WWII bunker, you'll find the bay with its thicket of banyan trees, as seen on TV's *Lost*. For the best swimming and snorkeling, keep walking to the middle of the bay. Kawela Bay is also accessible via a footpath from the Kamehameha Hwy.

◉ Sights & Activities

Kahuku Land Farms
Roadside Stand   MARKET

(📞808-232-2202; 56-781 Kamehameha Hwy; ⊙10am-5pm) A number of local farm stands group together just west of the Turtle Bay Resort entrance. Stop here for a fresh-cold coconut water ($3) and to peruse the unexpected selection of fruits (pitaya, pomelo…). It's a fun stop on your round-the-island trip, but getting a tad touristy.

Hans Hedemann Surf School   SURFING

(📞808-447-6755; www.hhsurf.com) Located at the entrance of the Turtle Bay Resort main building, this surfing and SUP school is an extension of Hans Hedemann's well-known Waikiki school (p150). It offers lessons for beginners and intermediates for both disciplines, virtually right outside the hotel. It also offers four-person outrigger-canoe trips to look for ocean life, such as green sea turtles.

Turtle Bay Golf   GOLF

(📞808-293-8574; www.turtlebayresort.com; Turtle Bay Resort, 57-091 Kamehameha Hwy; rates vary; ⊙by reservation only) Turtle Bay's two

North Shore & Central O'ahu

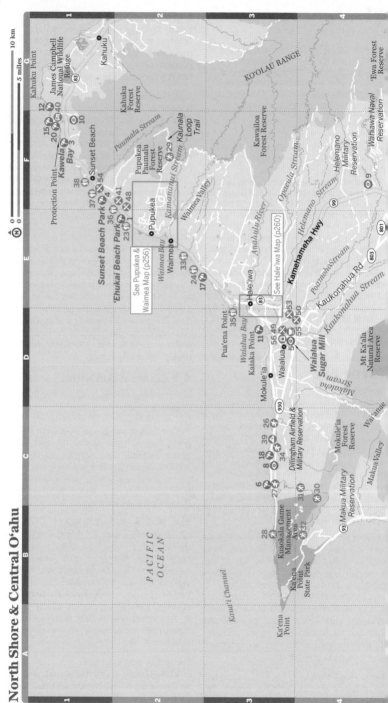

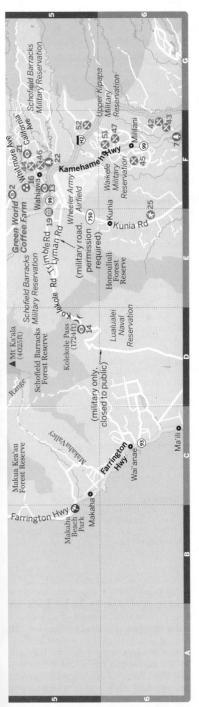

top-rated, par-72 courses abound in water views. The original Fazio Course, opened in 1972, is considered the more forgiving of the two. Opened in 1992, the Palmer Course is thought to be more challenging. There are different rates for hotel guests, residents of O'ahu and visitors. The Turtle Bay Amateur, open to all golfers, is in October.

Paradise Helicopters   SCENIC FLIGHTS
(☑808-969-7392; www.paradisecopters.com; Turtle Bay Resort, 57-091 Kamehameha Hwy; per person from $199; ☺7:30am-8pm) For a bird's-eye view of the North Shore, take a helicopter ride right from Turtle Bay Resort. This outfit has various options, including the Sunset Spectacular (30 minutes), the Valleys and Waterfall Explorer (40 minutes) and, for the whole hog, the Magnum Experience (one hour), which takes in the whole island of O'ahu.

Guidepost   OUTDOORS
(☑808-293-6020; www.turtlebayresort.com/about/guidepost; Turtle Bay Resort, 57-091 Kamehameha Hwy; ☺7am-7pm; ⊕) Swimming and snorkeling not exciting enough for you? Guidepost, the Turtle Bay Experience Center in the lobby of the resort, can organize everything from horseback rides to surfing lessons to Segway rentals, plus kayaking, fishing and helicopter tours. Contact them before you arrive, or have a chat with the friendly staff on site.

🛏 Sleeping & Eating

Besides the resort hotel, Turtle Bay has a number of private condos and vacation rentals around the grounds. Rates vary according to season and the amenities provided; many places have weekly and monthly discounts. Check out Estates at Turtle Bay (www.turtlebay-rentals.com) and Turtle Bay Condos (www.turtlebaycondos.com).

Excellent dining and drinking options are available at Turtle Bay Resort.

Turtle Bay Resort   RESORT $$$
(☑808-293-6000; www.turtlebayresort.com; 57-091 Kamehameha Hwy; r from $250, cottages/villas from $650/1050; ⓟ❄🛜🏊) Situated on a dramatic point, Turtle Bay Resort boasts impressive 800-acre surrounds. Each of the hotel-guest lodgings has an ocean view; deluxe rooms come with private lanai. Ocean villas have high ceilings, deep soaking tubs and a villa-guest-only private pool, in addition to sharing the resort's many other amenities. There are also beach cottages. Check for discounts online.

North Shore & Central O'ahu

★ **Roy's Beach House** FUSION $$
(☎808-293-7697; www.turtlebayresort.com; Turtle Bay Resort, 57-091 Kamehameha Hwy; lunch mains from $15; ⊙11am-10pm) On Bayview Beach, Roy Yamaguchi's Beach House is a casual yet classy place for resort guests, residents and visitors. The open-air restaurant is hard to beat and offers up fusion cuisine at lunch and dinner, bites in between (3pm to 5pm), and a takeout counter 11am to 4:30pm. Try the island-style ahi (yellowfin tuna) *poke* bowl.

Pa'akai SEAFOOD $$$
(☎808-293-6000; www.turtlebayresort.com; Turtle Bay Resort, 57-091 Kamehameha Hwy; mains from $30; ⊙5:30-10pm Tue-Sat; P) Turtle Bay Resort's top seafood restaurant, with a name that means 'sea salt', Pa'akai offers the best in local fish, prawns, lobster and scallops, as well as steak and lamb from the land. Try the pan-seared *kampachi* for a can't-miss dish. There's a full bar with signature cocktails and nightly live entertainment.

Casual resort wear is fine; reservations recommended.

Lei Lei's Bar & Grill
HAWAIIAN $$$

(☑ 808-293-2662; www.turtlebayresort.com; Turtle Bay Resort, 57-091 Kamehameha Hwy; dinner mains from $30; ⊙7am-10pm; ℗) Turtle Bay Resort's laid-back open-air bar and grill serves breakfast, lunch and dinner with impressive menus and an extensive wine list. For dinner, seafood, such as the grilled ahi steak ($36), may be a specialty, but it's hard to go past Lei Lei's signature prime rib (from $40). Reservations recommended for dinner.

🍷 Drinking & Nightlife

★ Surfer, the Bar
BAR

(☑ 808-293-6000; www.turtlebayresort.com; Turtle Bay Resort, 57-091 Kamehameha Hwy; pupu from $10; ⊙7pm-late Wed-Sat) Big-name North Shore musicians occasionally play live at the resort's Surfer, the Bar, where the stage is set for anything from karaoke to open-mike nights to surf-film screenings. Plenty of tasty *pupu* (snacks) and bar-food options. Try any of the '7 Mile Miracle Tropical Drinks' named after North Shore surf spots, or a variety of local Kona Brewing Co beers.

The Point Sunset & Pool Bar
HAWAIIAN

(☑808-293-6000; www.turtlebayresort.com; Turtle Bay Resort, 57-091 Kamehameha Hwy; ⊙cocktails 10am-10pm, food 11am-7pm) The Point is Turtle Bay Resort's drinks and dining bar at its stunning surf-side pool. Sunsets are gorgeous here looking west over Turtle Bay, often with surfers out catching their last rides of the afternoon. Signature and classic cocktails are the way to go. Nightly entertainment.

Sunset Beach to Hale'iwa

Revered for monster winter waves and some of the best surf breaks on the planet, the stretch of coastline from Sunset Beach to Hale'iwa is known as the 'Seven-Mile Miracle' and is a gathering point for the world's best surfers, ardent fans and enthusiastic wannabes.

Waimea Bay is so stunning that it's hard not to catch your breath when you round the highway curve and see it. Captain Cook's men, the first Westerners to sail into Waimea Bay, had the same reaction when they stopped by on the HMS *Resolution* in 1779 after Cook's death at Kealakekua Bay on the Big Island. Back then the valley was heavily settled, the lowlands terraced in taro, the valley walls dotted with house sites and the ridges topped with heiau (ancient stone temples). In those days the Waimea River emptied into the bay and served as a passage for canoes traveling to upstream villages.

🏖 Beaches

There's limited to no parking. For every beach parking lot you see, there are at least four more pedestrian-access paths tucked back into residential areas. Going by bicycle is the best way to explore them all.

★ Sunset Beach Park
BEACH

(59-104 Kamehameha Hwy) Like many beaches on the North Shore, Sunset Beach has a split personality. In winter big swells arrive, along with pro wave riders and the posse of followers these rock stars of the sea attract. The second leg of the Triple Crown of Surfing takes place here in late November and early December. In summer Sunset is a prime place to log beach time. Waves calm down, and there's a swimming channel before the reef and trees for shade.

In winter the tremendous surf activity causes the slope of the beach to become increasingly steep as the season goes on. Though the water looks more inviting in summer, be aware there are still some nasty currents about.

★ 'Ehukai Beach Park
BEACH

(59-337 Ke Nui Rd) The break off the park is known as Banzai Pipeline, Pipeline or just Pipe; it's probably the most famous surf site in the islands. For expert board riders who know what they're doing (no, a day of lessons at Waikiki Beach doesn't count), this could be surfing's ne plus ultra. The waves break only a few yards offshore, so spectators are front row and center. In the summer months everything calms down and there's even some decent snorkeling off this beach.

★ Waimea Bay Beach Park
BEACH

(61-031 Kamehameha Hwy) It may be a beauty, but it's certainly a moody one. Waimea Bay changes dramatically with the seasons: it can be tranquil and flat as a lake in summer, then savage in winter, with the island's meanest rip currents. Typically, the only time it's calm enough for swimming and snorkeling is from June to September, and maybe October. Winter water activities at this beach are *not* for novices – the waves at Waimea can get epically huge.

The beach plays host to the annual Eddie Aikau memorial surf competition between December and February. Eddie Aikau was a legendary waterman and Waimea lifeguard who died trying to save compatriots from a double-hull outrigger-canoe accident en route from Hawaii to Tahiti.

This is the North Shore's most popular beach, so parking is often tight. On weekends Waimea Valley across the street offers parking for $5. Don't park along the highway; police are notorious for towing away dozens of cars at once. Note, too, that jumping off the big rock formation at the southern end of the cove is technically forbidden. Facilities include showers, restrooms and picnic tables; there's a lifeguard on duty daily.

Laniakea Beach BEACH
(www.malamanahonu.org; Kamehameha Hwy) Between the highway's 3- and 4-mile markers, this narrow spit of sand is visited by basking *honu* (green sea turtles), who migrate here from French Frigate Shoals in the remote Northwestern Hawaiian Islands. Stay back at least 20ft from these endangered sea creatures, which are very sensitive to noise and human disturbance. Volunteers are on hand to answer questions. Most people park alongside the highway opposite the beach, but vehicle break-ins and theft are a risk.

◎ Sights & Activities

Waimea Valley GARDENS
(☏808-638-7766; www.waimeavalley.net; 59-864 Kamehameha Hwy; adult/child 4-12yr $18/12; ⊙9am-5pm; ℗⛹) ✐ Craving land instead of sea? This 1800-acre Hawaiian cultural and nature park, just inland from Waimea Bay,

---

TRIPLE CROWN OF SURFING

During the North Shore's **Triple Crown of Surfing** (www.vanstriplecrownofsurfing.com; ⊙Nov & Dec) championships, touring pros compete for pride – and megabucks in prizes. The kickoff is the Hawaiian Pro at Hale'iwa Ali'i Beach Park in mid-November. The competition's second challenge, the Vans World Cup of Surfing (late November to early December), rides at Sunset Beach. The final leg, the Billabong Pipe Masters, happens in early to mid-December at Pipeline. The Vans Pro, held at Sunset Beach in early November, is the official qualifying event for the Vans Triple Crown of Surfing.

---

is a sanctuary of tropical tranquility. Amid the jungle-like foliage you'll find up to 5000 native and exotic plant species. It's a 1.5-mile return walk up to Waimea Falls, where you can go swimming; there's a lifeguard in attendance. Wander the numerous paths alongside Kamananui Stream, checking out the Hawaiian cultural attractions. The valley is home to numerous ancient sites.

Equally interesting are the replicas of ancient Hawaiian dwellings and a restored heiau (temple) dedicated to Lono, the traditional god of fertility and agriculture. Golf-cart shuttles are available to Waimea Falls for $14/10 return/one way.

Pu'u o Mahuka Heiau State Historic Site TEMPLE
(www.hawaiistateparks.org; ⊙sunrise-sunset; ℗) ✐FREE A cinematic coastal panorama and a stroll around the grounds of O'ahu's largest ancient temple reward those who venture up to this national historic landmark, perched on a bluff above Waimea Bay. It's a dramatically windswept and lonely site. Though the ruined walls leave a lot to be imagined, it's worth the drive for the commanding views, especially at sunset.

Pu'u o Mahuka means 'Hill of Escape' – but this was a *luakini* heiau (temple dedicated to the war god Ku), where human sacrifices took place. Likely dating from the 17th century, the temple's stacked-stone construction is attributed to the *menehune* (the 'little people' who, according to legend, built many of Hawaii's fishponds, heiau and other stonework), who are said to have completed their work in just one night.

To get here, turn *mauka* (inland) onto Pupukea Rd by the Foodland supermarket; the monument turnoff is about half a mile uphill, from where it's another half mile of rough going to the heiau.

Sunset Point SURFING
One of O'ahu's best-known surf breaks, Sunset Point is good for intermediate to expert surfers, depending on the conditions. Because of its fame and dependability, it can get pretty crowded. The Kamehameha Hwy goes right past gorgeous Sunset Beach, where you can park and paddle out into the deep channel.

Velzyland SURFING
West of the University of Hawai'i Agricultural Station, Velzyland is a neighborhood fave, with a shore break at one end and a usually safe spot for swimming on the other. Always be cautious, year-round, when swimming on

the North Shore. Access the tiny parking lot off Waiale'e Beach Park Rd.

Banzai Pipeline   SURFING

Banzai Pipeline, aka Pipeline, aka Pipe – call it whatever you want, this place is known the world over as one of the biggest, heaviest and closest-to-perfect barrels in all of wave riding. When the strong westerly swells kick up in winter, the waves can reach mammoth proportions before breaking on the shallow reef below.

Ke Ala Pupukea Bike Path   CYCLING

A partly shaded bike path provides an excellent link between the beaches along part of the North Shore. Pie-in-the-sky plans are to expand it from Turtle Bay to Waialua. In the meantime, the trail runs roughly 3.5 miles on the *makai* (seaward) side of the Kamehameha Hwy, from O'opuola St in Sunset Beach to the northern end of Waimea Bay.

Backyards   SURFING

A smokin' surf break off Sunset Point, at the northern end of the beach near O'opuola St; under the right conditions Backyards draws top windsurfers. Note that there's a shallow reef and strong currents to contend with.

Pupukea   SURFING

One for experts only, Pupukea, just northeast of 'Ehukai Beach Park, is considered one of the best high-performance rights on the island. It's a popular spot, with good reason, and often crowded.

Leftovers, Rightovers & Alligator Rock   SURFING

These three breaks are seldom crowded and are good for intermediate to expert surfers. They are about 3.5 miles northeast of Hale'iwa and visible from the Kamehameha Hwy. Leftovers is a left-breaking wave over a shallow reef. Next up is Rightovers, which breaks right into a shallow channel. On the far side of the channel, Alligator Rock is a right-breaking wave.

Chun's Reef   SURFING

Chun's is about 3 miles from Hale'iwa up the Kamehameha Hwy, at the second opening where you can see beach and waves. It's good for beginners right through to experts, depending on the conditions, and can get pretty crowded. It's named after John Chun, who lived in a beach house in front of the surf break in the 1970s.

Laniakea   SURFING

The first beach you see on your left when heading up the Kamehameha Hwy from

TED'S

Quintessential North Shore **Ted's Bakery** (☑808-638-8207; www.tedsbakery. com; 59-024 Kamehameha Hwy; meals from $7; ☺7am-8pm; 🖪) is where surfers load up for breakfast, laid-back locals grab a snack, suntanned vacationers dig into plate lunches – and everybody goes for dessert. The chocolate-*haupia* (coconut pudding) cream pie is renowned across the island. Full-meal favorites include the meat-filled fried rice with eggs at breakfast and melt-in-your-mouth, lightly panfried garlic shrimp any other time.

Hale'iwa, Laniakea can get really busy with tourists who come to see the turtles. It can get busy offshore, too, but this is a spot for advanced and expert surfers, depending on the conditions. This is one of the North Shore's only true point breaks.

🛏 Sleeping & Eating

There are no hotels or motels along here, but O'ahu Family Rentals (www.oahufamily rentals.com) has a few options. For restaurant or cafe dining, head to Turtle Bay Resort or Hale'iwa; for food trucks, stop off in Pupukea.

Banzai Bowls   HEALTH FOOD $

(☑808-744-2849; www.banzaibowls.com; 59-186 Kamehameha Hwy; bowls from $8; ☺7am-8pm Mon-Fri, 8am-8pm Sat, 8am-7pm Sun) Healthy and super-delicious acai bowls, pitaya bowls and smoothies, served up just across from Sunset Beach beside the gas station. Buy your refreshing bowl, then head over and eat on the beach. Banzai Bowls has been successful in California and this was its first location in Hawaii.

North Shore Country Market   MARKET $

(www.northshorecountrymarket.ngo; Sunset Elementary School, 59 Kamehameha Hwy; ☺8am-1pm Sat) Small farmers market with fruit, vegetables, flowers, fresh-baked goods and handicrafts. Meet the locals at this North Shore favorite on Saturday mornings.

Pupukea

POP 4500

A largely residential area, Pupukea climbs from the coast further into the hills than you may think possible. There are a few services,

Pupukea & Waimea

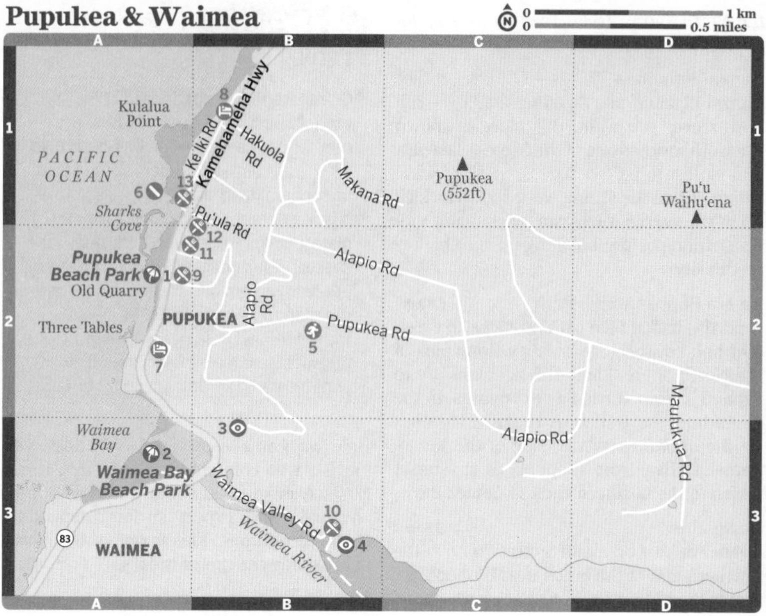

N 0 ———————— 1 km
0 ———————— 0.5 miles

Map with labels:

Kulalua Point

PACIFIC OCEAN

Sharks Cove

Pupukea Beach Park

Old Quarry

Three Tables

PUPUKEA

Waimea Bay

Waimea Bay Beach Park

83

WAIMEA

Ke iki Rd

Kamehameha Hwy

Hakuola Rd

Makana Rd

Pupukea (552ft)

Pu'u Waihu'ena

Pu'ula Rd

Alapio Rd

Alapio Rd

Pupukea Rd

Maulukua Rd

Alapio Rd

Waimea Valley Rd

Waimea River

---

including a big Foodland grocery store, along the highway. Pupukea Beach Park is popular, and higher up there are hiking opportunities and an ancient Hawaiian site.

🏖 Beaches

★ Pupukea Beach Park   BEACH
(59-727 Kamehameha Hwy) With deep-blue waters, a varied coastline and a mix of lava and white sand, Pupukea, meaning 'White Shell,' is a scenic stretch. The beach encompasses three areas: Sharks Cove to the north, Old Quarry in the center and Three Tables to the south. The waters off Pupukea Beach are protected as a marine-life conservation district.

The reef formation at **Sharks Cove** provides an excellent habitat for marine life, including sea turtles, and is good for snorkeling. When seas are calm, this is a great area for water exploring; make sure you always wear shoes to protect your feet from sharp coral. Despite the cove's name, the white-tipped reef sharks aren't usually a problem; just keep your distance and don't provoke them.

At low tide the rock features at **Old Quarry** appear as if they were cut by human hands, but rest assured that they are natural. Coastal tide pools are interesting microhabitats that are best explored at low tide during calm summer seas. Be careful, especially if you have kids in tow, because

the rocks are razor sharp. There are showers and restrooms in front of Old Quarry.

The flat ledges rising above the water give **Three Tables** its name. In summer (only) the area is good for snorkeling and diving. The best coral and fish, as well as some small caves, lava tubes and arches, are in deeper water further out. Access to Three Tables is just beyond Old Quarry, where there are a few unmarked parking spots.

🏃 Activities

Sharks Cove   DIVING
A popular cavern dive is accessed from Sharks Cove at Pupukea Beach Park. Some caves are very deep and labyrinthine, and several people have drowned, so divers should only venture into them with a local expert. Further west, outside Three Tables, the depth drops to 45ft; the many lava tubes and rock formations are ideal for scuba diving.

Kaunala Loop Trail   HIKING
(http://hawaiitrails.ehawaii.gov; ☉ sunrise-sunset Sat & Sun) This 5-mile loop hike (two to three hours) mixes an easy forest-valley walk with a moderate ridge climb for sweeping views of Waimea Bay. After spying the beauty of the bay from viewpoints atop this trail, it's easy to see why Hawaiian royalty considered it sacred. The trail is open to the public only on weekends and state and national

Pupukea & Waimea

holidays. To get here, travel 2.5 miles up Pupukea Rd from the Foodland supermarket. Park roadside before the Boy Scout Camp and follow the signage to the trailhead.

Happy Trails Hawaii HORSEBACK RIDING
(☑808-638-7433; www.happytrailshawaii.com; 59-231 Pupukea Rd; 1½/2hr ride $99/119; ⊙8am-5pm) Take to the mountainsides on horseback, over open pasture and near orchards, to reach panoramic views. Beginners are welcome; all rides start with orientation and instruction. Riders can sample tropical fruits such as strawberry guava, *liliko'i* (passion fruit), banana, star fruit, mangoes and mountain apples. Book online. At the Foodland corner, turn up Pupukea Rd for 1 mile.

🛏 Sleeping

BackPackers Hawaii HOSTEL $
(☑808-638-7838; www.backpackershawaii.com; 59-788 Kamehameha Hwy; dm $30, d $75, cabins per room from $85; ℗�r�) The only real budget option on the North Shore. If you care more about money and location than about the odd bit of peeling paint or modest-to-the-point-of-ramshackle furnishings, this backpacker-style village is for you. Hostel rooms are mostly located in the two main buildings. You don't have to do much more than cross the street to get to the beach.

★**Ke Iki Beach Bungalows** APARTMENT $$
(☑808-638-8229; www.keikibeach.com; 59-579 Ke Iki Rd; 1/2-bedroom apt from $205/230; ℗✳🕸) Smartly updated tropical decor adds to the retreat feel of this bungalow community on the white-sand beach just north of Pupukea Beach Park. Grassy lawns and a tropical garden complete the picture. Kick back on the shared beachfront lanai, nap in a hammock beneath the palm trees or head for a swim.

🍴 Eating

There are a lot of food-truck options, including North Shore Shrimp Truck, North Shore Tacos and Jerry's Pizza. As they all have wheels, there's a certain fluidity here. If you're into self-catering, there's a Foodland.

North Shore Shrimp Truck SEAFOOD $
(☑808-638-0390; 59-063 Pahoe Rd; meals from $12; ⊙11am-9:30pm) Owned and operated by a legendary local surfer, the North Shore Shrimp Truck is becoming just as legendary. You can get shrimp in three styles – garlic butter, lemon butter or spicy – each served with sushi rice and Pupukea green salad.

Sandy's Sandwiches SANDWICHES $
(www.sandyssandwiches.blogspot.com; 59-662 Kamehameha Hwy; sandwiches from $10; ⊙10am-5pm) This tiny green-and-blue trailer is incredibly popular and serves fresh sandwiches and a good selection of salads using organic and local products whenever possible. The chicken-pesto and turkey-and-brie sandwiches (each $10) are favorites. Look for the little trailer with Organic Sandwiches & Salads written on it. It's hard to miss.

Pupukea Grill HAWAIIAN $
(☑808-779-7943; www.pupukeagrill.com; 59-680 Kamehameha Hwy; meals from $9; ⊙11am-5pm Tue-Sun) A favorite lunch spot for pro surfers, locals and visitors, this bright-blue truck is covered in surf gear and features an intriguing menu. It's a kind of Japanese, Mexican and Hawaiian fusion that tends to keep everybody happy. Items such as acai bowls, grilled-fish tacos, panini sandwiches and *poke* bowls aren't typical food-truck fare.

Foodland SUPERMARKET $
(www.foodland.com; 59-720 Kamehameha Hwy; ⊙6am-11pm; ℗) Across from Pupukea Beach Park, you can pick up everything you need for a beach picnic from the deli or get groceries. This is the only supermarket along the North Shore east of Hale'iwa, so if you need anything, stock up here.

ⓘ Getting There & Away

Pupukea is about halfway between Hale'iwa and Turtle Bay on the Kamehameha Hwy. Get there on TheBus 55 from Ala Moana Center or Hale'iwa.

JL JAHN / SHUTTERSTOCK ©

1. Dragon fruit 2. Sunset Beach Park (p253) 3. Waimea Valley (p254) 4. Harbor at Hale'iwa (p260)

Lazy Days in North Shore & Central O'ahu

Hit the other side of O'ahu. From Hale'iwa east you've got the Seven-Mile Miracle with captivating beaches; head west from the North Shore's main town and things peter out to almost total seclusion at Ka'ena Point. Central O'ahu is a different look altogether, with military bases, plantations and suburbia.

The Seven-Mile Miracle

The 7-mile stretch from Hale'iwa to Sunset Beach – talk about a great place to kick back and enjoy yourself! Sun, sand... and, if it's summer, relaxed swimming on gorgeous beaches; if it's winter, watch the world's top surfers ride massive waves. Ted's Bakery (p255) offers iconic eats, while the food trucks in Pupukea (p257) will have you back for more.

Activities

If you've got time after all the beach relaxation, swimming and surfing, head west to Dillingham Airfield (p267) for skydiving, gliding or trike flights. Good hiking, horseback riding and uncrowded beaches out here, too. There's fishing, sailing, stand-up paddleboarding, kayaking and even shark cages out of Hale'iwa (p260). And don't forget golf and helicopter rides at Turtle Bay (p249).

Browsing & Shopping

Hale'iwa's main street (p262) will keep you busy for hours with surf shops, boutiques, art, souvenirs and more, along with a top selection of cafes and small restaurants. A tad west, Waialua's old sugar mill (p266) has been transformed into a fun collection of shops, while if you're a big-time shopper you'll need to head to Waikele Premium Outlets (p276), sheer heaven for brand hunters.

Hale'iwa

POP 4250

Originally a plantation-era supply town in the 1900s, Hale'iwa today is the de facto Surf City of the North Shore. It's all about the waves here and everyone knows it.

Beaches

Hale'iwa Beach Park BEACH

(62-449 Kamehameha Hwy) On the northern side of the harbor, this park is protected by a shallow shoal and breakwater, so it's usually a good choice for swimming. There's little wave action, except for the occasional north swells that ripple into the bay. The 13-acre park has basketball and volleyball courts, an exercise area, a softball field and a large parking lot.

Hale'iwa Ali'i Beach Park BEACH

(66-167 Hale'iwa Rd) This is home to some of the best surf on the North Shore, and waves can be huge. It's a popular spot for surf contests. In mid-November the Triple Crown of Surfing gets underway on this break. The 20-acre beach park has restrooms, showers, a wide grassy area with picnic tables, and lifeguards.

Kaiaka Bay Beach Park BEACH

(66-449 Hale'iwa Rd) Beachside trees a mile or so west of town offer shade, and turtles sometimes show up, but the swimming is better at the other local beaches. There are plenty of picnic areas and several designated campsites at the northern end of the peninsula in this spacious (53 acre) beach park. You'll need a permit to camp here.

Sights & Activities

If you're a beginner board rider, the North Shore has a few tame breaks such as Pua'ena Point (p262), just north of Hale'iwa Beach Park, and Chun's Reef (p255), about 3 miles northeast of town. Even if you've caught a few waves in Waikiki, it's smart to take a lesson with one of the many freelancing surfers to get an introduction to local underwater hazards. Ask around the beach, where surf-school vans rent gear and offer same-day instruction, or book ahead for surfing or SUP lessons. Expect to pay from $75 to $100 for two-hour group lessons, $100 to $180 for a private lesson and $30 to $45 to rent a board for the day ($60 with paddle).

Lili'uokalani Protestant Church CHURCH

(www.liliuokalanichurch.org; 66-090 Kamehameha Hwy) Hale'iwa's historic church, first built in 1832, takes its name from Queen Lili'uokala-ni, who spent summers on the shores of the Anahulu River and attended services here. The current building was built of wood in 1890, then rebuilt with cement in 1961. As late as the 1940s, services were held entirely in Hawaiian. Visitors are welcome.

North Shore Shark Adventures ADVENTURE SPORT

(☑808-228-5900; www.sharktourshawaii.com; Hale'iwa Small Boat Harbor; 2hr tour adult/child $120/60) Allow yourself to be submerged in a cage surrounded by sharks about 3 miles offshore from Hale'iwa. Shark sightings guaranteed. Return transportation from Waikiki is available for $55 plus tax per seat. Check out the website and book online for discounts.

Surf 'n' Sea WATER SPORT

(☑808-637-9887; www.surfnsea.net; 62-595 Kamehameha Hwy; ⊙9am-7pm) The big daddy of all surf shops, this colorful wooden building rents any kind of water gear you can think of: surfboards, paddleboard setups, wetsuits, car racks, snorkel sets, kayaks, beach umbrellas

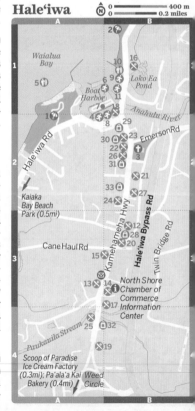

Hale'iwa

and chairs; it offers lessons and tours, too. Diving options include introductory dives and PADI certification courses from Open Water Diver through to Divemaster.

Rainbow Watersports
WATER SPORTS
(☑808-372-9304; www.rainbowwatersports.com; classes from $79; ⊙by reservation only) This local and original paddleboard company offers calm-water classes, glow-paddle twilight tours, SUP yoga, and 3½-hour coastal paddle tours (from $189). Board and kayak rentals available, too. Keep your eyes open for sea turtles when paddling up the Anahulu River. Its rainbow-colored van sits on the Kamehameha Hwy before Haleʻiwa Beach Park. This outfit wrote *The Stand-up Paddle Book*.

Chupu Sports Fishing
FISHING
(☑808-637-3474; www.chupu.com; Haleʻiwa Small Boat Harbor; half/full day from $700/950) The waters off the North Shore are legendary, as is the fishing. There's the possibility of catching *a'u* (Pacific blue marlin), *naiaragi* (striped marlin), *hebi* (shortbill marlin), *ono* (wahoo), mahimahi (dolphin fish), ahi (yellowfin tuna), *ahi po'onui* (big-eye tuna) and *aku* (skipjack tuna). The outfit has four boats and pricing is by the boat, not per person.

Haleʻiwa Small Boat Harbor
HARBOR
Haleʻiwa Small Boat Harbor sits at the western side of the mouth of the Anahulu River. Haleʻiwa Aliʻi Beach Park is immediately to its west. A number of tourist boats operate out of the harbor.

Watercraft Connection
WATER SPORTS
(☑808-637-8006; www.jetskishawaii.com; Haleʻiwa Small Boat Harbor; Jet Ski per 45min $100, kayak per 2hr $40; ⊙11am-5pm) Kayaks and Jet Skis are first-come, first-served; rent from the little booth at the harbor.

Surfing

There are surf schools all along the 'Seven-Mile Miracle.' Hans Hedemann Surf School (p249) is based at Turtle Bay Resort.

North Shore Surf Girls
SURFING
(☑808-637-2977; www.northshoresurfgirls.com; ⊙by reservation only) At this all-female-instructors surf school they teach girls, boys, women, men and families. The instructors include former pro surfers, lifeguards and *Bay Watch* stunt doubles; some even featured in the surf movie *Blue Crush*. Advanced lessons are available for more experienced surfers. They're especially great at teaching kids and other women to surf and stand-up paddle. Seven-day intensive learn-to-surf camps are also possible. Book online.

Sunset Surratt Surf Academy
SURFING
(☑808-783-8657; www.surfnorthshore.com) 'Uncle Bryan,' born and raised on the North Shore, has been coaching pro surfers for decades. He and his staff teach all levels from beginner to advanced, and stand-up paddlers. Rentals offered. His well-signed truck sits on the Kamehameha Hwy just before Haleʻiwa Beach Park – or could be elsewhere, depending on the waves. Book online.

Haleʻiwa

SURF MOVIES 101

The North Shore's epic waves have starred, or at least had cameos, in some of the best surf movies ever made.

Soul Surfer (2011) A girl's journey back to competition surfing after a shark attack.

Riding Giants (2004) This documentary surveys the history and lore of surfing.

The Ride (2003) A hit on the head sends one wave rider back to 1911, surfing with the Duke.

Blue Crush (2002) Can love come between a surfer and the Banzai Pipeline?

North Shore (1987) A big-wave wannabe braves a summer on the North Shore.

Five Summer Stories (1972) Eddie Aikau costars as a legendary local surfer – himself.

Endless Summer (1966) The original, existential, life-in-search-of-the-wave epic.

Hale'iwa   SURFING

Just off Hale'iwa Ali'i Beach Park and west of the boat harbor, this break is easily accessible to one and all. On small-wave days it's a good spot to learn to surf; on big days it turns into an epic wave fit only for experts and pros. It can get busy on weekends, but there's usually plenty of room.

Hosts the Hawaiian Pro, the first leg of the Triple Crown of Surfing, in mid-November.

Pua'ena Point   SURFING

A good spot to learn to surf – so much so that many surf schools head here. It's convenient to Hale'iwa and the waves can be much smaller during big swells than at other spots on the North Shore. It can get crowded.

Tours

Surf Bus   BUS

(808-226-7299; www.northshoresurfbus.com; adult/child from $124/98; tours 8am-4:30pm) Although it's totally easy to do these things on your own, you could let the Surf Bus do the driving on a full day of North Shore sightseeing or town shopping and add a variety of options such as snorkeling, hiking, bodyboarding, bike riding or SUP lessons.

North Shore Ecotours   HIKING

(877-521-4453; www.northshoreecotours.com; hiking tour adult/child from $95/75, driving tour

$95/75) Native Hawaiian guides lead easy to difficult hiking adventures on a rotating day-to-day basis. Driving adventures in a Swiss military off-road vehicle called a Pinzgauer are also on offer. Check it all out and make bookings direct on the website. Tours depart from North Shore Marketplace in Hale'iwa.

North Shore Catamaran   CRUISE

(808-351-9371; www.sailingcat.com; Hale'iwa Small Boat Harbor; adult/under 12yr from $60/45) Offers a variety of trips, including sunset cruises, whale-watching, turtle-watching and snorkeling, aboard a well-equipped catamaran sailboat. See the North Shore from the sea. Book online.

Historic Hale'iwa Tour   WALKING

(808-637-4558; www.gonorthshore.org; 66-434 Kamehameha Hwy; tours $10; by reservation) The Chamber of Commerce offers various historical tours. Reserve in advance for 90-minute walking tours with a local docent that take in the historic buildings of town. The visitor center sells illustrated tour maps ($2) that describe all the old structures and can be followed at your own pace.

Festivals & Events

Hale'iwa Arts Festival   ART

(www.haleiwaartsfestival.org; Jul) More than 100 artists gather at Hale'iwa one weekend to show and sell their wares. There's painting, photography, printmaking, ceramics, woodwork, jewelry, leatherwork, sculpture, glass and other art forms. Also music, food, cultural tours and hands-on demonstrations.

Sleeping

Hale'iwa has no hotels, but there are several vacation rentals in the area. As well as the standard websites, Team Real Estate (www.teamrealestate.com) has a number of options. The town is only a one-hour drive from Waikiki.

Kaiaka Bay Beach Park   CAMPGROUND $

(https://camping.honolulu.gov; 66-449 Hale'iwa Rd; 5-night campsite permit $52; 8am Fri-8am Wed; P) Advance permits required for the seven tent sites at Hale'iwa's only campground. The park has restrooms, outdoor showers and picnic tables. Good for surfing and fishing in season, but not such a great swimming spot.

Eating

There are plenty of good places to eat in Hale'iwa; think of it as the North Shore's dining capital. There are also plenty of food trucks around Hale'iwa town: expect to pay

68 to $14 for a plate; hours vary, but they're generally open 10am to 6pm. A number of restaurants with bars stay open late on Friday and Saturday nights, but if you're after a big night out, stick to Waikiki.

⭐ Waialua Bakery & Juice Bar
BAKERY $

📞 808-341-2838; www.waialuabakery.com; 66-200 Kamehameha Hwy; items from $1; ⏱ 10am-5pm Mon-Sat; 🖋️) This place is a real favorite. Many of the ingredients, such as bananas, papayas, mangoes, avocados, passion fruit, oranges, kale and mint, are grown at the owners' farm in Waialua. Cookies, treats, and breads for the piled-high sandwiches are all made from scratch. The acai bowls are seriously addictive. Choose to eat here at the convivial seating or take away.

⭐ Beet Box Cafe
HEALTH FOOD $

📞 808-637-3000; www.thebeetboxcafe.com; 66-443 Kamehameha Hwy; mains from $7; ⏱ 7am-4pm; 🖋️) 🌿 At the back of the town's karmically cool health-food store hides a popular vegetarian-friendly deli. Breakfast is served all day; lunch is hot plates, sandwiches or salads; and there's a great selection of smoothies, fresh juices and acai bowls.

Farm to Barn Cafe & Juicery
AMERICAN $

📞 808-354-5903; www.farmtobarncafe.com; 66-320 Kamehameha Hwy; bowls from $8.50; ⏱ 9am-3pm Sun-Thu, 9am-3pm & 5-8:30pm Fri & Sat) Amid a wide-open field of sunflowers, this unique venue's cheery, bright-red facade appears just like a farm from grandma's era – homey, welcoming and a bit old-fashioned. The farm stand is the North Shore's go-to place for premium locally grown produce, and it's a watering hole where locals and visitors come together to eat, shop and talk story.

Kono's Northshore
HAWAIIAN $

📞 808-637-9211; www.konosnorthshore.com; North Shore Marketplace, 66-250 Kamehameha Hwy; mains from $6; ⏱ 7am-2:30pm) If you like pork, this is as good as it gets – legendary *kalua* (pit-oven) pork cooked daily for over 12 hours. The triple crown sandwich ($15) features three kinds of pork, but the Hawaiian bowl ($10.75) with *kalua* pig, rice and guava barbecue sauce tops even that. Look for the logo of a pig on a surfboard.

Rajanee Thai Haleiwa
THAI $

📞 808-784-0023; www.facebook.com/rajaneethaihaleiwa; 66-111 Kamehameha Hwy, No 1001; mains from $12; ⏱ 12:30-9pm) Excellent Thai options here at the northern end of the main street range from soups, noodles and curries

to fried rice. It serves good-size dishes and there's a takeout window. Rajanee Thai has a branch (p271) in Mililani.

Giovanni's Shrimp Truck
SEAFOOD $

📞 808-293-1839; www.giovannisshrimptruck.com; 66-472 Kamehameha Hwy; shrimp meals $14; ⏱ 10:30am-5pm) Giovanni's can fairly claim to be the original shrimp truck, as it began plying area beaches with its sautéed garlic shrimp plates in 1993. It set up at a permanent spot in Hale'iwa in 1997. There are three shrimp options: the legendary garlicky shrimp scampi, hot and spicy shrimp and lemon-butter shrimp. This is where it's at!

Surf N Salsa
MEXICAN $

📞 808-692-2471; 66521 Kamehameha Hwy; tacos from $3.50; ⏱ 11:30am-7:30pm) Food-truck Mexican in Hale'iwa that gets a big thumbs-up from locals. It's good for dinner as it stays open later than most other food trucks, has parking and offers seating under umbrellas. The surf-and-turf burrito with shrimp and steak ($12) is a winner. You won't go hungry!

Killer Tacos
MEXICAN $

📞 808-637-4573; www.killertacos.com; 66-560 Kamehameha Hwy; tacos from $2.50; ⏱ 10am-8pm) Offering not only killer tacos but killer burritos. Try the longboard burrito ($9.50) with coconut rice and chicken, beef or *kalua* pig, plus all the other burrito goodies. Great value, tasty and filling. The fish burrito using Alaskan cod is also popular, and there's an array of other Mexican options. Friendly service.

Coffee Gallery
CAFE $

📞 808-637-5355; www.roastmaster.com; North Shore Marketplace, 66-250 Kamehameha Hwy; snacks & drinks from $2; ⏱ 6:30am-8pm; 🖥️) Coffee lovers rejoice over the house-roast beans and brews here at the back of the North Shore Marketplace. Be sure to poke your nose in for some marvelous odors: besides the hand-roasted coffee from all over, there's a bakery with pastries and snacks. Art is also on display. Try the iced honey latte.

Storto's Deli & Sandwich Shoppe
SANDWICHES $

📞 808-637-6633; www.stortoshaleiwa.com; 66-215 Kamehameha Hwy; sandwiches half/whole from $7/14; ⏱ 8am-5pm) The made-to-order submarine sandwiches here are delicious, using a secret recipe for the fresh-baked bread. Sandwiches are named after North Shore surf breaks, so you'll need to decide if you want a Laniakea, a Pipeline or a Sunset and if you want an 8in half or a 16in whole sandwich. The papaya-seed dressing rocks!

MEALS ON WHEELS

Hale'iwa boasts an incredible number of **food trucks** (meals $8-14) offering everything from shrimp to Cajun to hot dogs. If you're in a rental car, drive through town with your eyes open and see what's where. They can move, which makes them tricky to show on a map. On the south side of town, between the bridge and the roundabout, there's a food-truck corner, but you'll run into them all over town.

Kua 'Aina
BURGERS $

(☑ 808-637-6067; www.kua-ainahawaii.com; 66-160 Kamehameha Hwy; burgers from $10; ⊙11am-8pm; ⊕) There's no sure way of knowing that these are, as touted, the best hamburgers on the island, but they're definitely tasty and juicy, and they come with a variety of toppings. Give the pineapple burger, the *locomoco* burger (fried egg and a hamburger patty topped with gravy) or the mahimahi sandwich a go. There are four locations: Hale'iwa, London, Tokyo and Taipei.

Matsumoto's Shave Ice
SWEETS $

(☑ 808-637-4827; www.matsumotoshaveice.com; 66-111 Kamehameha Hwy; snacks from $2.75; ⊙9am-6pm; ⊕) O'ahu's classic circle-island drive just isn't complete without stopping for shave ice at this legendary store, which has undergone a big overhaul. Some families drive from Honolulu to the North Shore with one goal in mind: to stand in line here for a cone drenched with island flavors, such as *liliko'i*, banana, mango and pineapple.

Now part of the recently developed Hale'iwa Store Lots, Matsumoto's has lost a bit of its old-world tin-roof charm.

Hale'iwa Farmers' Market
MARKET $

(FarmLovers Farmers' Markets; ☑808-388-9696; www.farmloversmarkets.com; 59-864 Kamehameha Hwy, Waimea Valley; ⊙2-6pm Thu; ☑⊕) So much more than produce; here stacks of vendors sell artisan crafts, souvenirs and organic, seasonal edibles. At the time of writing the market was being held at Waimea Valley gardens (p254), but the intention is to eventually move back to Hale'iwa.

Cafe Haleiwa
AMERICAN $

(☑ 808-637-5516; www.cafehaleiwahawaiianislands.com; 66-460 Kamehameha Hwy; mains breakfast & lunch from $6; ⊙7am-1:30pm; ⊕) Locals have been fueling up at this laidback surf-style diner since the 1980s. A daily menu of fresh preparations focuses on local ingredients and may feature mains such as lamb or mahimahi. Here even the side-dish vegetables are stars.

★Uncle Bo's Bar & Grill
HAWAIIAN $$

(☑808-797-9649; www.unclebosrestaurant.com; 66-111 Kamehameha Hwy; dinner mains from $14; ⊙10am-9pm) This outpost of Uncle Bo's roaringly successful operation on Kapahulu Ave in Honolulu is earning its own loyal supporters with a great range of *pupu*, soups and salads, meat and fish mains, and desserts *Kalua*-pig fried rice is a simple dish, but it's outstanding here. So are the cocktails Plenty of free parking out the back.

Banzai Sushi Bar
JAPANESE $$

(☑808-637-4404; www.banzaisushibarhawaii.com North Shore Marketplace, 66-246 Kamehameha Hwy; mains from $12; ⊙noon-9pm) It's all about the food and the atmosphere at Banzai Sushi Bar. It has an appealing mantra: keep it real, keep it raw. Happy hour runs 4pm to 5pm Monday to Thursday, or give Sake Sundays a go, when sake-tinis are half price all day.

Haleiwa Joe's Seafood Grill
SEAFOOD $$

(☑808-637-8005; www.haleiwajoes.com; 66-011 Kamehameha Hwy; mains lunch /dinner from $10/15; ⊙11:30am-9:30pm Sun-Thu, to midnight Fri & Sat) With a superb location overlooking Halei'wa Small Boat Harbor, Joe's is the place for romantic dinners. The inventive *pupu* include black-and-blue ahi, a local favorite: blackened ahi is served chilled with wasabi ranch dipping sauce and pickled ginger. Aloha happy hour 4:30pm to 6:30pm Monday to Friday; late-night happy hour 10pm to midnight Friday and Saturday.

Haleiwa Beach House
HAWAIIAN $$$

(☑808-637-3435; www.haleiwabeachhouse.com; 62-540 Kamehameha Hwy; dinner mains from $30; ⊙11am-11pm) Over the bridge and across from the start of the beach, Haleiwa Beach House offers beautiful views from inside and outside dining areas. The menu is surf 'n' turf, with the quick-seared ahi ($33) and the *paniolo* rib eye ($38) popular eye-openers on the dinner menu. There's an upstairs bar. .

🔒 Shopping

From trendy to quirky, you'll find most of the North Shore's boutiques and galleries in Hale'iwa. The central shopping hubs are in the North Shore Marketplace in the center of town, and the newly redeveloped Hale'iwa Store Lots at the northern end of town.

★ Ukulele Site
MUSIC

(☑808-622-8000; www.theukulelesite.com; 66-560 Kamehameha Hwy; ⊙11am-6pm Mon-Sat, to 5pm Sun) The North Shore's top ukulele store, this place also has an excellent website and ships all over the world. Head to the store to see and try out a mind-boggling array of ukuleles. As good as it gets for ukulele fanatics!

North Shore Goodies
FOOD

(☑808-200-0575; www.northshoregoodies.net; 66-520 Kamehameha Hwy; ⊙10am-5pm) This family-owned and -operated business claims to be creator of the original coconut peanut butter. It was introduced at a local farmers market and things took off from there. It now makes more than 50 products. Try the peanut butter, syrups, jams and honeys. This is home base, but its products are available all over O'ahu.

Kai Ku Hale
HOMEWARES

(☑808-636-2244; www.kaikuhale.com; Hale'iwa Town Center, 66-145 Kamehameha Hwy; ⊙10am-6:30pm) Take island style home with you from this cute store on the main drag. The shop is packed with environmentally inspired Hawaiian art, wood wall carvings, homewares, jewelry, souvenirs and gifts.

Guava Shop
CLOTHING

(☑808-637-9670; www.guavahawaii.com; 66-111 Kamehameha Hwy; ⊙10am-6pm) This chic, upscale boutique for beachy women's apparel, such as gauzy sundresses and strappy sandals, has moved down the street into Hale'iwa Store Lots. You can also shop online.

Barnfield's Raging Isle Surf
CLOTHING

(☑808-637-7797; www.facebook.com/ragingisle; North Shore Marketplace, 66-250 Kamehameha Hwy; ⊙10am-6:30pm) Packed full of beachwear, surfboards, skateboards, accessories and anything else you might need for life on the North Shore, this local hot spot should cater for all your outdoors shopping needs.

Growing Keiki
CHILDREN'S CLOTHING

(☑808-637-4544; www.thegrowingkeiki.com; 66-051 Kamehameha Hwy; ⊙10am-6pm; 🖶) This kids' shop, in a 1930s-era building, has gear for junior surfers and beachgoers, including mini aloha shirts, trunks, Hawaiian books and wooden toys.

Hale'iwa Art Gallery
ARTS & CRAFTS

(☑808-637-3368; www.haleiwaartgallery.com; North Shore Marketplace, 66-252 Kamehameha Hwy; ⊙10am-6pm) Head here to see works by Pacific island, local and regional painters, photographers, sculptors, glassblowers and mixed-media artists. It's a little like a visit to an art museum.

V Boutique
CLOTHING

(☑808-637-1597; www.vboutiquehawaii.com; 66-165 Kamehameha Hwy; ⊙10am-6pm) Recently moved from the Waialua Sugar Mill complex, V Boutique offers fashionable clothing, bikinis, bags and jewelry designed by the owner, North Shore local Vanessa Pack. Expect Hawaiian themes at this cute little boutique.

ⓘ Information

First Hawaiian Bank (☑808-637-5034; www.fhb.com; Hale'iwa Town Center, 66-135 Kamehameha Hwy; ⊙8:30am-4pm Mon-Thu, to 6pm Fri) This branch is on the main street and has a 24-hour ATM.

North Shore Chamber of Commerce Information Center (☑808-637-4558; www.gonorthshore.org; 66-434b Kamehameha Hwy; ⊙10am-5pm Mon-Fri) The information center has free brochures and guides (including a North Shore map), historical displays, souvenirs and local gifts. There's also a clean public restroom here. The 90-minute docent-guided historical walking tours ($10) need to be booked at least 48 hours ahead.

Post Office (☑808-637-1711; 66-437 Kamehameha Hwy; ⊙9am-4pm Mon-Fri, to noon Sat) Small office at the south end of town.

ⓘ Getting There & Around

From Honolulu's Ala Moana Center, TheBus 52 runs to Hale'iwa via Mililani and Wahiawa once or twice hourly; the one-way ride from Honolulu takes 1¾ hours. Every hour, TheBus 55 trundles from Hale'iwa up to Turtle Bay, then down the Windward Coast, taking over two hours to reach the Ala Moana Center. By car, Hale'iwa is only an hour away from Waikiki.

North Shore Bike Rentals (☑808-226-1972; www.northshorebikerentals.com; adult/child per day $30/20) Delivers bikes anywhere on the North Shore free. Check the website and book online or call to discuss your options. Multiday rates available; locks and helmets included.

North Shore Airport Express (☑808-352-1818; www.northshoreairportshuttle.com; 1 way from $100) Book at least two days in advance for door-to-door shuttle service from Honolulu airport to Hale'iwa town ($100), Pupukea/Sunset Beach ($115) and Turtle Bay Resort ($125).

Waialua

POP 3850

If you find the relatively slow pace of life on the North Shore just too hectic, head over to Waialua. This sugar-mill town ground to a halt in 1996, when production ended. Since then, locals have transformed the old mill into a crafty, island-born shopping complex.

Festivals & Events

Waialua Bandstand in the Park
MUSIC
(www.waialuabandstand.com; 67-104 Kealohanui St; ☺4pm) The Friends of Waialua Bandstand in the Park organizes a concert in the bandstand on the first Sunday of each month. Check the website for schedules. US military bands, the Royal Hawaiian Band and local high-school bands are regulars.

✖ Eating & Drinking

There's a bit of food-truck fare, but if you're hungry, head into Hale'iwa – it's only a 10-minute drive away.

Waialua Farmers Market
MARKET $
(67-106 Kealohanui St; ☺8:30am-1pm Sat) Held at the Waialua Sugar Mill, the Waialua Farmers Market has strong support among the North Shore community. Get your fruit and veggies here, plus the *huli* chicken (Hawaiian-style grilled chicken) is superb.

Scoop of Paradise
Ice Cream Factory
ICE CREAM $
(☑808-637-3020; 66-935 Kaukonahua Rd; single scoop $4.20; ☺9am-6pm) Choose from exquisite homemade ice cream (in more than 50 flavors!), coffees, cakes and smoothies in the blue warehouse next to Pa'ala'a Kai Bakery. After careful research, we recommend the chocolate macadamia-nut ice cream. There's a shop in Hale'iwa, but this is the factory.

WORTH A TRIP

FROM SUGAR TO SHOPS

Waialua Sugar Mill (67-106 Kealohanui St; ☺9am-5pm Mon-Sat, 10am-5pm Sun) was the heart of the town for over a century until it closed in 1996, and has been redeveloped to house a number of shops and businesses. Waialua was home to one of the largest sugar plantations in Hawaii. Thousands of people from China, Japan, Korea, Portugal and the Philippines came to work and live in the plantation towns, raise their families and make Hawaii their home. You can still feel plenty of history.

If you're looking for the mill while driving, just keep an eye out for the towering smokestack.

Nui's Thai
THAI $
(☑808-224-1385; www.nuis-thai-food.business. site; 67-096 Kealohanui St; ☺10:30am-5pm Mon-Fri) A Bangkok-born cook oversees the kitchen squeezed into this roadside lunch truck. Flavors can be tame (ask for extra spicy), but the big plates of traditional curries, stir-fried noodles and savory salads are still satisfying. It's cash only at this semi-hidden gem. There are a few picnic tables out front.

Brew & Foam
CAFE
(☑424-234-2244; www.brewandfoam.com; unit 105, 67-292 Goodale Ave; ☺7am-1pm) A concept from an O'ahu married couple who are passionate about their lattes, Brew & Foam is a tiny storefront featuring a simple bar to sit at (most patrons get their grub and java to go) and a glass case of handmade goodies.

🛍 Shopping

North Shore Soap Factory
COSMETICS
(☑808-637-8400; www.northshoresoapfactory. com; 67-106 Kealohanui St; ☺9am-6pm Mon-Sat, 10am-5pm Sun) Located in the Bagasse bin (the huge, cone-shaped building at the front gate of the Waialua Sugar Mill), the North Shore Soap Factory is home to Hawaiian Bath & Body (www.hawaiianbathbody.com), selling natural and organic soap and skincare products handcrafted on the premises. All sorts of quality products are for sale at the store here.

It uses locally sourced ingredients such as macadamia and *kukui* (candlenut tree) oils, Pupukea tangerines, Waikane ginger root, Maui sugar and Big Island honey and guava.

Island X Hawaii
FOOD & DRINKS
(☑808-637-2624; www.islandxhawaii.com; 67-106 Kealohanui St; ☺9am-5pm Sun-Fri, from 8:30am Sat) In the rambling warehouse building at the far end of the parking lot of the Waialua Sugar Mill, Island X has all sorts of good stuff to interest visitors. Try locally made Waialua coffee, plus there's local chocolate, shave ice and all sorts of Hawaiiana for sale. The Waialua Coffee & Chocolate Mill is out back.

Third Stone
SPORTS & OUTDOORS
(Waialua Surf Shop; ☑808-391-9782; http://3rd stonehawaii.com; 67-106 Kealohanui St; ☺10am-5pm Mon-Fri, from 8:30am Sat) The various back buildings of the Waialua Sugar Mill are home to 14 companies operating in the surfboard industry, but right out front, in the car park, is Third Stone, selling boards, surf wear and outdoor gear. Make no mistake: these guys shape and make popular boards, but they also have a great shop and a super-friendly attitude.

CRAVING A 'SNOW PUFFY'?

Take a detour down a country road to find the family-run **Pa'ala'a Kai Bakery** (☏808-637-9795; www.pkbsweets.com; 66-935 Kaukonahua Rd; snacks & pastries from $2; ⊙5:30am-7pm), a pilgrimage for anyone craving a 'snow puffy' (flaky chocolate cream puff dusted with powdered sugar) or a hot *malasada* (Portuguese-style doughnut). There's also a tasty array of pastries, cakes, pies and sandwiches. Running since 1970, this is a Waialua institution that certainly keeps the locals happy.

Waialua Fresh   HEALTH & WELLNESS
(☏808-637-2379; www.facebook.com/waialua fresh; 67-701 Nauahi St; ⊙8am-7pm) Waialua Fresh is a breath of fresh air. Tucked into an unassuming strip mall, this shop boasts 80% local produce, most of it O'ahu grown, as well as Asian specialty foods, snacks, drinks and gift items. Gluten-free, vegan, vegetarian and numerous other offerings ensure that practically any diet can find something to tickle its fancy here.

ℹ Getting There & Away

You can get out here on TheBus 76 from Hale'iwa, but to make the most of your time, get some rental wheels.

Mokule'ia to Ka'ena Point

POP 1800

The further down the road you go, the fewer signs of habitation you'll see in this desolate corner of the island. Dillingham Airfield gets its fair share of air-adventure visitors, but once past there, the Farrington Hwy dead-ends into a chain across the road at a rocky, undeveloped spot 2.5 miles short of the island's western tip. Like the old railway, the highway used to go around Ka'ena Point, but it's now only a rocky path.

🏖 Beaches

Mokule'ia Beach Park   BEACH
(68-919 Farrington Hwy) The beach itself is a nice sandy stretch, but the rocky seabed makes for poor swimming. When waters are calm and flat in summer, snorkelers swim out along the shallow reef. Keen windsurfers and kitesurfers often congregate on this part of the shore, taking advantage of the consistent winds. The park has a large grassy area with picnic tables, restrooms and outdoor showers, but there aren't any lifeguards.

Army Beach   BEACH
(Farrington Hwy) Opposite the western end of Dillingham Airfield, this is the widest stretch of sand on the Mokule'ia shore, although it's not maintained and there are no facilities. The beach also has very strong rip currents, especially during high winter surf.

◉ Sights & Activities

Most of O'ahu's up-in-the-air adventures take off from Dillingham Airfield. Call ahead, as all are weather dependent.

Dillingham Airfield   AIRFIELD
(HDH; www.airnav.com/airport/PHDH; 68-760 Farrington Hwy) Operated by the Hawaii Department of Transportation under a 25-year lease from the US Army, Dillingham Airfield is mainly used for general aviation, gliding and skydiving operations. The runway was paved to 9000ft (2700m) during WWII and, by the end of the war, it could handle B-29 Superfortress bombers. These days, it is 5000ft (1500m) and still used by the military for night-vision training. The airfield has been used for filming in the television series *Lost* and *Hawaii Five-0*.

★**Honolulu Soaring**   SCENIC FLIGHTS
(☏808-637-0207; www.honolulusoaring.com; Dillingham Airfield; rides from $85; ⊙10am-5:30pm) Plenty of great options here at the western end of Dillingham Airfield, with piloted scenic flights for one or two passengers. Take a scenic tour over the North Shore, go for an aerobatic thrill ride or have a mini lesson in a glider. The outfit's been at Dillingham since 1970. Soaring operates year-round because of Hawaii's excellent flying conditions.

★**Pacific Skydiving Center**   SKYDIVING
(☏808-637-7472; www.pacificskydivinghonolulu.com; Dillingham Airfield, 68-760 Farrington Hwy; tandem jumps from $159; ⊙7:30am-2:30pm) Jumps attached to an instructor range from the regular tandem at 8000ft (15 to 20 seconds' free fall; $159) to the ultimate at 14,000ft (60-plus seconds' free fall; $189) to the extreme at 22,000ft to 24,000ft (100-plus seconds' free fall; $999; medical requirements!). Altitude is guaranteed and you pay after you jump. Your budget may well choose your jump for you. Includes free Waikiki pickup.

Paradise Air Hawaii   GLIDING
(☏808-497-6033; www.paradiseairhawaii.com; Dillingham Airfield, Farrington Hwy; per 30/45/60min $180/230/280; ⊙by reservation only) Soar like

a bird in an ultralight powered hang glider called a trike, accompanied by an instructor who may even let you pilot. They may look a tad flimsy, but these are full-on aircraft. The trikes are two seaters, so there's only one passenger. Reservations required; you'll need to find your own way to Dillingham Airfield.

Mokule'ia WINDSURFING
(Moks) An excellent, windy spot popular with windsurfers and kitesurfers, Moks is off Mokule'ia Beach Park. Winds are dependable, especially from April to September. Head out from the beach park.

Kealia & Kuaokala Trails HIKING
Beyond the Gate D entrance above Dillingham Airfield, the 2.5-mile, one-way Kealia Trail (Map p188; http://hawaiitrails.ehawaii.gov) switchbacks steeply up (there's a 1660ft elevation change) through exposed country with ocean views along the way. It connects to the 2.5-mile one-way Kuaokala Trail (p193), which brings hikers to a justly celebrated ridgetop viewpoint over the Makua Valley and Wai'anae Range. Note that access to the Kuaokala Trail is physically easier from the Wai'anae Coast but requires an advance permit to approach via the Ka'ena Point satellite-tracking station. Both trails are open to mountain bikes. Print out a topo map if you go; allow six hours for both. There's detailed trail information on the website.

Ka'ena Point Hike HIKING
(https://dlnr.hawaii.gov/dsp/hiking/oahu/kaena-point-trail) There are two ways to hike out to Ka'ena Point at the western tip of O'ahu. One is from the road's end at the termination of the Farrington Hwy on the Leeward Coast. The second is from the end of the Farrington Hwy here on the North Shore. It's a 2.5-mile one-way trip out to the point.

The Farrington Hwy and a railroad track used to run around Ka'ena Point, but both were washed out by a tsunami in 1946. This left a 5-mile gap in the highway. These days, with a bit of clever transport organization, hikers can walk right around the point, but in most cases they need to make a return journey from either road end. The walk from the North Shore end is relatively flat and features a couple of attractive secluded beaches along the way. Don't leave anything valuable in your car while out on this hike.

Hawaii Polo Trail Rides HORSEBACK RIDING
(☎808-220-5153; www.oahuhorsebackrides.com; 68-411 Farrington Hwy; rides from $88; ⊙1-7pm)

When the polo ponies aren't playing, you can take them for a ride around Hawaii Polo's 100-acre stomping grounds at the beach. Book online for sunshine rides ($98), sunset rides ($108), private rides ($128) or a polo lesson ($128). Long pants and closed-toed shoes are recommended. Everything you need to know is on the informative website.

🛌 Sleeping

Camp Mokule'ia CAMPGROUND $
(☎808-637-6241; www.campmokuleia.com; 68-729 Farrington Hwy; campsites per person from $10; ⊙office 8:30am-5pm Mon-Fri, 10am-5pm Sat; 🅿🏊) Looking for solace and solitude? This church-run seaside camp is open to travelers, by reservation only. Amenities for campers are basic, with outdoor showers and flushing toilets. Also on offer are 16 comfortable two-person lodge rooms with private bathroom ($125 per night), group cabins sleeping up to 22, and 'tent cabins' ($75 per night).

Central O'ahu

Central O'ahu is the island's forgotten backwater in terms of tourism. It's squeezed by enormous military bases: don't be surprised if you get passed on the highway by camo-painted Humvees or see Black Hawk choppers buzzing overhead. Many visitors race through on their way to the North Shore, but there are some interesting things going on here if you've got time up your sleeve.

👁 Sights & Activities

Kolekole Pass LANDMARK
(www.facebook.com/usaghawaii) At 1724ft, Kolekole Pass occupies the main gap in the Wai'anae Range. Film buffs may recognize the landscape, as this is where WWII Japanese fighters passed through on their way to bomb Pearl Harbor in the classic war film *Tora! Tora! Tora!* (In reality, the planes flew along the inside, not through, the mountain range.)

The pass, on military property above Schofield Barracks, can be visited on select weekends. Check the website to find open dates.

Bring photo ID and your rental-car contract or proof of vehicle insurance. Access is granted by the security guards at Lyman Gate on Kunia Rd. If you have problems with gate access, call 808-655-1434. Follow Lyman Rd for 5 miles to reach the pass.

KUNIA ROAD

If you're not in a hurry on your way to Wahiawa (and why would you be?), consider taking scenic Kunia Rd through rural plantations at the foot of the mountains. If you're coming from Honolulu on the H-1, take exit 5B and turn right onto Kunia Rd (Rte 750). The drive starts in sprawling suburbia but soon breaks free into an expansive landscape with 360-degree views. As you gain altitude, views of Honolulu and Diamond Head emerge; be sure to pull off somewhere and look back at the landscape. Cornfields gradually give way to enormous pineapple plantations, all hemmed in by the mountains to the west.

The rural landscape continues until you pass Schofield Barracks Military Reservation. This massive army base is the largest on the island and is a hive of activity. Onward from Wahiawa, two routes – rural Kaukonahua Rd (Hwy 803) and busy Kamehameha Hwy (Hwy 99) – lead through pineapple-plantation country to the North Shore.

Without military ID, you can't keep driving over to the coast.

From a dirt parking pull-off, a short, steep hiking path with wooden steps leads for 10 minutes up to a fine view of the Wai'anae Coast. En route you'll pass a large, ribbed stone rumored to have been used by ancient Hawaiians for ritual sacrifices of fallen warrior *ali'i* (chiefs). In Hawaiian mythology, the stone is believed to be the embodiment of a woman named Kolekole, who took this form in order to become the perpetual guardian of the pass – keeping intruders from the coast from entering the sacred lands of Wahiawa. Local lore has it that if you touch the stone, bad luck may follow.

Hawaii Country Club GOLF
(☑808-621-5654; www.hawaiicc.com; 94-1211 Kunia Rd; 18 holes from $25) The Hawaii Country Club, a challenging par 72, is the longest-operating public golf course on the island – and one of the most reasonably priced. Built on former pineapple fields and opened in 1957, it has a relatively relaxed atmosphere.

❶ Getting There & Around

You'll need your own wheels if you want to do much exploring in Central O'ahu. Most get here by car from Waikiki, Honolulu or the North Shore.

Wahiawa

POP 17,800

Wahiawa itself isn't the sort of place that travelers seek out, unless you're looking for a military buzz cut, a tattoo or a pawn shop. It's a tad dusty, and yes, maybe that was a tumbleweed you saw blowing down the street! Yet the land around town was considered sacred by ancient Hawaiians, who built temples, gave birth to royal chiefs and clashed in fierce battles here.

◉ Sights

★ **Green World Coffee Farm** PLANTATION
(☑808-622-2326; www.greenworldcoffeefarm.com; 71-101 Kamehameha Hwy; ◉6am-5pm Mon-Thu, to 6pm Fri, 7am-6pm Sat & Sun) **FREE** A must for coffee nuts, Green World roasts all its coffee on-site with homegrown beans and beans sourced from throughout the Hawaiian Islands. There's free sampling, free wi-fi and a great vibe in this roadside coffee extravaganza. It ships its vast range of products, including a huge variety of flavored coffee, all over the world.

Kukaniloko Birthstone State Monument ARCHAEOLOGICAL SITE
One of the most important ancient sites on the island, Kukaniloko Birthstone State Monument is located in a 5-acre field just north of Wahiawa township, on the western side of the Kamehameha Hwy. Wahiawa is considered the *piko* (navel) of O'ahu. The 180 lava-rock stones that make up the monument, once used as a royal birth site, are believed to possess the power to ease the pains of giving birth and are thought to be more than 900 years old.

Wahiawa Botanical Gardens GARDENS
(☑808-768-7135; www.honolulu.gov/parks/hbg.html; 1396 California Ave; ◉9am-4pm) **FREE** Started 80 years ago as an experiment by local sugarcane farmers, this 27-acre garden has evolved to showcase plants that thrive in a cool, moist climate. There's a mix of the manicured, with lawns and pruned ornamental plants, and the wild, with a gully of towering hardwoods, tropical ferns and forests of bamboo. Several paths, some wheelchair friendly, weave their way through the garden. It's located 1 mile east of the Kamehameha Hwy (Hwy 99).

PINEAPPLE TIDBITS

➡ In 1901 James Dole planted O'ahu's first pineapple patch in Wahiawa.

➡ Today, each acre of a pineapple field can support around 30,000 plants.

➡ The commercial pineapple variety grown in Hawaii is smooth cayenne.

➡ It takes nearly two years for a pineapple plant to reach maturity.

➡ Each plant produces just two pineapples, one in its second year and one in its third year.

➡ Pineapples are harvested year-round, but the long, sunny days of summer produce the sweetest fruit.

➡ Pineapples won't continue to ripen after they've been picked.

Dole Plantation AMUSEMENT PARK
(☎808-621-8408; www.dole-plantation.com; 64-1550 Kamehameha Hwy; visitor center free, adult/child 4-12yr maze $8/6, train ride $11.50/9.50, walking tour $7/6.25; ◷9:30am-5:30pm; ♿) Expect a sticky-sweet overdose of everything *ananas* (pineapples) when you walk into the Dole Plantation's visitor-center gift shop. After you've watched fruit-cutting demonstrations and bought your fill of pineapple potato chips and fruity trinkets, take your pineapple ice-cream sundae outside for more pineapple educational fun.

The small ornamental garden showcasing different species – including pink pineapple – is free; to see more, you'll have to pay to take the garden tour. On the 20-minute Pineapple Express open-air train ride, you chug along through the upland scenery while more of Dole's story is narrated. The Pineapple Garden Maze is meant purely as fun, as you find (or lose) your way among 14,000 Hawaiian plants on 1.5 miles of pathways. If you're hungry after that, you can stop at the plantation's self-service grill restaurant, which is surprisingly well priced.

Tropic Lightning Museum MUSEUM
(☎808-655-0438; https://home.army.mil/hawaii; Waianae Ave, Bldg 361, Schofield Barracks; ◷10am-4pm Tue-Sat) FREE This museum on Schofield Barracks remembers the proud achievements of the US Army's 25th Infantry Division, nicknamed 'Tropic Lightning.' The division was activated in 1941 in Hawaii. The museum has displays from the various campaigns that the 25th served in, including

WWII, and the occupation of Japan, Korea, Vietnam, Afghanistan and Iraq. Admission is free and the general public is welcome, but if you don't have a military ID there's a bit of rigmarole to get in. You'll need to enter Schofield Barracks' Lyman Gate on Kunia Rd with ID for everyone in the car, car registration and insurance (rental-car agreement) to obtain a visitor pass.

Keanianileihuaokalani Healing Stone RELIGIOUS SITE
(110 California Ave) FREE A small shrine on California Ave houses the Healing Stone of Wahiawa, also known as Keanianileihuaokalani. The history of the stone is somewhat cloudy, but Hawaiians believe that the stone has sacred healing properties. It is supposed to be watered to keep it clean as well as to maintain these properties. The spot where the shrine sits is open to the public.

Wahiawa Freshwater State Recreation Area PARK
(☎808-622-6316; www.hawaiistateparks.org/parks/oahu; 380 Walker Ave; ◷7am-7:30pm) FREE Despite being just beyond Wahiawa center, this park has an unspoiled countryside feel, and the picnic tables with views of Lake Wilson are oh-so-inviting. Public fishing is allowed in the waters stocked with bass and other fish. Turn east off Kamehameha Hwy (Hwy 99) onto Avocado St at the south end of town and then turn right onto Walker Ave.

🎊 Festivals & Events

Wahiawa Pineapple Festival FOOD & DRINK
(www.wahiawapinefest.com; ◷May) On a Saturday in early May everything pineapple is celebrated at this small-town community fair at the Wahiawa District Park on California Ave. A parade, music, food sales, games and demonstrations are all included.

🍴 Eating

Wahiawa has a number of small Asian eateries and fast-food joints. There are some good options 5 miles down the Kamehameha Hwy in Mililani town and Mililani Mauka.

Maui Mike's BARBECUE $
(☎808-622-5900; www.mauimikes.com; 96 Kamehameha Hwy; meals from $7.50; ◷10:30am-8:30pm) At Maui Mike's you have the choice of chicken, chicken or chicken – all free range, fire roasted and super fresh. Even the Cajun-spiced fries are 100% natural and trans fat free. Mike describes his chicken as

'mouth-watering eat-with-your-hands com-fort food' and that's spot on! There are a few tables inside, but most people grab and go.

Kilani Bakery BAKERY $
(☎808-621-5662; 704 Kilani Ave; pastries from $1; ☺4:30am-5:30pm Tue-Sun) Locally owned since 1959, Kilani Bakery is just the type of mom-and-pop, hole-in-the-wall establishment that you remember from growing up. Everything is made from scratch daily – try the chantilly cake, custard pies or *malasadas* (Portuguese doughnuts), or the famous brownies (said to be the best on the entire island).

Dots Restaurant HAWAIIAN $
(☎808-622-4115; www.dotswahiawa.com; 130 Mango St; mains from $10; ☺7am-late Wed-Mon) A local favorite since it opened in 1939, this legendary breakfast-to-dinner spot serves meals, has a cocktail lounge, holds ban-quets, and has regular events such as Ladies Nights @ Dots, Friday Night Live! and Tues-day Night Food Trucks in the car park. The food is a Hawaiian and Japanese mix, with kids' and seniors' menus, and there's a com-munity-minded vibe.

Shige's Saimin Stand NOODLES $
(☎808-621-3621; www.facebook.com/shiges saimin; 70 Kukui St; saimin from $4; ☺10am-10pm Mon-Thu, to 11pm Fri & Sat) Shige's may not look like much from the outside, but locals swear that these are the best saimin noodles around. Inspired by Chinese chow mein, Japanese ramen and Filipino *pancit,* saimin is a noodle-soup dish that was developed by immigrant groups in Hawaii. It became pop-ular during the plantation era. Shige's barbe-cue cheeseburger is also a winner.

Barrio Cafe MEXICAN $$
(☎808-622-3003; www.barriocafe808.business. site; 672 Kilani Ave; mains from $11; ☺7am-3pm Mon-Thu & Sat, 7am-3pm & 7-10pm Fri) This friendly, cozy Mexican *cocina* (kitchen), tucked away on an unassuming side street, serves authentic eats in generous portions amid bright and cheerful decor. Parking is limited in the lot, but ample street parking is available for diners.

❶ Getting There & Away

There are three roads heading north to Wahiawa from the south: the H-2 freeway, furthest east, is the fastest option; the Kamehameha Hwy, in the middle, takes you through suburbia; Kunia Rd (Hwy 750), the furthest west, is rural and the most scenic.

Mililani

Five miles south of Wahiawa down the Kamehameha Hwy, Mililani town has a com-pletely different feel. This designer town, west of the H-2, was built on old plantation fields in the 1960s and is like modern sub-urbia, with many residents commuting into Honolulu each day. Mililani hit boom times when the freeway into Honolulu was com-pleted in 1976. On the east side of the H-2 is Mililani Mauka, developed in the 1990s on fields that used to produce pineapples. Both areas have large shopping complexes that hide some surprisingly good eating options.

✖ Eating

⭐**Rise & Shine Cafe** HAWAIIAN $
(☎808-260-9312; http://riseandshinecafeoahu. com; 95-1057 Ainamakua Dr; meals from $10; ☺7am-3pm Mon-Sat, to 2pm Sun) In the Gate-way at Mililani Mauka shopping center, this is a popular family-run, home-style break-fast and lunch spot with a strong local fol-lowing. The sunny and positive atmosphere is reflected in the fine foods and desserts. Start your day with banana mac-nut pan-cakes with coconut syrup ($8.95) or try *furi-kake* fish with garlic aioli ($11.95) for lunch.

⭐**Mililani Farmers Market** MARKET $
(☎808-848-2074; www.hfbf.org/farmers-markets/ mililani; 95-1200 Meheula Pkwy; ☺8-11am Sun) Held in the lower parking lot at Mililani High School, this popular market doesn't see too many tourists. There's everything you'd expect to find at a local farmers market, with lots of produce for sale, plenty of eating op-tions and ample free parking.

Poke Stop SEAFOOD $
(☎808-626-3400; www.poke-stop.com; 95-1840 Meheula Pkwy; meals from $8; ☺8am-8:30pm Mon-Sat, to 7pm Sun) This excellent *poke* place is in the Gateway at Mililani Mauka shop-ping center, just off the H-2 on Meheula Pkwy. Load up here for a picnic of incredible *poke* or a gourmet plate lunch of blackened fish and garlic shrimp. There are a few ta-bles, so you can also eat in. Great spot!

Rajanee Thai Cuisine Mililani THAI $
(☎808-853-4724; www.facebook.com/rajanee thaicuisine; 95-390 Kuahelani Ave; meals from $10; ☺11am-8pm Mon-Sat) This popular Thai hole-in-the-wall place has a takeout counter tucked into the backside of Mililani Shop-ping Center. It's hard to find and there's
Continued on p276

CYCLING THE
SEVEN-MILE MIRACLE

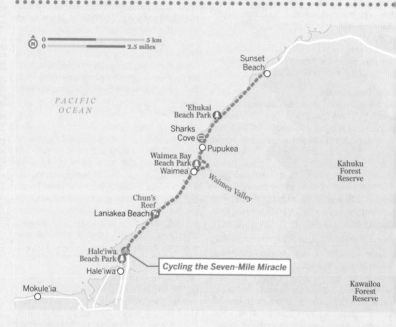

THE RIDE

START HALE'IWA BEACH PARK
END HALE'IWA BEACH PARK
DISTANCE 14 MILES
DIFFICULTY EASY

Both the Seven-Mile Miracle and this ride start at **Hale'iwa Beach Park** (p260), over the Anahulu River bridge at the northern end of Hale'iwa. You're looking at a 14-mile trip, with the turnaround point at Ted's Bakery just past Sunset Beach at the halfway point, where you'll have earned a rest and a chocolate-*haupia* (coconut pudding) cream pie.

ON YA BIKE!

The first section of the trip is along the Kamehameha Hwy with cars, so you'll want to be careful. If it's a busy day, you may well find yourself moving faster than the cars. Take a left heading out from Hale'iwa Beach Park, then another left at the major

intersection and start pedaling down the Kamehameha Hwy. The first sand you'll see on your left is **Laniakea Beach** (p254). Take a break and see if there are any *honu* (green sea turtles) down at the far corner of the beach. Volunteers from Malama na Honu, a Hawaiian sea-turtle-conservation group, are usually here to answer questions. A few minutes back on the bike and the next sand you'll see has **Chun's Reef** (p255), a legendary North Shore surf break, offshore. Spot the surfers.

Back on your bike, after a bit of a climb, gorgeous **Waimea Bay Beach Park** (p253) will come into view down on your left. If it's winter, marvel at the waves; if it's summer, this is a great spot for a dip in the sea. Waimea Bay can be a dangerous place to swim, however, so heed lifeguard warnings. There are showers and changing rooms here, so sort yourself out before getting back on your bike.

The name sounds like an ancient religious pilgrimage (and surfers may well worship this unique 7-mile stretch), but the 'Seven-Mile Miracle' that is the North Shore is best seen by bike.

If you want to go inland for a completely different look at the North Shore, head up the verdant **Waimea Valley** (p254). If time is on your side, check out the gardens and walk up to Waimea Falls in this tropical sanctuary with more than 5000 native and exotic plant species.

It's a short climb on your bike up to **Sharks Cove** (p256), a good place to stop for refreshments. If you're feeling peckish, choose from what looks good at the food trucks, or head into Foodland, the only supermarket you'll run into.

Across the road from Foodland is the beach, but you may want to hang on for your next swim as there are some cracker beaches coming up. Things are about to become a lot easier, as you should now be on the 3.5-mile **Ke Ala Pupukea Bike Path** (p255) that runs all the way to Sunset Beach, so you won't have to worry about cars. It's flat and mostly shaded, and the biggest decision you'll need to make is where to take a break for a swim.

Any time you can't resist the lure of the sand and the waves, head out and have a look. What a lineup! Next is **'Ehukai Beach Park** (p253). The break off the park is better known as **Banzai Pipeline** (p255), Pipeline or just Pipe. You don't have to be a surfer to have heard of it. Then comes legendary **Sunset Beach** (p253). Take your time and admire the miracle. Carrying on from Sunset, you'll hit **Ted's Bakery** (p255) in a few hundred yards, on your right. This is your cream-pie stop and turnaround point. If you're going to need more than a cream pie, tuck into one of Ted's superb plate-lunch options.

It's 7 miles back to Hale'iwa, but this time the action will be on your right. Enjoy it. It really is a miracle!

RENTAL BIKES

If you need to rent bikes, contact **North Shore Bike Rentals** (p265) and arrange times for your bikes to be dropped off and picked up at Hale'iwa Beach Park. The outfit delivers for free, and bike helmets and locks are included. It's also happy to drop off and pick up at other locations – you could do this trip one way or just do a return trip on the Ke Ala Pupukea Bike Path from Pupukea. These North Shore locals are full of helpful advice.

ROAD TRIP: OFF THE BEATEN PATH

Most visitors blast on through Central O'ahu on the H-2 freeway in a rush to get to Hale'iwa and the North Shore, but if you've got a couple of extra hours in hand, take a drive through O'ahu's old plantation country. Parts of it are now suburbia, but further north you'll run into military bases and rural O'ahu.

❶ Mililani Town

Coming from Waikiki or downtown Honolulu on the H-1, instead of going north on the H-2, head a tad further west and drive north up the Kamehameha Hwy (Hwy 99). The easiest thing to do is go past the H-2 turnoff north and get off at exit 7 (Waikele/Waipahu). Turn right at the Paiwa St traffic lights, then right again at the lights on Lumiaina St. Follow Lumiaina for almost a mile back east until it intersects with the Kamehameha Hwy. Turn left and you're on the route.

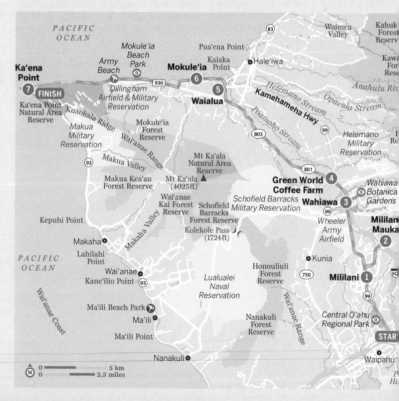

This is Waipio and Hawaiian suburbia. On your left you'll soon see **Central O'ahu Regional Park** (p276), a massive space full of sporting facilities. The highway then drops into a gulch before climbing up to **Mililani town**. This town was built on former plantation fields in the 1960s as a designed 'satellite city' developed to meet O'ahu's growing need for housing. It was a planned community, and when the H-2 freeway opened in 1976, halving driving times to Honolulu, Mililani boomed.

❷ Mililani Mauka

In the early 1990s, more plantation land was developed for Mililani Mauka, a newer planned development on the east side of the H-2. If you're feeling hungry, head right on Meheula Pkwy in Mililani town, cross over the H-2 to Mililani Mauka and satisfy your needs at either **Rise & Shine Cafe** (p271) or **Poke Stop** (p271) – both are good!

❸ Wahiawa

Back in Mililani town, continue heading north. The road will drop into another gulch, then climb again and on your left will be **Wheeler Army Airfield**, with its runway, helicopters and buildings. The Kamehameha Hwy then passes under the H-2 and you'll find yourself in the old plantation town of **Wahiawa** (p269). You're near Schofield Barracks, and you'll see plenty of military uniforms, buzz cuts, pawn shops and tattoo parlors. Compare this dusty town with the designer city of Mililani just down the road. To visit **Wahiawa Botanical Gardens** (p269), watch for the sign and turn right down California Ave. Back on the Kam Hwy, you could stop for chicken at **Maui Mike's** (p270).

❹ Green World Coffee Farm

Carry on through Wahiawa, down into a gulch, then up for a stop at **Green World Coffee Farm** (p269). It's at the first four-way intersection you'll come to. There are plenty of coffees to taste, examples of coffee plants in the garden, free wi-fi, and tasty edibles to tide you over.

❺ Waialua

Instead of turning right and taking Rte 99 to Hale'iwa, carry on straight along less-trafficked Kaukonahua Rd, then turn right when it joins Rte 803. You're now in for a lovely drive through pineapple plantations and rich volcanic soils to the sugar-plantation town of Waialua. Turn right at the roundabout and you'll soon spot the old **Waialua Sugar Mill** (p266) smokestack.

This historic mill closed in 1996 after over a century of operation and, to meet community needs, was cleverly redeveloped into a visitor attraction. Drop in and check out the **North Shore Soap Factory** (p266), **Third Stone surfboards** (p266), and **Island X Hawaii** (p266) for some more coffee tasting.

❻ Mokule'ia

Carry on down Goodale Ave to Rte 82 and turn left. The road winds its way west out to the Mokule'ia beach community and Crozier Dr, then narrows. There are plenty of speed bumps before you'll need to turn left on Mahinaai St out to the Farrington Hwy. Turn right and you'll soon pass **Hawaii Polo Trail Rides** (p268) and **Dillingham Airfield** (p267), with its skydiving and glider rides.

Opposite the airfield, **Mokule'ia Beach Park** (p267) may present great views of windsurfers and kitesurfers buzzing along, and at the far end of the field you may recognize **Army Beach** (p267) from its cameo in the television series *Lost*.

❼ Ka'ena Point

Not far to go now. Another mile or two and the road peters out at a locked gate and a small car park.

If you want to go any further, you'll have to walk the final 2.5 miles out to Ka'ena Point. A railway, opened in 1899, used to transport sugarcane around the point, but most of the tracks were destroyed by a tsunami in 1946.

This is the end of your drive. Retrace your route back to Mokule'ia, then head into Hale'iwa for refreshments.

ℹ SHOPPER'S BONANZA

Waikele Premium Outlets (☎808-676-5656; www.premiumoutlets.com/out let/waikele; 94-790 Lumiania St, Waipahu; ⊙9am-9pm) is the mother lode in terms of outlet stores. Lots of big brands are here and the place is so popular that there's direct transportation from Waikiki. Prepare to battle the shopper crowds for deals at over 70 stores and associated shopping rest-stop outlets.

If coming by car from Honolulu on the H-1, take exit 7 and turn right onto Paiwa St. There's stacks of free parking.

Continued from p271

not much seating, but it's good, winning an award as Central O'ahu's best neighborhood restaurant. Try the shrimp pad thai, and the fried coconut ice cream for dessert. Rajanee has a second restaurant in Hale'iwa (p263).

Freestyle Cafe　　　　　　　CAFE $
(☎808-800-6856; www.facebook.com/freestyle cafemililani; 94-780 Meheula Pkwy; smoothies & milk tea from $6.50; ⊙11am-8pm; P🛜) At the Mililani Marketplace shopping center, this cafe is decorated with black-and-white checkered flooring to complement its *Alice in Wonderland*–themed interior – all of which coincides perfectly with its fun (and sweet) menu selections of delicious milk teas, smoothies, mochi crepes (savory selections also available), coffees, lattes and more.

ℹ Getting There & Away

Coming from Honolulu, take the H-2's exit 5A and turn left for Mililani Town or right for Mililani Mauka. Alternatively, head straight up the Kamehameha Hwy (Hwy 99) to get to Mililani Town.

Waipio

Three miles south of Mililani on the Kamehameha Hwy and conveniently placed near the intersection of the H1 and H2 freeways, Waipio is home to an impressive park and sports facilities. Just west in Waikele is the incredible popular Waikele Premium Outlets; buses and tours run direct from Waikiki bringing those keen on a bargain.

🏃 Activities

Central O'ahu Regional Park　　　PARK
(☎808-676-6982; www.co.honolulu.hi.us/parks; 94-801 Kamehameha Hwy) Operated by the City and County of Honolulu, the Patsy T Mink Central O'ahu Regional Park is a 269-acre public space. The massive park houses a tennis and aquatic center, baseball diamonds, an archery range, a skateboard park and other sports fields. It's accessed off the Kamehameha Hwy (Hwy 99) that runs north from Waipahu to Mililani and Wahiawa.

🍴 Eating & Drinking

Black Sheep Cream Co　　　ICE CREAM $
(☎808-620-7904; 94-1235 Ka Uka Blvd, Waipahu; ⊙10am-9pm; P) Black Sheep makes craft ice cream in small batches daily. Every unique flavor has a kitschy name. Brave a single scoop ($4.50) of I Like Pig Butts and I Cannot Lie (maple cream with maple-bacon brittle) or Joe Gets Nuts (coffee cream with mac-nut brownie), or get an ice-cream flight ($10.50) of four scoops, served with hot fudge or caramel.

It also serves coffee and affogato.

Coffee or Tea?　　　　　　TEAHOUSE $
(☎808-676-6688; 94-1144 Ka Uka Blvd, Waipahu; ⊙10am-9pm Mon-Sat, to 7pm Sun; 🛜) Specializing in boba (also known as bubble tea, recognized by its mix-in of chewy tapioca balls or fruit jelly), Coffee or Tea? also offers milk tea ($3.75), iced tea, espresso, coffee, shakes, smoothies, and shave ice ($6), as well as non-caffeinated drinks. Another specialty is hot, thick toast slathered in a choice of toppings including condensed milk or coconut butter.

Auntie Pasto's　　　　　　ITALIAN $$
(☎808-680-0005; www.auntiepastosrestaurant. com; Kunia Shopping Center, 94-673 Kupuohi St, Waipahu; mains lunch/dinner from $9/10; ⊙11am-9pm) Have a large family in tow? The lively atmosphere here, with cheery red-checkered tablecloths and large variety of made-from-scratch Italian food such as pizza and pasta, are sure to satisfy, as will the cocktails. Check out daily deals on the website. The Kunia Shopping Center is just off the H-1 freeway, exit 5A.

ℹ Getting There & Away

From Honolulu, for Central O'ahu Regional Park, take exit 2 off the H-2 freeway and turn left. For Waikele Premium Outlets, take exit 7 off the H-1 and turn right.

Understand Honolulu, Waikiki & O'ahu

History

More than 2000 miles from the US mainland, Hawaii can feel like another country – and that's because it once was. Polynesians in canoes first colonized this tropical archipelago more than a millennium before Western explorers, whalers and missionaries arrived on ships. The tumultuous 19th century stirred a melting pot of immigrants from Asia, the United States and Europe even as it ended the Hawaiian kingdom founded by Kamehameha the Great. Throughout these times O'ahu was inevitably at the center of events.

Ancient Hawai'i

Temples & Sacred Sites

Kane'aki Heiau (Makaha)
....
Pu'u o Mahuka Heiau State Historic Site (Waimea)
....
Kea'iwa Heiau State Recreation Area ('Aiea)
....
Ulupo Heiau State Monument (Kailua)
....
Waimea Valley (Waimea)
....
Kukaniloko Birthstone State Monument (Wahiawa)

Almost nothing is known about the first wave of Polynesians (likely from the Marquesas Islands) who landed on this archipelago between 300 and 600 CE. A second wave of Polynesians from the Tahitian islands began arriving around 1000 CE, and they conquered the first peoples and obliterated nearly all traces of their history and culture. Legends of the *menehune* (an ancient race of 'little people' who built temples and great stoneworks overnight) may refer to these original inhabitants.

Although the discovery of Hawai'i may have been accidental, subsequent journeys were not. Tahitians were highly skilled seafarers, navigating more than 2400 miles of open ocean without maps, and with only the sun, stars, wind and waves to guide them. In their double-hulled canoes, they imported to the islands their religious beliefs, social structures and more than two dozen food plants and domestic animals. What they didn't possess is equally remarkable: no metals, no wheels, no alphabet or written language, and no clay to make pottery.

After trans-Pacific voyaging stopped completely around 1300 (for reasons unknown today), Hawaiian culture evolved in isolation. Nevertheless it retained a family resemblance to other Polynesian cultures. Ancient Hawai'i's highly stratified society was run by *ali'i* (chiefs) whose right to rule was based on their hereditary lineage from the gods. Clan loyalties trumped expressions of individuality, elaborate traditions of gifting and feasting conferred prestige, and a humanlike pantheon of gods inhabited the natural world.

TIMELINE	10 million BCE	300–600 CE	1000 CE
	Lava from an underwater volcano breaks the ocean's surface and O'ahu emerges as an island. From one million to 10,000 years ago, a period of renewed volcanism forms Le'ahi (Diamond Head).	The first human settlers – a small group of Polynesians, probably from the Marquesas Islands – arrive in the Hawaiian Islands.	Waves of immigration from Tahiti start around 1000 CE and continue into the mid-1400s.

Several layers of *ali'i* ruled each island, and life was marked by warring battles as they jockeyed for power and status. The basic political subdivision was the *ahupua'a*, a wedge-shaped slice of land from the mountains to the sea that contained all the resources each chiefdom needed. Below the chiefs were the kahuna (experts or masters), who included both the priests and the guild masters – canoe makers, healers, navigators and so on. *Maka'ainana* (commoners) did most of the physical labor, and were obligated to support the *ali'i* through taxes. Below all was a small class of *kaua* (outcasts).

Ancient Hawai'i's culture of mutuality and reciprocity infused what otherwise resembled a feudal agricultural society: chiefs were custodians of their people, and humans custodians of nature, all of which was sacred – the living expression (or mana, spiritual essence) of the universe's soul. Everyone played their part, through work and ritual, to maintain the health of the community and its relationship to the gods. In practice, a strict code of ritualized behavior – the *kapu* (taboo) system – governed every aspect of daily life; violating the *kapu* could mean death. Hawaiians also enjoyed life immensely, cultivating rich traditions in music, dance and athletic sports.

The First Westerners

British explorer Captain James Cook spent a decade traversing the Pacific Ocean over the course of three voyages. His ostensible goal was to locate a fabled 'northwest passage' between the Pacific and Atlantic Oceans. However, his were also self-conscious voyages of discovery, and he sailed with a full complement of scientists and artists to document the places, plants and peoples they found. In 1778, and quite by accident, Cook chanced upon O'ahu and two other islands. He dubbed the archipelago the Sandwich Islands in honor of his patron, the Earl of Sandwich.

Cook's arrival ended nearly 500 years of isolation, and it's impossible to overstate the impact of this, or even to appreciate now what his unexpected appearance meant to Hawaiians. Cook's arrival at Kealakekua Bay on Hawai'i, the Big Island, happened to coincide with the *makahiki*, an annual harvest festival in honor of the god Lono. Cook's ships were greeted by a thousand canoes, and Hawaiian chiefs and priests honored Cook with feasting, religious rituals and deference suggesting that they perhaps considered him to be an earthly manifestation of the god.

When Cook set sail some weeks later, he encountered storms that damaged his ships and forced him to return. Suddenly, the islanders' mood had changed: no canoes rowed out to meet the ships, and mistrust replaced welcome. A series of small conflicts escalated into an angry confrontation on the beach, and Cook, in an ill-advised fit of pique, shot to

An interesting legacy has John Montagu, 4th Earl of Sandwich. He was a great supporter of Captain James Cook, and the explorer named Hawaii 'the Sandwich Islands' in his honor in 1778. The earl is also credited with inventing the sandwich: the first example of the lunchtime staple was apparently a piece of salted beef between two slices of toasted bread.

HISTORY THE FIRST WESTERNERS

1450	1778–79	1790	1795
Ma'ilikukahi, the ancient *mo'i* (high chief) of O'ahu, moves his capital to Waikiki, a coastal wetland known for its fertile farmlands and abundant fishing, as well as being a place of recreation and healing.	Captain James Cook becomes the first Western explorer to reach the Hawaiian Islands. O'ahu is one of three islands he initially spots. He gets no further east on this voyage.	Kamehameha launches a military campaign to gain control over all the Hawaiian Islands.	Kamehameha the Great conquers O'ahu, nearly completing the unification of the Hawaiian kingdom. The islands of Kaua'i and Ni'ihau, ruled by Kaumuali'i, resist paying tribute until 1810.

death a Hawaiian while surrounded by thousands of native people, who immediately descended on Cook, killing him in return.

Kamehameha the Great

In the years following Cook's death, a small, steady number of trading ships sought out Hawaii as a mid-Pacific supply point, and increasingly the thing that Hawaiian chiefs traded for most was firearms. Bolstered with muskets and cannons, Kamehameha, one of the chiefs on the Big Island, began a tremendous military campaign in 1790 to conquer all the Hawaiian Islands. Other chiefs had tried this and failed, but Kamehameha not only had guns but was prophesied to succeed, and he possessed an unyielding, charismatic determination.

Within five bloody years Kamehameha had conquered all the main islands but Kaua'i (which eventually joined peacefully). The bloody campaign on O'ahu started with a fleet of war canoes landing on the shores

VOYAGING BY THE STARS

In 1976 a double-hulled wooden canoe and its crew set off from O'ahu's Windward Coast, aiming to recreate the journey of Hawaii's first human settlers and to do what no one had done in more than 600 years: sail 2400 miles to Tahiti without the benefit of radar, compass, satellites or sextant. Launched by the Polynesian Voyaging Society, this modern reproduction of an ancient Hawaiian long-distance seafaring canoe was named *Hokule'a* (Star of Gladness).

The canoe's Micronesian navigator, Mau Piailug, still knew the art of traditional Polynesian wayfaring at a time when such knowledge had been lost to Hawaiian culture. He knew how to use horizon or zenith stars – those that always rose over known islands – as a guide, then evaluate currents, winds, landmarks and time in a complex system of dead reckoning to stay on course. In the mind's eye, the trick is to hold the canoe still in relation to the stars while the island sails toward you.

Academic skeptics had long questioned whether Hawaii's early settlers really were capable of journeying back and forth across such vast, empty ocean. After 33 days at sea, the crew of the *Hokule'a* proved those so-called experts wrong by reaching their destination, where they were greeted by 20,000 Tahitians. This historic achievement helped spark a revival of interest in Hawaii's Polynesian cultural heritage.

Since its historic 1976 voyage, the *Hokule'a* has served as a floating living-history classroom. The canoe made a number of transoceanic voyages, sailing throughout Polynesia and to the US mainland, Canada, Micronesia and Japan. From 2014 to 2017 the *Hokule'a* undertook a circumnavigation of the globe, and after returning to Hawaii has continued to sail around the Hawaiian Islands to reconnect with local communities and schools and to share stories and lessons learned on the worldwide voyage. Learn more at www.hokulea.com.

1810	1819	1823	1843
Kamehameha the Great unites the major Hawaiian Islands into one sovereign kingdom. O'ahu is his last major conquest; he moves his seat of power to O'ahu.	Kamehameha the Great dies, leaving his kingdom to son Liholiho, with his favorite wife, Queen Ka'ahumanu, as regent. The *kapu* (taboo) system is abolished and many heiau (ancient temples) are destroyed.	After allowing the first Christian missionaries to land on O'ahu in 1820, Kamehameha II (Liholiho) fatefully becomes the first Hawaiian king to travel abroad, dying of measles in London in 1824.	Hawaii's only 'invasion' by a foreign power occurs when George Paulet, an upstart British commander upset about a petty land deal involving a British national, sails into Honolulu and seizes O'ahu for six months.

of Waikiki in 1795. Kamehameha then led his warriors up the Nu'uanu Valley to meet the entrenched O'ahuan defenders. The O'ahuans, who were prepared for spear-and-stone warfare, panicked when they realized that Kamehameha had brought in a handful of Western sharpshooters with modern firearms. Fleeing up the cliffs in retreat, they were forced to make a doomed last stand.

Some O'ahuan warriors, including King Kalanikupule, escaped into the upland forests. When Kalanikupule surfaced a few months later, Kamehameha offered the fallen king as a human sacrifice to his war god Ku. Kamehameha's victory marked the end of an era. The O'ahu invasion was the last battle ever fought between Hawaiian troops, and saw the beginning of Hawaii's emergence as a united kingdom. It also set the stage for the center of power to shift to O'ahu.

Founding of Honolulu

In 1793 the English frigate *Butterworth* became the first foreign ship to sail into what is now called Honolulu Harbor. Its captain, William Brown, named the protected harbor Fair Haven. Ships that followed called it Brown's Harbor. Over time the name Honolulu, which means 'Sheltered Bay,' came to be used for both the harbor and the seaside district that the Hawaiians had called Kou.

As more and more foreign ships found their way to Honolulu, a harborside village of thatched houses sprang up. Shops selling food and other simple provisions to the sailors opened along the waterfront. The port soon became a focal point for the lucrative trade conducted by Yankee clippers, those merchant ships that plied the seas between the US and China. The wealth of manufactured goods the ships carried – from iron cannons to ornate furniture – was unlike anything the Hawaiians had ever seen.

In 1809 Kamehameha the Great, who had been living in his royal court in Waikiki, decided to move to the Honolulu Harbor area, which by then had grown into a village of almost 1800 people. The king wanted to maintain control over the growing foreign presence and make sure Hawaiians got a fair deal in any trade. To keep an eye on all the commercial action flowing into and out of the harbor, he set up a residence near the waterfront on what today is the corner of Bethel and Queen Sts.

Kamehameha traded Hawaii's highly prized sandalwood, which was shipped to China, mostly for weapons and luxury goods. As the trade grew, the king built harborside warehouses to store his acquisitions, and he introduced wharfage fees to build up his treasury. New England Yankees, who dominated the sandalwood trade, quickly became the main foreign presence in Honolulu.

Honolulu Historical Buildings

....

'Iolani Palace

....

Hawaiian Mission Houses Historic Site

....

Kawaiaha'o Church

....

Washington Place

....

Cathedral of St Andrew

HISTORY FOUNDING OF HONOLULU

1854	1863	1866	1885
Kamehameha IV ascends the throne. He passes a law mandating that all children be given a Christian name along with their Hawaiian name; this statute stays on the books until 1967.	Kohala Sugar Company, O'ahu's first sugar plantation, is established. Soon sugarcane crops cover much of central and northern O'ahu and remain a key part of the economy until well after WWII.	The first group of patients with Hansen's disease (formerly known as leprosy) are exiled from O'ahu's Kahili Hospital to Moloka'i's Kalaupapa Peninsula. This policy of forced isolation continues until 1969.	Captain John Kidwell plants pineapples in the Manoa Valley. A decade later, James Dole starts a plantation in Wahiawa. Pineapples remain a major part of O'ahu's agriculture until the 1980s.

By the time of Kamehameha the Great's death in 1819, nearly 3500 people lived in Honolulu and it continued to boom as more foreigners arrived. Honolulu, the city that built up around the harbor, was firmly established as the center of Hawaii's commerce. To this day Honolulu Harbor remains the most important commercial harbor in the state.

Traders, Whalers & Soul Savers

By 1820 whaling ships sailing the Pacific began to pull into Honolulu for supplies, liquor and women. To meet their needs, shops, taverns and brothels sprang up around the harbor.

To the ire of the whalers, Christian missionaries came ashore in their wake. Hawaii's first missionary ship sailed into Honolulu on April 14, 1820, carrying staunch Calvinists who were set on saving the Hawaiians from their 'heathen ways.'

Although both the missionaries and the whalers hailed from New England, they had little else in common and were soon at odds. The missionaries were intent on saving souls and the whalers were intent, after months at sea, on satisfying more earthly desires. To most sailors, there was 'no God west of the Horn.'

In time the missionaries gained enough influence with Hawaiian royalty to have laws enacted against drunkenness and prostitution. In response, by the peak whaling years of the mid-1800s, most whaling boats had abandoned Honolulu, preferring to land in Lahaina on Maui, where whalers had gained the upper hand over the missionaries.

Interestingly, both groups left their mark on Honolulu. To this day the headquarters of the Protestant mission sits placidly in downtown Honolulu, while only minutes away Honolulu's red-light district continues to attract sea-weary sailors and wayward souls. Kawaiaha'o Church, built by those first missionaries, sits opposite the royal palace and still holds services in the Hawaiian language.

Downtown Honolulu also became the headquarters for emerging corporations that eventually gained control of Hawaii's commerce. It's no coincidence that their lists of corporate board members – Alexander, Baldwin, Cooke and Dole – read like a roster from the first mission ships, for indeed it was the sons of missionaries who became the power brokers in the new Hawaii.

Immigration

Ko (sugarcane) arrived in Hawaii with the early Polynesian settlers. Although the Hawaiians enjoyed chewing the cane for its juices, they never refined it into sugar.

In 1835 a Bostonian, William Hooper, saw a bigger opportunity in sugar and set out to establish Hawaii's first sugar plantation. Hooper

The popular radio program *Hawaii Calls* introduced the world to Hawaiian music. It broadcast from the banyan-tree courtyard of Waikiki's Moana Hotel between 1935 and 1975. CD compilations are available through www. mele.com.

1889	1893	1901	1912
A group of 150 Hawaiian royalists attempts to overthrow the 'bayonet constitution' by occupying 'Iolani Palace. It was called the Wilcox Rebellion after its part-Hawaiian leader, who surrendered after just one day.	Queen Lili'uokalani is overthrown. The son of an American missionary declares himself leader of the provisional government. A group of US sailors marches on 'Iolani Palace, aiming guns at the queen's residence.	The Moana Hotel, Waikiki's first tourist hotel, opens to guests arriving at Honolulu Harbor on cruise ships. The resort is built atop a former royal Hawaiian compound.	Champion surfer Duke Kahanamoku wins his first gold medal in the 100m freestyle swim at the Stockholm Olympics.

convinced Honolulu investors to put up the money for his venture and then worked out a deal with Kamehameha III to lease 980 acres of land for $300. His next step was to negotiate with the *ali'i* (royalty and chiefs) for the right to use Hawaiian laborers, as Hawaii was still a feudal society.

The new plantation system, which introduced the concept of growing crops for profit rather than subsistence, marked the advent of capitalism and the introduction of wage labor in Hawaii. The sugar industry emerged at the same time that whalers began arriving in force, and together they became the foundation of Hawaii's economy.

While the sugar industry boomed, Hawaii's native population declined, largely as the result of diseases introduced by foreigners. To expand their operations, the plantation owners looked overseas for a labor supply. They needed immigrants accustomed to working long days in hot weather, and for whom the low wages would seem like an opportunity.

In 1852 the plantation owners began recruiting laborers from China. In 1868 they went to Japan and in the 1870s they brought in Portuguese from the Azores. After Hawaii's 1898 annexation to the USA resulted in restrictions on Chinese immigration, plantation owners turned to Puerto Ricans and Koreans. Filipinos were the last group of immigrants brought to Hawaii to work the fields; the first wave came in 1906, the last in 1946. O'ahu plantation towns, such as Waipahu and Waialua, grew up around the mills, with barber shops, beer halls and bathhouses catering to the workers. Even today a drive through these sleepy towns, with their now-defunct mills (both closed in the 1990s), offers a glimpse of plantation history.

Honolulu as Capital

In 1845 Kamehameha III, the last son of Kamehameha the Great, moved the capital of the Hawaiian kingdom from Maui to Honolulu. Kamehameha III, who ruled from 1825 to 1854, established Hawaii's first national legislature, provided for a supreme court and passed the Great Mahele Land Act, which established religious freedom and gave all (male) citizens the right to vote.

Hawaii's only 'invasion' by a foreign power occurred in 1843 when George Paulet, an upstart British commander upset about a petty land deal involving a British national, sailed into Honolulu commanding the British ship *Carysfort* and seized O'ahu for six months. In that short period, he anglicized street names, seized property and began to collect taxes.

To avoid bloodshed, Kamehameha III stood aside as the British flag was raised and the ship's band played 'God Save the Queen.' Queen Victoria herself wasn't flattered. After catching wind of the incident, she dispatched Admiral Richard Thomas to restore Hawaiian independence.

History Museums

Bishop Museum (Honolulu)

'Iolani Palace (Honolulu)

Hawaiian Mission Houses Historic Site (Honolulu)

Pearl Harbor National Memorial (Pearl Harbor)

US Army Museum of Hawai'i (Waikiki)

Hawaii's Plantation Village (Waipahu)

HISTORY HONOLULU AS CAPITAL

1920s	1936	1941	1955
After winning more Olympic medals for swimming, Duke Kahanamoku gives surfing demonstrations, popularizing a sport that had been limited mostly to O'ahu. He uses a 16ft longboard made of redwood.	Pan American airlines flies the first passenger flights from the US mainland to Hawaii. This aviation milestone ushers in the transpacific jet age and mass tourism on O'ahu, mainly at Waikiki Beach.	Japanese forces stage a surprise attack on Pearl Harbor, catapulting the USA into WWII. Under martial law, around 1250 Japanese residents of Hawaii are forced into internment camps on O'ahu and the Big Island.	The first part of what was to become Hilton Hawaiian Village opens on what had been the home of Duke Kahanamoku. As it grows to today's 3000-plus rooms it spurs mass tourism at Waikiki.

WWII's 442nd Second Regimental Combat Team, comprising Japanese Americans, was the most decorated unit in US history. Honolulu's own Senator Daniel Inouye lost an arm in the fighting.

Admiral Thomas raised the Hawaiian flag in Honolulu again at the site of what is today Thomas Sq.

As the flag was raised, Kamehameha III uttered the words 'Ua mau ke ea o ka aina i ka pono,' meaning 'The life of the land is perpetuated in righteousness,' which remains Hawaii's official motto.

In an 1853 census Honolulu registered 11,450 residents, a full 15% of the Hawaiian kingdom's population. Though still a frontier town with dusty streets and simple wooden buildings, Honolulu was both the commercial and political center of the kingdom.

In the decades that followed, Honolulu took on a modern appearance as the monarchy erected a number of stately buildings in the city center, including St Andrew's Cathedral, 'Iolani Palace and the supreme-court building Ali'iolani Hale.

Fall of the Monarchy

As much as any other monarch, King David Kalakaua, who reigned from 1874 to 1891, fought to restore Hawaiian culture and native pride. With robust joy, he resurrected hula and its attendant arts from near extinction (earning himself the nickname 'the Merrie Monarch'), much to the dismay of missionaries. He cared not a whit about placating the plantation oligarchy either. The king spent money lavishly and piled up massive debt. Wanting Hawaii's monarchy to be equal to any in the world, he built Honolulu's 'Iolani Palace, holding an extravagant coronation ceremony in 1883. Foreign businessmen considered these actions to be egotistical follies.

Kalakaua was a mercurial decision-maker given to summarily replacing his entire cabinet on a whim. A secret, antimonarchy group of mostly non–Native Hawaiian residents calling itself the Hawaiian League formed, and in 1887 it forced Kalakaua to sign a new 'bayonet' constitution that stripped the monarchy of most of its powers, and changed the voting laws to include only those who met certain income and property requirements – effectively disenfranchising all but wealthy, mostly Caucasian, mostly O'ahu-based business owners. To ensure economic profitability, the Hawaiian League was ready to sacrifice Hawaiian sovereignty.

When King Kalakaua died in 1891, his sister and heir, Princess Lili'uokalani, ascended the throne. The queen fought against foreign intervention and control as she secretly drafted a new constitution to restore Native Hawaiian voting rights and the monarchy's powers. In 1893, before Lili'uokalani could present this constitution to Hawaii's people, a hastily formed 'Committee of Safety' put into violent motion the Hawaiian League's long-brewing plans to overthrow the Hawaiian government. Without an army to defend her, and opting to avoid bloodshed, the queen stepped down.

1959	1961	1968	1971
Hawaii becomes the 50th US state; Honolulu's Daniel Inouye is elected first Japanese American in Congress. In 1963 he moves up to the Senate and serves until 2012.	Barack Obama is born and spends much of his childhood in Honolulu. In 2008 he is elected as the 44th US president. He enjoys many family vacations in Kailua on O'ahu's Windward Coast.	With one of TV's most memorable opening sequences, Hawaii Five-O premieres and runs for 12 seasons. Set on O'ahu, it makes 'Book 'em, Danno' a catchphrase. A reboot launches in 2010.	The first Hawaiian Masters surfing competition, a precursor to the Triple Crown of Surfing, is held at Sunset Beach on O'ahu's North Shore. Legendary big-wave rider Eddie Aikau is named O'ahu's Lifeguard of the Year.

After the coup, the new provisional government immediately requested annexation by the US. However, much to its surprise, President Grover Cleveland reviewed the situation and refused: he condemned the coup as illegal, conducted on a false pretext and against the will of the Hawaiian people, and he requested that Lili'uokalani be reinstated. Miffed but unbowed, the Committee of Safety instead established its own government, the Republic of Hawaii.

Annexation, War & Statehood

For five years, Queen Lili'uokalani pressed her case (for a time while under house arrest at 'Iolani Palace) – even collecting an anti-annexation petition signed by the vast majority of Native Hawaiians – to no avail. In 1898, spurred by President McKinley, the US approved a resolution for annexing the Republic of Hawaii as a US territory.

In part, the US justified this colonialism because the ongoing Spanish-American War had highlighted the strategic importance of the islands as a Pacific military base. Indeed, some Americans feared that if the US didn't take Hawaii, another Pacific Rim power (such as Japan) just might. The US Navy quickly established its Pacific headquarters at Pearl Harbor and built Schofield Barracks, at that time the largest US army base in the world, in Central O'ahu. The military soon became the leading sector of O'ahu's economy.

Pan American airlines flew the first passenger flights from the US mainland to Hawaii in 1936, an aviation milestone that ushered in the transpacific air age. Waikiki was now only hours away from the US West Coast and was on the verge of becoming a major tourism destination. Everything was put on hold when on December 7, 1941, a wave of Japanese bombers attacked Pearl Harbor, jolting the USA into WWII.

The war brought Hawaii closer to the center stage of American culture and politics. The prospect of statehood had long been an important topic, but to the overwhelmingly white and largely conservative Congress, Hawaii's multiethnic community was too exotic and foreign to be thought of as 'American.'

In March 1959 the US Congress finally passed legislation to make Hawaii a state. On June 27 a plebiscite was held in Hawaii, with more than 90% of the islanders voting for statehood. On August 21, 1959, after 61 years of territorial status, Hawaii became the 50th state of the USA.

Modern O'ahu

In the early 1970s O'ahu began to experience a resurgence of cultural pride not seen since the reign of King Kalakaua. It is difficult to pinpoint one event or activity that caused this resurgence, but the retracing of the Hawaii migration routes by the *Hokule'a* was certainly a catalyst. This

In 1935 Amelia Earhart became the first person to fly solo from Honolulu to California, spanning the distance in 13 hours.

1976	1980	1990	1993
The Hawaiian renaissance flowers and is symbolized by the successful wayfaring voyage of the *Hokule'a* canoe to Tahiti, first launched from the Windward Coast.	Tom Selleck and too-short men's shorts become all the rage as *Magnum, P. I.* hits US TV. Much of the action takes place on O'ahu's Windward Coast.	Hawaii tourism hits seven million people a year, with most (five million) spending time in Waikiki. The enormous industry replaces sugar, pineapples and the military as O'ahu's main source of income.	President Clinton signs 'Apology Resolution,' recognizing the illegal overthrow of the kingdom in 1893. It acknowledges that 'the Native Hawaiian people never directly relinquished... their claims to inherent sovereignty.'

project required the learning of ancient navigational skills and sailing techniques that had been nearly forgotten.

In 1976 a group of activists illegally occupied Kaho'olawe, aka 'Target Island,' which the US government had taken during WWII and used for bombing practice ever since. During another protest occupation attempt in 1977, two activist members of the Protect Kaho'olawe 'Ohana (PKO) – George Helm and Kimo Mitchell – disappeared at sea, instantly becoming martyrs. Saving Kaho'olawe became a rallying cry, and it radicalized a nascent Native Hawaiian rights movement that continues today.

When the state held its landmark Constitutional Convention in 1978, it passed several amendments of special importance to Native Hawaiians. For example, it made Hawaiian the official state language (along with English) and mandated that Hawaiian culture be taught in public schools. At the grassroots level, the islands were simultaneously experiencing a revival of Hawaiian culture, with a surge in residents – of all ethnicities – joining hula *halau* (schools), learning to play Hawaiian music and rediscovering traditional island crafts such as feather-lei making.

Revival of the Hawaiian language has been a focal point of the Hawaiian renaissance. By the 1970s the pool of native Hawaiian speakers had dropped to fewer than 1000 individuals statewide. In an effort to reverse this trend, Hawaiian-language immersion schools began to emerge and the University of Hawai'i began offering Hawaiian-language classes.

Music has also been affected by the ongoing Hawaiian renaissance, and leading contemporary musicians, such as Hapa and Keali'i Reichel, sing in the Hawaiian language. Many have also become interested in relearning nearly lost arts, such as the making of *kapa* (bark cloth), drums, feather lei, wooden bowls and other traditional items. Many people feel that if this renaissance hadn't occurred, Hawaiian language and culture would now be nearly extinct.

A heightened consciousness created by the 1993 centennial anniversary of Queen Lili'uokalani's overthrow served as a rallying point for a Hawaiian sovereignty movement intent on righting some of the wrongs of the previous century. Plenty of discussion has taken place since, but agreement on what form sovereignty should take and who qualifies as a Native Hawaiian has yet to emerge.

Meanwhile, 70% of Hawaii's 1.4 million residents live on O'ahu. Old sugar plantations have been turned into subdivisions, but some people can already see the day when the supply of land suitable for housing is exhausted. And while people debate ways to diversify the economy, tourism is still the main industry on O'ahu, attracting millions of North Americans and Asians to a beautiful island that's considered 'safe' in an unsettled world.

The Historic Hawai'i Foundation has an online map of historic sites across O'ahu and the other islands. It also has features, walking tours and more. See www.historichawaii.org.

1996	2004	2012	2019
The last remaining sugar mill on O'ahu, built at Waialua on the North Shore in 1898, closes its doors after rising labor costs drive the sugar industry to Mexico and the Philippines.	The TV show *Lost* premieres and runs for six seasons. The show about the survivors of an airplane crash is filmed on O'ahu, especially at isolated beaches in the north.	President Obama is reelected. He again wins more than 70% of the vote in Hawaii – more than in any other state. Later he rules out locating his presidential library on O'ahu, disappointing many.	The latest budget forecast for the troubled Honolulu Rail Transit project puts the cost at over $8 billion, more than twice the original estimate.

People of O'ahu

Everything you imagine when you hear the name Hawaii is probably true. Whatever your postcard idyll might be – a paradise of white sandy beaches, emerald cliffs and azure seas, of falsetto-voiced ukulele strummers, graceful hula dancers and sun-bronzed surfers – it exists somewhere on the islands. But beyond the frame of that magical postcard is a startlingly different version of Hawaii, a real place where real people live.

Slow Down, This Ain't the Mainland

O'ahu is a Polynesian island, yes. But one with shopping malls, landfills, industrial parks, cookie-cutter housing developments, military bases and ramshackle small towns. In many ways it's much like the rest of the US, and a first-time visitor stepping off the plane may be surprised to find a place where interstate highways and McDonald's look pretty much the same as back on 'da mainland.'

Above Prince Kuhio Day celebrations

Underneath the veneer of an imported consumer culture is a different world, a world defined by – and proud of – its cultural separateness, its geographical isolation, its unique mix of Polynesian, Asian and Western traditions. While those cultures don't always blend seamlessly, there are very few places in the world today where so many different ethnicities, with no one group commanding a substantial majority, get along so well.

Perhaps it's because they live on a tiny island in the middle of an ocean that O'ahu residents strive to treat one another with aloha, act politely and respectfully, and 'no make waves' (ie be cool). Smiling or waving at complete strangers is not that unusual here. As Native Hawaiians say, 'We're all in the same canoe.' No matter their race or background, everyone shares an awareness of living in one of the earth's most extraordinary spots.

Island Identity

Who are you?

A haole is a white person (except local Portuguese). The term 'haole' can be insulting or playful, depending on context.

Honolulu is 'the city,' not only for those who live on O'ahu but for all of Hawaii. Far slower paced than New York City or Los Angeles, Hawaii's capital can still be surprisingly cosmopolitan, technologically savvy and fashion conscious. Right or wrong, Honoluluans see themselves as at the center of everything; they deal with the traffic jams and high-rises because along with them come better-paying jobs, vibrant arts and cultural scenes, trendy shops and (relatively tame) nightlife. Ritzy suburbs sprawl along the coast east of Waikiki, while military bases are found around Pearl Harbor to 'Ewa in the west and in Wahiawa in the island's center.

If it weren't for the occasional ride into the city to pick up supplies, the lifestyle of rural O'ahuans would be as 'small town' as you'd find anywhere else in Hawaii. O'ahu's Windward Coast, North Shore and Leeward Coast are considered 'the country.' (Though in a landscape as compressed as this island, 'country' is relative: rural areas are not too far from the urban or suburban, and there are no vast swaths of wilderness as on the mainland.) Here, status often isn't measured by a Lexus but by a monster truck.

'Hawaiian time' – the stereotype that everyone and everything in the islands moves a bit more slowly than on the mainland – may be a bit of a joke, but locals are proud of their laid-back lifestyle, and proud that they can slow down and enjoy life on their gorgeous island with their *'ohana* (extended family and friends).

'Ohana is important everywhere, but in small towns it's often the center of life. Even in Honolulu, when locals first meet they don't ask 'What do you do?' but 'Where you wen' grad?' (Where did you go to high school?). Like ancient Hawaiians comparing genealogies, locals define themselves in part by the communities to which they belong: extended family, island, town, high school. And when two locals happen to meet outside Hawaii, there's an automatic bond, often based on shared homesickness. But wherever they go, they're still part of Hawaii's extended *'ohana*.

Multiculturalism

Who are you?

Hapa is a person of mixed ancestry, often *hapa haole* (literally 'half white').

During the 2008 US presidential election, Barack Obama, who spent much of his boyhood in Honolulu, was lauded by locals because of his calm demeanor and his respect for diversity. He also displayed true devotion to his *'ohana* by suspending his campaign and visiting his sick grandmother in Honolulu. She died days before the election. To locals, these are the things that count. What didn't matter to Hawaii was what the rest of the nation seemed fixated on: his race.

That Obama is mixed race was barely worth mentioning. Of course he's mixed race – who in Hawaii isn't? One legacy of the plantation era is Hawaii's unselfconscious and inclusive mixing of ethnicities; cultural differences are freely acknowledged, even carefully maintained, but they don't normally divide people. Depending on your perspective, Honolulu is either America's most Asian city or Polynesia's most American city.

Honolulu's Chinatown (p94)

Hawaii is as ethnically diverse as and more racially intermixed than California, Texas and Florida, but without the large African American and Latino populations that help define those states.

Among older locals, plantation-era stereotypes still inform social hierarchies and interactions. During the plantation days, whites were the wealthy owners, and for years afterwards people would half-seriously joke about the privileges that came with being a haole (Caucasian) 'boss.' Hawaii's youth often dismiss racial distinctions even as they continue to speak plantation-born pidgin. With intermarriage, it's not uncommon to meet locals who can rattle off several ethnicities in their ancestry – for example, Native Hawaiian, Chinese, Portuguese and haole.

Lifestyle

The values of tolerance and acceptance extend beyond race – they apply also to religion and sexual orientation. While for many years Hawaii was politically behind the curve in its treatment of gay, lesbian and transgender people, especially in some tight-knit rural communities, today the right to same-sex civil unions is guaranteed by state law.

Most voters are middle-of-the-road Democrats who vote along party, racial, ethnic, seniority and local/nonlocal lines. In everyday life, most don't jump into a controversial topic just to argue the point. At community meetings and activist rallies, the most vocal liberals are often mainland transplants. Yet as more mainlanders settle on O'ahu, especially around Kailua and Kane'ohe on the Windward Coast, traditional stereotypes are fading.

Native Hawaiians still struggle with the colonial legacy that has marginalized them in their own homeland. Hawaiians constitute a disproportionate number of those homeless and impoverished. Native Hawaiian schoolchildren tend to score below state averages in reading and math and are more likely to drop out of school. Hawaiian charter schools were created in part to address this problem. However, many Native Hawaiians feel that some form of sovereignty is necessary to correct these deeply entrenched inequities.

Who are you?

A Hawaiian is a person of Native Hawaiian ancestry. Don't use the term 'Hawaiian' as a catchall for all island residents.

Beach sunset in Honolulu

Honolulu's Chinatown still has its seedy edges, just as in the 19th-century whaling days, with skid rows of drug addicts, sex workers and panhandlers. The use of 'ice' (methamphetamine, aka crystal meth) became rampant in the 1990s, in both urban and rural communities, where it's an ongoing social and law-enforcement challenge. Homelessness and a lack of affordable housing are also serious social and political issues, with hundreds of O'ahuans encamped semipermanently at public beaches, especially on the Wai'anae Coast.

Language
Hawaiian

A melodious Polynesian language, Hawaiian almost disappeared when, soon after the overthrow of the Hawaiian kingdom in 1893, a law was passed to make it illegal to teach in schools in anything but the English language. English replaced Hawaiian as the official language of government, business and education. Over the last few decades, however, as part of the Hawaiian renaissance, there has been a determined movement to revitalize Hawaiian. While there has been good progress, very few Native Hawaiians on O'ahu can speak Hawaiian fluently.

Visitors will mostly run into Hawaiian when encountering words that have become commonly used in modern language, such as aloha, hula lei and *mahalo* (thank you).

You'll also run into Hawaiian place or road names, such as Kapi'olani Park, Kalakaua Ave, Kapahulu Ave and the Kamehameha Hwy. Don't just blank out when you see these long Hawaiian words starting with 'K'. Locals will appreciate efforts to pronounce Hawaiian names properly. They won't give you a hard time if you make a mistake, and it's not as hard as it looks. In fact, the Hawaiian language uses only 12 letters: the five vowels – a, e, i, o, u – and seven consonants – h, k, l, m, n, p, w. When missionaries found

Who are you?
A *kama'ina* is a person who is native to a particular place. Commonly, 'kama'ina' discounts' apply to any island resident (ie anyone with a state driver's license).

that the Hawaiians had no written language, they formulated a simple way to phonetically write everything down. Interestingly, 45 years earlier, when Captain Cook turned up in 1778, he wrote Hawaii as 'Owhyhee'.

The upside-down apostrophe is called an *okina;* it indicates a glottal stop or abrupt break in the middle of a word: Kapi'olani Park, Nu'uanu Ave, and the island's name, O'ahu.

When you're feeling confident, here's the name of Hawaii's state fish to work on: *humuhumunukunukuapua'a.* It's a gorgeous kind of trig-gerfish and a lot easier to pronounce if broken up with hyphens: *humu-humu-nuku-nuku-apua-a.* If it's all too much, *humuhumu* will do.

English/Pidgin

Basically, English is the primary language spoken on O'ahu but, depend-ing on who you're talking to, you could find it noticeably different to the English you're used to hearing. The Hawaiian version has been enriched with words and accents introduced by immigrant groups such as the Chi-nese, Japanese, Filipinos, Koreans, Okinawans, Portuguese, Puerto Ricans, Samoans and Tongans. Pidgin is an ever-evolving language and new words are being introduced all the time. If you have the chance to listen to two locals talking, listen in and see if you can understand what they're saying.

Nonverbal Communication

Language isn't all words. Here are a couple of non-verbal forms of com-munication you're likely to run into:

Raising-of-the-eyebrows greeting Common throughout Polynesia. You're likely to see it in greetings between Pacific Island peoples.

The shaka A hand gesture done by extending the pinkie and thumb while curling the three middle fingers. It's friendly – a Hawaiian version of the thumbs-up – and in no way should be interpreted as an 'up yours' gesture.

THE NUMBERS

➡ About 70% of Hawaii's population of 1.4 million people live on O'ahu (980,000).

➡ Although it is the third-largest of Hawaii's islands, the land area of O'ahu is less than 10% of the land area of the state of Hawaii.

➡ O'ahu's population density is 1600 people per square mile; Maui has the second-densest population of the Hawaiian islands at 200 people per square mile.

Where on O'ahu?

In very approximate figures:

➡ 450,000 people live in greater Honolulu, from 'Aiea down to Koko Head, including Waikiki.

➡ 100,000 live in the Kane'ohe and Kailua area on the Windward Coast.

➡ 100,000 live in Mililani and Wahiawa in Central O'ahu.

➡ 70,000 live in Pearl City and Waipahu, west of Honolulu.

➡ 40,000 live on the Leeward Coast.

Military Numbers

➡ About 375,000 military and civilian personnel are assigned to US Indo-Pacific Command (USPACOM), which is based in Honolulu. USPACOM is responsible for an area covering more than 100 million square miles, about 52% of the earth's surface.

Visitor Numbers

➡ Of the nine million visitors to Hawaii annually (over six times the state's population!), nearly all pass through O'ahu and more than half stay on the island.

➡ On average, there are 90,000 to 100,000 visitors on O'ahu each day.

SSGUY / SHUTTERSTOCK ©

Top Polynesian Cultural Center (p238)

Bottom Residential community near Pearl City (p181)

Arts & Crafts

The islands' arts are all around you. Any night in Waikiki you might catch a slack key guitar great in concert. But you also may overhear an impromptu ukulele performance at a rural beach park or happen upon a hula *halau* (school) performing at a farmers market. Keep your eyes and ears open: the local music, hula, native crafts and storytelling are a great way to experience Hawaiian culture.

Hula
Waikiki is the best place to reliably catch hula performances. Bars, restaurants and hotels often include hula in their evening entertainment, and the Kuhio Beach Torchlighting & Hula Show (p167) is free. Another way to experience hula is to attend a luau; the Polynesian Cultural Center (p238), at La'ie on the Windward Coast, has the most authentic performances. You may also be lucky enough to see a *halau* performing at a local festival; always check event calendars.

Island Music
In Honolulu, for classic and contemporary Hawaiian music tune into KINE Radio (105.1 FM). You can browse for recordings online at Mountain Apple Company (www.mountainapplecompany.com) or Mele (www.mele.com). Also check out recent winners of the Na Hoku Hanohano Awards (www.nahokuhanohano.org), Hawaii's version of the Grammys.

Traditional Crafts
Many modern painters, printmakers, photographers and graphic and textile artists draw inspiration from Hawaii's cultural heritage, as showcased at the multimedia Hawai'i State Art Museum in downtown Honolulu. Also check out the contemporary island art galleries in nearby Chinatown. Arts and crafts fairs take place island-wide throughout the year. The Honolulu Made in Hawaii Festival (www.madeinhawaiifestival.com) happens over a weekend in August.

Island Writings
Bamboo Ridge Press (www.bambooridge.com) has launched many local writers' careers.

➡ Honolulu-born Kiana Davenport's works are well recommended; *Song of the Exile* follows two fictional families from WWII through US statehood.

➡ Kaui Hart Hemmings, also O'ahu born, made a splash when her first novel, *The Descendants,* was made into a movie.

➡ Lois-Ann Yamanaka, author of the award-winning anthology *Saturday Night at the Pahala Theatre,* has caused controversy with the gritty depictions of local life in her novels and poetry.

Best Live Local Acts

Jack Johnson

Jake Shimabukuro

Ekolu

Jerry Santos & Friends

Kelly Boy De Lima with Kapena

Henry Kapono

Natural Vibrations (Natty Vibes)

O'AHU ON SCREEN

The Descendants (2011) George Clooney in an Academy Award winner.

Blue Hawaii (1961) Elvis Presley on Waikiki.

Tora! Tora! Tora! (1970) Dramatization of the Pearl Harbor attack.

Highwater (2009) Documentary about the Triple Crown of Surfing competition.

50 First Dates (2004) Romantic comedy filmed near Moli'i Fishpond.

From Here to Eternity (1953) Burt Lancaster and Deborah Kerr embrace in the surf.

Lots of television programs, such as **Magnum, P.I.**, **Hawaii Five-O** and **Lost**.

Art on O'ahu

Honolulu and the island of O'ahu as a whole have some amazing art institutions. There are several galleries in Chinatown, and you'll find impressive statues in public places in Honolulu, Waikiki and around the island. Check out the following:

Honolulu Museum of Art (p96) Exceptional fine-arts museum with galleries, cafe, shop and theater.

Hawai'i State Art Museum (p88) Traditional and contemporary art from Hawaii's multiethnic communities in the downtown area.

Bishop Museum (p100) Remarkable array of cultural and natural-history exhibits west of downtown.

Honolulu Museum of Art at First Hawaiian Center (p93) Features fascinating mixed-media exhibits of modern and contemporary works by Hawaii artists.

Louis Pohl Gallery (p130) Paintings by contemporary island artists and works by former 'living treasure' of Hawaii Louis Pohl.

Pegge Hopper Gallery (p130) Distinctive colorful prints and paintings depicting island women.

Art on the Zoo Fence (p169) Dozens of artists hang their works along the fence on the ocean side of the Honolulu Zoo every weekend, weather permitting.

Nohea Gallery (p169) High-end gallery in Waikiki selling O'ahu-produced paintings, glassware, pottery and woodwork.

Shangri La (p201) Doris Duke's Islamic-art extravaganza at Black Point, east of Diamond Head.

John Young Museum of Art (p99) Collection of ceramics, pottery and culture from around the world at the University of Hawai'i.

Sunshine Arts Gallery (p231) Works by over 100 island artists near Kahulu'u on the Windward Coast.

Hale'iwa Art Gallery (p265) Art by Pacific-island, local and regional painters, photographers, sculptors and glassblowers on the North Shore.

Gyotaku by Naoki (p229) Magnificent Japanese-style fish prints in a tiny studio in Kane'ohe.

Above Lei made from plumeria

Lei

Greetings. Devotion. Respect. Peace. Celebration. Love. A Hawaiian lei – a handcrafted garland of tropical flora – can signify myriad meanings. Giving or receiving a lei is a symbol of heartfelt aloha, not a throwaway gesture. Fragrant and fleeting, lei exemplify the beauty of nature and the embrace of *ʻohana* (extended family and friends). When offered to visitors, a lei means 'welcome!'

The Art of the Lei

In choosing their materials, lei makers express emotions and tell stories, since flowers and other natural artifacts often embody Hawaiian places and myths. Traditional lei makers use feathers, nuts, shells, seeds, seaweed, vines, leaves and fruit, in addition to fragrant flowers. The most common methods of making lei are by knotting, braiding, winding, stringing or sewing raw materials together.

Worn daily, lei were integral to ancient Hawaiian society. They were important elements of sacred hula dances and given as special gifts to loved ones, as healing medicine to the sick and as offerings to the gods, all practices that continue today. So powerful a symbol were they that on ancient Hawaii's battlefields, a lei could bring peace to warring armies.

Today, locals wear lei for special events, such as weddings, birthdays, anniversaries and graduations. It's no longer common to make one's own lei, unless you belong to a hula *halau* (school). For ceremonial hula, performers are often required to make their own lei, gathering raw materials by hand, never taking more than necessary and always thanking the tree and the gods.

Modern Celebrations

For visitors to Hawaii, the tradition of giving and receiving lei dates back to 19th-century steamships that brought the first tourists to the islands. Later, disembarking cruise-ship passengers were greeted by vendors who would toss garlands around the necks of *malihini* (newcomers).

In 1927, the poet Don Blanding and Honolulu journalist Grace Tower Warren called for making May 1 a holiday to honor lei. Every year, Lei Day is still celebrated across the islands with Hawaiian music, hula dancing, parades, and lei-making workshops and contests.

The tradition of giving a kiss with a lei began during WWII, allegedly when a hula dancer at a USO (United Services Organization) club was dared by her friends to give a military serviceman a peck on the cheek when offering him a flower lei.

Shopping for Lei

Flower lei are in high demand on O'ahu as nearly all visitors to Hawaii arrive on the island, mostly at Honolulu airport. While there are lei shops at the airport, the best leis are made in Chinatown, where there is a group of tiny stores, mostly on Maunakea St. Cindy's Lei Shoppe (p128) is very good; order online and arrange a curbside pickup on your way to the airport.

Hawaii Flower Lei (www.hawaiiflowerlei.com) is a Honolulu company that will deliver lei both locally and to the mainland using a 'lei cooler' and FedEx.

O'ahu's special flower is the *'ilima (Sida fallax)*, which blooms year-round and ranges in color from pastel yellow to burnt orange. Originally, *lei 'ilima* were reserved for royalty since they looked very much like the yellow feather lei worn only by *ali'i*, the hereditary line of rulers.

On O'ahu, it's a tradition for passengers to throw their lei into the sea as their departing ship passes Diamond Head. If the flowers of their lei float back toward the beach, it's said that they'll return to Hawaii someday.

The yellow-orange *'ilima* is the island's official flower, and a symbol of Laka, the Hawaiian goddess of hula dancing. Once favored by royalty, an *'ilima* lei may be made of up to a thousand small blossoms strung together.

LEI: DOS & DON'TS

➡ Do not wear a lei hanging down like binoculars around your neck. Instead, drape a closed (circular) lei over your shoulders, making sure equal lengths are hanging over your front and back.

➡ When presenting a lei, bow your head slightly and raise the lei above your heart. Do not drape it with your own hands over the head of the recipient because this isn't respectful; let them do it themselves.

➡ Never refuse a lei, and do not take one off in the presence of the giver.

➡ Resist the temptation to wear a lei intended for someone else. That's bad luck.

➡ Closed lei are considered unlucky for pregnant woman, so give an open (untied) lei or *haku* (head) lei instead.

➡ When you stop wearing your lei, don't trash it. Remove the string and return the lei's natural elements to the earth (eg scatter flowers in the ocean, bury seeds or nuts).

Landscapes & Wildlife

With a total land area of 594 sq miles, O'ahu is the third-largest Hawaiian island. Though it accounts for less than 10% of Hawaii's total land mass, roughly 70% of state residents call 'The Gathering Place' home. The City and County of Honolulu incorporates the entire island, as well as the Northwestern Hawaiian Islands – dozens of small, unpopulated islands and atolls stretching more than 1200 miles across the Pacific.

Geography

The island of O'ahu is really two separate shield volcanoes that arose about two million years ago and formed two mountain ranges: Wai'anae in the northwest and Ko'olau in the southeast. O'ahu's last gasp of volcanic activity occurred between 10,000 and one million years ago, creating the tuff cone of Diamond Head, Southeast O'ahu's most famous geographical landmark. The forces of erosion – wind, rain and waves –

Above Diamond Head (p199)

subsequently added more geologic character, cutting valleys, creating beaches and turning a mound of lava into paradise. Oʻahu's highest point, Mt Kaʻala (4025ft), is in the central Waiʻanae Range.

All of this oceanic-plate tectonic activity can really shake things up. Small earthquakes are not uncommon here, but Honolulu tends to be safely distant from the epicenter and feels only minor shocks. That doesn't mean that Oʻahu is completely safe, though. The Pacific Tsunami Warning Center (PTWC) that is responsible for the entire Pacific Ocean is on Ford Island in Pearl Harbor. It was set up in 1949, following a 1946 Aleutian Islands earthquake and tsunami that killed 165 people and wiped out the railway and road that went around Kaʻena Point at Oʻahu's western tip.

An Evolving Ecosystem

Hawaii is the northernmost point of the triangle of Pacific islands known as Polynesia ('Many Islands' in Greek); the other points are New Zealand in the south and Rapa Nui (Easter Island) in the east.

It has been said that if Darwin had arrived in Hawaii first, he would have developed his theory of evolution in a period of weeks instead of years. Hawaii is even more remote than the Galápagos Islands, and the archipelago boasts thousands of species of bird, plant and insect that are found nowhere else on earth.

Each of the volcanic Hawaiian Islands was formed by underwater volcanic eruptions that built them up from the sea floor over hundreds of thousands of years. They broke the sea's surface as lumps of lava with no forms of life and, out in the middle of the ocean, it wasn't easy for life-forms to get there.

Plants probably arrived by hitchhiking across the Pacific on floating debris. It's thought that birds and insects came on mid-altitude air currents, but it must have been a long journey as many species didn't make it – only a small number of bird species are represented in Hawaii. The islands have no native reptiles, ants, termites, cockroaches or scorpions, and only one mammal, the ʻopeʻapeʻa (hoary bat). For those who did make it, they found they were in paradise.

Almost all the plants, birds and insects carried by wind and waves across the vast ocean adapted so uniquely to these remote volcanic islands that they evolved into new species endemic to Hawaii. For example, the 56 known species of honeycreeper bird all descended from a single type of finch. Unfortunately, these days, only 18 of those species survive, and six are on the endangered list.

Birds didn't need to fly, so they didn't. Large flightless ducks, called *moa-nalo,* became ground birds and the main herbivores on the island.

BOX-JELLYFISH CALENDAR

The main danger out there in the water may not be the one you think it is. Box jellyfish, with a very nasty sting, turn up eight to 10 days after the full moon each month; you will not want to be in the water then. Check out the Waikiki Aquarium Box Jellyfish Calendar (www.waikikiaquarium.org/interact/box-jellyfish-calendar) for when they'll be out there. They particularly affect beaches on the south shore and around to Kailua Beach on the Windward Coast.

There will be signs on the beaches when the jellyfish are around, and lifeguards have vinegar spray, which can reduce pain. If stung, get medical help in case you suffer from a severe reaction: jellyfish stings can cause anaphylactic shock or even death. Get the help of a lifeguard or call 911.

Similar to a jellyfish, the Portuguese man-of-war also causes a painful sting. It has a purplish body and is commonly found on windward (eastern) beaches as the prevalent northeastern trade winds blow them close to shore. There is no calendar predicting their arrival.

Hawaiian monk seal (p300)

And it wasn't just birds. Hundreds of species lost the ability to fly – there were flightless moths, flightless wasps and even flightless flies! Weirdest of all, a plant-eating caterpillar evolved to become a predator, eating flies. Plant species also changed due to the lack of grazing animals. Prior to human contact, the Hawaiian Islands had no native mammals, save for monk seals and *'ope'ape'a*.

The first Polynesian voyagers turned up in canoes between 300 and 600 CE, probably from the Marquesas Islands, 2400 miles to the south. They brought pigs, dogs, rats, coconuts, bananas, taro and about two dozen other plants, and, of course, themselves. Hawaii's native creatures were completely unprepared for the carnivorous new arrivals.

Having evolved with limited competition and few predators, native species fared poorly among these aggressive introduced flora and fauna. After having thrived for three million years, the flightless *moa-nalo* was gone within 500 years of the arrival of humans – eaten to extinction, much like the moa in New Zealand centuries later.

Things got worse after Captain Cook made the first European discovery of Hawaii in 1778. The pace of alien-species introduction escalated with the arrival of European missionaries and settlers, who brought cattle, goats, mongooses, mosquitoes, foreign songbirds and more. Nearly every species introduced has been detrimental to the local environment.

Today, Hawaii is the 'extinction capital of the USA,' accounting for 75% of the nation's documented extinctions. Most environmentalists agree that the next big potential threat to O'ahu is from the brown tree snake, which has led to the extinction of all native birds on the Pacific island of Guam.

Mongoose

Animals
Marine Life

Up to 10,000 migrating North Pacific humpback whales come to Hawaii waters for calving each winter; whale-watching is a major highlight. The world's fifth-largest whale, the endangered humpback can reach lengths of 45ft and weigh up to 50 tons. Other whales (such as rarely seen blue and fin whales) also migrate through.

O'ahu waters are home to a number of dolphins, the most notable of which is the spinner dolphin that likes the western waters off Leeward O'ahu. These acrobats are nocturnal feeders that come into sheltered bays during the day to rest. They are sensitive to human disturbance, and federal guidelines recommend that swimmers do not approach closer than within 50yd.

One of the Pacific's most endangered marine creatures is the Hawaiian monk seal, named both for the monastic cowl-like fold of skin at its neck and for its solitary habits. The Hawaiian name for the animal is *'ilio holo kai,* meaning 'the dog that runs in the sea.' Adults are more than 7ft long and 500lb of toughness, some with the scars to prove they can withstand shark attacks. Once nearly driven to extinction, they now number around 1300. Although monk seals breed primarily in the remote Northwestern Hawaiian Islands, they have begun hauling out on the northwestern beaches and may be spotted at Ka'ena Point in Leeward O'ahu. Even more exciting, they occasionally turn up at Kaimana Beach, Waikiki. For their well-being, keep at least 50yd from these endangered creatures, limit your observation time to 30 minutes, and never get between a female and her pup.

Native Hawaiians traditionally revere the green sea turtle, which they call *honu.* Often considered a personal *'aumakua* (protective deity), a *honu* frequently appears in petroglyphs (and today in tattoos). For ancient Hawaiians they were a prized source of food, caught in accordance with religious and traditional codes. Adults can grow more than 3ft long and weigh more than 200lb. Young turtles are omnivorous, but adults (unique among sea turtles) become strict vegetarians. This turns their fat green – hence their name. Green sea turtles can be seen along the North Shore, commonly at Laniakea Beach and sometimes swimming up the Anahulu River at Haleʻiwa. Note that they are endangered and protected by federal law. Keeping a distance of 50ft is advised.

Oʻahu's nearshore waters also harbor hundreds of tropical fish, including rainbow-colored parrot fish, moray eels and ballooning puffer fish, to name just a few.

Land Animals

All of Hawaii's land animals have been introduced by humans. The first Polynesian arrivals, sometime between 300 and 600 CE, brought themselves, pigs, dogs and rats. Later, from the late 1700s, settlers brought horses, goats, cattle, cats, and reptiles such as geckos, anoles and chameleons. The introduction of all these animals has had detrimental consequences for Oʻahu's native species and natural environment. Fortunately, there are no snakes (yet). Hawaii strictly enforces a no-snake rule, and planes, especially those from Guam, are frequently inspected for snakes.

Feathered Friends

Endemic birdlife has suffered greatly since the arrival of humans. That said, Hawaii still has a number of magnificent birds, including 18 species of honeycreeper (very difficult to spot!), the *koloa* (Hawaiian duck), the ʻalae kea (Hawaiian coot), and the pueo (Hawaiian owl), which, unlike other owl species, is active during the day.

Most of the islets off Oʻahu's Windward Coast are sanctuaries for seabirds, including terns, noddies, shearwaters, Laysan albatrosses and boobies.

Birds introduced to Hawaiʻi include sparrows, cardinals, doves and mynas.

Plants

Oʻahu blooms year-round. The classic hibiscus is native to Hawaii, but many of the hundreds of varieties growing here have been introduced. Other exotic tropical flowers commonly seen include blood-red anthurium, brilliant-orange bird-of-paradise, showy bougainvillea and numerous varieties of heliconia. Strangely enough, while Hawaii's climate is ideal for orchids, there are only three native species. Most of the

Best Natural Preserves

Ka'ena Point State Park (p267)

Diamond Head State Monument (p199)

Waimea Valley (p254)

Ho'omaluhia Botanical Garden (p228)

Lyon Arboretum (p99)

Hanauma Bay Nature Preserve (p207)

Koko Crater Botanical Garden (p210)

THE MONGOOSE

A classic example of putting economics before the environment was the introduction of the Indian mongoose to Hawaii. Brought to the archipelago in 1883 from India to control the rat population in the sugar plantations, the mongoose thrived and today is widespread across the state. Introducing the mongoose has proved to be a major mistake, as the animal has heavily preyed upon the ground-nesting birds, bird hatchlings, eggs and endangered turtles of the islands. Even worse, the mongoose never did what it was brought to Hawaii to do – rats are nocturnal, while the mongoose is active during the day and sleeps at night!

If you want see a mongoose in the wild on Oʻahu, go to Hanauma Bay. Sit near the vegetation at the top of the sand and watch the wriggling bags belonging to snorkelers who have left their gear on the beach with food inside. Troops of mongooses turn up daily to sneak into snorkelers' bags and steal a snack.

Red hibiscus

agricultural plants associated with the island, such as the pineapple, were introduced. Other endemic species you might see include the following:

'Ohi'a lehua A native shrub or tree with bright-red, tufted pompom flowers; thought to be sacred to the goddess Pele.

'Ilima The island's official flower; a native ground cover with delicate yellow blossoms that are often strung into lei.

Koa Tall, upland tree with flat, crescent-shaped mature leaves; its wood is used to make canoes, ukuleles and exquisite bowls.

Naupaka A common shrub with oval green leaves and a small pinkish-white, five-petal flower. It's said that the mountain variety and the beach variety were once a young male and female, separated and turned into plants because of Pele's jealousy of their love.

National, State & County Parks

O'ahu has no national parks, but the federal government manages the Pearl Harbor National Memorial, as well as the James Campbell National Wildlife Refuge at the edge of the North Shore. About 25% of the island's land is protected, although some tension exists between the government and a few rural communities that want more land for affordable housing and farming. From Diamond Head near Waikiki to Ka'ena Point on the remote northwestern tip of the island, a rich system of state parks and forest reserves is loaded with outdoor opportunities, especially hiking. Dozens of county beach parks offer all kinds of aquatic adventures. The state's Department of Land and Natural Resources (www.dlnr.hawaii. gov) has useful information about hiking, history and aquatic safety.

Survival
Guide

Directory A–Z

Accessible Travel

➡ Bigger, newer hotels and resorts in Hawaii have elevators, TDD-capable phones and wheelchair-accessible rooms (reserve these well in advance).

➡ Telephone companies provide relay operators (dial 711) for those with impaired hearing.

➡ Many banks provide ATM instructions in braille.

➡ Traffic intersections have dropped curbs and audible crossing signals in cities and some towns, as well as all along Waikiki's beachfront.

➡ Honolulu's Department of Parks and Recreation (www.honolulu.gov/parks.html) provides all-terrain beach mats and wheelchairs for free (call ahead to make arrangements) at several beaches, including Ala Moana, Hanauma Bay, Kaimana (Sans Souci), Kailua and Kualoa.

➡ Guide dogs and service animals are not subject to the same quarantine requirements as pets; contact the Department of Agriculture's Animal Quarantine Station (www.hdoa.hawaii.gov) before arrival.

Transportation

➡ All public buses on O'ahu are wheelchair accessible and will 'kneel' if you're unable to use the steps – just let the driver know that you need the lift or ramp.

➡ If you have a disability parking placard from home, bring it with you and hang it from your rental car's rearview mirror when using designated disabled-parking spaces.

➡ Some major car-rental agencies offer hand-controlled vehicles and vans with wheelchair lifts. You'll need to reserve these well in advance.

Addresses

Street addresses on some island highways may seem random, but there's a pattern. For hyphenated numbers, such as 4-734 Kuhio Hwy, the first part of the number identifies the post-office district and the second part identifies the street address. Thus, it's possible for 4-736 to be followed by 5-002; you've just entered a new district, that's all.

Customs Regulations

Currently, each international visitor is allowed to bring the following into the USA duty-free:

➡ 1L of liquor (if you're over 21 years old).

➡ 200 cigarettes (one carton) if you're over 18.

Amounts higher than $10,000 in cash, money orders and other cash equivalents must be declared. For more information, check with US Customs and Border Protection (www.cbp.gov).

Most fresh fruits and plants are restricted from entry into Hawaii (to prevent the spread of invasive species). At Honolulu airport, customs officials strictly enforce both import and export regulations. Because Hawaii is a rabies-free state, pet quarantine laws are draconian. Questions? Contact the Hawaiian Department of Agriculture (www.hdoa.hawaii.gov).

Agricultural Inspection

All checked and carry-on bags leaving Hawaii for the US mainland must be checked by an agricultural inspector using an X-ray machine. You cannot take out gardenia, jade vine or Mauna Loa anthurium, even in lei, although most other fresh flowers and foliage are permitted. With the exceptions of pineapples and coconuts, most fresh fruit and vegetables are banned. Also not allowed to enter mainland states are plants in soil, fresh coffee berries (roasted beans are OK), cactus and sugarcane. For more information, go to www.hdoa.hawaii.gov.

Electricity

Type A
120V/60Hz

Type B
120V/60Hz

Etiquette

Hawaii may be a relaxed and laid-back place, but it pays to show good manners on your visit.

➡ Two words you will hear every day are aloha (hello and goodbye) and *mahalo*

(thank you). Use them with sincerity.

➡ If you are given a lei, always accept and wear it with gratitude and never take it off in the presence of the person who gave it to you.

➡ Hawaii is a US state, so gratuities are expected in accordance with American standards. For example, 15% to 20% tips are the norm in restaurants.

➡ If you are invited into someone's home, always remove your shoes before going inside.

➡ Be respectful at Native Hawaiian historic, sacred or religious sites.

➡ Don't damage the coral by touching it or stepping on it.

➡ Don't take lava rocks or black sand – it is considered to bring bad luck.

➡ Use public access at beaches – don't cross private land to get to them.

➡ Always pick up and properly dispose of garbage. You will upset locals if you trash their treasured environment.

➡ Don't honk your horn in traffic unless it's absolutely necessary and let faster traffic by if you are driving slowly.

➡ Surf carefully – give way to local surfers and be careful

of others on the beach and in the water.

➡ Hawaiian people have great respect for their elders – visitors should show deference to the elderly too.

Insurance

Getting travel insurance to cover theft, loss and medical problems is highly recommended. Some policies do not cover 'risky' activities such as scuba diving and motorcycling, so read the fine print. Make sure your policy at least covers hospital stays and an emergency flight home.

Paying for your airline ticket or rental car with a credit card may provide limited travel-accident insurance. If you already have private US health insurance or a homeowner's or renter's policy, find out what those policies cover and only get supplemental insurance. If you have prepaid a large portion of your vacation, trip-cancellation insurance may be a worthwhile expense.

Worldwide travel insurance is available at www.lonelyplanet.com/travel-insurance. You can buy, extend and claim online anytime – even if you're already on the road.

Internet Access

➡ In listings, the internet symbol @ indicates that a terminal is available, while the wifi symbol 🛜 indicates a hot spot; either may be free or fee based.

➡ Most hotels and resorts, and many coffee shops, bars and other businesses, offer public wi-fi (sometimes free only for paying customers).

➡ Honolulu, Waikiki and a few island towns have business centers with pay-as-you-go internet terminals (typically $6 to $12 per hour) and sometimes wi-fi.

➡ Hawaii's public libraries (www.librarieshawaii. org) provide free internet access via their computer terminals, but you will need a temporary nonresident library card ($10). Some library branches now offer free wi-fi (no card required).

Legal Matters

If you are arrested, you have the right to an attorney; if you can't afford one, a public defender will be provided free. The Hawaii State Bar Association (www.hsba.org) can make attorney referrals.

➡ If you are stopped by the police while driving, be courteous. Don't get out of the car unless asked.

➡ It's illegal to have open containers of alcohol (even empty ones) in motor vehicles; unless containers are still sealed and have never been opened, store them in the trunk.

➡ Bars, nightclubs and stores may require photo ID to prove you're of legal age (21 years) to buy or consume alcohol.

➡ Drinking alcohol in public anywhere besides a licensed premises (eg bar, restaurant), including at beaches and parks, is illegal.

➡ In Hawaii, anyone caught driving with a blood alcohol level of 0.08% or greater is guilty of driving under the influence (DUI), a serious offense that may incur heavy fines, a suspended driver's license, jail time and other stiff penalties.

➡ The possession of marijuana (except for medical reasons) and nonprescription narcotics is illegal. Foreigners convicted of a drug offense face immediate deportation.

➡ Public nudity (as at beaches) and hitchhiking are illegal, but sometimes police ignore them.

LGBTIQ Travelers

The state of Hawaii has strong minority protections and a constitutional guarantee of privacy that extends to sexual behavior between consenting adults. Same-sex couples also have the right to civil unions. But showing affection toward a same-sex partner in public isn't common.

Waikiki is without question the epicenter of O'ahu's LGBTIQ nightlife, but this laid-back 'scene' is muted by US mainland standards.

Honolulu Pride is celebrated in October with two weeks of events leading up to a parade and festival. As well as the vibrant parade, the event features a lineup of talented live acts, and various participating bars and local restaurants provide tropical drinks and specialty dishes.

Visitors should check out the Hawai'i LGBT Legacy Foundation website (http:// hawaiilgbtlegacyfoundation. com), which features a community calendar and a list of projects and volunteer positions.

Hawai'i LGBT Center Honolulu (www.hawaiilgbt legacyfoundation.com/ lgbtq-center-honolulu) is located at Waikiki Community Center. It's a gathering place for Hawaii's LGBTIQ community, hosting meetings, educational programs, trainings, film screenings, talk-story events and more.

Helpful DIY resources include the website Go Gay Hawaii (www.gogayhawaii. com).

Purple Roofs (www.pur pleroofs.com) is a gay-travel website and accommodations directory. You'll find O'ahu gay-friendly and lesbian- and gay-owned B&Bs, inns, hotels, vacation rentals and other accommodations. It also lists O'ahu travel agents and tour operators,

---

KUMU HINA

Kumu Hina – A Place in the Middle (www.kumuhina. com) is an acclaimed 2014 documentary in which a transgender Hawaiian teacher and cultural icon inspires a girl to lead the school's male hula troupe. With a wonderful Hawaiian-music playlist, the film explores gender-diverse cultures. It looks at the role of *mahu* (who identify their gender between male and female) in Hawaiian society through the eyes of a Native Hawaiian who is deeply rooted in the traditions of her ancestors and committed to living a meaningful life. *Mahu* have been part of Hawaiian culture for centuries, much as in other Polynesian cultures – *fa'afafine* in Samoa and *fakaleiti* in Tonga. Hawaiian songs often contain deeper meanings, called *kaona*, that refer to love and relationships that don't conform to contemporary Western definitions of male and female gender roles.

as well as local gay-travel events, gay-travel news and much more.

Money

ATMs are all over the place and credit cards are accepted just about everywhere.

Bargaining

Haggling is not normal practice on O'ahu. The only place you may get somewhere if you try to bargain over prices is the Aloha Stadium Swap Meet in 'Aiea, where hundreds of outdoor-store holders, mostly owner-operators, are competing for your dollars.

Tipping

In Hawaii, tipping practices are the same as on the US mainland, roughly as follows:

Airport and hotel porters $2 per bag, minimum of $5 per cart.

Bartenders 15% to 20% per round, minimum of $1 per drink.

Housekeepers $2 to $4 per night, left under the card provided; more if you're messy.

Parking valets At least $2 when your keys are returned.

Restaurant servers 18% to 20%, unless a service charge is already on the bill.

Taxi drivers 15% of the metered fare, rounded up to the next dollar.

Opening Hours

The following standard hours apply; variances are noted in listings.

Banks 8:30am to 4pm Monday to Friday; some to 6pm Friday and 9am to noon or 1pm Saturday.

Bars and clubs Noon to midnight; some to 2am Thursday to Saturday.

Businesses and government offices 8:30am to 4:30pm Monday to Friday; some post offices open 9am to noon Saturday.

Restaurants Breakfast 6am to 10am, lunch 11:30am to 2pm, dinner 5pm to 9:30pm.

Shops 9am to 5pm Monday to Saturday, some also noon to 5pm Sunday; malls keep extended hours.

Post

The US Postal Service is inexpensive and reliable. Mail delivery to/from Hawaii usually takes slightly longer than on the US mainland.

Public Holidays

On the following holidays, banks, schools and government offices (including post offices) close, and transportation and museums operate on a Sunday schedule. Holidays falling on a weekend are usually observed the following Monday.

New Year's Day January 1

Martin Luther King Jr Day Third Monday in January

Presidents' Day Third Monday in February

Easter March or April

Prince Kuhio Day March 26

Memorial Day Last Monday in May

King Kamehameha Day June 11

Independence Day July 4

Statehood Day Third Friday in August

Labor Day First Monday in September

Columbus Day Second Monday in October

Veterans Day November 11

Thanksgiving Fourth Thursday in November

Christmas Day December 25

Safe Travel

Box jellyfish (p298) These turn up eight to 10 days after the full moon of each month. Follow beach signage and talk to lifeguards. See www. waikikiaquarium.org/interact/box-jellyfish-calendar.

Car break-ins Absolutely do not leave anything visible in a rental car. Car break-ins are common. Hiding things in the trunk is only effective if you do so before getting to your parking spot.

Beaches Do not leave valuables on the beach while you swim; slippers and towels are usually left alone.

Swimming at waterfalls Hazards include falling rocks and leptospirosis (an infection caused by corkscrew-shaped bacteria).

Telephone

Check with your service provider about using your cell phone in Hawaii. Among US providers, AT&T, Verizon, T-Mobile and Sprint are good. Cell coverage may be spotty or nonexistent in rural areas, on hiking trails and at remote beaches.

International travelers need a multiband GSM phone in order to make calls in the USA. With an unlocked multiband phone, popping in a US prepaid rechargeable SIM card is usually cheaper than using your own network. SIM cards are available at any major telecommunications or electronics store. These stores also sell inexpensive prepaid phones, including some airtime.

Time

Hawaii-Aleutian Standard Time (HAST) is GMT minus 10 hours. Hawaii doesn't observe daylight-saving time (DST). The euphemism 'island time' means taking things at a slower pace, or occasionally being late.

Toilets

Hawaii uses standard Western-style sit-down toilets. Public toilets are sometimes hard to come by in places like downtown or Chinatown in Honolulu. Shopping malls, restaurants and beach parks usually have toilet facilities.

Tourist Information

In the arrivals area at Honolulu airport there are tourist-information desks with helpful staff. Tourist brochures and magazines, such as *101 Things to Do* (www.101thingstodo.com), *This Week* (www.thisweekpublications.com) and *Spotlight's O'ahu Gold* (www.spotlighthawaii.com), are packed with discount coupons. These magazines, as well as plenty of others, are also readily available in Waikiki.

For pretrip planning, browse the Hawaii Tourism Authority's information-packed website Go Hawaii (www.gohawaii.com).

Visas

➡ Visa and passport requirements change often; double-check *before* you come.

➡ For current info, check the visa section of the US Department of State (www.travel.state.gov) and US Customs and Border Protection (www.cbp.gov/travel) websites.

➡ Travelers who don't qualify for the Visa Waiver Program (VWP) must apply for a tourist visa. The process of applying for a tourist visa is not free, involves a personal interview and can take several weeks, so apply early.

➡ Upon arrival, most foreign visitors must have electronic fingerprints and a digital photo taken; the process usually takes less than a minute.

Passports

➡ A machine-readable passport is required for all foreign citizens to enter Hawaii.

➡ Passports must be valid for six months beyond expected dates of stay in the USA.

➡ Any passport issued or renewed after October 26, 2006, must be an 'e-passport' with a digital photo and an integrated biometric data chip.

Visa Waiver Program (VWP)

➡ For VWP countries, visas are not required for stays of less than 90 days. To see which countries are VWP countries, visit www.dhs.gov/visa-waiver-program-requirements.

➡ Under the VWP you must have a return ticket (or an onward ticket to any foreign destination) that is nonrefundable in the USA. All VWP travelers must register online at least 72 hours before arrival with the Electronic System for Travel Authorization (ESTA; https://esta.cbp.dhs.gov/esta), which currently costs $14.

➡ Registration is valid for two years.

Transportation

GETTING THERE & AWAY

Most visitors to Oʻahu arrive via Daniel K Inouye International Airport. Flights, cars and tours can be booked online at lonelyplanet.com/bookings.

Air

Honolulu is the gateway to Hawaii. It has flights from major North American cities as well as from Asia and the Pacific. It is also a hub of interisland service for flights serving the neighbor islands.

Daniel K Inouye International Airport (HNL; ☑808-836-6411; www.airports.hawaii.gov/hnl; 300 Rodgers Blvd; 🛜), formerly known as Honolulu International Airport, is Oʻahu's main commercial airport, about 6 miles northwest of downtown Honolulu and 9 miles northwest of Waikiki. The main terminal is a series of interconnected large buildings with dozens of gates. There's also a Commuter Terminal (Terminal 3), used by small interisland carrier Mokulele Airlines. It's about a 200m walk or free shuttle-bus ride from the main terminal.

Hawaiian Airlines (☑800-367-5320; www.hawaiianairlines.com) Nonstop flights between the Hawaiian Islands and various spots on the US mainland. The largest airline flying between the main islands, Hawaiian uses all jets; its subsidiary Ohana serves smaller islands such as Lanaʻi and Molokaʻi with prop planes.

Southwest Airlines (www.southwest.com) There's a lot more competition in the interisland flying market now that Southwest has jumped in with cheap flights between Oʻahu and the other major Hawaiian islands.

Mokulele Airlines (www.mokuleleairlines.com) Uses single-engine Cessna 208EX Grand Caravans to fly to secondary airports such as Molokaʻi and Hana (on Maui). Many flights do not require passengers to go through security, and the rides can be thrilling as you get up-close views of the islands.

GETTING AROUND

The public-transit system is comprehensive and convenient. You can get a bus to most parts of Oʻahu, but to explore thoroughly and reach off-the-beaten-path sights, you'll need your own wheels.

To/From the Airport

From Daniel K Inouye International Airport you can reach Honolulu or Waikiki by airport shuttle, public bus or taxi/Uber/Lyft (fares $35 to $45). For other points around Oʻahu, it's more convenient to rent a car.

Roberts Hawaii Airport Shuttle (☑808-439-8800; www.airportshuttlehawaii.com;

CLIMATE CHANGE & TRAVEL

Every form of transport that relies on carbon-based fuel generates CO_2, the main cause of human-induced climate change. Modern travel is dependent on airplanes, which might use less fuel per mile per person than most cars but travel much greater distances. The altitude at which aircraft emit gases (including CO_2) and particles also contributes to their climate change impact. Many websites offer 'carbon calculators' that allow people to estimate the carbon emissions generated by their journey and, for those who wish to do so, to offset the impact of the greenhouse gases emitted with contributions to portfolios of climate-friendly initiatives throughout the world. Lonely Planet offsets the carbon footprint of all staff and author travel.

fare to Waikiki one way $17) operates 24-hour shuttles to Waikiki hotels departing every 20 to 60 minutes.

You can reach downtown Honolulu, the Ala Moana Center and Waikiki via The-Bus routes 19 or 20. Buses run every 20 minutes from 6am to 11pm; the regular fare is $2.75. Luggage is restricted to what you can hold on your lap or stow under the seat (maximum size 22in by 14in by 9in).

Bicycle

It's possible to cycle around O'ahu, but consider taking TheBus to get beyond Hon-olulu metro-area traffic. All buses have front-loading racks that accommodate two bicycles at no extra charge – just let the driver know first.

Honolulu has a shared-bicycle scheme called **Biki** (www.gobiki.org). There are dozens of stations for the distinctive turquoise bikes all over Honolulu and Waikiki. As with other bike-sharing schemes worldwide, you can pick up a bike at one station and drop it off at another.

Pay for the service with a credit card at the station or by using the handy app. Biki rates for non-Hawaii residents are $4 for the first 30 minutes and $4.50 for every 30 minutes after that. Or you can buy 300 minutes of use for $25, which can consist of multiple trips – by far the best value.

Hawaii's Department of Transportation publishes excellent and comprehensive Bike O'ahu route maps online at www.hidot.hawaii.gov/highways/bike-map-oahu. If you plan to do any riding, these maps can be viewed online and are essential ways to determine how bike-friendly you'll find your intended route. A handy three-color system gives routes ratings of green (good for novices), yellow (best for experienced cyclists) and red (not suited to bikes at all).

Cyclists will find O'ahu to be a fairly rider-friendly place. There are many local cyclists on the roads and drivers are used to seeing people riding along the shoulder.

That said, roads, especially away from Honolulu and Waikiki, can be narrow, so riders who are unaccustomed to sharing the asphalt with cars might find some routes challenging. Otherwise, conditions will be familiar to riders: heavy traffic at rush hour and in cities, breezy freedom away from south O'ahu in the countryside.

Roads are not outlandishly hilly, except if you choose to ride over the mountains between Honolulu and Kail-ua. That's why many people stick to coastal roads for this route. One recommendation from locals is to use TheBus to get you and your bike out of the Honolulu/Waikiki madness and then start riding in more cycle-friendly areas such as Pearl Harbor and 'Aiea to the west, and the southeast of O'ahu, centered on Hawai'i Kai.

Waikiki has several good bicycle-rental shops. They include the following:

EBikes Hawaii (☑808-722-5454; www.ebikeshawaii.com; 3318 Campbell Ave; rental per day $23-35; ☺10am-6pm Mon-Sat, 11am-5pm Sun) Based

USEFUL BUS ROUTES

ROUTE NO	DESTINATION
A City Express!	University of Hawai'i Manoa, Ala Moana Center, downtown Honolulu, Chinatown, Aloha Stadium
E Country Express!	Waikiki, Ala Moana Center, Waterfront Plaza, Aloha Tower, downtown Honolulu
2 & 13	Waikiki, Kapahulu Ave, Honolulu Convention Center, downtown Honolulu, Chinatown; also Honolulu Museum of Art & Bishop Museum (bus 2)
4	Waikiki, UH Manoa, downtown Honolulu, Queen Emma Summer Palace
6	UH Manoa, Ala Moana Center, downtown Honolulu
8	Waikiki, Ala Moana Center
19 & 20	Waikiki, Ala Moana Center, Ward Center, Waterfront Plaza, Aloha Tower, downtown Honolulu, Chinatown, Honolulu airport; also USS Arizona Memorial (bus 20)
22 ('Beach Bus')	Waikiki, Diamond Head, Koko Marina, Hanauma Bay, Sandy Beach, Sea Life Park
23	Ala Moana Center, Waikiki, Diamond Head, Hawai'i Kai (inland), Sea Life Park
42	Waikiki, Ala Moana Center, downtown Honolulu, Chinatown, USS Arizona Memorial (limited hours)
52 & 55 ('Circle Isle' buses)	Ala Moana Center, North Shore, Windward Coast
57	Ala Moana Center, Queen Emma Summer Palace, Kailua, Waimanalo, Sea Life Park

just off Kapahulu Ave, this shop is a center for electric bikes. Hourly, daily and weekly rates are available.

Hawaiian Style Rentals
(☑866-916-6733; www.hawaii bikes.com; 2556 Lemon Rd, Waikiki Beachside Hostel; rental per day from $25; ☺8:30am-5pm) Rents a large range of bikes; half-day, daily and weekly rates are available and include helmets, locks and more. An excellent source of O'ahu cycling info, both at the shop and online.

Should you want to bring your own bike, most airlines will allow this for an extra fee (that varies widely). You may also face special packing regulations.

Finally, bikes have the same rules of the road in Hawaii as cars; eg no riding against traffic.

Bus

O'ahu's public bus system, **TheBus** (☑808-848-5555; www.thebus.org; adult $2.75; ☺infoline 5:30am-10pm), is extensive and easy to use. The Ala Moana Center is Honolulu's central bus-transfer point. The system covers most points on the island along the main roads, and it's a great way to experience O'ahu's best trips, such as the classic North Shore and Windward Coast loop. However, many trailheads, wilderness areas and viewpoints are not served.

Buses run regularly on major routes, seven days a week, and from early morning into the evening. The website has full schedule and route info.

All buses are wheelchair accessible.

Bus Passes
The one-way adult fare is $2.75 (for children aged six to 17 it's $1.25). Use coins or $1 bills; bus drivers don't give change. A free transfer good for two connections is available from the driver.

A monthly pass ($70), valid for unlimited rides during a calendar month (not just any 30-day period), is sold at **TheBus Pass Office** (☑808-848-5555; www.thebus. org; Kalihi Transit Center, cnr Middle St & Kamehameha Hwy; ☺7:30am-4pm Mon-Fri), 7-Eleven convenience stores and Foodland and Times supermarkets.

Seniors (65 years and older) and anyone with a physical disability can buy a $10 discount ID card at TheBus Pass Office, entitling them to pay $1 per one-way fare or $6 for a pass valid for unlimited rides during a calendar month (or $35 for a year).

Car & Motorcycle

All major car-rental companies have locations at Daniel K Inouye International Airport, either in the parking garage across from the terminals or on nearby access roads. Rates are very competitive.

Most major car-rental agencies also have multiple branch locations in Waikiki, usually in the lobbies of resort hotels. Although the best rental rates are usually offered at Honolulu's airport, Waikiki branches can be less hassle (and less expensive, given steep overnight parking costs at Waikiki hotels) if you're only renting a car for a limited time.

In Waikiki, independent car-rental agencies (p171) may offer lower rates. They also are more likely to rent to drivers under 25. Some also rent mopeds and motorcycles, and a few specialize in Smart cars and hybrid vehicles.

Hawaii Campers (☑808-222-2547; www.hawaiicampers. net) has rental camping cars you can take all over O'ahu for $155 per night plus tax.

Times vary depending on traffic, but following are typical driving times and distances from Waikiki:

Destination	Miles	Time (min)
Diamond Head	3	10
Hale'iwa	37	55
Hanauma Bay	11	25
Honolulu airport	9	25
Ka'ena Point State Park	46	70
Kailua	17	30
Ko Olina	29	45
La'ie	38	65
Nu'uanu Pali Lookout	11	20
Sunset Beach	43	65
USS Arizona Memorial	15	30

Driver's License
➡ US citizens with a driver's license from another state can legally drive in Hawaii if they are at least 18 years old.

➡ International visitors can legally drive in Hawaii with a valid driver's license issued by their home country (minimum age 18).

➡ Car-rental companies will generally accept foreign driver's licenses written in English with an accompanying photo. Otherwise, be prepared to present an International Driving Permit (IDP), obtainable in your home country, along with your foreign driver's license.

Insurance
➡ Required by law, liability insurance covers any people or property that you might hit. It's usually included in comprehensive rental insurance policies. It can add up to $30 per day to the rental cost.

➡ A collision damage waiver (CDW) does not include liability insurance and costs an extra $15 to $20 a day.

➡ If you decline CDW, you will be held liable for any damage up to the full value of the car.

➡ Even with CDW, you may be required to pay the first $100 to $500 for repairs; some agencies will also charge you for the rental cost of the car during the time it takes to be repaired.

➡ If you have vehicle insurance at home, it likely covers any liability needs and usually covers collision and damage costs as well. Check your policy to confirm this.

➡ Many credit cards offer coverage for car rentals. This is usually in addition to your primary coverage via your own auto insurance. In real terms this means that your credit-card policy will pick up any deductible and other fees not covered by your primary policy. Again, confirm these details in advance.

➡ Rentals over 15 days or 'exotic' models (eg performance cars, 4WD Jeeps) may not be covered by personal and credit-card policies.

➡ The best advice is to simply confirm what coverage you have in advance; then you'll know if you can confidently decline the coverage rental outfits may try to sell you at the counter. It's a major source of profit.

Road Rules

Slow, courteous driving is the rule in Hawaii. Locals usually don't honk (unless they're about to crash), don't follow close (ie tailgate), and let other drivers pass and merge. Do the same, and you may get an appreciative *shaka* (Hawaiian hand greeting sign) from other drivers.

➡ Drive on the right-hand side of the road.

➡ Speed limits are posted and enforced. If you're stopped for speeding, expect a ticket, as police rarely just give warnings.

➡ Turning right on red is allowed (unless a sign prohibits it).

➡ At four-way stop signs, cars proceed in order of arrival. If two cars arrive simultaneously, the one on the right has the right of way. When in doubt, politely wave the other driver ahead.

➡ For one-lane-bridge crossings, one direction of traffic usually has the right of way, while the other must obey the posted yield sign.

➡ Downhill traffic must yield to uphill traffic where there is no sign.

➡ Diamond-marked carpool lanes are reserved for high-occupancy vehicles during morning and afternoon rush hours.

➡ When emergency vehicles (ie police, fire or ambulance) approach from either direction, carefully pull over to the side of the road.

Safety Laws

➡ Texting on a handheld device (eg cell phone) while driving is illegal. Talking on a cell phone is only allowed for adult drivers (age 18 and over) who use a hands-free device.

➡ Driving under the influence (DUI) of alcohol or drugs is a serious criminal offense. It's illegal to carry open containers of alcohol (even if they're empty) inside a car. Unless the containers are still sealed and have never been opened, store them in the trunk instead.

➡ The use of seat belts is required for the driver and all passengers, even those riding in the back seat.

➡ Child safety seats are mandatory for children aged three and younger. Those aged four to seven must ride in a booster or child safety seat, unless they weigh over 80lb, in which case they must be secured by a lap-only belt in the back seat.

Avoiding Car Break-ins

When visiting O'ahu's beach parks, hiking trails or 'secret' spots off the side of the highway, take all valuables with you. Don't leave anything visible inside your car or stowed in the trunk. Car break-ins are common all over the island and can happen within minutes. Some locals leave their cars unlocked to avoid the hassles of broken windows or damaged door locks.

Taxi, Uber & Lyft

Taxis have been struggling in competition with Uber and Lyft.

Taxis have meters and charge $3.50 at flag fall, plus $3.60 per mile and 50¢ per suitcase or backpack. They're readily available at the airport, resort hotels and shopping centers. Otherwise, call for one.

TheCab (☎808-422-2222; www.thecabhawaii.com) Offers island-wide service.

Charley's Taxi (☎808-233-3333, 877-531-1333; www.charleystaxi.com) Limos, vans and SUVs. Book online for flat rates from the airport to Waikiki ($29) and downtown Honolulu ($20).

Behind the Scenes

SEND US YOUR FEEDBACK

We love to hear from travelers – your comments keep us on our toes and help make our books better. Our well-traveled team reads every word on what you loved or loathed about this book. Although we cannot reply individually to your submissions, we always guarantee that your feedback goes straight to the appropriate authors, in time for the next edition. Each person who sends us information is thanked in the next edition – the most useful submissions are rewarded with a selection of digital PDF chapters.

Visit **lonelyplanet.com/contact** to submit your updates and suggestions or to ask for help. Our award-winning website also features inspirational travel stories, news and discussions.

Note: We may edit, reproduce and incorporate your comments in Lonely Planet products such as guidebooks, websites and digital products, so let us know if you don't want your comments reproduced or your name acknowledged. For a copy of our privacy policy visit lonelyplanet.com/legal.

WRITER THANKS

Craig McLachlan

A hearty *mahalo* to everyone who helped out during my O'ahu research. A special thanks, as always, to my exceptionally beautiful wife Yuriko, who keeps me focused – and to our good friends Paul and Nezia. Cheers (and a few mai tais too!) to co-writer Ryan and to Vicky Smith at Lonely Planet.

Ryan Ver Berkmoes

Thanks to the dozens of people who showed real aloha answering my questions and revealing their favorites. And special thanks to the Pearl Harbor guard who politely stopped my explorations as I was about to (accidentally) wander into a restricted area and get arrested. And huge thanks to Alexis Ver Berkmoes, who is the orgeat syrup in my mai tai.

ACKNOWLEDGEMENTS

Climate map data adapted from Peel MC, Finlayson BL & McMahon TA (2007) 'Updated World Map of the Köppen-Geiger Climate Classification', *Hydrology and Earth System Sciences*, 11, 1633–44.

Cover photograph: Lanikai Beach (p221), Tomas Del Amo/Shutterstock©

THIS BOOK

This 6th edition of Lonely Planet's *Honolulu, Waikiki & O'ahu* guidebook was researched and written by Craig McLachlan and Ryan Ver Berkmoes. The previous two editions were written by Sara Benson, Lisa Dunford, Craig McLachlan and Ryan Ver Berkmoes. This guidebook was produced by the following:

Senior Product Editors Vicky Smith, Sandie Kestell

Regional Senior Cartographer Corey Hutchison

Product Editor Kate James

Book Designer Fergal Condon

Cover researcher Brendan Dempsey-Spencer

Assisting Editors Sarah Bailey, James Bainbridge, Grace Dobell, Bailey Freeman, Charlotte Orr, Kirsten Rawlings, Gabrielle Stefanos

Cartographers Valentina Kremenchutskaya, Mark Griffiths

Thanks to Sasha Drew, Samuel McMahon

Index

Map Legend

Sights
- Beach
- Bird Sanctuary
- Buddhist
- Castle/Palace
- Christian
- Confucian
- Hindu
- Islamic
- Jain
- Jewish
- Monument
- Museum/Gallery/Historic Building
- Ruin
- Shinto
- Sikh
- Taoist
- Winery/Vineyard
- Zoo/Wildlife Sanctuary
- Other Sight

Activities, Courses & Tours
- Bodysurfing
- Diving
- Canoeing/Kayaking
- Course/Tour
- Sento Hot Baths/Onsen
- Skiing
- Snorkeling
- Surfing
- Swimming/Pool
- Walking
- Windsurfing
- Other Activity

Sleeping
- Sleeping
- Camping

Information
- Bank
- Embassy/Consulate
- Hospital/Medical
- Internet
- Police
- Post Office
- Telephone
- Toilet
- Tourist Information
- Other Information

Geographic
- Beach
- Gate
- Hut/Shelter
- Lighthouse
- Lookout
- Mountain/Volcano
- Oasis
- Park
- Pass
- Picnic Area
- Waterfall

Population
- Capital (National)
- Capital (State/Province)
- City/Large Town
- Town/Village

Transport
- Airport
- BART station
- Border crossing
- Boston T station
- Bus
- Cable car/Funicular
- Cycling

Routes
- Tollway
- Freeway
- Primary
- Secondary
- Tertiary
- Lane
- Unsealed road
- Road under construction
- Plaza/Mall
- Steps
- Tunnel
- Pedestrian overpass
- Walking Tour
- Walking Tour detour
- Path/Walking Trail

Boundaries
- International
- State/Province
- Disputed
- Regional/Suburb
- Marine Park
- Cliff
- Wall

Hydrography
- River, Creek
- Intermittent River
- Canal
- Water
- Dry/Salt/Intermittent Lake
- Reef

Areas
- Airport/Runway
- Beach/Desert

OUR STORY

A beat-up old car, a few dollars in the pocket and a sense of adventure. In 1972 that's all Tony and Maureen Wheeler needed for the trip of a lifetime – across Europe and Asia overland to Australia. It took several months, and at the end – broke but inspired – they sat at their kitchen table writing and stapling together their first travel guide, *Across Asia on the Cheap*. Within a week they'd sold 1500 copies. Lonely Planet was born.

Today, Lonely Planet has offices in the US, Ireland and China, with a network of over 2000 contributors in every corner of the globe. We share Tony's belief that 'a great guidebook should do three things: inform, educate and amuse'.

OUR WRITERS

Craig McLachlan

Southeast O'ahu, Windward Coast, North Shore & Central O'ahu Craig has covered destinations all over the globe for Lonely Planet for two decades. Based in Queenstown, New Zealand for half the year, he runs an outdoor activities company and a sake brewery, then moonlights overseas for the other half, leading tours and writing for Lonely Planet. Craig has completed a number of adventures in Japan and his books are available on Amazon. Describing himself as a 'freelance anything', Craig has an MBA from the University of Hawai'i and is also a Japanese interpreter, pilot, hiking guide, tour leader, karate instructor, marriage celebrant and budding novelist. Check out www.craigmclachlan.com.

Ryan Ver Berkmoes

Honolulu, Waikiki, Pearl Harbor & Leeward O'ahu Ryan Ver Berkmoes has written more than 110 guidebooks for Lonely Planet. He grew up in Santa Cruz, California, which he left at age 17 for college in the Midwest, where he first discovered snow. All joy of this novelty soon wore off. Since then he has been travelling the world, both for pleasure and for work – which are often indistinguishable. He has covered everything from wars to bars. He definitely prefers the latter. Ryan calls New York City home. Read more at ryanverberkmoes.com and at @ryanvb.

Published by Lonely Planet Global Limited
CRN 554153
6th edition – April 2021
ISBN 978 1 78657 8563
© Lonely Planet 2021 Photographs © as indicated 2021
10 9 8 7 6 5 4
Printed in China

31192022524688

rm by any means, electronic,
may be sold or hired, without the
are registered in the US Patent and
mercial establishments, such as